口译实训教程

主 编 肖 辉 陶长安
编 者 陈芙蓉 王 怡
　　　　张 宇 陶驷腾

东南大学出版社
·南京·

图书在版编目(CIP)数据

口译实训教程 / 肖辉,陶长安主编. —南京:东南大学出版社,2014.1
ISBN 978-7-5641-4668-9

Ⅰ.①口… Ⅱ.①肖…②陶… Ⅲ.①英语—口译—教材 Ⅳ.①H315.9

中国版本图书馆 CIP 数据核字(2013)第 289655 号

口译实训教程

出版发行:	东南大学出版社
社　　址:	南京市四牌楼 2 号　邮编:210096
出 版 人:	江建中
责任编辑:	史建农
网　　址:	http://www.seupress.com
电子邮箱:	press@seupress.com
经　　销:	全国各地新华书店
印　　刷:	兴化印刷有限责任公司
开　　本:	787mm×1092mm　1/16
印　　张:	22
字　　数:	535 千字
版　　次:	2014 年 1 月第 1 版
印　　次:	2014 年 1 月第 1 次印刷
书　　号:	ISBN 978-7-5641-4668-9
定　　价:	46.00 元

本社图书若有印装质量问题,请直接与营销部联系。电话:025-83791830

前 言

随着中外交流的日益频繁,口译——这一语言交际能力也愈显重要。口译是一种通过口头表达形式,将所听到(间或读到)的信息准确而又快速地由一种语言转换成另一种语言,进而达到传递与交流信息之目的的交际行为,是人类在跨文化、跨民族交往活动中所依赖的一种基本的语言交际工具。人类的口译活动不是一种机械地将信息的来源语符号转换为目标语符号的"翻语"活动,而是一种积极的、始终以交流信息意义为宗旨的、具有一定创造性的"译语"活动。因此,口译不是孤立地以词义和句子意义为转换单位的单一性语言活动,而是兼顾交际内容所涉及的词语意义、话语上下文意义、言外寓意、语体含义、体语含义、民族文化含义等信息的综合性语言活动。从这个意义上说,口译不仅仅是语言活动,而且还是文化活动、心理活动和社交活动。因为有了口译人员的"搭桥",科学技术可以得到现场的交流、商务贸易能够进行当面的洽谈、双方的信息可以得到即时的沟通、友谊则会呈现为具体现实。中国加入世界贸易组织(WTO)后,我国的经济活动以及社会生活必将加快全球化进程。在日益频繁的对外交流和国际交往过程中,英语口译已经成为全社会的迫切需要。为满足英语专业学生和业余口译人员的需要,满足英语学习者想有效地掌握英语口译理论知识、技能的需要,我们组织了实力派骨干教师编写了《口译实训教程》。

《口译实训教程》是一本实用英汉口译书。全书共分15个单元:第一单元 接待口译(Interpreting for Reception Service);第二单元 礼仪祝辞(Ceremonial Speech);第三单元 参观访问(Tour and Visit);第四单元 人物访谈(Interview);第五单元 饮食文化(Catering Culture);第六单元 外交政策(Foreign Policy);第七单元 商务谈判(Business Negotiation);第八单元 新闻发布会(Press Conference);第九单元 广告宣传(Advertising and Publicity);第十单元 医疗(Medical Care);第十一单元 环境保护(Environmental Protection);第十二单元 法律事务(Legal Affairs);第十三单元 外贸政策(Foreign Trade Policy);第十四单元 科技(Science & Technology);第十五单元 网络时代(Network Times)。

每个单元推出独特的单元要点、理论难点提示、选文 A(中、英文对话或文章)、选文 A 的重难点评析和译文、选文 B(中、英文文章)、选文 B 的重难点评析和译文、拓展阅读、选文 A(中、英文文章)译文;选文 B(中、英文文章)译文。

该书取材广泛，内容新颖，时效性强，语言素材与日常生活、工作紧密结合，语言材料真实、重点突出、将理论与实践有机结合、实用性强。读者通过本书的学习，不仅可以受到涵盖上述15个方面的英语口语、口译训练，而且可以学到相应的理论知识和策略，可收举一反三之效，提升口译理论和实践的能力。

《口译实训教程》是一本实用英语口译书，本书的使用对象为全国大专院校英语专业高年级学生和硕士研究生、英语教师、涉外工作人员以及广大英语爱好者。它还可用作中高级口译证书助考材料。

本书为安徽省人力资源和社会保障厅口译项目指定用书。

囿于编者的学识，加之编写时间仓促，其中遗漏错误在所难免，恳请广大读者不吝赐教。

编　者

2013年12月

目 录

第一单元　接待口译（Interpreting for Reception Service） ... 1
　单元要点 ... 1
　理论难点提示 ... 1
　　选文 A ... 1
　　重难点评析 ... 2
　　译文 ... 3
　　选文 B ... 4
　　重难点评析 ... 5
　　译文 ... 6
　外事口、笔译的特点综述 ... 7
　口译听辨技巧 ... 11
　拓展阅读 ... 14
　　选文 A ... 14
　　译文 ... 14
　　选文 B ... 14
　　译文 ... 15

第二单元　礼仪祝辞（Ceremonial Speech） ... 18
　单元要点 ... 18
　理论难点提示 ... 18
　　选文 A ... 18
　　重难点评析 ... 19
　　译文 ... 22
　　选文 B ... 24
　　重难点评析 ... 25
　　译文 ... 25
　口译记忆 ... 26
　公共演讲 ... 28
　拓展阅读 ... 32
　　选文 A ... 32
　　译文 ... 32
　　选文 B ... 33
　　译文 ... 34

第三单元　参观访问（Tour and Visit） ... 35
单元要点 ... 35
理论难点提示 ... 35
选文 A ... 35
重难点评析 ... 36
译文 ... 38
选文 B ... 39
重难点评析 ... 41
译文 ... 42
Qualifications for Being a Good Guide-interpreter ... 43
口译笔记理论与技巧（一） ... 44
拓展阅读 ... 47
选文 A ... 47
译文 ... 48
选文 B ... 49
译文 ... 50

第四单元　人物访谈（Interview） ... 51
单元要点 ... 51
理论难点提示 ... 51
选文 A ... 51
重难点评析 ... 52
译文 ... 54
选文 B ... 57
重难点评析 ... 59
译文 ... 61
口音听辨技巧 ... 62
口译笔记理论及技巧（二） ... 66
拓展阅读 ... 71
选文 A ... 71
译文 ... 73
选文 B ... 74
译文 ... 76

第五单元　饮食文化（Catering Culture） ... 78
单元要点 ... 78
理论难点提示 ... 78
选文 A ... 78
重难点评析 ... 80
译文 ... 81
选文 B ... 84

重难点评析 ………………………………………………………… 85
　　译文 …………………………………………………………………… 86
　中文菜单英文翻译的原则 ……………………………………………… 87
　翻译的语言转换理论 …………………………………………………… 89
　拓展阅读 ………………………………………………………………… 92
　　选文 A ………………………………………………………………… 92
　　译文 …………………………………………………………………… 93
　　选文 B ………………………………………………………………… 94
　　译文 …………………………………………………………………… 95

第六单元　外交政策（Foreign Policy）………………………………… 97
　单元要点 ………………………………………………………………… 97
　理论难点提示 …………………………………………………………… 97
　　选文 A ………………………………………………………………… 97
　　重难点评析 ………………………………………………………… 99
　　译文 …………………………………………………………………… 100
　　选文 B ………………………………………………………………… 102
　　重难点评析 ………………………………………………………… 104
　　译文 …………………………………………………………………… 105
　听辨与解析 ……………………………………………………………… 106
　重译法 …………………………………………………………………… 114
　拓展阅读 ………………………………………………………………… 117
　　选文 A ………………………………………………………………… 117
　　译文 …………………………………………………………………… 119
　　选文 B ………………………………………………………………… 121
　　译文 …………………………………………………………………… 123

第七单元　商务谈判（Business Negotiation）………………………… 126
　单元要点 ………………………………………………………………… 126
　理论难点提示 …………………………………………………………… 126
　　选文 A ………………………………………………………………… 126
　　重难点评析 ………………………………………………………… 127
　　译文 …………………………………………………………………… 128
　　选文 B ………………………………………………………………… 130
　　重难点评析 ………………………………………………………… 131
　　译文 …………………………………………………………………… 133
　英汉双语的衔接和连贯 ………………………………………………… 134
　词序调整法 ……………………………………………………………… 139
　拓展阅读 ………………………………………………………………… 142
　　选文 A ………………………………………………………………… 142
　　译文 …………………………………………………………………… 143

选文B ··· 144
　　译文 ··· 145

第八单元　新闻发布会（Press Conference） ······························· 147
　单元要点 ··· 147
　理论难点提示 ··· 147
　　选文A ··· 147
　　重难点评析 ··· 149
　　译文 ··· 150
　　选文B ··· 154
　　重难点评析 ··· 156
　　译文 ··· 157
　倍数表示法 ··· 159
　分译法 ··· 161
　　译文 ··· 167
　拓展阅读 ··· 169
　　选文A ··· 169
　　译文 ··· 172
　　选文B ··· 179
　　译文 ··· 185

第九单元　广告宣传（Advertising and Publicity） ························· 190
　单元要点 ··· 190
　理论难点提示 ··· 190
　　选文A ··· 190
　　重难点评析 ··· 191
　　译文 ··· 192
　　选文B ··· 195
　　重难点评析 ··· 196
　　译文 ··· 197
　重组与表达 ··· 198
　增译法和减译法 ·· 206
　拓展阅读 ··· 210
　　选文A ··· 210
　　译文 ··· 211
　　选文B ··· 213
　　译文 ··· 214

第十单元　医疗（Medical Care） ··· 216
　单元要点 ··· 216
　理论难点提示 ··· 216
　　选文A ··· 216

重难点评析 ………………………………………………………………… 218
　　　译文 ……………………………………………………………………… 220
　　　选文 B …………………………………………………………………… 223
　　　重难点评析 ………………………………………………………………… 224
　　　译文 ……………………………………………………………………… 225
　速记 ………………………………………………………………………………… 226
　词类转移法 ………………………………………………………………………… 228
　拓展阅读 …………………………………………………………………………… 231
　　　选文 A …………………………………………………………………… 231
　　　译文 ……………………………………………………………………… 233
　　　选文 B …………………………………………………………………… 237
　　　译文 ……………………………………………………………………… 237

第十一单元　环境保护（Environmental Protection） …………………………… 239
　单元要点 …………………………………………………………………………… 239
　理论难点提示 ……………………………………………………………………… 239
　　　选文 A …………………………………………………………………… 239
　　　重难点评析 ………………………………………………………………… 241
　　　译文 ……………………………………………………………………… 242
　　　选文 B …………………………………………………………………… 245
　　　重难点评析 ………………………………………………………………… 245
　　　译文 ……………………………………………………………………… 246
　中国地名英译的注意事项 ………………………………………………………… 247
　外国政要译名的策略 ……………………………………………………………… 252
　拓展阅读 …………………………………………………………………………… 255
　　　选文 A …………………………………………………………………… 255
　　　译文 ……………………………………………………………………… 256
　　　选文 B …………………………………………………………………… 258
　　　译文 ……………………………………………………………………… 259

第十二单元　法律事务（Legal Affairs） …………………………………………… 261
　单元要点 …………………………………………………………………………… 261
　理论难点提示 ……………………………………………………………………… 261
　　　选文 A …………………………………………………………………… 261
　　　重难点评析 ………………………………………………………………… 263
　　　译文 ……………………………………………………………………… 263
　　　选文 B …………………………………………………………………… 265
　　　重难点评析 ………………………………………………………………… 267
　　　译文 ……………………………………………………………………… 268
　口译中的跨文化因素 ……………………………………………………………… 270
　法庭口译的类别和特点 …………………………………………………………… 274

拓展阅读 ··· 276
      选文 A ·· 276
      译文 ·· 277
      选文 B ·· 278
      译文 ·· 281

第十三单元　外贸政策（Foreign Trade Policy） ······························ 284
   单元要点 ·· 284
   理论难点提示 ·· 284
      选文 A ·· 284
      重难点评析 ·· 285
      译文 ·· 286
      选文 B ·· 287
      重难点评析 ·· 289
      译文 ·· 290
   数字口译 ·· 292
   拓展阅读 ·· 299
      选文 A ·· 299
      译文 ·· 300
      选文 B ·· 301
      译文 ·· 302

第十四单元　科技（Science & Technology） ····································· 304
   单元要点 ·· 304
   理论难点提示 ·· 304
      选文 A ·· 304
      重难点评析 ·· 305
      译文 ·· 306
      选文 B ·· 308
      重难点评析 ·· 309
      译文 ·· 310
   科技口译的特点 ·· 311
   口译前准备工作概述 ·· 312
   拓展阅读 ·· 313
      选文 A ·· 313
      译文 ·· 314
      选文 B ·· 316
      译文 ·· 318

第十五单元　网络时代（Network Times） ······································· 319
   单元要点 ·· 319
   理论难点提示 ·· 319

选文 A ··· 319
　　重难点评析 ··· 321
　　译文 ··· 322
　　选文 B ··· 325
　　重难点评析 ··· 327
　　译文 ··· 328
口译员的临场应变策略 ·· 329
中文网络流行词汇英文译解 ·· 330
拓展阅读 ··· 332
　　选文 A ··· 332
　　译文 ··· 334
　　选文 B ··· 338
　　译文 ··· 338

第一单元 接待口译
(Interpreting for Reception Service)

单元要点

本单元共分五个层次,分别是:汉英互译一篇;欢迎致辞口译一篇;外事口、笔译的特点综述;口译听辨技巧;拓展阅读(汉译英、英译汉各一篇)。第一、二部分提供接待口译的例文及其翻译和重难点评析;第三、四部分主要是相关口译理论与技能的介绍;第五部分的拓展阅读中,提供汉、英原文和参考译文。

理论难点提示

1. 外事口、笔译的特点综述。
2. 口译听辨的技巧。

选文A

(在机场迎接)

王(interpreter): Excuse me, but aren't you Mr. Smith, head of the US delegation?

Smith: Yes. I'm John Smith from the United States of America.

王: How do you do, Mr. Smith? My name is Wang Min, an interpreter from the Foreign Affairs Office of our company. Allow me to introduce you to our general manager, Mr. Zhao. 赵总,这位是史密斯先生。

Smith & 赵(together while shaking hands): How do you do? 您好!

赵: 史密斯先生,我很高兴地欢迎您及您的代表团来访,祝您此行愉快。

Smith: Thank you very much for coming to meet me. We are very honored to have this opportunity to come here. Just call me John.

赵: 好的,你们旅途一切可好?

Smith: Not too bad. But we are later than expected. Our plane delayed taking off as we ran into a storm. We were held up for several hours at the airport, waiting for the storm to clear up. But on the whole, we had good flying weather.

赵: 飞行了这么久一定很累了吧,我们直接开车去宾馆吧。

Smith: Yes, I'm a bit tired. But I'll be all right by tomorrow.

赵: 考虑到你们的方便和舒适,我们已为你们安排住在公司附近的宾馆,那里从设计到装潢都非常具有中国古典特色,我相信你们一定会喜欢的。

Smith: I think I will. Thank you so much.

(在宾馆客房)

赵：希望你们对这里的住宿和服务感到满意。这是我们为代表团安排的日程草案，请您看一看。如果要作任何变动，或有什么事情要办，可以联系我们的翻译员王敏。为了照顾代表团，他将陪同你们住在宾馆。

Smith：Good．None of us knows any Chinese beyond a few polite formulas such as"你好"and"谢谢"．I'm afraid that's hardly enough to get by．

赵：是的。史密斯先生，我公司今晚七点将设宴欢迎代表团，王敏将陪同你们前往。希望代表团所有成员都能出席。

Smith：I think so．Everyone of us wants to make the most of this visit．Let me thank you on behalf of our delegation．

赵：请不要客气。好吧，我该走了，你们好好休息吧。今晚的宴会上见。

重难点评析

1．"Allow me to introduce you to our general manager，Mr．Zhao．"译为"请允许我介绍一下，这位是我公司的赵总经理。"作为译员为双方作介绍的时候可以说：I'd like to introduce you to...／I would like you to meet...／May I introduce you to...

2．"我很高兴地……"译为"I'm very happy to.../I'm delighted to.../I'm so pleased to.../It's a great pleasure to..."等等。

3．"祝您此行愉快。"可以译为"I hope you'll have a pleasant visit here．/I wish you a pleasant trip here．/I hope you'll enjoy your visit here．"等等。

4．"be honored to"是接待口译常用语，译为"对于某事感到非常的荣幸"。

5．"旅途一切可好？"译为"How was the journey？/Did you enjoy your trip？/Did you have a pleasant trip？"等等。

6．"run into a storm"译为"突遇暴雨"。"run into sth．"译为"突然遇到（意料之外的）某事）"。

7．"We were held up for several hours at the airport，waiting for the storm to clear up．"译为"我们那里突然下大暴雨，飞机推迟起飞，我们在机场等了好几个小时才等到天气转好。"be held up 译为"被某个原因阻碍、滞留等"；clear up 译为"天气转好"。

8．"...we had good flying weather．"译为"……飞行途中天气很好。"

9．"考虑到你们的方便和舒适"译为"for your convenience and comfort"。

10．"为你们安排住在公司附近的宾馆"译为"We accommodate you in the hotel located very close to our company．""安排某人入住"可以译为"accommodate sb"，如果要表达的是为某人预订好了住处（如宾馆客房等），也可以译为"reserve for sb a suite"等。

11．"从设计到装潢都非常具有中国古典特色"译为"It is a classic Chinese residence designed and decorated in the architectural style of ancient China．""从设计到装潢"直接译为并列的"designed and decorated"，简明且符合英文的表达习惯。

12．"希望你们对这里的住宿和服务感到满意"译为"I hope you find the accommodations and service satisfactory．"accommodations用复数形式，指的是"食宿"。

13．"如果要作任何变动，或有什么事情要办，可以联系我们的翻译员王敏。"译为"If

you should want anything changed or done, just speak to Wang Min."这里将"事务变动"和"办事"两个意思进行了合译"want anything changed or done",流畅而简洁。

14. "为了照顾代表团,他将陪同你们住在宾馆。"译为"He will be staying here to see to your needs and comfort."这里"照顾"的意思是指照顾到代表团在访期间的各种要求,不是指照料他们,所以应非常地道地译成"see to your needs and comforts",而不是"take care of you"。

15. "a few polite formulas"译为"一些礼貌用语或客套话"。

16. "I'm afraid that's hardly enough to get by."译为"这些(几句礼貌用语)恐怕是不够应付的。"get by 译为"通过,混过"。例如:I hope I can get by in a dark suit for this formal occasion. 我希望我能穿一件深色的衣服把这个正式场合应付过去。How does she get by on such a small salary? 她靠那么一点儿薪水怎么过活?

17. "我公司今晚七点将设宴欢迎代表团。"译为"We'll host a reception banquet in honor of your delegation this evening at seven.""设宴"译为"host a reception banquet",这里是非常正式的译法,在有些场合也可以说"host/give a reception dinner/banquet"。

18. "Everyone of us wants to make the most of this visit."译为"我们每个人都希望能从此次访问中充分受益。"make the most of 译为"充分利用"。

译 文

(Meeting at the airport)

王(翻译员):请问,您是美方代表团的团长史密斯先生吗?

Smith:是的。我是来自美国的约翰·史密斯。

王:您好,史密斯先生。我叫王敏,是我们公司外事办公室的翻译员。请允许我介绍一下,这位是我公司的赵总经理。Mr. Zhao, this is Mr. Smith.

Smith & 赵(边握手边说):您好! How do you do?

赵:Mr. Smith, I'm very happy to welcome you and all the other members of your delegation. I hope you'll have a pleasant visit here.

Smith:非常感谢您来机场接我。能有机会来到这里,我们感到非常的荣幸。叫我的名字约翰就可以。

赵:OK. Did you enjoy your trip?

Smith:还可以,但还是误点了。我们那里突然下大暴雨,飞机推迟起飞,我们在机场等了好几个小时才等到天气转好。总的来说,飞行的天气还不错。

赵:I suppose you must be very tired after the long trip. Shall we drive directly to the hotel?

Smith:是的,我是有点累了,但明天就可以恢复了。

赵:For your convenience and comfort, we have accommodated you in the hotel located very close to our company. It is a classic Chinese residence designed and decorated in the architectural style of ancient China, and I'm sure you'll like it.

Smith:我想我会的。非常感谢你。

(In Mr. Smith's suite)

赵:I hope you find the accommodation and service satisfactory. This is a tentative schedule we've worked out for your tour. Please have a look to see whether it suits you. If you want anything changed or done, just contact our interpretor Wang Min. He will be staying here to see to your needs and comfort.

Smith:太好了。我们中间没有人懂中文,最多能讲几句像"你好"、"谢谢"等客套话。这些恐怕是不够应付的。

赵:I suppose so. Well, Mr. Smith, we'll host a reception banquet in honor of your delegation this evening at seven. Wang Min will accompany there. We hope every member of your delegation will be able to come.

Smith:我看没问题。我们每个人都希望能从此次访问中充分受益。让我代表我们代表团的所有成员向您表示感谢。

赵:You're welcome. Now, I'm sure you need a good rest. I suppose I have to go now. See you at the banquet tonight.

选文B

驻英国大使刘晓明在陈晓东公使离任暨秦刚公使到任招待会上的讲话

2010年9月13日,中国驻英国使馆

女士们,先生们:

感谢大家出席今天的招待会,与我们一道欢送陈晓东公使,欢迎秦刚公使。

陈公使是我的老同事、老朋友,早在九年前我们就在中国驻埃及大使馆共事。此次在伦敦再度聚首,虽然相处只有半年多,但陈公使的出色表现使我充满感激。

临别之际,我愿用"五好"来评价陈公使:首先,他是一位好同事。他以对英国的深入了解、对中英关系的准确把握,为我到任以来的工作提供了许多不可或缺的帮助。

其次,他是一位好领导。中国驻英使馆有十多个部门、一百多人,陈公使协调得力,管理有方。

再者,他是一位好外交官。他广交朋友,善于沟通,为人谦和,一会儿佩里先生将代表48家集团俱乐部向陈公使授予"破冰者"荣誉称号,这是英国朋友对陈公使在英工作的最好评价。

最后,他是一位好丈夫和好父亲。当然,由于工作繁忙,他没有很多时间来照顾家人。这里我向陈公使夫人张斌女士表示歉意,同时对你和你们的女儿始终理解、支持陈公使的工作表示衷心的感谢,也对你们的女儿伊莎今年考入名校表示祝贺。

我为有陈公使这样的好同事、好朋友感到高兴,也对他离任感到惋惜。我衷心地祝福他,祝他鹏程万里,再立新功。

今天,我还要热烈欢迎秦刚公使。可能在场的许多人都认识、熟悉秦刚公使。一则他曾是中国外交部发言人,是外交部出镜率最高的几个人之一,不仅部内外知名度高,在中国还有众多"粉丝"。

二则他与英国颇有渊源,这是他第三次来英国常驻,是一位名副其实的"英国通"。他的到来为驻英使馆增添了新鲜血液,他的经验、人脉、知识和卓识将使他在对英工作中大显身手。我预祝他工作顺利,为中英关系发展谱写更多新的篇章。

当前,中英关系处在新的历史起点上,面临着新的发展机遇。我们愿与英方一道,抓好机遇,扩大交流,深化合作,推动中英战略合作关系不断向前发展。

最后,我再次感谢英国各界朋友们对陈公使的热心支持和帮助,希望你们继续给予秦刚公使大力支持与通力合作。

谢谢!

重难点评析

1. "欢送"在这里译为"bid farewell to",是正式场合的常用语,另有如"farewell dinner/banquet"。

2. "在伦敦再度聚首",根据实际情况来看,这里仍然是"共事"的意思,故译为"to be colleagues again"。

3. "陈公使的出色表现使我充满感激"译为"I must say I have nothing but thanks to him for the dedication and competence he has shown in performing his duties.""出色表现"具体地译为"dedication and competence"(奉献精神和工作能力),非常贴切说话人本意。

4. "我愿用'五好'来评价陈公使",中文经常有"评价某人"的说法,没有直译成"estimate",说话人的原意是陈公使的五种好品质给他留下了深刻印象,而不是要对陈公使做什么评估,故译为"I have been impressed by the 'five good qualities' of Minister Chen."

5. "对英国的深入了解、对中英关系的准确把握"译为"his broad understanding of Britain and solid grasp of China-UK relations",也可译为"his thorough understanding of Britain and accurate grasp of China-UK relations"。

6. "他是一位好领导",译者将"一位好领导"作了补译"a good team leader well-liked and respected by colleagues"。

7. "中国驻英使馆有十多个部门、一百多人,陈公使协调得力,管理有方",在翻译时使用了合译法"He has done an excellent job in smoothly coordinating the work of more than 100 diplomats across a dozen sections within the embassy."整个句子意义明晰,结构紧凑。

8. "他广交朋友,善于沟通,为人谦和",译者根据自己对实际情况的理解将这三者之间的关系译成了因和果的关系,再次采用了合译法译为一个整句"His modesty, professionalism and ability to communicate has won him many friends in Britain."

9. "向陈公使授予'破冰者'荣誉称号"译为"present him with the Icebreaker Award","present someone with something"译为"(尤指在正式场合)向某人颁发、授予、赠送"。

10. "这是英国朋友对陈公使在英工作的最好评价",将"英国朋友"进行了省译,并针对"对陈公使在英工作的最好评价"进行了意译"recognizing his achievements"。

11. "同时对你和你们的女儿始终理解、支持陈公使的工作表示衷心的感谢"译为"I am sincerely thankful to her and to their daughter Yisha for their consistent understanding and support to Minister Chen.""为某事向某人致谢"可表达为"be thankful to someone/thank someone for something"。

12. "也对你们的女儿伊莎今年考入名校表示祝贺"译为"And I also wish to take this opportunity to congratulate Yisha on being recently admitted to a prestigious university in

London.""为某事向某人致以祝贺"可表达为"congratulate someone on something","名校"可表达为"prestigious/top/topnotch university"。

13. "他与英国颇有渊源"译为"His association with the UK dates back many years." "date back many years"译为"追溯到很多年前"。

14. "他的经验、人脉、知识和卓识将使他在对英工作中大显身手",为了照顾译文前后意群的连贯,此句采用了分译法译为"..., he has brought with him his knowledge, insight and experience of Britain and of its people. I am sure he will do a good job..."

15. "我预祝他工作顺利,为中英关系发展谱写更多新的篇章。"译为"I wish him every success and greater contribution to China-UK relations."中文里常说的"谱写新的篇章"采用了意译"greater contribution"更加符合英语的习惯。

16. "抓好机遇,扩大交流,深化合作,推动中英战略合作关系不断向前发展",这是外事致辞的常用排比句,译为"... to grasp these opportunities to expand exchanges and cooperation and take our strategic partnership to a new level."战略合作关系可表达为"strategic partnership"。

译 文

Remarks by H. E. Ambassador Liu Xiaoming at the Farewell Reception for Minister Chen Xiaodong and Welcoming Reception for Minister Qin Gang

13 September 2010, Chinese Embassy

Ladies and Gentlemen,

Thank you for joining us in bidding farewell to Minister Chen Xiaodong and welcoming Minister Qin Gang.

Minister Chen has been a close colleague and good friend of mine for many years. Nine years ago, we worked together at the Chinese Embassy in Egypt. We are more than pleased to be colleagues again in London, though this time only for six months. I must say I have nothing but thanks to him for the dedication and competence he has shown in performing his duties.

For years, I have been impressed by the "five good qualities" of Minister Chen. Firstly, he is a good colleague. He has been a source of advice and support to me. Since I arrived in London, I have benefitted a great deal from his broad understanding of Britain and solid grasp of China-UK relations.

Secondly, he is a good team leader well-liked and respected by colleagues. He has done an excellent job in smoothly coordinating the work of more than 100 diplomats across a dozen sections within the embassy.

Thirdly, he is a good diplomat. His modesty, professionalism and ability to communicate has won him many friends in Britain. In a little while Mr. Stephen Perry, Chairman of the 48 Group Club, will present him with the Icebreaker Award, recognising his achievements during his posting in London.

Lastly, but definitely not least, he is a good husband and a good father, though he has often been too busy to leave much time for his family. For that I must say sorry to his wife Madame Zhang Bin. I am sincerely thankful to her and to their daughter Yisha for their consistent understanding and support to Minister Chen. And I also wish to take this opportunity to congratulate Yisha on being recently admitted to a prestigious university in London.

Whilst I am sorry to say goodbye to such a good colleague, I am also proud that Minister Chen is leaving us to take on a position of important responsibilities. I wish him the best of luck in his new endeavours.

It now gives me great pleasure to introduce to you Minister Chen's successor, Mr. Qin Gang. Although I am sure many of you know, or know of him through his previous high-profile role as the Chinese Foreign Ministry spokesman. I hear that he has lots of fans in China.

His association with the UK dates back many years. This is his third posting in London. Being an expert on UK affairs, he has brought with him his knowledge, insight and experience of Britain and of its people. I am sure he will do a good job as Deputy Head of Mission. I wish him every success and greater contribution to China-UK relations.

Today China-UK relations stand at a new starting point and are blessed with new opportunities. We are ready to work with British colleagues to grasp these opportunities to expand exchanges and cooperation and take our strategic partnership to a new level.

To conclude, I wish to thank all of you once again for your support and assistance to Minister Chen. I do hope that Minister Qin can continue to enjoy your support and cooperation.

Thank you!

外事口、笔译的特点综述

一、翻译的种类和外事翻译的特点

翻译活动的范围很广。就其翻译方式来说,有汉语译成外语(简称"汉译外")和外语译成汉语(简称"外译汉")两种。就其工作方式来说,有口头翻译(简称"口译",interpretation)和笔头翻译(简称"笔译",translation)之分。口译包括交替传译(简称"交传",consecutive interpretation)和同声传译(简称"同传",simultaneous interpretation 或 conference interpretation)两种。就其程度而言,可分为全文翻译(full translation)和部分翻译(partial translation),如摘译。上述种种翻译既有共同之处,又有其特点。

外事翻译的内容主要是在各种外交、外事场合上口头和书面的讲话和文件。在外事场合,口、笔译往往同时使用。比如建交谈判、关于国际公约的谈判,都要求译员既能口译,又能将所谈的内容和结果落实到文字上,成为公报、公约、条约、备忘录、协议等。有时是先口译,然后产生文件;有时则在讲话、演讲前将稿件译好,再到现场作口译。

外事翻译的内容决定了它具有有别于其他领域翻译的特点：

首先，外事翻译政治性和政策性强。无论是口译，还是笔译，外事翻译的内容多是国家的立场、政策。稍有差错，就可能影响到一个国家的政治和经济利益、形象、声誉、地位及其国际关系等，就可能给国家和人民造成无可挽回的损失。因此，译者一定要严肃认真对待每次翻译。

其次，外事翻译的时效性很强。口译工作的最大特点是时间紧，要求译员当场完成翻译过程。笔译也往往有时限要求。有时前台在与某国谈判建交问题，后台同时在翻译建交公报，随时根据前台的谈判情况进行修改，随时打出清样交前台使用。很多时候在领导人出访前不久，才把出访时要用的讲话稿交译员去翻，译员需要在短时间内完成翻译定稿、打字、校对等多道程序。有时我国国家领导人参加国际性首脑会议，在开会现场根据会议进程和情况亲自手写即席发言稿或修改事先草拟的发言稿，写完立即从会场传出来由在场外的笔译同志译成外语后，交至会场上的同声传译译员手中，以保证翻译效果。

再者，外事翻译的政治性还决定了它的保密性强的特点。作为翻译，经常要翻译尚未正式发表的讲话稿及其他文件，决不应该向外界透露文件内容。

二、外事笔译

笔译是指书面翻译。外事笔译的内容主要是各种外交、外事场合的讲话稿，如在国家会议上的讲话稿，在宴会、招待会上的祝酒词，以及外交上交涉用的说帖、声明，国家间的照会、信函、公报、协议、条约等正式外交文件。笔译的工具过去用手动和电动打字机，后来改用文字处理机，现在则是使用电脑。笔译的成果是书面译文，它是供对外提供、公开发表、长期保存的，必须经得起审查、琢磨和推敲。政府或外交部声明、领导人讲话稿、祝酒词等政策性很强。公报、协议、条约、议定书、国际会议文件等则具有国际法律性质。所以，对笔译要求很高，不仅要求译文正确、准确、完整、严谨，而且要求译文通顺、优美。译出的中文应是地地道道的中文，要符合中文的习惯；译出的外文应是地道的外文，要符合外文的用语。这就要求笔译人员应具有较高的外语功底和母语基础。

三、外事口译

口译，又称口头传译，就是现场翻译。外事口译的主要任务是，担任我国领导人出访或外国领导人来访时双方或多方谈判、会谈、交谈时的现场翻译，在各种场合的演讲、讲话或参观访问时的介绍即席翻译。在双边会谈中，这种翻译通常采用交替传译方式。在国际研讨会、国际大会、国际组织的年会等各种会议上通常采用同声传译。

要成为一个合格的口译译员，除具有翻译的一般素质外，还必须具有一些特别的素质。对于从事外事口译工作的同志来说，无论是交替传译，还是同声传译，翻译的第一个环节是听。只有听明白了原话，才能进行翻译。因此，口译译员有敏锐的听觉是极其重要的。译员有好的听力，还需要有良好的收听条件。做交替传译的同志往往坐或站在领导人的后边或旁边，做同声传译的同志大多坐在会场上面的同传厢子里。这样的位置有利于译员听清楚。但译员有时不得不在各种环境里进行翻译，如：在大型记者招待会上，译员需要听明白记者从远距离提出的问题。在领导人参观访问时，译员有时不得不在机器的轰鸣声中或人声嘈杂的多方中进行翻译。做同声传译的也不是每次都有具有隔音效果的同传厢，有时不得不在会场一角、直接面对与会人员做同声传译。所有这些情况都会影响收听效果。对于这些影响收听的因素,译员在大多数情况下是无能为力的。为了确保较好地完成口译任务,译员应该提前到场,做好装备工作。在可能的情况选择一个较佳的位置。对同传译员来说,应事先做好检查耳机是否接插无误、电钮的位置是否准确等准备工作。但更重要的是平时采取有针对性的措施,提高自己的听力,如:多听带各种口音的外语,总结规律、熟悉口音。扩大知识面、熟悉情况和所谈问题,能够有助于根据所听的大概的声音进行"合理"的猜测(intelligent guess),以求准确理解原话。

1. 外事交传

进行交替传译时,讲话者每讲几句话或一段话就会停下来,让译员进行翻译。在外事活动中,这种翻译方式主要用在中、外领导人进行会见、会晤、会谈、对话、磋商、谈判、交涉及参观访问等场合。现场翻译时间紧,没有翻译斟酌的时间,这就要求翻译反应快、语言水平高、语言转换能力强。在大多数外交谈话中,特别是会谈、对话、磋商、谈判、交涉时,中、外领导人主要是讨论双边关系和交换对国际形势、国际问题的看法。他们的谈话内容往往政策性很强,有时十分敏感。在这种场合,翻译必须准确无误、完整无漏,从政策高度把握分寸。在参观游览、观看演出、进餐陪车等私下随便交谈时,有时可以翻得灵活一些。

2. 外事同传

同声传译是指举行国际会议时,在发言人讲话的同时,由译员进行传译。发言人不间断地讲话,译员边听边译。同声传译是口译中最难的。

同声传译始于1919年的巴黎和会。那次会议第一次聘用了正式同声传译译员。从1919年到第二次世界大战结束,这一期间的国际会议使用英、法两种语言的译员进行同声传译。1945年,联合国成立,规定汉语、英语、法语、俄语及西班牙语为正式语言和工作语言,后又增加阿拉伯语。由于美国及一些西方国家的阻挠,中国在联合国的合法席位一直被蒋介石集团所窃据。当时,美国纠集一些国家对中国实行孤立、封锁政策,新中国在五六十年代参加的国际会议不多。因此,在那段时期,新中国基本没有自己的同声传译人员。1971年,第26届联合国大会以压倒多数通过了"恢复中华人民共和国在联合国的一切合法权利、并立即将国民党集团的代表从联合国一切机构中驱逐出去"的2758号决议。自那以来,中国积极参加联合国及其专门机构的活动,积极参加各种国际会议,所以迫切需要同声传译人才。1979年,中国政府与联合国总部委托北京外国语学院开办联合国译员培训班,这是中国历史上首次正规地培训国际组织、国际会议的口、笔译人员。现在,中国有一批同声传译人员长期为联合国等国际机构工作。国务院许多部委都有自己的同声传译人员。

四、笔译与口译、交替传译与同声传译的不同特点

笔译可以查字典、找参考资料、与同事商讨,可以反复研究、体会原文,可以琢磨、推敲、斟酌字句。但口译,无论是交传还是同声传译,都要在讲话人讲话的同时听清、领会讲话的内容,记住讲话的原话、原词,并立即用另一种语言清楚、准确地表达出来。他们没有思考的时间,没有查找字典、资料和与他人探讨的条件。再者,人们讲话往往有口音,讲话的风格也各不相同。有的喜欢用简单明了的短句,有的则爱用一句套一句的复杂句;有的口齿伶俐、发音清楚,有的则口齿含混、吞音吃音;有的说话慢条斯理、有板有眼,有的说话则像开机关枪,速度很快,句与句之间没有停顿。但在任何情况下,人们都期待译员能够迅速、完整、准确地翻译出来。口译译员在工作时,必须保持注意力高度集中,不能有片刻松懈、

走神,否则,必然会漏听、漏译。他们还必须学会在听的同时做笔记,并一开始便将所听到的内容在脑子里译成另一种语言。也就是说,译员必须学会同时做三件事——认真听、记笔记、思考翻译。这确实是一项高度紧张的脑力劳动,要求译员不但听力好、理解力强,而且要记忆力好、反应快。

同样是口译,交替传译与同声传译又各有特点。做交传时,听与表达可以分阶段进行。有人讲话时,口译译员最重要的是集中注意力听,力求听懂,抓住讲话的主要内容、重点。同时,适当记一些笔记。如果没有听清楚,可以请发言者再说一遍,或自己重复一遍,请发言者确认。当讲话人停下来让译员翻译时,译员再集中精力翻译。译的时候,要抓重点,要注意意思准确、完整,语言通顺易懂,讲话速度适中,不带拖音、嗯音,不拖泥带水,不胡编乱造、不懂装懂。实在听不懂或想不出对应词的时候,可以请教在座的中外人士。而同声传译需要听、说同时进行,边听边译。他们不能等待发言者讲完一句话后再翻,那样就会跟不上,来不及。译员与发言人只能有一两个词组、最多半句话的差距。发言人讲完一句话,译员也应尽快译完这句话。而且,不管前半句是如何开始翻的,都应该设法使后半句能够接得上,使翻译的句子基本通顺,而不致于断句,或是词组、短语的堆砌,凌乱无序。尽管同声传译也可以丢掉一些啰嗦、重复的东西,以及一些无关紧要的修饰词,可以进行适当的概括,甚至可以省略无关紧要的内容,但不能抓不住中心意思。同声传译的速度是由发言人来决定的,译员只能适应。总之,交传必须翻得准、全、顺。而同传则难以做到准、全、顺。因此,只要保证主要意思不丢、能够译出百分之七八十,就可以过得去,被接受。语言也不必完全忠实于发言人的说话风格,而是应该学会将长句切成几个短句来译,但不能不成句。

与同声传译相比,交替传译有一个有利条件。译员听不明白的时候可以客气地请讲话者重复一遍或适当进行一些解释。而同声传译的译员坐在同传厢子里,对有些字句未听懂或漏听时,是无法要求发言人重复的。与同声传译和笔译相比,交替传译的另一个优势是,译员还可以借助声调、手势等来说明意思,达到传神传意的目的。坐在同传厢子里的同传译员和在幕后从事笔译的同志都是无法借助手势的。在做翻译的时候,交传译员如果不知道某一个词或字,还可以稍加解释,把意思译出来就行。要求与发言人同步说话的同传译员是绝没有时间进行解释的。可以说,交替传译的表达方式可以比同声传译和笔译灵活一些,丰富一些。三者相比,笔译的翻译质量要求最高,交替传译次之,同声传译更次之。但从翻译的时间上来看,这个次序就颠倒过来了。同传译员最没有斟酌和思考的时间;交传译员还可以在听的同时边做笔记,边思考;笔译尽管常常有时限,但思考时间相对充裕一些,还可以查字典、咨询他人。

交替传译、同声传译、笔译,既有许多共同的特点和共同的要求,又有不少差异,对从事不同翻译工作的人有不同的要求。正因为如此,在联合国系统、欧盟以及其他一些国家,从事口、笔译的人员是分开的。他们分属于不同的部门,如在欧盟,从事会议翻译的人属于会议翻译总司,而从事笔译的人则属于笔译总司。我国外交部翻译室的绝大多数同志历来是多面手,他们兼做交替传译、同声传译和笔译。当然,鉴于年龄、翻译水平、工作需要等多方面因素的考虑,不同的人在不同的时期可能有不同的侧重。一般情况下,年轻的同志口译做得多一些,年长一点的同志多做一些笔译。也有一些同志各方面的条件都很好,语言功底深厚,可以交传、同传、笔译齐头并进。但不管侧重于哪一方面,每一个同志都必须从事笔译,因为,笔译是基础。有平时笔译经验的积累,才能练出口译所需要的快速反应和熟练的语言转换能力。反过来,经常从事口译工作,经常接触活的语言,跟上形势的发展,才能不断丰富语言,提高笔译水平。两者是相辅相成的。因此,译员应力争使自己成为"全才",成为交传、同传、笔译都行的全面翻译。

五、汉外对译

汉译外(translation from Chinese into a foreign language)和外译汉(translation from a foreign language into Chinese),是两个不同的翻译程序。汉译外,首先要理解汉语的原文、原话的意思,再用外语表达出来。而外译汉正好相反,先理解外语的原文、原话的意思,再用中文表达出来。对于绝大多数人来说,外语学得再好,也不如母语讲得好。表达一般比理解要难一些。因此,联合国聘用语文专业人员有一条规定:翻译审校要一律以母语为译入语言(在联合国机构里,中国人只从事外译中,而中译外是聘请外国人从事的)。

口译听辨技巧

"听辨"(listening and information receiving),顾名思义,不仅要"听"还要"辨",即思考、分析。"听辨"是口译过程中的第一阶段。在这个过程中我们接收到源语信息,并通过种种分析手段把接收到的信息纳入到我们的理解范畴,以便储存和输出。毫无疑问,口译的成败在很大程度上取决于听辨过程。所以,大家首先要先对口译的听辨过程有一个透彻的认识,以便有针对性地进行练习,提高自己的听辨能力。

口译中的听辨过程和大家平时英语学习中所接受的听力训练不同,但两者又有一定联系。

首先,具备良好的听力水平是培养良好听辨能力的基础。换句话说,如果一个人的外语听力有问题,那么无论他的语言表达能力有多强,他都很难胜任口译工作。其次,光有好的听力还不够,因为听辨过程还涉及其他方面的能力。这一点可以从听力训练与听辨过程的区别中看出来。

一、听力训练与听辨过程的区别

1. 英语听力训练中比较注重语言层面,也就是说他们会十分注意语音、语调和语言的表达及用法。而译员在听辨过程中所注重的是意思,或是讲话者的意图,而不是具体的词句表达。所以译员在听到一段话之后在头脑中形成的是一个有逻辑关系的语意整体,而不仅仅是词句的简单集合。

2. 听力练习中主要启动听觉系统,理解只是一个被动而附带的过程。而译员在听辨过程中不仅要启动听觉系统,还要启动大脑中的分析理解机制和记忆机制。也就是说,译员要边听、边分析、边理解、边记忆。所以,与一般的外语学习相比较而言,专业译员要具有更强的分析能力,要会"一心多用"。

3. 就一般听力而言,信息接收是被动和跟随性的,对信息的反应略显滞后,而译员的听辨过程是积极主动的,在听的过程中伴有很大程度的预测和判断行为,常常需要调动非语言因素对所听内容进行分析、整理、补充和联想。

4. 通常,用作听力训练的材料,信息比较清晰,杂音干扰较少。而译员在口译工作中所处的信息环境是现场性的,不确定性因素较多;信息干扰、信息缺失时有发生。而且,讲话者以交流为唯一目的,在信息发布过程中并不照顾或考虑译员的状态。

综上所述,口译听辨过程较一般外语听力训练要复杂得多,要求也高得多。大家需要建立这样一个意识,即口译过程不是一个信息背诵加字词翻译的过程,而是一个通过听辨将信息接收、理解,再用译入语将理解的信息加以表达的过程。以下提供一些方法供大家参考。

二、英语听辨能力训练的方法

1. 可以选择一些英文有声资料(最好是现场讲话)或是请练习搭档模拟现场发言。听过一段话后,在不记笔记的情况下用源语(英文)进行复述。注意在听的过程中要把注意力从词句表达上移开,而专注于整段话的逻辑意思。在复述时不要拘泥于原文词句,更不要试图背原话,意思和逻辑关系要尽量复述得准确完整。

2. 在听辨训练的初级阶段,如果还不能完全掌握边听、边分析、边记忆的技能,可采取就所听内容进行提问的方式建立逻辑关系。比如,可以将注意力放在 What, Who, When and Where, How and Why 等几个要素上。通过这种方式增强逻辑分析意识,努力跟上讲话人的思路,从而对所听语篇有一个正确的理解。

3. 每段讲话的长度可随熟练程度的增强而逐步增加,比如从听几句话到听一小段,从一小段到一大段,再到数段等。并可以尝试听各种不同风格的讲话。选题也可以从比较熟悉的领域逐步扩展到比较陌生的领域,以培养临场适应能力和综合分析能力。

4. 练习听辨能力可以从标准的英语视听资料开始。练习者对标准语音都比较适应,因此听力方面的障碍较小,可以将更多的精力放在分辨、整理讲话内容方面。在对标准英文的听辨练到一定程度之后,可以逐渐引入带有各种口音的英文视听资料。现场工作中,很多时候讲话者的英文带有浓重的地方或个人口音,如果平时练习只针对标准英文发音,在实际工作中遇到"非标准"英语时就会因准备不足而影响口译任务的完成。

三、听辨训练的逻辑线索

口译中的逻辑分析指的是对讲话内容进行纵向和横向的分析。纵向分析是指分清关键信息和辅助信息,即找出逻辑的层次;横向分析则是明确各信息点之间的逻辑关系,如因果关系、对比对照、举例说明等。逻辑分析的目的是为了透彻地理解原语讲话的内容,对信息的点(具体的信息内容)、线(各点之间的联系)和面(即整体概念)进行全面的把握,以便于记忆和表达。信息经过分析加工,便能在记忆中留下更深的印象。

逻辑分析练习可分为纵向分析和横向分析练习。纵向分析的训练方法和概述练习有些类似,但侧重点不一样。纵向分析要求进行逻辑分层训练,即在听完一篇讲话后首先用一句话概括出讲话的中心内容,这是逻辑的最上层;围绕这一中心问题讲话人谈了哪几个方面的内容,这是第二层关系;而每个方面又具体谈了些什么,这是逻辑的下一个层次。将信息一层一层地剖析下去,形成一个清晰的逻辑线路图,然后按照逻辑线路对原语讲话进行复述,复述时不必拘泥于原语的顺序和结构。

横向分析的练习则要求我们找出信息之间的逻辑关系。一般的信息结构都遵从一定的逻辑关系模式,如:概括(generalization)、分类(classification)、因果(cause-effect)、对比对照(compare & contrast)、按照时间、空间、步骤、重要性的顺序排列(sequencing)、列举(simple listing)、提出问题—解决问题(problem—solution)等。找逻辑关系可以根据线索词汇,如英文里表示概括关系的线索词汇有:to sum up, in summary, in conclusion, in brief, in short, on the whole 等;表示顺序的词汇有:first, second, furthermore, before, preceding, during, when, finally, meanwhile 等;表示对比的词汇有:likewise, as well as, in common with, both, similarly, compared to 等;表示对照的词汇有:on the other hand, on the contrary, otherwise, instead, still, yet, whereas, differently 等;表示因果的词汇则有:so, since, because, as a result, consequently, lead to 等等。

逻辑分析要求在听取信息时不是被动地接收,而是在全神贯注地收听的同时,结合自己对口译情境和讲话人背景的了解,进行合理的分析和预测,这样才能更好地跟上讲话人的思路,缓解"听"的压力,使口译理解更轻松、更准确。

四、十类标志词

学习口译必不可少的就是听力训练,听讲座、演讲、新闻等等,而据研究有90%以上的语篇小话题都是由标志词引导或提示的,因此在语段听力中听到下列标志词时要引起高度的重视,集中注意力听清标志词前后的句子。

1. 最高级标志词

形容词、副词最高级

most/chief/primary/main/leading...

2. 唯一级标志词

only/unique/prefer/every/one/of all/perfect...

3. 因果项标志词

cause/lead to/contribute to/thanks to/owing to/question/answer/why/reason/其他形式的问句...

4. 转折项关键词

despite/in spite of/instead/while/from...to.../although...(yet).../not only...but also...

5. 序数项标志词

所有的序数词(first,second)/another/the other/next/last/in addition/on the other hand...

6. 时间项标志词

when/today/as/before/after/since/then/until...

7. 解释项标志词

or/namely/in other words/that is/that is to say...

8. 目的项标志词

to/for...

9. 总结项标志词

all in all/in brief/to conclude/at last/in summary/in short...

10. 强调项标志词

副词:especially/particularly/almost/always/usually...

动词:show/remember/note/notice/say/pronounce...

拓展阅读

选文A

（在机场送行）

赵：时间过得真快，好像你们昨天刚下飞机似的，可是现在就要说再见了，真是遗憾。

Smith：Can't be half as sorry as we shall be to be leaving. Really, it's been a most interesting and rewarding visit.

赵：听您这么说，我真高兴。欢迎你们随时再来。对朋友，我们的门是永远敞开的。

Smith：Glad to hear that. We all want to thank you and all those concerned for the generous hospitality and accompanying us on the tour around the city.

赵：能接待你们，我们感到很愉快。这次我们谈得很成功，我也很高兴。

Smith：Thanks again for making this trip such a success. If you have time around Christmas, please come to New York. I'll show you around our city.

赵：谢谢您的邀请。我会考虑的。

Smith：There's the last call for boarding. I guess we must say goodbye now.

赵：再见！祝你们一路平安。

译文

(Seeing off at the airport)

赵：How time flies! It seems as if it was only yesterday that you got off the plane and now you are leaving us. I'm really sorry.

Smith：我们要离开贵国更感到遗憾。真的，这是一次很有趣也很有收获的访问。

赵：I'm so glad to hear that. You are welcome to visit us again any time. Our door is always open to friends.

Smith：很高兴听您这么说。我们非常感谢您和相关人员对我们的盛情款待以及陪同我们观光这座城市。

赵：It was a real pleasure having you with us. I'm also very excited about our successful talks.

Smith：再次感谢你们使得此行如此成功。圣诞节的时候如果有空，欢迎到纽约来。我可以带你看看我们的城市。

赵：Thanks for the invitation. I'll think about it.

Smith：这是最后一次登机广播了。我们得说再见了。

赵：Goodbye and have a nice flight.

选文B

何亚非大使在到任招待会上的讲话
2010年3月16日

女士们，先生们，朋友们，

首先欢迎并感谢大家光临。

第一单元 接待口译(Interpreting for Reception Service)

　　日内瓦湖光山色,国际组织云集,国际会议众多,是重要的多边外交舞台。作为中国新任常驻代表,很高兴来日内瓦这个美丽的城市工作。

　　日内瓦对我并不陌生,20多年前,我曾有幸在日内瓦国际问题高等学院学习一年。至今我仍能忆起当年学习生活的美好时光,忆起日内瓦人民的热情和友善。

　　日内瓦也是中国多边外交起步的地方。1954年,周恩来总理率团出席日内瓦会议,新中国从这里走上国际舞台。多年来,中国全面、深入参与多边事务,成为国际体系的重要参与者和积极建设者。中国与驻日内瓦各联合国机构和国际组织的关系不断发展,为推动相关领域的国际合作做出了积极贡献。

　　女士们,先生们,当今世界正处于经济大动荡、体系大变革、格局大调整时期。国际经济危机阴霾未散。气候变化、能源资源、公共卫生安全等全球性问题日益突出和多元化。国际和地区热点问题此起彼伏。2010年更是继续应对国际金融危机、推动世界经济复苏非常重要的一年。

　　新形势下,任何国家都难以独善其身。继续推进人类和平与发展的崇高事业,需要各国加强合作,协调行动。正如中国外交部长杨洁篪日前在中外记者会上指出的:"冷战思维、零和博弈这样的思想不合时宜,同舟共济、互利共赢才是生存和发展之道。"

　　女士们,先生们,中国一贯倡导多边主义,坚定支持联合国在维护世界和平与安全、促进共同发展、保障人权等方面发挥的积极作用,主张合作应对全球挑战。过去的一年里,中国积极参加应对国际金融危机、气候变化等国际合作,在一系列重大多边会议上发挥了独特的建设性作用。

　　在刚刚结束的中国第十一届全国人大三次会议上,中国总理温家宝在《政府工作报告》中指出,2010年,中国"将继续以20国集团金融峰会等重大多边活动为主要平台,积极参与国际体系变革进程,维护发展中国家利益。统筹协调好双边外交与多边外交、国别区域外交与各领域外交工作,推动中国与各大国、周边国家和发展中国家的关系全面深入发展","进一步做好应对气候变化、能源资源合作等方面的对外工作,在妥善解决热点问题和全球性问题中发挥建设性作用"。

　　女士们,先生们,新形势下,日内瓦这个多边舞台更加广阔,更加重要。中方愿进一步全面、深入参与日内瓦多边外交各领域活动,服务中国国内社会经济发展,并为推动世界持久和平和共同繁荣做出自己的贡献。我本人和中国代表团愿意成为大家了解中国的窗口,更愿成为促进中国与各方加强交流与合作的桥梁。

　　2010年上海世博会将于5月1日开幕。本届世博会将是探讨人类城市生活的盛会,是一曲以创新和融合为主旋律的交响乐,将成为人类文明的一次精彩对话。我借此机会热烈欢迎各位届时赴上海参观世博会。

　　谢谢大家。

译 文

Remarks by H. E. Ambassador He Yafei at a Reception Marking His Assumption of Office

2010-03-16

Excellencies,

Ladies and Gentlemen and friends,

　　I am very much delighted to have you here today at the Chinese Mission. Thank you for honouring me with your presence upon my assumption of office.

I am most privileged and honoured to be accredited as China's new Permanent Representative to Geneva, not only because of its beautiful lakes and mountains, but most importantly, its position as home to many international organizations with numerous international conferences. Geneva is an important stage for multilateral diplomacy.

Geneva is not unfamiliar to me. I was here in Geneva with the Graduate School of International Studies as a student about 20 years ago. The happy time of my school life as well as the warmth and friendship of the local people are memorable.

Geneva is also a place that started China's multilateral diplomacy. In 1954, as you may recall, late Premier Zhou Enlai led the Chinese delegation to the Geneva Conference, ushering China onto the multilateral diplomatic stage. And China has, over the years, fully engaged itself in multilateral affairs on all fronts. It is not only an active participant, but also an important contributor to the relevant international systems and regimes. The Chinese Mission here has also worked hard and contributed to expanding its relations and cooperation with the UN agencies and other international organizations based in Geneva.

Ladies and Gentlemen, the present world is witnessing major economic challenges, coupled with major structural changes or adjustments. The impact of the global economic crisis is still with us, while global challenges such as climate change, energy and resources, public health security have become increasingly prominent. In addition, the present world is also witnessing international or regional hot issues here and there. 2010 is a very important year for the international efforts to combat financial crisis in promotion of early world economic recovery.

Collective efforts are essential, under the present new circumstances, if the above global problems are to be put behind us. No country can do it alone. To further advance the noble course of peace and development for humanity, intensified cooperation and coordinated actions are called for on the part of the international community. The Chinese Foreign Minister Yang Jiechi said during a recent press conference, "The cold-war mentality and zero-sum game theory have become anachronistic. And the right way to survive and thrive is stick together in tough times like passengers in the same boat and pursue mutual benefit and win-win progress."

Ladies and Gentlemen, China has all along championed multilateralism, and we have been resolute in supporting the positive role of the United Nations in maintaining world peace and security, promoting common development and safeguarding human rights. We've also stood for intensified international cooperation to meet global challenges. Over the last year, China has, for its part, actively participated in the international cooperation to address international financial crisis and climate change, and played a unique and constructive role in a series of major international conferences.

At the just-concluded Third Session of the 11th National People's Congress, Premier Wen Jiabao said in his Report of the Work of the Government, that, in 2010, "China will continue to use the G20 financial summit and other major multilateral activities as our main platforms for actively participating in the process of change in international systems and safeguarding the interests of developing countries. We will make overall plans for coordinating bilateral and multilateral diplomacy as well as promote further, comprehensive development of our relations with major powers, neighboring countries, and developing countries. We will continue to carry out diplomatic work in climate change, energy and resources cooperation, and other areas, and play a constructive role in finding proper solutions to hot issues and global problems".

Ladies and Gentlemen, Geneva, under new circumstances, will be an even more important multilateral stage with broader agenda. We, for our part, stand ready to work closely with our friends here in a bid to advance the multilateral diplomatic work on all fronts, so as to help serve China's domestic social and economic development, and to contribute to the durable peace and common prosperity of the world. I myself and the Chinese Mission are willing to serve as a window, through which, to promote the understanding, exchanges and cooperation between China and the world.

The Expo 2010 Shanghai is going to unveil on 1 May this year in China. With the theme of "Better City, Better Life", Expo 2010 represents the common aspiration of all mankind for a better living in future urban environments. And it will also be a wonderful occasion for dialogues between human civilizations. I'd like to take this opportunity to warmly welcome you all to the Shanghai Expo.

Thank you.

第二单元　礼仪祝辞
（Ceremonial Speech）

单元要点

　　本单元共分五个层次，分别是：礼仪祝辞汉译英一篇；礼仪祝辞英译汉一篇；口译记忆；公共演讲；拓展阅读（汉译英、英译汉各一篇）。第一、二部分提供礼仪祝辞口译的例文及其翻译和重难点评析；第三、四部分主要是相关口译理论与技能的介绍；第五部分的拓展阅读中，提供汉、英原文和参考译文。

理论难点提示

1. 口译记忆。
2. 公共演讲。

选文A

胡锦涛在庆祝新中国成立60周年大会上的讲话
中共中央总书记、国家主席、中央军委主席　胡锦涛
北京天安门城楼
2009年10月1日

全国同胞们，同志们，朋友们：

　　今天，我们隆重集会，庆祝中华人民共和国成立60周年。在这个喜庆而又庄严的时刻，全国各族人民都为伟大祖国的发展进步感到无比自豪，都对实现中华民族伟大复兴的光明前景充满信心。

　　在这里，我代表党中央、全国人大、国务院、全国政协和中央军委，向一切为民族独立和人民解放、国家富强和人民幸福建立了不朽功勋的革命先辈和烈士们，表示深切的怀念！向全国各族人民和海内外爱国同胞，致以热烈的祝贺！向关心和支持中国发展的各国朋友，表示衷心的感谢！

　　60年前的今天，中国人民经过近代以来100多年的浴血奋战终于夺取了中国革命的伟大胜利，毛泽东主席在这里向世界庄严宣告了中华人民共和国的成立。中国人民从此站起来了，具有5 000多年文明历史的中华民族从此进入了发展进步的历史新纪元。

　　60年来，在以毛泽东同志、邓小平同志、江泽民同志为核心的党的三代中央领导集体和党的十六大以来的党中央领导下，勤劳智慧的我国各族人民同心同德、艰苦奋斗，战胜各种艰难曲折和风险考验，取得了举世瞩目的伟大成就，谱写了自强不息的壮丽凯歌。今天，一个面向现代化、面向世界、面向未来的社会主义中国巍然屹立在世界东方。

新中国60年的发展进步充分证明,只有社会主义才能救中国,只有改革开放才能发展中国、发展社会主义、发展马克思主义。中国人民有信心、有能力建设好自己的国家,也有信心、有能力为世界作出自己应有的贡献。

我们将坚定不移地坚持中国特色社会主义道路,全面贯彻执行党的基本理论、基本路线、基本纲领、基本经验,继续解放思想,坚持改革开放,推动科学发展,促进社会和谐,推进全面建设小康社会进程,不断开创中国特色社会主义事业新局面,谱写人民美好生活新篇章。

我们将坚定不移地坚持"和平统一、一国两制"的方针,保持香港、澳门长期繁荣稳定,推动海峡两岸关系和平发展,继续为实现祖国完全统一这一中华民族的共同心愿而奋斗。

我们将坚定不移地坚持独立自主的和平外交政策,坚持和平发展道路,奉行互利共赢的开放战略,在和平共处五项原则基础上同所有国家发展友好合作,继续同世界各国人民一道推进人类和平与发展的崇高事业,推动建设持久和平、共同繁荣的和谐世界。

中国人民解放军和人民武装警察部队要发扬光荣传统,加强自身建设,切实履行使命,为维护国家主权、安全、领土完整,为维护世界和平再立新功。

历史启示我们,前进道路从来不是一帆风顺的,但掌握了自己命运、团结起来的人民必将战胜一切艰难险阻,不断创造历史伟业。

展望未来,中国的发展前景无限美好。全党、全军、全国各族人民要更加紧密地团结起来,高举中国特色社会主义伟大旗帜,与时俱进,锐意进取,继续朝着建设富强民主文明和谐的社会主义现代化国家、实现中华民族伟大复兴的宏伟目标奋勇前进,继续以自己的辛勤劳动和不懈奋斗为人类作出新的更大的贡献!

伟大的中华人民共和国万岁!

伟大的中国共产党万岁!

伟大的中国人民万岁!

重难点评析

1. "隆重集会"译为"hold a grand celebration"。注意这里翻译中的词性转换,副词"隆重"译文中为形容词"grand"。

2. "庆祝中华人民共和国成立60周年"译为"to mark the 60th anniversary of the founding of the People's Republic of China"。

3. "全国各族人民都为伟大祖国的发展进步感到无比自豪,都对实现中华民族伟大复兴的光明前景充满信心",译文中用了两个形容词短语"be proud of"和"be confident of"并列连接两个成分。"实现中华民族伟大复兴的光明前景"译为"the Chinese nation's bright prospect on the road to revival",注意这里使用了省译法,因为无须将"实现"实译出来。

4. "党中央、全国人大、国务院、全国政协和中央军委",注意这些重要机构的正确英译,应译为"the CPC Central Committee, the National People's Congress, the State Council, the Chinese People's Political Consultative Conference and the Central Military Commission"。

5. "向一切为民族独立和人民解放、国家富强和人民幸福建立了不朽功勋的革命先辈和烈士们,表示深切的怀念!"译为"I hereby pay tribute to all the revolutionary pioneers of

older generations and martyrs who made great contributions to realizing national independence and liberation of the people, the country's prosperity and strength and happy life of the people.""向某人(尤指已逝世者)致以敬意、悼念"译为"pay tribute to","民族独立和人民解放、国家富强和人民幸福"译为"national independence and liberation of the people, the country's prosperity and strength and happy life of the people",在意义上两两相关,故分别译成由 and 连接的两组名词短语。

6. "向全国各族人民和海内外爱国同胞,致以热烈的祝贺!"译为"I send warm congratulations to people from all ethnic groups in the country and patriotic compatriots from home and abroad.""向某人致以热烈祝贺"译为"send warm congratulations to sb","全国各族人民"译为"all ethnic groups in the country","海内外爱国同胞"译为"patriotic compatriots from home and abroad"。

7. "100 多年的浴血奋战"译为"more than one hundred years of blooded struggle"。

8. "毛泽东主席在这里向世界庄严宣告了中华人民共和国的成立。"翻译时使用了强调句"It was here that Chairman Mao Zedong solemnly declared to the world the founding of the People's Republic of China.""向世界庄严宣告"译为"solemnly declare to the world"。

9. "具有 5 000 多年文明历史的中华民族从此进入了发展进步的历史新纪元"译为"the Chinese nation with over 5,000 years of civilization began a new page of development and progress in history","进入新纪元"译为"begin a new page/step into a new era"。

10. "60 年来,在以毛泽东同志、邓小平同志、江泽民同志为核心的党的三代中央领导集体和党的十六大以来的党中央领导下,勤劳智慧的我国各族人民同心同德、艰苦奋斗,战胜各种艰难曲折和风险考验,取得了举世瞩目的伟大成就,谱写了自强不息的壮丽凯歌。"译文也是一个长句"In the past sixty years, with the three generations of Party leadership with Comrade Mao Zedong, Comrade Deng Xiaoping and Comrade Jiang Zemin as a core, and with the leadership of the Central Committee formed after the 16th National Congress of the CPC, with hard work and wisdom of all ethnic groups of the country, the Chinese people have joined hands to overcome the great hardship and made great contributions that have been recognized by the world, and proved our perseverance and endurance.""党的十六大"译为"the 16th National Congress of the CPC","同心同德、艰苦奋斗,战胜各种艰难曲折和风险考验"译文采用了意译,译成一个简洁的短句"the Chinese people have joined hands to overcome the great hardship","谱写了自强不息的壮丽凯歌"同样采用了意译"proved our perseverance and endurance"。

11. "面向现代化、面向世界、面向未来"译为"marching towards modernization, embracing the world and future",同一个动词"面向"在译文中根据英文的习惯分别译成了"march toward"和"embrace"。

12. "我们将坚定不移地坚持中国特色社会主义道路,全面贯彻执行党的基本理论、基本路线、基本纲领、基本经验,继续解放思想,坚持改革开放,推动科学发展,促进社会和谐,推进全面建设小康社会进程,不断开创中国特色社会主义事业新局面,谱写人民美好生活新篇章。"原文是个长句子,在翻译时根据意群断开采用了分译法将其译成了三个英文句子,"We will unswervingly follow our path on socialism with Chinese characteristics and

comprehensively implement the ruling party's basic theory, basic line, basic program and basic experience. We will maintain our policies of emancipating our thoughts, of reform and opening-up, pushing forward scientific development and promoting social harmony. We will push forward the process of comprehensively building a moderately well-off society, turning new pages in the endeavor of socialism with Chinese characteristics, and opening new chapters in making the people's life better."了解以下几个中国政治常用语：坚持中国特色社会主义道路 follow our path on socialism with Chinese characteristics, 党的基本理论、基本路线、基本纲领、基本经验 the ruling party's basic theory, basic line, basic program and basic experience, 解放思想 emancipate our thoughts, 改革开放 reform and opening-up, 小康社会 a moderately well-off society, 开创新局面 turn new pages, 谱写新篇章 open new chapters; 此外, 还要注意"坚持""贯彻""推动""促进""推进"等中国政治常用动词的正确翻译。

13. "坚持'和平统一、一国两制'的方针"译为"stick to the policy of 'peaceful reunification' and 'one country, two systems'", "坚定不移地坚持"译为"stick to/abide by/pursue unswervingly"。

14. "推动海峡两岸关系和平发展"译为"seek peaceful development of cross-strait relations", "推动"译为"seek/push forward/promote/advance"。在翻译时注意, 如果中文的同一个动词重复出现时要注意选用不同的词来翻译。

15. "我们将坚定不移地坚持独立自主的和平外交政策, 坚持和平发展道路", 这里的两个"坚持"为避免重复, 分别译成了"maintain"和"follow", "独立自主的和平外交政策"译为"an independent foreign policy of peace"。

16. "和平共处五项原则"是政治常用语, 固定译法为"the five cardinal Principles of Peaceful Co-existence"。

17. "中国人民解放军和人民武装警察部队"固定译法为"The Chinese People's Liberation Army and People's Armed Police Force"。

18. "为维护国家主权、安全、领土完整, 为维护世界和平再立新功", 根据上下文, 译文将此句译为由"so as to"连接的目的状语"so as to make new contributions to safeguarding national sovereignty, security and territorial integrity, as well as world peace"。"国家主权、安全、领土完整"为政治常用语, 固定译法为"national sovereignty, security and territorial integrity"。

19. "展望未来, 中国的发展前景无限美好"在翻译时采用了主语转换, 增译主语"我们", 译为"Looking forward to the future, we envision bright prospect for China's development."

20. "全党、全军、全国各族人民要更加紧密地团结起来, 高举中国特色社会主义伟大旗帜, 与时俱进, 锐意进取, 继续朝着建设富强民主文明和谐的社会主义现代化国家、实现中华民族伟大复兴的宏伟目标奋勇前进, 继续以自己的辛勤劳动和不懈奋斗为人类作出新的更大的贡献！"这是一个很长的句子, 译者根据意群将其断开分译成了两个句子, 将两个"继续"的内容归为后半句, 译为"The whole Party, the army and people of all ethnic groups will unite more closely, holding up the great banner of building a socialism with Chinese

characteristics, and advance with the times and with enterprising spirit. Let's continue to build up socialist modern nation with prosperity, democracy and harmony, move forward to realize the great goal of rejuvenation of the Chinese nation and make new great contributions to the well being of humanity with our diligent work and unremitting efforts.""与时俱进,锐意进取"译为"advance with the times and with enterprising spirit","实现中华民族伟大复兴的宏伟目标"译为"realize the great goal of rejuvenation of the Chinese nation"。

译文

Speech at the Celebration for the 60th Anniversary of the Founding of the People's Republic of China

President Hu Jintao

Tian'anmen Rostrum in Central Beijing

Oct. 1, 2009

Fellow countrymen, comrades and friends,

Today, we hold a grand celebration to mark the 60th anniversary of the founding of the People's Republic of China. At this cheerful and solemn moment, people from all over the country's ethnic groups are extremely proud of our great nation's development and progress and are confident of the Chinese nation's bright prospect on the road to revival.

On behalf of the CPC Central Committee, the National People's Congress, the State Council, the Chinese People's Political Consultative Conference and the Central Military Commission, I hereby pay tribute to all the revolutionary pioneers of older generations and martyrs who made great contributions to realizing national independence and liberation of the people, the country's prosperity and strength and happy life of the people. I send warm congratulations to people from all ethnic groups in the country and patriotic compatriots from home and abroad, and express heartfelt thanks to the friends from other countries who care about and support China's development.

Sixty years ago on this day, the Chinese people achieved great victory of the Chinese revolution after more than one hundred years of blooded struggle. It was here that Chairman Mao Zedong solemnly declared to the world the founding of the People's Republic of China. At that moment, the Chinese people stood up and the Chinese nation with over 5,000 years of civilization began a new page of development and progress in history.

In the past sixty years, with the three generations of Party leadership with Comrade Mao Zedong, Comrade Deng Xiaoping and Comrade Jiang Zemin as a core, and with the leadership of the Central Committee formed after the 16th National Congress of the CPC, with hard work and wisdom of all ethnic groups of the country, the Chinese people have joined hands to overcome the great hardship and made great contributions that have been recognized by the world, and proved our perseverance and endurance. Today, a socialist China is standing firm in the east as marching towards modernization, embracing the world and future.

The sixty years of development of New China has proved that only socialism can save China, only reform and opening up can develop China, develop socialism and develop Marxism. The Chinese people are confident and are capable of building our own country and make due contributions to the world.

We will unswervingly follow our path on socialism with Chinese characteristics and comprehensively implement the ruling party's basic theory, basic line, basic program and basic experience. We will maintain our policies of emancipating our thoughts, of reform and opening-up, pushing forward scientific development and promoting social harmony. We will push forward the process of comprehensively building a moderately well-off society, turning new pages in the endeavor of socialism with Chinese characteristics, and opening new chapters in making the people's life better.

We will unswervingly stick to the policy of "peaceful reunification" and "one country, two systems" to help Hong Kong and Macao remain prosperous and stable, to seek peaceful development of cross-strait relations, and to work for the complete reunification of the motherland, which is the common aspiration of the Chinese nation.

We will unswervingly maintain an independent foreign policy of peace. We will follow a path of peaceful development. We will seek a strategy of win-win cooperation based on the five cardinal Principles of Peaceful Co-existence. We will develop friendly relations and cooperation with all nations. We join hands with the people from all over the world in pushing forward the lofty cause of making the world more peaceful and progressive and building a harmonious world of long-lasting peace and prosperity.

The Chinese People's Liberation Army and People's Armed Police Force should uphold their glorious traditions, build up their own strength and fulfill their missions practically so as to make new contributions to safeguarding national sovereignty, security and territorial integrity, as well as world peace.

History has shown us that the road ahead may not always be as smooth as what we expect. But the Chinese people who are united and are masters of the destiny will overcome all difficulties and obstacles and will continue to create great historic undertakings.

Looking forward to the future, we envision bright prospect for China's development. The whole Party, the army and people of all ethnic groups will unite more closely, holding up the great banner of building a socialism with Chinese characteristics, and advance with the times and with enterprising spirit. Let's continue to build up socialist modern nation with prosperity, democracy and harmony, move forward to realize the great goal of rejuvenation of the Chinese nation and make new great contributions to the well being of humanity with our diligent work and unremitting efforts.

Long live the great People's Republic of China!

Long live the great Communist Party of China!

Long live the great Chinese people!

选文B

Speech at the Official Welcoming Ceremony for President Hu Jintao
by Barack Obama, President of the United States
January 19, 2011

Good morning, everyone. President Hu, members of the Chinese delegation, on behalf of Michelle and myself, welcome to the White House. And on behalf of the American people, welcome to the United States.

Three decades ago, on a January day like this, another American President stood here and welcomed another Chinese leader for the historic normalization of relations between the United States and the People's Republic of China. On that day, Deng Xiaoping spoke of the great possibilities of cooperation between our two nations.

Looking back on that winter day in 1979, it is now clear. The previous 30 years had been a time of estrangement for our two countries. The 30 years since have been a time of growing exchanges and understanding. And with this visit we can lay the foundation for the next 30 years.

At a time when some doubt the benefits of cooperation between the United States and China, this visit is also a chance to demonstrate a simple truth. We have an enormous stake in each other's success. In an interconnected world, in a global economy, nations — including our own — will be more prosperous and more secure when we work together.

The United States welcomes China's rise as a strong, prosperous and successful member of the community of nations. Indeed, China's success has brought with it economic benefits for our people as well as yours, and our cooperation on a range of issues has helped advance stability in the Asia Pacific and in the world.

We also know this: History shows that societies are more harmonious, nations are more successful, and the world is more just, when the rights and responsibilities of all nations and all people are upheld, including the universal rights of every human being.

Mr. President, we can learn from our people. Chinese and American students and educators, business people, tourists, researchers and scientists, including Chinese Americans who are here today — they work together and make progress together every single day. They know that even as our nations compete in some areas, we can cooperate in so many others, in a spirit of mutual respect, for our mutual benefit.

What Deng Xiaoping said long ago remains true today. There are still great possibilities for cooperation between our countries. President Hu, members of the Chinese delegation, let us seize these possibilities together. Welcome to the United States of America. Hwan-ying.

重难点评析

1. "on behalf of..., welcome to..."是致辞的惯用语,译为"我谨代表……欢迎你们来到……"。

2. "...another American President stood here and welcomed another Chinese leader for the historic normalization of relations between the United States and the People's Republic of China."这是一个很长的句子,翻译员采用了分译法将其译成了两个短句,"另一位美国总统站在这里欢迎另一位中国领导人,标志着美国和中华人民共和国关系正常化的历史时刻。"这更符合中文的习惯。

3. "The previous 30 years had been a time of estrangement for our two countries."注意这里的时态是过去完成时,指的是"1979年邓小平访美之前的30年,是两国关系僵持的一段时期"。

4. "The 30 years since have been a time of growing exchanges and understanding."这是一个现在完成时的句子,是指"邓小平访美之后的30年,是两国之间交流与理解不断发展的时期"。

5. "some doubt the benefits of cooperation"译为"有些人对两国合作是否有利表示怀疑"。

6. "We have an enormous stake in each other's success."译为"我们与对方的成功利益攸关。""have a stake in"译为"与……有利害关系"。

7. "China's rise"译为"中国的崛起"。

8. "the community of nations"译为"国际大家庭/国际社会"。

9. "our cooperation on a range of issues"译为"我们在一系列问题上的合作"。

10. "History shows that societies are more harmonious, nations are more successful, and the world is more just, when the rights and responsibilities of all nations and all people are upheld, including the universal rights of every human being."考虑到中文的表达习惯,这句话采用倒译法进行翻译,因和果之间的关系一目了然。译文为"历史表明,当各国的权利和责任、各国人民的权利——包括每个人的普遍权利——得到维护时,社会就更和谐、国家就更繁荣、世界就更公正。"

11. "in a spirit of mutual respect"译为"本着相互尊重的精神"。"in a spirit of"是外交致辞与演讲中的常用语,译为"本着……的精神"。

译 文

2011年1月19日美国总统奥巴马在正式欢迎胡锦涛主席访美仪式上的致辞

大家早上好!胡主席、中国代表团成员们,我谨代表米歇尔和我自己欢迎你们来到白宫,并代表美国人民欢迎你们来到美国。

30年前,在像今天这样的一个1月的日子里,另一位美国总统站在这里欢迎另一位中国领导人,标志着美国和中华人民共和国关系正常化的历史时刻。在那一天,邓小平谈到了我们两国间巨大的合作机会。

回首1979年那个冬日,现在一切都非常清晰。在那之前的30年是我们两国关系的僵持时期。在那之后的30年是交流与理解不断发展的时期。胡主席的此次访问能够让我们为未来30年奠定基础。

正当有人怀疑美中两国间的合作是否有利的时候,此次访问也提供了展示一个简单事实的机会。我们与对方的成功利益攸关。在一个相互依存的世界、在全球经济中,如果我们齐心协力,各国——包括我国——将会更加繁荣、更加安全。

美国欢迎中国崛起成为国际大家庭中的一个强大、繁荣、成功的成员。事实上,中国的成功已经既给你们的人民,也给我国人民带来了经济好处;我们在一系列问题上的合作帮助增进了亚太地区和世界的稳定。

我们也很清楚:历史表明,当各国的权利和责任、各国人民的权利——包括每个人的普遍权利——得到维护时,社会就更和谐、国家就更繁荣、世界就更公正。

主席先生,我们可以向我们的人民学习。中国和美国的学生和教育工作者、商界人士、旅游者、研究人员和科学家,包括今天在场的华裔美国人——他们一道努力,每天都在共同取得进步。他们知道,虽然我们两国在某些领域相互竞争,但我们能够在其他那么多领域本着相互尊重的精神,为着我们的共同利益而合作。

邓小平多年前所说的话今天依然正确。我们两国之间仍然有着巨大的合作机会。胡主席、中国代表团成员们,让我们共同抓住这些机会。欢迎你们来到美利坚合众国,欢迎!

口译记忆

一、口译记忆的机制

良好的记忆力是译员必须具备的技能,是译员得以施展其口译能力的前提条件。记忆包括输入、储存和重现三个过程,一般可分为瞬时记忆、短时记忆和长时记忆。

有研究表明,瞬时记忆只能使语言信息保持0.25秒至2秒,之后记忆的信息便会消失,它是大脑最短的记忆。做口译,尤其是同声传译,要求译者反映迅速,其实就是强调译者要有瞬时获取信息的能力,这也是口译人员需要具备的基本素质之一。在同传训练初期,教师会要求学生做一个月左右的跟读训练,即在讲话者开始讲话后,学生等待五六个词的时间,然后复述讲话者刚刚讲过的内容。在整个跟读练习过程中,学生始终要与讲话者保持五六个词的间隔,不许缩短,但可以适当延长。这种练习就是要着力训练学生瞬间捕捉信息的能力。

短时记忆启动后,捕捉到的关键瞬时信息得以暂时储存。虽然信息保持的时间短,但对口译人员来说,该时段的记忆相当重要,它是译者进行高强度脑力活动的关键时刻。此时,译者对源语的记忆还十分清楚,可以利用这一时段将捕捉到的瞬时信息迅速进行各种关联并进一步完成由源语到目的语的转化。短时记忆除了可以获取谈话者正在讨论的信息,还可以激活长时记忆中的相关信息。但短时记忆的特点是容量小和持续时间短,因此,该时段记忆的信息应尽快使用,否则,时间拖延久了便会遗忘。鉴于短时记忆的这一特点,译者在做交传时应用笔记来帮助大脑储存信息。笔记记录的是类似于路标一样的信息,译员在阅读时,相关信息将存储在大脑中的短时记忆激活,并指引其将信息进行分析和整合,最终予以传译。

最后,经过加工的语言信息进入长时记忆阶段。长时记忆的信息容量要大得多,信息的保持可以从短时直至终生,是大脑长期保持信息的重要手段。在口译的记忆过程中它配合短时记忆共同完成大脑的记忆工作。长时记忆对我们口译的影响很大。长时记忆的信息都是经验性的,人们听过、看过、经历过的事情都可以留在长时记忆中,随时可提取出来与正在听到的信息相结合,从而帮助人们更透彻地理解信息。对口译员来讲,大脑储存的知识越多,经验知识越丰富,就越能在口译时发挥出最佳的水平。

概括来讲,三种记忆机制在口译过程中各司其职。瞬时记忆由瞬间感知信息、接收外界信号,所以通常与源语听辨有关;短时记忆与长时记忆都有一定的持续时间,所以与译员对源语信息的储存有关;而长时记忆的持续时间最长,有积累和相互重叠的特点,所以与译员长期以来的语言学习和知识积累有关。就记忆而言,"瞬时记忆"是口译的前提,"短时记忆"是口译的关键,"长时记忆"是口译的基础。

译员在口译时并不是机械地记忆接收到的语音信息,而是需要从长时记忆中提取相关的语言和专题知识对信息进行理解后才能将其意义储存在短时记忆中。如果所听到的词汇和信息是译员平时反复使用且非常熟悉的,那么这些内容在长时记忆中处于一种活跃状态,口译中这部分内容就很容易被激活,提取速度快,理解也会更容易、更透彻,记忆储存效果也会相应更好。反之,如果碰上平时很少接触或使用的词汇和题材,即这些内容在长时记忆中处于不活跃状态,译员的理解就会更费时费力,记忆效果也会大打折扣。可见,长时记忆是口译理解的基础,而口译理解则是口译记忆的前提。

口译记忆的困难一般可以归结为三个方面的原因:一是短时记忆的局限性,二是长时记忆中储存的信息处于不活跃状态,三是心理压力大。

了解口译记忆的这些特点,能够帮助我们找到提高口译记忆效率的途径。

二、口译记忆的训练方法

口译记忆有三种类型:瞬时记忆、短时记忆和长时记忆。一般来讲,记忆的效果与记忆材料的类型有一定的关系。比如逻辑关系清晰、结构紧凑的语料记忆起来就比较容易,记忆保持的效果也比较理想。另外,记忆的效果还与待识记语料是否具有形象性有关。人们对贴近生活实景生动、形象的描述记忆起来会比较容易,印象也比较深刻。考虑到记忆的不同类型和影响记忆的种种因素,大家不妨采取以下几种方法进行相关的记忆训练。

1. 信息视觉化和现实化训练

这种训练是针对大脑对意像语料的敏感性而设计的,旨在训练译员通过将信息内容现实化、视觉化来记忆信息的能力。比如听到以下一段内容:

I was walking in the park with a friend recently, and his cell phone rang, interrrupting our conversaiton. There we were, walking and talking on a beautiful sunny day and — poof! — I became invisible, absent from the conversation. The park was filled with people talking on their cell phones. They were passing other people without looking at them, saying hello, noticing their babies or stopping to pet their puppies. Evidently, the untethered electronic voice is preferable to human contact.

听到这一段生动形象的描述之后，译员便可在头脑中勾画这样一幅图景：自己正与一位朋友在公园中散步、闲谈。突然，谈话被朋友的手机打断。然后放眼四周，发现到处是只顾自己拿着手机讲话而无暇互相交流的人们。译员就这样通过现实化、形象化的方法将一篇复杂的描写转化成生活中一个再熟悉不过的镜头摄入了头脑。然后，译员再用译语将眼前的这幅图景按照自己的方式描述出来即可。这样不仅记忆深刻、全面，而且译员也不会陷入机械的"找词翻译"的误区。

2. 逻辑分层记忆训练

通常，人们能较好地识记逻辑层次清晰、结构紧凑的篇章，我们不妨从一些条理清晰的篇章入手，锻炼自己的逻辑思维和整理识记的能力。在逻辑分析和记忆能力都有所提高之后，再逐渐降低待识记信息的条理性和逻辑性，以提高自己对逻辑层次一般甚至较差的普通讲话的适应能力，并最终能将逻辑思维能力作为一种"半自动化"的技能加以掌握，即在听到一段讲话后能够"本能"地对其进行逻辑层次的分析并加以记忆。

以上两种具体的记忆训练（信息视觉化和逻辑分层记忆训练），均建议采用"复述法"的步骤进行。

（1）由训练者（或练习伙伴）以适当的语速现场发布源语信息，长度应掌握在1至5分钟之内。

（2）接受训练者凭记忆储存源语内容，并尽量用译语记忆。

（3）接受训练者用译语对原文的内容进行要点复述。

（4）复述后可进行讲评、切磋，探讨遗漏信息的性质和原因。

（5）练习可分阶段进行。复述的内容逐渐由大意进入细节，并逐渐提高对细节准确性的要求。

（6）整个过程中不允许记笔记。

公共演讲

一、发声训练

一名优秀的译员必须同时是一位杰出的演讲者。译员作为次级讲话人（secondary speaker），与发言人同时出现在听众面前，必须要将发言人的发言效果（impact）体现出来。这不仅仅指语言内容要准确，也指译员要合理运用声音、姿势、动作、眼神等。出色的译员能通过良好的演讲表现增加听众对其翻译能力和译作质量的信任度。

但是，译员与一般讲演者有所不同。译员对于发言的题目、内容和发言目的没有决定权，也不能随意更改发言内容，只能通过翻译尽量达到讲者要传达的发言效果。

因此，口译训练中的演讲技巧注重表述能力，它包含口头表述（vocal rendering）和体态语言（body language）两个方面，指的是译员借助有声和无声的手段达到良好的演讲效果的能力。表述训练是为了增强听众对译员的信任度，提高译文的效果。

译员口头表述的训练重点是发声（voice projection）和吐字（articulation）。发声和吐字是有声语言表达的重要载体。动听的声音和标准的吐字发音是我们练好有声语言表达的重要环节。通常所说的"字正腔圆"指的就是这两个方面。

在发声训练上要注意以下几个要素：

1. 音色

译员要具备良好的嗓音条件，圆润清亮是最理想的，尖细或嘶哑的声音让人听了不舒服。

2. 音高

音高即声音的高低，有高、中、低之分。高音具有高亢、明亮的特点，多用来表示惊疑、欢乐、赞叹等情感；中音比较丰富充实，多用来表示平和舒缓的感情；低音则比较低沉、宽厚，多用来表示沉郁、压抑、悲哀之情。对口译来说，适中的音高是最理想的，但是准确地把握高音、中音、低音的运用规律可以恰如其分地传情达意。

3. 音量

音量的大小由发音时振动用力的大小来决定。一般来说，口译时语音要响亮，送音有力。不能大到声嘶力竭，也不能小到无法听清。

4. 语调

语调指声音高低升降的变化，一般是和句子的语气紧密结合的，其中以结尾的升降变化最为重要。语调是口语表达的重要手段，它能辅助语言表情达意。语调的选择和运用，必须切合思想内容，符合语言环境，考虑现场效果。译员应准确地掌握演讲的内容和情感，恰当地运用语调，做到贴切、自然。

5. 语速

口译速度要避免太快和太慢两个极端。太快，一则听众难以跟上，时间长了容易使听众对讲话逐渐失去兴趣，不愿继续倾听；二则也使人产生怀疑，认为译员太紧张，因为人们胆怯紧张时往往语速较快。当然也不能太慢，太慢就显得拉腔拖调，犹豫不决，听众也会因为听得很累而失去耐心。口译员必须保持心态平和，语速适中。

6. 停顿

停顿不只是译员在生理上正常换气的需要，也是表情达意的需要。口译时要连贯流畅，适当停顿。停顿得当，不仅可以清晰地显示语意，而且可以调节语言节奏，给听众留下回味的余地。停顿不当，往往影响语意的表达。

7. 变化

同样一句话，由于语调轻重、高低长短、急缓抑扬等的不同变化，在不同语境里，可以表达出种种不同的思想感情。利用音高、音量、语调、语速等的变化可表示强调或引起听众特别注意，避免单调乏味，能更准确地表达思想感情，加强译文效果，保持听众的注意力。

吐字强调的是口齿清楚、发音准确。吐字的技巧不仅关系到音节的清晰度，而且关系到声音的圆润、饱满。要吐字清楚，首先要熟练地掌握常用词语的标准音。其次，要力求克服发音含糊、吐字不清的毛病。平时多练习绕口令有助于练好吐字的基本功。

另外，由于译员工作时大多通过麦克风传递声音，因此要注意"麦克风礼仪"(microphone manners)。译员的嘴巴应与麦克风之间保持一定的距离以把握适当的音量，防止音效失真和出现气爆杂音(pop noise)，要注意不能对着麦克风喘粗气、吸鼻子、咳嗽或大声翻阅资料。

二、体态语

体态语又称身势语或形体语言，是人们利用姿态、动作、面部表情来传递信息的非言语行为。体态语是人类社会交际的信息载体。人们借助体态语来表达和交流信息、感情、态度,因此体态语也是演讲语言的组成部分。译员不仅要有较强的口语表达能力,也要善于用体态语言来表情达意。

译员登上讲台,首先给听众的是视觉形象。仪表、姿态、神情、动作,全都呈现在听众面前。译员灵活自如、优美协调的体态动作,能很好地辅助口语,弥补有声语言表达的不足,使有声语言表达的内容更准确、生动、完整。译员的体态语言主要包括以下几个方面:

1. 仪表与风度

仪表与风度是一种无声的体态语言。译员一上台,听众首先通过视觉观察其形象,根据他的仪表和风度,产生了一连串的心理活动,形成"第一印象",这直接影响听讲效果。因此,译员应讲究风度,以得体的形象出现在听众面前,这种行为本身就显示出对听众的尊重。这种无声的信息传递,能很自然地缩短译员与听众的心理距离,赢得听众的关注和尊重,形成融洽和谐的气氛。

2. 身体姿态

无论站、坐、走,都要稳重、自然。站时两脚自然平立,体形端庄,精神抖擞;切忌低头弯腰,扭怩局促或将手插在衣袋中,左摇右晃;切不可斜肩、偏头、曲颈。入座时声音要轻,要坐正坐稳,身体不宜后倾或斜躺,不宜前探后望,左顾右盼,也不宜玩弄手指、衣角等。

3. 手势

不要使用过多的手势,否则令人眼花缭乱,显示译员处于紧张状态,会无形中分散听众注意力,引起听众反感。手势动作还不可过大或过小。过大,显得"张牙舞爪";过小,又显得"缩手缩脚"。对于那些习惯性动作和毫无意义的下意识动作,如抓耳挠腮、不自觉地挥舞等应尽量避免。

4. 眼神交流

眼睛是"心灵的窗户",能准确、生动地表达出复杂微妙的思想感情。译员不能只顾埋头看笔记或材料,必须通过眼神交流观察听众的反应,接受听众的信息反馈。如听众东张西望,显然是心不在焉;如听众往后一靠,双手交叉在胸前,可能是对讲话内容不甚赞同,或对译文不认可;如听众露出迷惑不解的神情,译员就要思考是否是译文不到位的缘故。进行眼神交流时要自然、从容,表现出信心和活力;看听众与看材料应交替进行。

5. 表情

表情应体现出庄重大方、从容自信、亲切热情。运用面部表情,要求自然真实,切不可过分夸张,矫揉造作,那样会令人感到虚伪滑稽;也不可毫无表情,冷若冰霜,使人感到枯燥压抑。译员一般应面带微笑以示从容、友好。为了有效地传递信息、交流感情,要尽量避免傲慢、沮丧、苦恼、不耐烦和无可奈何的表情,如皱眉、做鬼脸、吐舌头、叹气、一脸苦相等,这些都会在听众中产生不良影响,形成离心效应。

总之,译员在平时训练和实际工作中一定要注意恰如其分地使用体态语,避免出现因为不得体的体态动作而影响口译效果的情形。

三、现场常见问题和应对策略

问:口译时应站在什么立场上说话?

答:第一人称。不论是汉译英,还是英译汉,口译者都可以站在发言者的角度口译,说

"我"、"我方"、"我们"等,而不是"他"、"对方"或"他们"。第一人称的优点是亲切和融洽。例如,I'm thinking about the possibility of further cooperation. 这句话最好译为"我正在考虑有没有可能与贵方继续合作"。这远远胜过"他说他正在考虑与我方继续合作的可能性"。

问:口译语速应该快还是慢?

答:口译者说话的速度应该大致等同于发言者的速度。口译者的反应要快,但说话不宜过快,原因有三:说话太快会造成听众没听清楚意思;说得过快会造成速度的不均衡(会的说得快,而不会说的,不得不慢下来);说话太快给人以放机关枪和抢时间的感觉(难道还有一场口译要做?)。

问:如何对付口译怯场?

答:口译者怯场主要有以下几种原因:心理因素的影响(自我期望过高,或容易受挫);情面观念太重(在熟人面前怕丢面子);外语基础不过硬;知识面狭窄;性格内向,胆小怕事;仓促上阵,无备而战。鉴于这些怯场因素,我们认为,口译者必须端正态度,抛弃面子观念,巩固专业知识,扩大知识面,广交朋友,多练习对话、发言、作报告,做好口译前的准备工作。

问:口译时没有听清楚怎么办?

答:一方面,任何人都不能保证听力不出现任何问题,所以任何人都要不断地学习。另一方面,如果由于人多嘴杂或发言者发音不清楚等原因而没有听清楚,那么,口译者应该判断这个词、短语或句子是否很重要。如果能够忽略(如在 that is to say 前后的词语或句子),就连猜带混;如果不能忽略(如数字、地名、人名),就要问发言者。问的时候,不要说"我没听懂"或 I beg your pardon、因为发言者不知道你没听懂的是哪个词或词组,最好是以确认为目的的问题请求发言者解释或重复。如,发言者说:Adolescents, especially female adolescents, are particularly vulnerable, however, becuase they are new and inexperienced consumers and are the prime targets of many advertisements. 假设第一个词没听清楚,或者没听懂,如果说 I beg your pardon, 发言者就会不知所措。口译者应该说 You mean "young people"? 或者说 What does "adolescent" mean? 发言者一定会解释说:young men and women, usually teenagers 或者 children or school boys and girls.

问:口译者发现前面出现错译怎么办?

答:口译不容易,错误在所难免,因此口译者要永远学习给自己充电。万一出现错误,就予以纠正。至于怎么纠正,要看情形。如果是一个小错,可以在下面的口译中伺机更正。例如,前头把 New York State 译成了"纽约",下面就说"纽约州"或"纽约州,不是纽约市"。如果前面把它说成了"华盛顿",那么就要说"纽约州,对不起,不是华盛顿,而是纽约州"。在汉译英的错误纠正过程中,可以用 I mean/meant 或 I'm sorry 来纠正。在非正式的口译场合,小错蒙混过关或频繁纠正都不会造成很恶劣的影响,只要不出现大错就行了。在正式或大型的口译场合,小错要及时纠正;大错更要纠正,还要为此向发言者和听众道歉。至于原则错误、政治错误、政策错误,就更要防微杜渐。有条件最好是两个口译者同时参加双边会谈。一个口齿伶俐的口译者当主要口译者,另一个当辅助口译者,遇到大错时,辅助口译者可以帮助伙伴纠正。当然,也可以一段一段地交替口译。至于各方带口译,例如,英语国家一方的口译者翻译英语成汉语,我方口译者把汉语翻译成英语,这是可行的,也是受口译者欢迎的。

拓展阅读

选文A

香港特区行政长官曾荫权在礼宾府新春酒会的致辞
2010年2月22日

各位嘉宾、朋友：

大家好！新春佳节，我先祝大家新年进步，希望大家在新一年好像老虎一样，充满干劲和力量，龙精虎猛，虎虎生威。

刚过去的牛年，充满起落和变化。记得去年农历新年时，全球经济受到金融海啸的严重冲击，前景极不明朗，市民过节的心情大受影响。

其后，各国政府推出的刺激经济措施开始发挥作用，加上内地经济保持高增长，好消息陆续传来。本港经济在第二季出现反弹后，持续有所改善。第四季本地生产总值后日预算案才揭晓，预料将回复按年正增长。

虎年伊始，祝愿香港以及全球经济如虎添翼，屡创佳绩。上星期公布的数据显示就业情况持续改善，最新一季的失业率维持4.9%，是去年年初以来的低位。另外，香港新股上市集资额跃升全球第一位，消费市道亦回复畅旺。

早前一项调查发现，超过六成的受访者预期新一年香港整体发展会有改善，人数较去年大幅上升了近五成。有研究指出，乐观是成功的要素之一，见到大家对前景投下信心一票，固然值得高兴，不过，乐观归乐观，我们都要未雨绸缪，时刻保持警惕。

目前的经济状况虽然有所改善，但复苏的步伐仍然未稳：外围经济仍存有变数，各地的退市政策亦可能令市场出现波动，再加上资金流入，本港资产价格上升，令通胀的风险再次浮现。这些问题，我们都不能掉以轻心，我和我的同事会很小心评估和处理。

乐观的人在每个困难中都会看到机会。新一年虽然充满挑战，但同时亦充满机遇和希望，我会像广大市民那样，抱乐观的态度面对。大家一起努力，好好发挥香港人过去成功的要素——就是自强不息，不断提升自己，为香港寻找更多发展机遇。

牛年，令我们可以在"经济大萧条"的阴霾下重见"牛市"。如果生肖真是这样奇妙，我祝愿虎年大家都能发挥老虎的勇气和力量，为21世纪第二个十年，迈出成功的第一步。

译文

Speech at the Spring Reception at Government House by the Chief Executive of HKSAR, Mr Donald Tsang

February 22, 2010

Distinguished guests, ladies and gentlemen,

Good afternoon. In this festive season, let me start by wishing you all good progress and good health in the Year of the Tiger.

According to the Chinese zodiac, the ox is supposed to stand for steadiness and stability. Yet the past year, the Year of the Ox, turned out to be full of fluctuations and changes. I remember during the last Spring Festival, the global economy was hard hit by the financial tsunami and the uncertain economic outlook dimmed our festive mood.

Then the massive stimulus measures launched by governments around the globe began to take effect. Coupled with sustained high economic growth on the Mainland, Hong Kong's economy continued to improve at the heels of a rebound in the second quarter. The GDP for the fourth quarter will be announced on the Budget Day. We expect it to return to a year-on-year positive growth.

As we begin the new year of the Tiger, which symbolises prowess, I hope that local and global economies can continue to improve. The latest statistics indicate that the labour market is improving continuously — the jobless rate for the latest quarter remained at 4.9%, the lowest since the beginning of last year. Moreover, Hong Kong ranked first globally in terms of amount of IPO raised last year. Consumers' confidence has also picked up.

A survey conducted earlier revealed that more than 60% of the respondents expect improvement in Hong Kong's overall development in the coming year, a surge of nearly 50% over the figure last year. Studies show that optimism is an essential element for success, so I am glad that you have cast a vote of confidence in Hong Kong. Having said that, we must stay vigilant and brace ourselves for possibly rough times ahead.

Despite signs of improvement, the steadiness of economic recovery remains uncertain. The external economic environment is subject to change and market fluctuations may occur when countries begin to withdraw their stimulus packages. Influx of capital will push up local asset prices and incur inflation risks. All these factors cannot be taken lightly. My colleagues and I will assess and handle them with care.

An optimist sees the opportunity in every difficulty. Looking ahead, we may see a year filled with challenges, and yet it may also be a year of opportunities and hope. Like my fellow citizens, I will embrace the future with optimism. Let's work together to give full play to our strengths — always persevere, always strive for excellence, and always look for opportunities for the betterment of Hong Kong.

In the past year, the Year of the Ox, we witnessed the return of a "bull market" amid the looming threat of a "great depression". If the Chinese zodiac is that prescient, I wish you all the courage and strength of the tiger to stride into the second decade of the 21st century.

选文B

Christmas Greeting from Canadian Prime Minister Stephen Harper 2009

Christmas is always a special time, a time when Canadians celebrate the bonds of family, faith and friendship.

This year, we have even more reasons to give thanks — a challenging year ended well and a new year brings hope and promise.

We shall be the site of the next G-8 and G-20 summits, where the world's most powerful leaders will set a new course toward sustainable growth and prosperity.

And Canada will welcome the world at the Winter Olympic Games in Vancouver and Whistler. Young Canadians, already winners of the contests to represent our country, will face off against the best athletes in the world. Their eyes are on gold and our hearts are with them.

Their courage makes us proud. Their determination inspires us and when they take the podium, they will tell us something of our country: in a tough, competitive world Canada can lead. Every great thing to which our nation should aspire is within our reach if we have the spirit of an Olympian.

Laureen, Ben, Rachel and I join in wishing you a very Merry Christmas.

And we ask that you remember in your thoughts and prayers our men and women in uniform who risk their lives in the service of our country and their loved ones here at home who anxiously await their return.

And to them, and all of you, we wish a happy and prosperous New Year.

译文

加拿大总理史蒂芬·哈珀2009年圣诞致辞

圣诞节始终是一个特殊的时刻,在这一天加拿大人为家庭纽带、信念和友谊而庆祝。

今年,我们有更多的理由去感谢——充满挑战的一年圆满地结束了,新的一年带来了希望和承诺。

我们将举办下一次G8和20国集团首脑会议,期间世界上最强大的各国领导人将建设一条通向可持续增长和繁荣的新道路。

同时,加拿大将在温哥华和惠斯勒举办的冬季奥运会上欢迎世界宾朋。年轻的加拿大人,比赛的获胜者们,将代表我们的国家,去面对世界上最优秀的运动员。他们的目光集中在金牌上,而我们的心与他们在一起。

他们的勇气让我们为之骄傲,他们的决心激励着我们。当他们站上领奖台的一刻,他们会告诉我们这个国家所具有的信心,那就是在这样一个充满艰难和竞争的世界里,加拿大敢当人先。如果我们具有奥林匹克的精神,我们渴望取得的每一件伟大的事情都能办到。

劳润,本,瑞切尔和我一起祝愿你们圣诞快乐!

我们也请大家在思念和祈祷时,记得祝福我们那些不畏艰险为国效力的男女军人们,祝福那些依然在焦急地等待着他们回家的亲人们。

衷心祝愿各位新年快乐,万事如意!

第三单元 参观访问
(Tour and Visit)

单元要点

本单元共分五个层次,分别是:旅游组织大会讲话汉译英一篇;旅游胜地介绍英译汉一篇;导游口译特点介绍;口译笔记理论与技巧(一);拓展阅读(汉译英、英译汉各一篇)。第一、二部分提供参观访问口译的例文及其翻译和重难点评析;第三、四部分主要是相关口译理论与技能的介绍;第五部分的拓展阅读中,提供汉、英原文和参考译文。

理论难点提示

1. 导游口译特点介绍。
2. 口译笔记理论与技巧(一)。

选文A

2003年温家宝在世界旅游组织15届大会开幕式上的讲话

世界旅游组织秘书长弗朗加利先生,
联合国常务副秘书长弗莱切特女士,
各位代表,女士们,先生们:

十月的北京,天高气爽,秋色宜人。世界旅游组织第15届全体大会今天在这里隆重开幕。我代表中国政府,向各位来宾表示诚挚的欢迎!向大会表示热烈的祝贺!

旅游是一项集观光、娱乐、健身为一体的愉快而美好的活动。旅游业随着时代进步而不断发展。20世纪中叶以来,现代旅游在世界范围迅速兴起,旅游人数不断增加,旅游产业规模持续扩大,旅游经济地位显著提升,旅游活动日益成为各国人民交流文化、增进友谊、扩大交往的重要渠道,对人类生活和社会进步产生越来越广泛的影响。

古往今来,旅游一直是人们增长知识、丰富阅历、强健体魄的美好追求。在古代,中国先哲们就提出了"观国之光"的思想,倡导"读万卷书,行万里路",游历名山大川,承天地之灵气,接山水之精华。新中国成立后特别是改革开放以来,中国政府高度重视旅游工作,旅游业持续快速发展,已经成为一个富有蓬勃活力和巨大潜力的新兴产业。目前,中国入境旅游人数和旅游外汇收入跃居世界前列,出境旅游人数迅速增加,已经成为旅游大国。今年上半年,尽管我国遭遇了一场突如其来的非典疫情冲击,但我们一手抓防治非典,一手抓经济建设,及时采取有力扶持政策,使一度受到重创的旅游业得以迅速恢复和发展。

中国是一个历史悠久的文明古国,也是一个充满时代生机的东方大国,拥有许多得天独厚的旅游资源。自然风光旖旎秀美,历史文化博大精深,56个民族风情浓郁,目前已被列入世界文化遗产地和世界自然遗产地达29处。在改革开放的推动下,现代化建设突飞猛进,城乡面貌日新月异。古代中国的风采神韵与现代中国的蓬勃英姿交相辉映。这些都为发展国内外旅游创造了优越的条件。

21世纪头20年,是中国全面建设小康社会、加快推进社会主义现代化的重要战略机遇期,也是中国旅游业发展的有利时期。我们要把旅游业培育成为中国国民经济的重要产业,合理保护和利用旅游资源,努力实现旅游业的可持续发展。中国政府欢迎各国朋友到中国旅游观光,我们将全力保障广大旅游者的健康和安全;同时鼓励更多的中国人走向世界。我们愿同各国广泛开展合作,推动世界旅游业的发展。

多年来,世界旅游组织为促进全球旅游业的繁荣与发展,做出了积极而富有成效的努力。最近,世界旅游组织成为联合国专门机构,我们谨表示衷心祝贺。我们相信,这次大会必将对实现全球旅游业的更大繁荣和发展,起到重要的推动作用。

祝世界旅游组织第15届全体大会圆满成功!

谢谢大家!

重难点评析

1. "十月的北京,天高气爽,秋色宜人。"译为"At this October time when Beijing is offering us its charming autumn scenery in a most fresh air and clear weather."采用了倒译法,将"天高气爽"处理成了状语,句子简洁,意思清晰。

2. "集观光、娱乐、健身为一体"译为"combine sightseeing, recreation and health care"。

3. "20世纪中叶以来,现代旅游在世界范围迅速兴起"译为"Since the middle of the 20th century, modern tourism has been growing at a fast pace around the world…","迅速兴起"译为"grow at a fast pace/spring up"。

4. "旅游活动日益成为各国人民交流文化、增进友谊、扩大交往的重要渠道,对人类生活和社会进步产生越来越广泛的影响。"译为"Tourism serves gradually as an important bridge of cultural exchange, friendship and further exchanges and exerts more and more extensive influence on the human life and social progress among various countries.""交流文化、增进友谊、扩大交往的重要渠道"译为"an important bridge of cultural exchange, friendship and further exchanges/an important bridge of exchanging cultures, furthering friendship and expanding mutual contacts and exchange"。

5. "在古代,中国先哲们就提出了'观国之光'的思想,倡导'读万卷书,行万里路',游历名山大川,承天地之灵气,接山水之精华。"在译文中,由于"提出"和"倡导"的宾语都比较长,分译成了两个句子"In ancient times, Chinese thinkers raised the idea of 'appreciating the landscape through sightseeing'. Ancient people also proposed to 'travel ten thousand li and read ten thousand books', which shows they found pleasure in enriching themselves mentally and physically through traveling over famous mountains and rivers.""观国之光"采用了意译"appreciating the landscape through sightseeing"。"游历名山大川,承天地之灵气,接山水之精华",译者根据上下文的逻辑关系采用了补译法将这三个排比处理成了一个定语从句,并将"承天地之灵气,接山水之精华"进行了意译。

6. "目前,中国入境旅游人数和旅游外汇收入跃居世界前列,出境旅游人数迅速增加,已经成为旅游大国。"根据意群译为两个分句"Presently, China ranks among the top destinations in the world in terms of both tourist arrivals and foreign currency receipts; our outbound tourists are also increasing rapidly and China is now a big tourism country."
"在某方面位于前列"译为"rank among the top destinations in terms of","旅游外汇收入"译为"foreign currency receipts"。

7. "一手抓防治非典,一手抓经济建设"采用意译"... we spent all our efforts in preventing and controlling SARS while continuing with our economic construction."例如,我们常说的"一手抓改革开放,一手抓经济建设。"可以译为"We should promote reform and opening up to the outside world and at the same time strengthen the construction of economy."

8. "自然风光旖旎秀美,历史文化博大精深,56个民族风情浓郁,目前已被列入世界文化遗产地和世界自然遗产地达29处。"采用分译法译成了两个独立的句子,"Besides the picturesque natural scenery, profound history and extensive culture, China embodies the different folk customs of 56 nationalities. Now, there are 29 places that have been listed as World Cultural and Natural Heritages sites."旅游业常用语"世界文化遗产地和世界自然遗产地"译为"World Cultural and Natural Heritages sites."

9. "古代中国的风采神韵与现代中国的蓬勃英姿交相辉映。这些都为发展国内外旅游创造了优越的条件。"译为"The ancient glory of China and its modern boom add radiance and charm to each other, joining to create a most favorable condition for developing our domestic and international tourism."交相辉映 add radiance and charm to each other。类似的例子有:湖光山色交相辉映。译为"The lake and the hills add radiance and beauty to each other."

10. "21世纪头20年,是中国全面建设小康社会、加快推进社会主义现代化的重要战略机遇期"采用倒译法,将"重要战略机遇期"先译,接着用and连接两个不定式"The first 20 years of the 21st century represents an important strategic period for China to achieve all-round construction of a better-off society and to speed up its socialist modernization."意义表达清晰,结构简洁紧凑。

11. "我们要把旅游业培育成为中国国民经济的重要产业,合理保护和利用旅游资源,努力实现旅游业的可持续发展。"译为"We shall bring up tourism as an important industry in China's national economy, properly protect and utilize our tourism resources and try to achieve sustainable tourism development." "中国国民经济"译为"China's national economy","合理保护和利用"译为"properly protect and utilize","实现旅游业的可持续发展"译为"achieve sustainable tourism development"。

12. "多年来,世界旅游组织为促进全球旅游业的繁荣与发展,做出了积极而富有成效的努力。"采用了词性的换译,将动词"促进"处理成了名词"promotion",使得译文更简明清楚,"For many years, the World Tourism Organization has made active and effective efforts to the promotion of tourism prosperity and development around the globe." "做出了积极而富有成效的努力"是常用语,译作"have made active and effective efforts"。

译 文

Speech at the Opening Ceremony of the 15th General Assembly Session of the World Tourism Organization

Mr. Francesco Frangialli, Secretary-General of the World Tourism Organization,
Ms. Louise Frechette, Deputy Secretary-General of the United Nations,
All Delegates, Ladies and Gentlemen,

At this October time when Beijing is offering us its charming autumn scenery in a most fresh air and clear weather, the 15th General Assembly Session of the World Tourism Organization is officially opened here. On behalf of the Chinese government, I would like to extend our sincere welcome to all the guests here and to express our warm congratulations on the convening of this session.

Tourism represents a kind of popular and pleasant activity that combines sightseeing, recreation and health care. Tourism has been developing all along with the progress of the times. Since the middle of the 20th century, modern tourism has been growing at a fast pace around the world. The number of tourists has ever been on the rise, the scale of the tourism industry has been on constant expansion, and the position of tourism in the economy has been obviously raised. Tourism serves gradually as an important bridge of cultural exchange, friendship and further exchanges and exerts more and more extensive influence on the human life and social progress among various countries.

From ancient times till now, tourism has demonstrated the happy wish of the people for more knowledge, varied experience and good health. In ancient times, Chinese thinkers raised the idea of "appreciating the landscape through sightseeing". Ancient people also proposed to "travel ten thousand li and read ten thousand books", which shows they found pleasure in enriching themselves mentally and physically through traveling over famous mountains and rivers. After the founding of New China, especially since the opening up to the outside world and the reform, the Chinese government has given profound attention to the tourism work, which has been undergoing steady and fast growth as a newly emerging dynamic and potentially strong industry. Presently, China ranks among the top destinations in the world in terms of both tourist arrivals and foreign currency receipts; our outbound tourists are also increasing rapidly and China is now a big tourism country. In the first half of this year, although China was affected by the sudden outbreak of SARS, yet we spent all our efforts in preventing and controlling SARS while continuing with our economic construction. By implementing strong supportive policy measures, the tourism industry, which suffered greatly for a time, has been on fast recovery and development.

As a country with a long civilized history, China is also one big oriental country full of modern vitality, not to mention its unique, rich and varied tourism resources. Besides the picturesque natural scenery, profound history and extensive culture, China embodies the different folk customs of 56 nationalities. Now, there are 29 places that have been listed as World Cultural and Natural Heritages sites. Thanks to the further push by the opening up and reform, China's modern construction is surging ahead and the cities and the country are experiencing daily changes. The ancient glory of China and its modern boom add radiance and charm to each other, joining to create a most favorable condition for developing our domestic and international tourism.

The first 20 years of the 21st century represents an important strategic period for China to achieve all-round construction of a better-off society and to speed up its socialist modernization. It also provides a favorable time for the further development of China's tourism industry. We shall bring up tourism as an important industry in China's national economy, properly protect and utilize our tourism resources and try to achieve sustainable tourism development. The Chinese government welcomes all international friends to visit China. We shall do our best to protect their health and safety; and at the same time encourage more Chinese people to go abroad for visits. We are ready to develop extensive cooperation with other countries and contribute to global tourism growth.

For many years, the World Tourism Organization has made active and effective efforts to the promotion of tourism prosperity and development around the globe. The World Tourism Organization will soon become a specialized agency of the United Nations. We would like to offer our sincere congratulations. We believe this WTO General Assembly Session will give a major push to the further tourism prosperity and development in the world.

Finally, I wish a full success of the 15th General Assembly Session of the World Tourism Organization.

Thank you.

选文B

A Brief Introduction to the Tourism Industry of the Republic of Vanuatu
Vanuatu's President Iolu Johnson Abbil

It is my privilege as President to introduce you to the Republic of Vanuatu. My country is an archipelago of 83 islands, situated in the southwest Pacific Ocean, about 2.5 flying hours from the east coast of Australia, north of New Zealand, not far from the Fiji Islands, and a little over 7,000 km southeast of Shanghai.

The people of Vanuatu are very special. Having travelled the vast Pacific Ocean to land on these islands over 2,000 years ago, the Ni Vanuatu as we are called, from the Melanesian race, have lived for centuries in close harmony with the environment.

In this 21st century, Vanuatu won an international accolade as the happiest country in the world, based upon an independent assessment of the low environmental footprint caused by its people, the long life expectancy, and high quality of life and sense of community experienced by its people. It is indeed the natural welcoming smile of the Ni Vanuatu, their openness and friendliness to outsiders, that makes Vanuatu a special place to visit.

After living in splendid isolation for centuries, Europeans visited then settled in the country. Vanuatu was one of the few places that were colonized jointly by two countries. In our case we were a colony of France and Britain for 75 years until independence in 1980. Since Vanuatu's independence, the nation has rapidly matured in terms of its institutions of state, the development of a mature economy, and its engagement with the outside world as an independent nation of about 200,000 people.

Because of its beauty and culture, the country has become a popular tourist destination in the southwest Pacific. Tourists like Vanuatu for its diversity, the potential for soft adventure in its islands, whether visiting beauty spots, scuba diving or snorkeling the ever present coral reefs, sailing, fishing, hiking through magnificent scenery, observing traditional culture up close, or just sitting under a massive banyan tree on the beach admiring the unspoilt world. There is accommodation ranging from large luxury resorts in the major centres of Port Vila or Luganville through to small local family-owned bungalows on the outer islands. The general feeling is of an unspoilt destination.

Agriculture is the second largest sector, providing both the local food supply, and some exports, mostly, copra, sandalwood, and kava, the latter a specialised root crop that produces the social drink of choice around the Pacific and now in places around the world, and on sample at World Expo 2010 Shanghai. Vanuatu kava is renown around the Pacific as the most noble variety.

Vanuatu is a world leader in the adoption of coconut oil as a replacement for diesel fuel. Manufacturing in Vanuatu is small, but specialized, and largely derived from natural products. Specialized medicines produced from the Beche-La-Mar or Sea Cucumber are produced in Vanuatu and sold around the world, with major research now being undertaken by the US Food and Drug Administration, to establish the effectiveness of some of these medicines for treating cancer. Vanuatu is a high quality coffee exporter, and produces many health care products.

Vanuatu strongly promotes private-sector-led growth. Many of the major international accounting firms and a number of major international financial institutions have representation in the capital of Port Vila, and the second city, Luganville.

The Ni Vanuatu are happy people and this happiness is infectious. We invite you to share this happiness, by coming to our exhibit at World Expo 2010 Shanghai, and participating in our events during Expo. We hope that from the sharing of our lifestyle experience, we can help inspire city dwellers to reinvigorate their sense of being an important member and contributor to the well-being of their community environment.

重难点评析

1. "It is my privilege as President to introduce you to the Republic of Vanuatu."译为"我很荣幸以总统的身份向您介绍瓦努阿图共和国"。"It is my privilege to..."译为"我很荣幸……"。类似的表达诸如：It's my honor to.../I feel honored to...

2. "an archipelago of 83 islands"译为"由83个岛屿组成的群岛"。

3. "Having travelled the vast Pacific Ocean to land on these islands over 2,000 years ago, the Ni Vanuatu as we are called, from the Melanesian race, have lived for centuries in close harmony with the environment."采用了分译法，译成了两个独立的句子，并且第二句话采用了主语补译，使得意思清楚，译为"2 000多年前，在游历过浩瀚的太平洋后，瓦努阿图人民在这片土地上定居下来。我们称他们为尼—瓦努阿图，他们来自美拉尼西亚种族，到现在已经在这片土地上和谐居住了长达几个世纪之久"。"in (close) harmony with"译为"与……相和谐"。

4. "In this 21st century, Vanuatu won an international accolade as the happiest country in the world, based upon an independent assessment of the low environmental footprint caused by its people, the long life expectancy, and high quality of life and sense of community experienced by its people."这句话采用了分译法，并且第二句话增补了主语，译为"获得这一荣誉是因为……"，后面自然罗列出四个原因，自然流畅，更符合中文的习惯。"win an international accolade"译为"赢得国际赞誉"，"(be) based upon"译为"基于某种原因"。

5. "After living in splendid isolation for centuries, Europeans visited then settled in the country."译者没有根据字面意思直译，而是结合历史知识对内容作了增补，译成"经过数百年与世隔绝的生活，这片土地迎来了第一批欧洲人，他们随后在此定居"。

6. "that were colonized jointly by two countries"译为"由两个国家共同殖民"。

7. "Since Vanuatu's independence, the nation has rapidly matured in terms of its institutions of state, the development of a mature economy, and its engagement with the outside world as an independent nation of about 200,000 people."译者并没有根据 in terms of 而译成"就以下各方面而言迅速成熟"，如此必然不够简洁通畅。译者在这里采用了词性的转换，将 development 和 engagement 分别译成了动词"发展"和"交往"，译成了排比的主谓短语句式，"自从瓦努阿图独立以来，国家机构迅速成熟，经济日益发展，与世界其他各国开始交往，并且拥有了20万人口"。

8. "There is accommodation ranging from large luxury resorts in the major centres of Port Vila or Luganville through to small local family-owned bungalows on the outer islands.""range from... to..."要视具体语境，一般译为"包括，从……到……，既有……又有……"等。这里译为"既有维拉港和卢甘维尔的大型豪华度假村，又有小型的建筑在小岛上的家庭式平房"。

9. "Agriculture is the second largest sector, providing both the local food supply, and some exports, mostly, copra, sandalwood, and kava, the latter a specialised root crop that produces the social drink of choice around the Pacific and now in places around the

world, and on sample at World Expo 2010 Shanghai."这是个长句,采用分译法译成了四个独立的句子,并且反复采用了增译法使得各个句子意思更清楚,各句之间的联系更紧密。译文为"农业是瓦努阿图的第二大产业,为当地人民提供食物,也向国外出口产品。这其中大部分是椰干、檀香和卡瓦。卡瓦是一种专门制作饮料的块根作物,这种饮料在太平洋区域很流行。现在已经在全世界推广,并且将会出现在2010年上海世博会上"。

10. "Manufacturing in Vanuatu is small, but specialized, and largely derived from natural products."译为"瓦努阿图的制作业虽小,但很专业,主要处理自然产物"。"be derived from"意思是"来源于……";这里译者没有采用直译成"制作业主要来源于自然产物",不符合中文的表达,而是根据下文内容的理解译为"主要处理自然产物"。

11. "Specialized medicines produced from the Beche-La-Mar or Sea Cucumber are produced in Vanuatu and sold around the world, with major research now being undertaken by the US Food and Drug Administration, to establish the effectiveness of some of these medicines for treating cancer."这个长句被分译成了两个句子。第一句本是被动语态,采用了倒译法并增补了主语"人们",倒译法常常被应用于被动语态的句子。第二句将原句中 with 引导的状语独立出来译成一个句子并增补了主语"这些药品"。

12. "We invite you to share this happiness, by coming to our exhibit at World Expo 2010 Shanghai, and participating in our events during Expo."采用了倒译法,将介词 by 引导的很长的位于句尾部分的内容译在前面,符合中文的习惯。译文为"我们邀请大家参观瓦努阿图在上海世博会的展馆,并且参与我们的活动,分享我们的快乐"。

译 文

瓦努阿图共和国旅游概况
瓦努阿图总统 尤路·约翰逊·阿比尔

我很荣幸以总统的身份向您介绍瓦努阿图共和国。瓦努阿图共和国坐落于太平洋的西南部,由83个岛屿组成。从澳大利亚东海岸或新西兰北部乘飞机约花费2个半小时,和斐济群岛相距不远,在上海的东南方向7 000公里多一些的地方。

瓦努阿图人民是非常特殊的。2 000多年前,在游历过浩瀚的太平洋后,瓦努阿图人民在这片土地上定居下来。我们称他们为尼—瓦努阿图,他们来自美拉尼西亚种族,到现在已经在这片土地上和谐居住了长达几个世纪之久。

在21世纪,瓦努阿图被国际社会誉为世界上最快乐的国家。获得这一荣誉是因为瓦努阿图人民尽可能地不对自然环境产生影响,还因为瓦努阿图人民的平均寿命很长,以及瓦努阿图人民高品质的生活和丰富的社会认知。瓦努阿图人民的真挚笑容和开放友好的态度,使得瓦努阿图成为您旅游的好去处。

经过数百年与世隔绝的生活,这片土地迎来了第一批欧洲人,他们随后在此定居。瓦努阿图是少数几个由两个国家共同殖民的国家之一。瓦努阿图作为法国和英国的殖民地长达75年,直到1980年获得独立。自从瓦努阿图独立以来,国家机构迅速成熟,经济日益发展,与世界其他各国开始交往,并且拥有了20万人口。

由于风景迷人,文化独特,瓦努阿图已成为西南太平洋受欢迎的旅游目的地。游客们喜欢瓦努阿图,因为这个国家的多样性,因为可以到未知小岛上去探险,因为可以参观名胜、潜水或浮潜、帆船、钓鱼、登山观看壮丽的风景、近距离地观察传统文化,或者坐在海滩的大榕树下欣赏未被破坏过的世界。在这里,既有维拉港和卢甘维尔的大型豪华度假村,又有小型的建筑在小岛上的家庭式平房。这些都是最亲近自然的选择。

农业是瓦努阿图的第二大产业,为当地人民提供食物,也向国外出口产品。这其中大部分是椰干、檀香和卡瓦。卡瓦是一种专门制作饮料的块根作物,这种饮料在太平洋区域很流行。现在已经在全世界推广,并且将会出现在2010年上海世博会上。瓦努阿图的卡瓦,作为高贵的品种闻名于太平洋区域。

在通过使用椰子油代替柴油作为燃料方面,瓦努阿图是世界的领先者。瓦努阿图的制作业虽小,但很专业,主要处理自然产物。人们从海参中提取元素,制成药品,销往世界各地。这些药品现由美国食品药物监督管理局进行研究,以便确认这些药物治疗癌症的功效。瓦努阿图还是一个高品质咖啡的出口国,并生产了许多保健产品。

瓦努阿图大力促进私营经济的增长。很多大型国际会计公司和一些主要的国际金融机构已经在首都维拉港以及第二大城市卢甘维尔设立了自己的代表处。

瓦努阿图的人民是快乐的民族,快乐是可以传染的。我们邀请大家参观瓦努阿图在上海世博会的展馆,并且参与我们的活动,分享我们的快乐。我们希望通过分享我们的生活经验,可以帮助激发城市居民重新找回作为社区环境一员和贡献者的幸福感。

Qualifications for Being a Good Guide-interpreter

Tourism is a comprehensive economic undertaking and it plays a very important role in a country's economic construction; and it is at the same time a part of foreign relations work, as it offers an effective means for people-to-people diplomacy.

Failure or success of tourism industry, therefore, bears on a country's image abroad in terms of its political reputation and of the opportunity of earning foreign exchange for a country's economic construction.

Tourism in China started from scratch, although China surpasses those countries where tourism is well-developed in terms of resources of tourism. China's huge amount of cultural relics, its scenery known far and wide for its quiet beauty, the splendor of its ancient arts and culture, its traditional multi-national arts and crafts and food prepared on various local recipes — all these have attracted foreign visitors for a long time. However, as tourism in China has just developed, there isn't sufficient transportation and other facilities. In addition, we still have a lot of problems to be solved in the management of tourism, in the quality of service and in the quality and English level of guide-interpreters. With all these problems gradually settled, China's tourism will surely advance to a high stage of development along the pattern uniquely Chinese.

In fact, guide-interpreters are in direct service of foreign visitors and their quality and service play a decisive role in the development of tourism industry in China. Their speech and behavior directly influence foreign visitors' mood in traveling. In a sense, the function of a tour guide is similar to that of a diplomat of the people. His or her duty is to try his or her utmost to make foreign visitors enjoy their trip in China and at the same time let them understand China's history, geography, people's customs and its cultural tradition better through their interpreting and efforts. Therefore, a tour guide's service is the key link of tourism industry.

The guide should be the spirit of mountains and rivers, envoy of friendship, disseminator of culture and civilization of the motherland and publicity agent of the new idea and morale of socialism. If a tour guide's service is satisfactory, foreign visitors would have a good impression of China and the travel agency, so that they would plan their second trip to China for other sights and furthermore, they would urge others to come along to see China with their own eyes. A travel agency would, of course, employ as many such competent and qualified interpreters as possible so as to make their business thrive with each passing day.

A tour guide should be able to act as an attendant, publicity agent, investigator and defender while accompanying foreign visitors. So, he or she has to have a perfect mastery of our Party's policies and political ideology, foreign language and knowledge. He or she must be honest and upright, free from corruption, prudent and careful in his or her work, diligent and assiduous in his or her working style.

口译笔记理论与技巧(一)

笔记法是口译当中的必备技能之一,特别是当我们听到很长的一个段落,短时记忆不够用,必须用笔辅助大脑记忆。大多数学生刚开始练笔记法时都很认真,可是往往过分专注于做笔记,忽略了文章的整体意思,结果反倒影响了脑记和传译。初学口译笔记的人经常会遇到以下问题:

1. 记笔记的速度跟不上发言人说话的速度。
2. 自己记的笔记自己看不懂。
3. 记笔记干扰听和理解的过程。

关于第一个问题,很多发言人说话本来就快,笔记要记全本来就难。其实口译笔记只不过是记几个关键字,觉得跟不上发言人肯定是记得太多。口译笔记不是速记,而是记关键字和主干。另外,手的速度是永远比不上耳朵和大脑的速度。很多信息都要靠你的大脑来处理和记忆,不能完全依赖笔记。

第二个问题,自己的笔记自己看不懂,大概有两个原因:一是,笔记记得太潦草。二是,听的过程中没有理清关系,没有理解发言人所说的内容,回忆起来自然有困难。

第三个问题,做口译要求译员能够一心二用,无论是做交替传译还是同声传译都有这个要求。记笔记会干扰听是因为还没有达到一心二用的境界,多练习会有所改善。在练习中会发现记忆熟悉的话题比记忆不熟悉的话题要容易得多。所以平时要注意扩大知识面,熟悉各种话题,做口译的时候才能驾轻就熟。

另外,口译笔记是很个人的东西,即便是看了口译笔记的书籍,也要把别人的方法和符号融入自己的笔记系统中,否则一到实战还是手忙脚乱。平时自己练习的时候可以找各种题材的听力材料,自己多琢磨。做口译是三分靠笔记,七分靠脑记。不能过分依赖笔记。

一、脑记为主,笔记为辅

首先我们要认识到,笔记是用于辅助大脑记忆的。口译笔记的主要内容是概念、命题、名称、数字、组织机构和逻辑关系(如大小、先后、上下、正反、升降、因果关系等),切忌整句整段地记录源语信息,否则不但时间来不及,还会影响对句子结构的理解。其次,脑记时要重点关注段落句子的整体信息,顺带注意一些没有用笔记下来的细节。为什么说顺带呢?简单的一个例子:"表示热烈的欢迎和衷心的感谢",我们只要把欢迎和感谢的速记符号一写就行,"热烈"和"衷心"这些词很容易就在大脑中形成印象。

二、平静心态,循序渐进

刚开始接触笔记,肯定是很生疏的。不熟悉笔记符号,不会一心二用,恨不得把每个词都写下来等等,这些问题都是非常正常的。特别是在做英翻汉的时候,练一通下来,也没弄懂听到的东西,也看不懂自己记的东西,都是普遍存在的现象。这时候,我们首先不要心急,千万不要刚开始就找篇诸如 VOA standard 之类来操练笔记。可以一步一步来,找一些经典的口译材料,先看着它,把该记的笔记列出来,然后慢速地放着听,再列一遍笔记。或者先慢速地放一遍,尽量记一些,然后多放几遍进行改进,再对照原文研究一下哪些词是应该记下来的,用常见符号还是用缩写,用怎样的结构好等等,如此多次反复。当然,练到一定程度后,对常用笔记符号熟练了,创造出自己熟悉的笔记系统,就可以慢慢提高速度增加难度。

三、辅助练习,坚持不懈

练笔记的同时呢,当然要辅助别的练习,比如每天锻炼一心二用的能力,做些视译和短时记忆的练习等等。还是那句话,Practice makes perfect! 万事开头难,但是只要坚持下去,就会慢慢走上正轨。要养成好的习惯,以至平时听新闻、听评论、听对话的时候都想快速把它们记下来。

口译笔记的六要

一、笔记要少而精,清晰易读

记录的应当是能提示整个意群的字(如"不断扩大"四个字,只要记录"扩",或者用上升符号代表),反映逻辑关系的字和数字等要求精确的细节词。写字要尽量快,但不能为了速度牺牲清晰,读不懂的笔记还不如根本没有记录。

二、要学会借助画线和符号,表示常用词汇以及句中逻辑关系

例如,"V"可以表示 success,"/"可以表示 of,所以当我们听到 success of the American society 时,我们可以写下 V/A;又如,在一个动词下面加一条下画线,可以表示进行时态,如"正在进行改革"就可以记录成"改"。不难看出,合理地使用符号对于口译成功非常重要。

三、要少线多指,即用同一种符号代表多种相互关联的意思

例如,Φ(意指一条横线穿过圆圆的地球)可以表示 across the world, worldwide,

global, international, universal, the earth；而 globalization 便可用 Φn 来表示。这样，避免了使用过多符号反而更复杂。

四、要少横多竖，即按照意群，勤换行，尤其是列举的时候，竖着记录更为清晰

例如，We'll invest in schools, colleges, universities, libraries and our communities. 最好记录成：

|-sch
|-col
{-uni
|-libr
|-comm.

五、快速书写

毋庸置疑，在保证清晰的基础上，笔记应该尽量快。

六、明确结束

在每一段结束后，画上一道线，或者隔开一段距离再记录下一段的内容。

口译笔记的六不要

初学者往往会陷入一些笔记的误区，造成口译的困难。

一、不要把笔记作为目的，占用大量脑力，重心一定要放在听懂上面

脑记和笔记的协调是需要大量练习才能提高的，但是把握整体意思、结构的重要性永远大过将部分字句记录下来。

二、不要力图把每一个字都记下来

除非熟练掌握速记，否则不可能做到把口译的内容都记下来进行视译（sight interpretation）。因此，笔记要记的是反映核心意义的关键信息以及细节信息，如数字、专有名词等等。

三、不要在一段话结束后拼命把最后几个字都写全

初学者往往喜欢这样做，但实际上，这样做既不必要，又不合理。按照心理学上记忆的规律，最后一句话已经没有倒摄抑制（retroactive inhibition），是不容易遗忘的；如果花了几秒钟记录最后几个字，浪费宝贵时间，是非常可惜的。

四、不要书写得过于拥挤，以免过后难以辨认

五、不要刻意追求使用符号

符号有很多优点，但是创造过多的符号，以至于听到某个词之后脑力用在了回忆其符号上，就成了本末倒置。

六、不要现场发明符号

经验表明，在口译现场大脑高度紧张的状态下，从未使用过的符号在事后口译时往往会难以再现其含义。因此，包含符号的笔记系统，一定要平时建立、熟练应用，而临场不要创造符号。

拓展阅读

选文A

西藏旅游发展情况

西藏自治区旅游局副局长　邓　珠

西藏旅游业自20世纪80年代起步以来，从小到大，率先在西藏各产业中实现了跨越式发展，已成为促进西藏转变发展方式的动力产业，成为推进西藏经济结构升级优化的优势产业，成为推动西藏经济跨越式发展的支柱产业。

一、西藏旅游资源开发建设情况

目前，西藏已有国家4A级旅游景区8个（布达拉宫、大昭寺、罗布林卡、西藏博物馆、扎什伦布寺、巴松错、珠穆朗玛峰、桑耶寺），3A级旅游景区2个（娘热度假村、敏珠林寺），2A级景区3个（然乌湖旅游景区、孜珠寺、岗坚寺），1A级旅游景区2个（热堆寺卓玛拉康、色乌沟寺）；有国家级自然保护区6个（珠穆朗玛自然保护区、羌塘自然保护区、察隅慈巴沟自然保护区、色林错自然保护区、雅江中游河谷自然保护区、雅鲁藏布大峡谷自然保护区），国家地质公园2个（易贡国家地质公园、扎达土林国家地质公园）；中国优秀旅游城市一座（拉萨市），可供旅游者游览的景点297处，形成了以拉萨为中心，辐射西藏的旅游资源开发利用格局，为发展观光旅游、民俗旅游、生态旅游以及徒步、探险、朝圣等专项旅游奠定了坚实的基础。旅游客源市场也由发展之初单一接待外宾型发展到今天集入境、出境、国内三大市场为一体的旅游客源体系。

二、旅游产业规模

截至2009年，西藏拥有各类旅游企业1 430家，其中，国际国内旅行社80家，星级饭店（宾馆）142家，各类旅游豪华汽车2 745辆，全行业固定资产超过50亿元。在西藏，旅游直接从业人员2.84万人，间接从业人员14.2万人，其中，藏族从业人员占62.8%，汉族和其他少数民族从业人员占37.2%，建立起了一支以藏族为主体的旅游从业队伍。发展旅游业已成为许多地方加快发展的成功之路，成为西藏广大农牧民增收的重要途径。目前西藏从事旅游的农牧民达到4 664户，34 979人，旅游收入达到6 094万元，户均收入达13 066元，人均现金收入达到1 742元，一大批农牧民吃上了旅游饭，走上了致富路。

三、旅游经济发展态势

1980年到2008年，西藏旅游累计收入188.98亿元，旅游收入增幅高于西藏生产总值增幅23%，仅"十五"期间旅游总收入就比西藏"六五"期间国民生产总值还要多。特别是自2006年青藏铁路通车以来，旅游产业规模迅速扩大，增长速度强势攀升，发展质量显著提高。据统计，2007年接待中外游客达到创记录的402万人次，旅游总收入增长到48.5亿元，占西藏生产总值的14.2%，基本确立了旅游业在国民经济中的支柱产业地位。

四、下一步发展计划

未来旅游业的发展将以政府投入为主，发挥市场配置资源的基础性作用，全力推进旅游基础设施和配套设施建设；完善体制、优化环境、培养队伍，确保在旅游设施管理与服务水平等方面有实质性提升,实现从旅游资源优势向旅游产品优势的跨越,把西藏建设成享誉海内外的精品旅游胜地。

西藏将紧紧抓住机遇,以深厚的文化、精优的产品、优质的服务,打造"世界屋脊、神奇西藏"的旅游主题形象。

译文

The Development of Tourism in Tibet

Dengzhu, Vice Director of the Tourism Bureau of Tibet Autonomous Region

Since its outset in the 1980s, the tourism of Tibet has developed from small to large, taking the initiate of a leap development among all industries in Tibet. Now it has become an impetus industry for Tibet to change its development model, an advantageous industry to boost the upgrading and optimization of economic structure in Tibet, and a backbone industry to motivate the leap development of Tibetan economy.

1. The Development and Construction of Tourist Resources in Tibet

At present, there are in Tibet 8 national 4 As level tourist scenic areas (the Potala Palace, the Jokhang Monastery, the Norbulingka Garden, the Tibet Museum, the Tashilhunpo Monastery, the Pagsum Co Lake, the Qomolangma Peak, and the Samye Monastery), two 3 As tourist scenic areas (the Nyangrain Holiday Village and the Mindroling Monastery), three 2 As tourist scenic areas (the Rawok Co National Forest Park, the Zezhol Monastery and the Kang Gyan Monastery), and two 1 A tourist scenic areas (the Drolma Lhakhang Part of the Rato Monastery, and the Sewugou Monastery). In addition, there are 6 national natural reserves (the Qomolangma National Nature Preserve, the Chang Tang Nature Reserve, the Cibagou Nature Reserve in Zayu County, the Siling Co National Nature Reserve, the Yarlung Zangbo River Middle Reaches Black-necked Crane Nature Reserve, and the Yarlung Zangbo Grand Canyon National Nature Reserve), two national geological parks (the Yigong National Geopark and the Zanda Clay Forest National Geopark). What is more, Lhasa is a famous tourist city of China, where there are as many as 297 tourist scenic sites. All the afore-mentioned scenic areas have formed a network centered on Lhasa and extending all over Tibet, and they have laid a reliable foundation for the development of sightseeing tours, folk customs tours and ecological tours, as well as of special tours such as pedestrian tours, exploration and pilgrimages. And its tourist resources have also developed from the simple reception of foreign visitors at the outset to a comprehensive one of tourists who enter and leave China or travel around in China.

2. The Scale of Tourist Industry

Up to 2009, there have been 1,430 various tourist enterprises in Tibet, of which are 80 international and domestic traveling agencies and 142 star-level hotels, with 2,745 luxurious tourist vehicles and more than five billion RMB fixed assets in the whole industry. In Tibet, people directly engaged in tourist industry number 28,400, and those indirectly in tourist industry 142,000. Among these members, Tibetan people amount to

62.8%, and people of Han and other minority ethnic groups 37.2%. So, a tourist service team with Tibetan people as a mainstay has been established. Now, to develop tourist industry has become a way to successfully speed development in many places, and an important means for the many peasants and herdsmen in Tibet to increase their incomes. At present, there have been as many as 4,664 peasant and herdsman households and 34,979 people engaged in tourist services in Tibet, and the incomes from tourism have reached 60.94 million RMB, with household incomes averaging 13,066 RMB, and per capita incomes in cash 1,742 RMB. A large group of peasants and herdsmen have been making a living and even become rich thanks to the development of tourism.

3. The Trend of Tourist Economy

From 1980 to 2008, the tourist revenues in Tibet added up to 18.898 billion RMB, with the tourist income increasing 23% higher than that of the gross production in Tibet; the total revenues from tourism only during the 10th Five-year Plan period exceeded the gross production during the 6th Five-year Plan period in Tibet. Especially after the Qinghai-Tibet Railway was open to traffic in 2006, the tourist industry has been enlarged rapidly, its growth has been accelerated vigorously, and its quality has been improved obviously. According to the statistics, 2007 witnessed a 4.02 million person/times tourist reception for travelers both from home and abroad, which created a new record in the development of Tibetan tourism; and the total revenues from tourism increased up to 4.85 billion RMB in the same year, covering 14.2% of gross production in Tibet. Tourism has essentially established its mainstay industrial position in the economy of Tibet.

4. A Plan for Further Development

The future development of Tibet tourism will mainly come from the governments. Meanwhile, the market will play its basic role of configuring resources, and the whole industry will exert itself to boost tourist infrastructure and supplementary facility construction. The system will be improved, the environment will be optimized, and related talents will be trained. With all these done, it will guarantee an essential improvement in the management of tourist facilities and services, and realize a stride from advantageous tourist resources to superior tourist products, building Tibet into a quintessential tourist resort famous both at home and abroad.

Tibet will make full use of the opportunities to build such a tourist subject as "the World Roof in the Wonderful Tibet" with its profound culture, quintessential products and high-quality services.

选文B

Secretary-General's Message on World Tourism Day

27 September 2010

I am delighted that the UN World Tourism Organization is celebrating this year's World Tourism Day under the theme "Tourism and Biodiversity". Despite repeated global pledges to protect the planet's species and habitats — and the goods and services they provide — the variety of life on Earth continues to decline at an unprecedented rate. Human activities are the cause. This year — the International Year of Biodiversity — provides a timely opportunity to focus on the urgency of safeguarding biodiversity for the wealth, health and well-being of people in all regions of the world.

Tourism and biodiversity are closely intertwined. Millions of people travel each year to experience nature's splendour. The income generated by sustainable tourism can provide important support for nature conservation, as well as for economic development. Furthermore, sustainable tourism can help to raise awareness among tourists and local communities of the importance of biodiversity to our everyday lives.

Through initiatives such as its "Sustainable Tourism — Eliminating Poverty" project, and its collaboration with the UN family, national tourism authorities and the private sector, the World Tourism Organization is helping to highlight the links between tourism, poverty alleviation and biodiversity. The tourism community is becoming increasingly aware of its responsibility. And indeed there is much the sector can contribute to protecting biodiversity, including by integrating simple measures such as managing tour groups to minimize disturbance to wildlife or buying supplies only from sustainable sources.

On this World Tourism Day, I commend the tourism community for its growing recognition of the importance of conserving the diversity of life on Earth, and I urge all partners to strengthen their commitment to sustainability.

译文

联合国秘书长潘基文2010世界旅游日致辞

2010年9月27日

我高兴地看到,联合国世界旅游组织在"旅游与生物多样性"的主题下纪念今年的世界旅游日。尽管一再做出全球承诺,要保护地球上的物种和生境及其提供的货物和服务,但生物种类继续以史无前例的速度减少。其根源在于人类的活动。今年是国际生物多样性年,为世界各地人民的财富、健康和福祉提供了一个适时的机会来集中注意保护生物多样性的紧迫。

旅游与生物多样性密切相连。每年有千百万人为领略壮丽的自然风光而旅游。可持续旅游业产生的收入可以为保护自然和发展经济提供重要的支持。此外,可持续旅游业还有助于游客和地方社区更多地认识到生物多样性在日常生活中的重要作用。

世界旅游组织通过诸如"可持续旅游业——消除贫穷"这样的项目以及同联合国系统、各国旅游主管部门和私人部门的合作,正在帮助突出宣传旅游、扶贫和生物多样性之间的联系。旅游界正日益意识到自己的责任。这个行业确实可以为保护生物多样性做出很大贡献,包括为此实行一些简单的措施,例如通过对旅游团的管理来尽量减少对野生物的干扰,或仅从可持续来源购买用品。

值此世界旅游日之际,我赞扬旅游界日益认识到保护地球生物多样性的重要意义,并促请所有合作伙伴加强对可持续性的承诺。

第四单元　人物访谈

（Interview）

单元要点

本单元共分五个层次,分别是:中国商务部部长陈德铭接受专访的汉译英一篇;美国国务卿希拉里·克林顿接受专访的英译汉一篇;口音听辨技巧;口译笔记理论与技巧(二);拓展阅读(汉译英、英译汉各一篇)。第一、二部分提供人物访谈口译的例文及其翻译和重难点评析;第三、四部分主要是相关口译理论与技能的介绍;第五部分的拓展阅读中,提供汉、英原文和参考译文。

理论难点提示

1. 口音听辨技巧。
2. 口译笔记理论与技巧(二)。

选文A

中国商务部部长陈德铭就访非情况和当前中非经贸合作有关问题接受新华社记者专访
2011年2月17日

记者:陈部长,您连续三年每年年初率中国政府经贸代表团访问非洲,这是出于什么考虑?

陈德铭:经贸合作是中非友谊的重要基石。非洲是中国传统友好朋友和可信赖的经贸合作伙伴,中国是非洲第一大贸易伙伴国、重要投资来源地和主要援助提供国。巩固和发展同非洲国家的友好、务实合作,是中国对外政策的重要立足点,理所当然地成为我们开展对外经济交往优先考虑的工作重点。

记者:当前中非经贸合作面临什么新形势?此次出访非洲主要任务是什么?

陈德铭:今年是我国"十二五"计划的开局之年,也是中非合作论坛成立后第二个十年的开始。根据温家宝总理2009年11月在中非合作论坛第四届部长级会议宣布的加强对非务实合作新八项举措,我国将继续加强与非洲国家的务实合作,特别是要积极开展农业、医疗卫生、人力资源开发等有利于改善当地民生的项目合作。

今年是我国大力推进对外援助新模式、新方式的第一年。根据去年召开的全国对外援助工作会议精神,我国将进一步增加对外援助资金,优化对外援助结构,创新对外援助方式,提高对外援助的质量和效益。我们在坚持把对外援助视为发展中国家之间相互帮助的同时,一方面要通过对外援助增强受援国自主发展能力,另一方面带动我国企业"走出去",实现互利共赢。在援助资金的具体使用上要更加突出重点,无偿援助和无息贷款主要用于援建民事福利性项目、社会公共设施等项目,优惠贷款主要用于有经济效益的生产型项目、资源能源开发项目。

今年也是中国加入世界贸易组织10周年。中国政府将进一步提高对外开放水平,并通过积极参与多哈回合谈判,努力维护广大发展中国家的利益。在扩大对非合作方面,我国确定了从2010年开始用三年左右时间减免非洲最不发达国家95%的关税、在国内设立非洲产品展销中心、与多个非洲国家启动中小企业发展专项贷款合作等一系列扩大开放的措施。我们还将进一步推进贸易自由化、便利化,出台更具针对性的扩大对非进口新举措。

总体上看,当前中非经贸合作正处在互利共赢的新起点上,为实现对非经贸务实合作新跨越,中国政府推出了一系列新举措。我希望通过此次访问,向非洲政府和民众传达中国政府发展对非关系的真诚愿望和采取的新举措,了解非洲朋友的真实需求,探讨在新形势下如何深化双边务实合作,进一步推动中非经贸关系健康稳步发展。

记者:您这次访问非洲三国,取得了哪些具体成果?

陈德铭:此次访问的三个非洲国家都具有显著的区位优势,且与中国的经贸合作关系日益密切。摩洛哥作为地处北非的阿拉伯国家,是经济持续稳定发展的经济体,也是非洲通往欧洲和中东地区的重要通道;赤道几内亚是中非国家经济共同体和中部非洲关税和经济联盟成员,是中非地区近年来经济稳定、快速发展的国家;加纳是西非国家经济共同体的重要成员,近年来发展势头良好。

访问期间,我拜会了三国领导人,与三国政府相关部门分别举行了对口会谈,重点探讨了如何推动一些新领域的合作,并考察了一些在建项目和当地市场。虽然此次访问日程紧凑,但内容丰富,成效明显,达到了预期目的。

一是与三国领导人、政府部门和企业界进行了广泛的接触和交流,与非洲朋友共同探讨新形势下加强双边经贸合作的新途径、新方式,达成了许多新共识。在摩洛哥,双方就扩大磷肥进口、举办开发区建设高级官员研讨班等议题达成合作意向;在赤道几内亚,双方就人力资源开发、农业渔业合作等议题形成了共识;在加纳,双方同意就基础设施建设、电信合作和融资合作以新方式展开合作。此外,还与三国共同探讨了加强农业领域多层次合作、开展区域项目设计和区域规划等多项议题。

二是更深入地了解了中方务实合作各项举措的实施情况,推动了中非合作论坛第四次部长级会议新举措的落实。访问期间,中国政府相关机构和企业与三国分别签署了多个经贸合作协议,推进了一批双方关注的重点项目。

三是围绕新形势下如何进一步开展双边务实合作进行了深入调研,通过实地考察在建的重大项目、走访不同档次的当地市场以及与中资企业交流,获得了许多切合实际的意见和建议。

四是通过正式会谈会见、接受记者采访、召开媒体座谈会等方式,耐心细致介绍我对非经贸政策和对有关热点问题的立场,增进了非洲国家和国际社会对中国对非政策的理解和支持。

重难点评析

1. "您连续三年……"应灵活地译为"It is the third year that you…",此处可能不少人的第一反应就是"for three years"。译文应注意中文是"连续三年每年都率团访问",而不是

"率团访问了三年"。

2. "巩固和发展同非洲国家的友好、务实合作,是中国对外政策的重要立足点,理所当然地成为我们开展对外经济交往优先考虑的工作重点。"译为"It is an important foothold for China's foreign policies to consolidate and develop the friendly and pragmatic cooperation with African countries so that we will give priority to it in our development of foreign economic exchanges.""巩固和发展同非洲国家的友好、务实合作,是中国对外政策的重要立足点",此句中主语很长,为避免头重脚轻,译文中用 it 作形式主语,to 引导的真正的主语放在句末。"理所当然地成为我们开展对外经济交往优先考虑的工作重点",在译文中采用 so that 引导结果状语从句,与前文内容紧密相连。

3. "根据温家宝总理 2009 年 11 月在中非合作论坛第四届部长级会议宣布的加强对非务实合作新八项举措,我国将继续加强与非洲国家的务实合作,特别是要积极开展农业、医疗卫生、人力资源开发等有利于改善当地民生的项目合作。"译为"In accordance with the eight new measures on enhancing the pragmatic cooperation with Africa proposed by Chinese Premier Wen Jiabao in the 4th Ministerial Conference of FOCAC, China will continue enhancing its pragmatic cooperation with African countries, especially the cooperation in the projects that are beneficial for the improvement of local livelihood in agriculture, medical care and development of human resources."这是一个长句,译文为了内容完整和结构简洁,前后采用了两次倒译法。第一次倒译将"新八项举措"之前的很长的定语进行了后置,第二次倒译将"项目合作"之前的定语进行了后置,符合英文的习惯。

4. "我们在坚持把对外援助视为发展中国家之间相互帮助的同时,一方面要通过对外援助增强受援国自主发展能力,另一方面带动我国企业'走出去',实现互利共赢。"译为"While holding on foreign aid as the mutual help among developing countries, China will strengthen the capacity of independent development of aided countries and drive up domestic enterprises 'going global' through foreign aid to realize the mutual benefit and win-win outcome.""坚持视为"译为"hold on sth as","走出去"译为"go global","互利共赢(外交常用语)"译为"mutual benefit and win-win outcome"。

5. "……,无偿援助和无息贷款主要用于援建民事福利性项目、社会公共设施等项目,优惠贷款主要用于有经济效益的生产型项目、资源能源开发项目。"译为"..., free aid and interest-free loans for social welfare projects and social public facilities, concessional loans for production projects with economic effects and projects of resources and energy."

6. "中小企业发展专项贷款"译为"special loan for small and medium-sized enterprise development","进一步推进贸易自由化、便利化"译为"further boost the liberalization and facilitation of trade"。

7. "总体上看,当前中非经贸合作正处在互利共赢的新起点上,为实现对非经贸务实合作新跨越,中国政府推出了一系列新举措。"采用了分译法译为两个句子,"To put it in a nutshell, it is a new start for Sino-Africa trade and economic cooperation of mutual benefit and win-win outcome. For another leap and bound in the pragmatic cooperation in trade and economy with Africa, China launched a series of new measures.""总体上看"译为"to put it in a nutshell","为实现新跨越"译为"for another leap and bound","经贸务实合作"译

为"pragmatic cooperation in trade and economy"。

8. "此次访问的三个非洲国家都具有显著的区位优势"译为"The three countries have featured regional advantages"。译文中 feature 作为动词用,意为"以……为特征"。

9. "中非国家经济共同体"译为"Economic Community of Central African States","中部非洲关税和经济联盟"译为"Central African Customs and Economic Union","西非国家经济共同体"译为"Economic Community of West African States"。

10. "虽然此次访问日程紧凑,但内容丰富,成效明显,达到了预期目的。"译为"Despite the compact schedule, the visit is abundant, effective and successful.""内容丰富,成效明显,达到了预期目的"在译文中以三个形容词并列,简洁明了。

11. "达成共识"译为"make consensus on/reach consensus on","达成合作意向"译为"achieve the intention of cooperation","多层次合作"译为"multi-level cooperation"。

12. "三是围绕新形势下如何进一步开展双边务实合作进行了深入调研,通过实地考察在建的重大项目、走访不同档次的当地市场以及与中资企业交流,获得了许多切合实际的意见和建议。"第一个逗号后的部分进行了倒译,用 by 引导一个很长的介宾短语作为句子的方式状语并根据英文的习惯置于句尾,译为"Thirdly, we made in-depth investigation into how to further develop bilateral pragmatic cooperation under the new situation and acquired many pragmatic suggestions by field inspections in ongoing projects and local markets and talks with Chinese-funded enterprises in Africa."

13. "四是通过正式会谈会见、接受记者采访、召开媒体座谈会等方式,耐心细致介绍我对非经贸政策和对有关热点问题的立场,增进了非洲国家和国际社会对中国对非政策的理解和支持。"译文的句型特点与前一个要点基本相似,同时,定语从句的应用使得整个句子结构更紧凑、意义更明确。"Fourthly, we carefully and patiently introduced China's measures on trade and economy with Africa and standpoints on some hot issues by means of official meetings, interviews and media symposium, which further enhanced the understanding and support of African countries and international society in China's relevant measures."

译 文

Minister Chen's Exclusive Interview by Xinhua News Agency on Sino-Africa Trade and Economic Cooperation

February 17, 2011

Reporter: Minister Chen, it is the third year that you head the Chinese government trade and economic delegation to visit Africa at the beginning of the year. What's your consideration?

Chen Deming: The trade and economic cooperation is the important cornerstone of Sino-Africa friendship. Africa is China's good friend and reliable trading partner while China is Africa's first largest trading partner, important investment source and principal provider of aid. It is an important foothold for China's foreign policies to consolidate and develop the friendly and pragmatic cooperation with African countries so that we will give priority to it in our development of foreign economic exchanges.

Reporter: What's the new situation that Sino-Africa trade and economic cooperation faces with? And what are the major tasks of this visit?

Chen Deming: The year of 2011 is the first year of China's "12th Five-Year-Plan" and the second decade since the establishment of FOCAC. In accordance with the eight new measures on enhancing the pragmatic cooperation with Africa proposed by Chinese Premier Wen Jiabao in the 4th Ministerial Conference of FOCAC, China will continue enhancing its pragmatic cooperation with African countries, especially the cooperation in the projects that are beneficial for the improvement of local livelihood in agriculture, medical care and development of human resources.

It is the first year for China to vigorously push forward new methods for foreign aid. China will, based on the spirits of National Foreign Aid Working Conference last year, further increase the capital for foreign aid, optimize the structure and innovate the way so as to improve the effectiveness of foreign aid. While holding on foreign aid as the mutual help among developing countries, China will strengthen the capacity of independent development of aided countries and drive up domestic enterprises "going global" through foreign aid to realize the mutual benefit and win-win outcome. In addition, the specific use of aid capital should emphasize the highlights, free aid and interest-free loans for social welfare projects and social public facilities, concessional loans for production projects with economic effects and projects of resources and energy.

This year is also the 10th anniversary of China's accession into the WTO. The Chinese government will open wider to the rest of the world and strive to maintain the interests of developing countries by its participation into Doha Round Negotiations. On expansion of the cooperation with Africa, China determined to grant zero-tariff measure on 95% products from the least developed countries in Africa in three years since 2010, set up exhibition center for African products in the Mainland and initiate the cooperation about special loan for small and medium-sized enterprise development with quite a number of African countries. Besides, China will further boost the liberalization and facilitation of trade and launch more targeted measures on expanding import from Africa.

To put it in a nutshell, it is a new start for Sino-Africa trade and economic cooperation of mutual benefit and win-win outcome. For another leap and bound in the pragmatic cooperation in trade and economy with Africa, China launched a series of new measures. I hope to extend the Chinese government's sincere wishes on the development of Sino-Africa relations and new measures to African countries and people, understand the real demands of our friends, discuss how to deepen bilateral pragmatic cooperation under the new situation and further promote the sound and steady development of Sino-Africa trade and economic relations by this visit.

Reporter: What achievements do you make after your visit to the three countries?

Chen Deming: The three countries have featured regional advantages and their trade and economic cooperation with China is ever closer. Morocco, as an Arab country in North Africa, has a steady economy with constant development. It is also the important channel between Africa and Europe and Middle East. Equatorial Guinea, whose economy developed rapidly and steadily in recent years, is the member of Economic Community of Central African States and Central African Customs and Economic Union. And Ghana is an important member of Economic Community of West African States and its development momentum is sound.

During the visit, I called upon leaders of the three countries, held matching talks on how to boost the cooperation in new fields with relevant departments of the three governments respectively and made inspection in some ongoing projects and local market. Despite the compact schedule, the visit is abundant, effective and successful. Here are the main fruits:

Firstly, we had expansive exchanges with leaders, government departments and business communities of the three countries and made quite a number of new consensuses in the discussion on new methods of enhancing bilateral trade and economic cooperation under the new situation. In Morocco, the two sides achieved the intention of cooperation in the issues of expanding the import of phosphate fertilizer and sponsoring symposium for senior officials of developing zones; in Equatorial Guinea, the two sides reached consensus on the development of human resources and cooperation in agriculture and fishery; in Ghana, the two sides agreed to take new methods in cooperation in infrastructure construction, telecommunication and financing. In addition, more issues were discussed with the three countries, like enhancing multi-level cooperation in agriculture, regional planning and design of projects.

Secondly, we got more deep information about the fulfillment of Chinese measures on pragmatic cooperation and promoted the implementation of new measures proposed in the 4th Ministerial Conference of FOCAC. During the visit, relevant institutions of the Chinese government and enterprises signed quite a number of trade and economic cooperation agreements with the three countries and pushed forward a batch of key projects of common concern.

Thirdly, we made in-depth investigation into how to further develop bilateral pragmatic cooperation under the new situation and acquired many pragmatic suggestions by field inspections in ongoing projects and local markets and talks with Chinese-funded enterprises in Africa.

Fourthly, we carefully and patiently introduced China's measures on trade and economy with Africa and standpoints on some hot issues by means of official meetings, interviews and media symposium, which further enhanced the understanding and support of African countries and international society in China's relevant measures.

The U.S. and China Working Toward Clean Energy
Hillary Rodham Clinton, Secretary of State,
Online Chat Moderated by Professor Qi Ye, Hosted by China Daily
Beijing, China
February 22, 2009

PROFESSOR QI: First of all, our netizens are very much interested in learning how your family — you know, you, your family, former President Clinton, Chelsea — do the environment — the energy conservation.

SECRETARY CLINTON: Well, first of all, let me thank you for having me be able to speak to the netizens — I like that phrase — and I am so pleased that you are focusing on such an important topic as energy efficiency and climate change.

In our own lives, we have tried to be much more conscious of what we should do. So, for example, we use compact fluorescent bulbs, which are less of a drain on the electricity grid. We have installed more high-energy resistant windows, more insulted windows. We have, obviously, insulated our utilities and our homes. We have also recycled, so that we are trying not to add to the landfill waste more than absolutely necessary.

And my husband, of course, with the Clinton Foundation, is running a climate change program with, I think, 40 cities around the world working on higher energy efficiency, and so much else. So, we have tried to do more, but we are constantly asking ourselves what more we can do.

PROFESSOR QI: Great, thank you. And during this trip you have emphasized this cooperative — this positive cooperation. Would you mind to elaborate a little bit on that, you know, how that is going to work for this China-U.S. cooperation on environment, energy, and climate change?

SECRETARY CLINTON: Well, as part of the agreement in principle that we announced yesterday between myself and Foreign Minister Yang, we will enter into strategic and economic dialogues co-chaired by myself and the Treasury Secretary.

And one of the most important tracks will be clean energy and climate change. We wish to create a series of actions and partnerships between our countries, between our businesses, our academic institutions, our citizens. And we hope to work together in the lead-up to Copenhagen at the end of this year, with a new climate treaty. We hope that there will be many opportunities, as I saw for myself yesterday, for partnerships between American companies and Chinese companies to produce cleaner energy. And our new Energy Secretary, Dr. Steven Chu, wants to work to help create more intellectual property that would be jointly designed and implemented by Chinese and American researchers.

So, we are just at the beginning of this cooperative relationship on clean energy and climate change. But I am very hopeful that it will continue to grow.

PROFESSOR QI: Great. Does this mean the 10-year framework, the cooperative effort developed during the strategic economic dialogue is going to continue, and is going to work through all these areas related to environment, climate change, and energy conservation?

SECRETARY CLINTON: Yes, and we are going to build on the 10 year strategic dialogue about climate change and clean energy. We want to expand it even more and I was heartened by the commitments shown by the Chinese government to Copenhagen, that they want to participate and look for how the Chinese economy and the Chinese policies can contribute to lowering emissions.

PROFESSOR QI: Right. You made this same statement yesterday — which I very much agree on — when speaking to the students and scholars at Tsinghua University. You said, you know, "China and U.S. should work together to avoid the kind of mistakes that the U.S. made in the past."

I wonder if you could name some of those mistakes, and how we're going to work together to avoid that.

SECRETARY CLINTON: Well, I will give you one example. Back in the early 1970s, when the price of oil shot up, and the cost of gasoline shot up, individuals and governments under President Carter — and President Ford before him — tried to impose conservation measures, and tried to encourage the development of higher gas mileage cars, and more energy efficiency.

In the early 1980s, the price of gasoline went down. So everybody in America said, "Oh, well, we don't have to worry about that any more, and we don't have to have gas-efficient cars, we can continue to have very inefficient cars." And it was a mistake. It set us back.

Now, if you compare what our entire country did with what one state did — California kept pushing energy conservation. California tried to push higher gas mileage cars. And, today, California still has a lower-per-capita use of electricity because of efficiency measures than the rest of the United States.

So, we made a mistake. People thought, "Oh, we don't have to worry about it any more." We know we have to worry and we are trying to be good partners, and coordinate with other countries, including making our own changes.

PROFESSOR QI: Right, right. Well, that's a great point. Moving into the next phase, Copenhagen. IPCC, the Intergovernmental Panel on Climate Change, proposed 25 to 40 percent of cuts in greenhouse gas emissions for the developed countries in order to avoid a dangerous deterioration of the climate. Do you think that's possible for the U.S. — that 25 to 40 percent cut by the year 2020?

SECRETARY CLINTON: I think that a great deal is possible. Very much of it is technically possible. Our challenge now is to make it politically and personally possible. And that is what President Obama is committed to doing, is, with our stimulus money, which was a very significant down payment on modernizing our electric grid, on incentivizing changes in building construction and design, and retrofitting federal buildings.

The science and technology is possible for us to be much more energy efficient. In fact, concentrating on energy efficiency more than renewable energies is a very obvious way of trying to move toward our targets. We just have to convince enough of our fellow citizens to agree with us.

You started by asking what my family does. Well, we have tried to change our mental attitude — turning off appliances, turning off lights. My late father grew up with the belief that you didn't waste things like electricity. So, we would turn off the furnace at night. We would turn off all the lights when we left a room.

And then, I confess, we got a little bit less aware. And I think most Americans did. So we weren't paying attention. We had so many utensils, appliances plugged into the walls and draining electricity all the time, and we would walk out of a room with all the lights on, and our big buildings would be lit all night long, and we wasted a lot of energy and we wasted a lot of money. We can't do that.

And so, being more efficient will take us a long way toward what we need to achieve. But it is also clear that it is not only the developed countries, it is economies like China and India that have to become full partners. How you do it, given your challenges, is something we want to work on, because we will have different approaches. And Kyoto recognized that. Different approaches to common objectives is how we have to consider the Copenhagen treaty.

PROFESSOR QI:Great. And it is great to see such a great level of optimism. And thank you so much for being with us.

SECRETARY CLINTON:Thank you. It's a pleasure.

重难点评析

1. "compact fluorescent bulbs"译为"紧凑型荧光灯",比白炽灯(incandescent light bulb)节电;"insulted windows"译为"隔热窗"。

2. "We have also recycled, so that we are trying not to add to the landfill waste more than absolutely necessary."so that 引导目的状语从句,意为"目的是"。译文中进行的省译是考虑到中文的说话习惯和译文的流畅,"我们也做垃圾回收,若非必要,我们尽量减少需要填埋的垃圾。"

3. "And we hope to work together in the lead-up to Copenhagen at the end of this year, with a new climate treaty."译为"我们希望在年底哥本哈根气候变化会议之前这段时间通力合作,能达成新的气候变化协定。""in the lead-up to"译为"在……到来之前的一段时间",例如:The international media showed intense interest in Hong Kong in the lead-up

to, and during, the handover."对于在回归前及回归期间的香港,国际传媒尤为关注。

4. "And our new Energy Secretary, Dr. Steven Chu, wants to work to help create more intellectual property that would be jointly designed and implemented by Chinese and American researchers."定语从句很长,在翻译时遵从了中文的习惯进行了倒译将其前置,"而且我们(美国)新上任的能源部长朱棣文,也希望通过努力发展更多由美中双方的研究人员共同设计执行的专利技术产品。"

5. "Does this mean the 10-year framework, the cooperative effort developed during the strategic economic dialogue is going to continue, and is going to work through all these areas related to environment, climate change, and energy conservation?"原句很长,句子成分也较多、较复杂,译文采用了合译法将其整合成一个简洁的整句,"这是不是意味着双方在战略经济对话合作框架下达成的有关环保、气候、能源领域的10年合作框架还会继续下去?"

6. "... when the price of oil shot up, and the cost of gasoline shot up, ... tried to impose conservation measures, ..." "shoot up"译为"暴涨,迅速增长";"conservation measures"译为"节能措施"。

7. "And, today, California still has a lower-per-capita use of electricity because of efficiency measures than the rest of the United States." "per capita"译为"人均",例如:"per capita income"译为"人均收入";"per capita consumption"译为"人均消费量";"efficiency measures"译为"节能措施"。

8. "... proposed 25 to 40 percent of cuts in greenhouse gas emissions for the developed countries..."在翻译时将名词"cuts"进行了词性的换译,变成了动词"削减",更符合中文的表达习惯。"……提出发达国家要在1990年基础上将温室气体排放量削减25%到40%……"

9. "And that is what President Obama is committed to doing, is, with our stimulus money, which was a very significant down payment on modernizing our electric grid, on incentivizing changes in building construction and design, and retrofitting federal buildings."译为"这也是奥巴马总统一直努力的方向。我们用于经济刺激计划的投资,很大一部分用来建设现代化的电网,用于鼓励对建筑及其设计做出改造,用于翻新联邦政府的办公楼,以使其能效更高。"

10. "The science and technology is possible for us to be much more energy efficient."考虑到中文的表达习惯使用了倒译,"更多的节能在科学技术上来说是可能的。"

11. "We just have to convince enough of our fellow citizens to agree with us." "agree with us"即指前句说的"节能",采用了意译,"但同时我们必须说服每个公民都要做到节约能源。"

12. "grow up with the belief that..."译为"一直有一个信念"。

13. "We had so many utensils, appliances plugged into the walls and draining electricity all the time..."译为"那么多的电器插座一直通着电在浪费……"。

14. "But it is also clear that it is not only the developed countries, it is economies like

China and India that have to become full partners."强调句的结构,译为"此外不仅是发达国家,还有像中国和印度这些经济体,都需要有所作为"。

二、译 文

美国国务卿希拉里·克林顿就中美共同致力清洁能源等相关问题
接受清华大学齐晔教授在中国日报网《环球对话》节目的专访

2009年2月22日

齐晔:首先,我们的网民非常感兴趣地想了解您的家庭——您,还有克林顿总统、女儿切尔西在环保、节约能源方面的做法是什么?

希拉里·克林顿:首先谢谢您让我有机会能和(中国的)网民交谈,非常高兴看到您把重点放在能源效率和气候变化这么重要的话题上。

在平常的生活中,我们努力有意识地做一些力所能及的事。譬如说我们会用一些紧凑型的荧光灯泡,这相对不太耗电。另外我们安装了隔热窗,我们也做垃圾回收,若非必要,我们尽量减少需要填埋的垃圾。

另外,我丈夫克林顿的基金会正在世界各地40多个城市推行一个与气候变化有关的项目,他们从事着提高能源效率及其相关的工作。我们在为此付出更多的努力,同时我们也在不停地问自己,我们还能做些什么。

齐晔:谢谢,您在此次访问中强调了积极合作,您能否对中美如何推进在环保、能源以及气候领域的合作做一下详细的说明?

希拉里·克林顿:原则上来讲,作为我和杨洁篪外长昨日宣布的协议的一部分,(中美之间)要继续进行战略经济对话,美方由我和财政部长共同牵头。

(在这一对话机制中)最重要的轨道之一就是清洁能源和气候变化,我们想在两国以及两国的商业机构、学术机构和公民之间建立一系列的伙伴关系,举行一系列的活动。我们希望在年底哥本哈根气候变化会议之前这段时间通力合作,能达成新的气候变化协定;也希望能像昨天我看到的一样,发掘更多美中企业间合作发展清洁能源的机会。而且我们(美国)新上任的能源部长朱棣文,也希望通过努力发展更多由美中双方的研究人员共同设计执行的专利技术产品。

美中双方在清洁能源和气候变化领域的合作关系还刚刚起步,但我希望双方的合作能继续开展下去。

齐晔:太好了。这是不是意味着双方在战略经济对话合作框架下达成的有关环保、气候、能源领域的10年合作框架还会继续下去?

希拉里·克林顿:是的,我们将在《中美能源环境十年合作框架》的基础上进一步扩大双方的合作。我很高兴看到中国政府对参与哥本哈根会议所做出的努力,我也想看看中国的经济和政策会对减排做出怎样的贡献。

齐晔:您昨天在和清华大学的学者和学生交流时说了这句话,我非常同意您的看法。您说美中两国应该共同努力,来避免美国过去所犯的那种错误。

您能不能再说一下,过去的那些错误指的是什么,我们应该怎样通过共同努力来避免错误再发生?

希拉里·克林顿：我举一个例子：在20世纪70年代的时候，当石油价格开始猛升，汽油价格也跟着上升，卡特总统，包括之前的福特总统领导下的人民和政府都努力实施节能措施，鼓励发展比较省油的车和提高能效。

可是80年代初，汽油的价格就降下来了，这时候美国人说："好了，我们不要再去在意油价，我们不是非得开省油的车，可以继续开油耗高的车。"可是这是一个错误，一下倒退了回去。

如果作个比较的话，和全国的情况不同，加利福尼亚州一直推行节约能源，一直要求推广油耗低的汽车。如今加利福尼亚的人均耗电量还是比美国其他地方低，就是因为他们坚持采用节能措施。

美国犯过这个错误，原本以为不用再在意油耗，但是现在知道我们不得不在意。美国要做"好的合作伙伴"，美国要和其他国家合作，自己也要做出改变。

齐晔：是的，这正是很重要的一点。现在让我们进入下个话题。联合国政府间气候变化委员会（IPCC）提出，到2020年，发达国家要在1990年基础上将温室气体排放量削减25％到40％，以避免气候进一步恶化。您认为2020年美国能达到这个要求吗？

希拉里·克林顿：我认为还是很有可能的，技术上来讲是可以实现的。现在我们面临的挑战就是如何在政治上和日常生活中实现这个目标，这也是奥巴马总统一直努力的方向。我们用于经济刺激计划的投资，很大一部分用来建设现代化的电网，用于鼓励对建筑及其设计做出改造，用于翻新联邦政府的办公楼，以使其能效更高。

更多的节能在科学技术上来说是可能的。事实上，致力于提高能效而不仅仅着眼于可再生能源，是能使我们达到目标的一个很显然的办法。但同时我们必须说服每个公民都要做到节约能源。

你刚才问到我自己的家庭怎么做的，我们是先从改变观念做起，我们会关掉不用的电器，关上灯。我已故的父亲一直有一个信念，不应该浪费电以及其他能源，所以晚上火炉要关掉，离开房间所有的灯要关掉。

但是我得承认，后来我们变得不是那么在意，我想大部分美国人也是这样不太注意这些事。那么多的电器插座一直通着电在浪费，离开房间也不关灯，办公楼的灯整夜地开，我们浪费了很多能源和钱。我们不可以那样做。

在节约能源这方面，我们还有很多要改进的地方。此外不仅是发达国家，还有像中国和印度这些经济体，都需要有所作为，要实事求是因地制宜，不同的国家做法也不尽相同。这种不同在《京都议定书》里就有所体现，如何用不同的方法来应对共同的目标，也是在哥本哈根协议中所要考虑到的。

齐晔：我完全同意。非常高兴看到您对此这么乐观，感谢您作客《环球对话》，和我们的网友交流，谢谢。

希拉里·克林顿：谢谢，非常荣幸。

口音听辨技巧

一、英语语音变体

正如汉语在中国的各个地区存在不同的方言和口音，英语在世界范围内也存在着各种语言变体,这里的变体既包括词汇表达上的微小差异,也包括语音语调上的多样变化。作为口译员,在实战中不可避免地要接触来自不同国家、地区,操持不同英语口音的人士的发言和讲话。

我们可以简单地将英语口音归纳为三个语言圈:

核心圈:英式英语(British English)及以英式英语为主的澳洲英语(Australian English)
美式英语(American English)及以美式英语为主的加拿大英语(Canadian English)

British English 与 American English 目前被普遍接受为"标准英语"。

次级圈:由于历史的原因,还有很多国家或地区也以英语作为官方语言,但受到本民族语言的影响,它们的英语带有较为明显的发音变化。

西亚:印度英语(Hindi English)受到印地语的影响,巴基斯坦英语(Pakistani English)受到乌尔都语的影响。

东南亚:新加坡、马来西亚等地以英式英语为主,菲律宾英语(Taglish)以美式英语为主,但都各自体现本民族语言的痕迹。

非洲:英语受到来自本民族语言和各种占领国外来语的影响。

外围圈:由于政治、经济、文化等往来,以下国家将英语作为重要的外语进行推广:

欧洲:法国、德国、意大利、西班牙、俄罗斯

亚洲:中国、日本、韩国

南美洲:阿根廷、巴西

这些地区的人讲的英语都带有很浓重的本民族语言痕迹。

二、英式英语与美式英语的语音和拼写区别

Ⅰ.语音的区别

1. 音素

A. /t/ → /d/   writer latter metal plenty Ottawa little
   /ɑː/ → /æ/   after bath pass fast laugh can't demand France
   /o/ → /ʌ/   hot dog pot lock dock
   /juː/ → /uː/ student tune tube

B. -r /~r/   card sport four teacher brother poor bear beer
   -ary /rɪ/ → /ərɪ/   secretary military dictionary necessary
   -on /ən/ → /ɑn/   polygon pentagon automaton
   -ile /aɪl/ → /il/   mobile fragile hostile juvenile

C. /ʃ/ → /ʒ/   version Asia
   /w/ → /hw/ white whether

2. 重音

A. 以-ary 和-ory 结尾的词,英音重音放在第二音节,美音放在第一音节:
laboratory [英] /leˈbɔrətrɪ/ [美] /ˈlæbrətɔrɪ/   centenary [英] /senˈtiːnərɪ/ [美] /ˈsentɪnərɪ/

B. 以-ate 结尾的词,英音重音放在第二音节,美音放在第一音节

dictate [英] /dɪkˈteɪt/ [美] /ˈdɪkteɪt/ donate [英] /dəʊˈneɪt/ [美] /ˈdəʊneɪt/

C. 以-arily 结尾的词，美音重音放在该词缀上，英音放在前面正常重音位置：
necessarily [英] /ˈnesəserɪlɪ/ [美] /nesəˈserɪlɪ/

D. 大多数复合词英音中的重音放在后，美音放在前：

[英] beefˈsteak elseˈwhere inˈland meanˈtime midˈday
[美] ˈbeefsteak ˈelsewhere ˈinland ˈmeantime ˈmidday

个别一些词例外，刚好相反：

[英] ˈbaseball ˈfingernail ˈfireproof ˈmidsummer
[美] baseˈball fingerˈnail fireˈproof midˈsummer

3. 个别单词发音

anti capsule clerk herb leisure lever
[英] /ˈæntɪ/ /ˈkæpsjuːl/ /klɑːk/ /hɜːb/ /ˈleʒə/ /ˈliːvə/
[美] /ˈæntaɪ/ /ˈkæpsʊl/ /klɜːrk/ /ɜːb/ /ˈlɪʒə/ /ˈlevər/

medicine missile progress schedule tomato vase
[英] /ˈmedsɪn/ /ˈmɪsaɪl/ /ˈprəʊgres/ /ˈʃedjuːl/ /təˈmɑːtəʊ/ /vɑːz/
[美] /ˈmedɪsɪn/ /ˈmɪsəl/ /ˈprɒgres/ /ˈskedʒʊl/ /təˈmeɪtəʊ/ /veɪs/

Ⅱ. 拼写的区别

1. -our → -or colour/color favourite/favorite neighbour/neighbor
2. -re → -er centre/center metre/meter theatre/theater
3. -ce → -se defence/defense offence/offense licence/license
4. -gramme → -gram kilogramme/kilogram programme/program
5. -i(y)se → -i(y)ze analyse/analyze organise/organize memorise/memorize
6. -l-/ -ll- dialled/dialed travelling/traveling jewellery/jewelry

三、各国英语口音概述

1. 英国口音

英国口音的特点，就是抑扬顿挫，几乎每个音节都发得清清楚楚，长韵母音和短韵母音有十分明显的区别。而美式英语里面则有点含糊不清，大部分的长韵母音都被截短。比如说 class 中的 a 音，属于长韵母音，英国人一般都发得比较完整，而美国人往往读成短音，听上去和 bad 里面的 a 音差不多。又如 aunt，美国人几乎无一例外发成 ant，让人搞不清楚他们到底是说自己的阿姨，还是家门口的蚂蚁。

英国口音往往对位于弱音节上的清辅音发得十分清晰，美国人则经常把清辅音读成浊辅音。比如 battery，美国人读来就如同 baddery。

2. 美国东部口音

美东的发音，由于地理上靠近英国，因此很多方面更类似英国口音。尽管如此，因为美国东部开发较早，人口流动性比较大，口音混杂得很厉害。

语言学上有 rhotic 和 non-rhotic accent 的说法。rhotic accent（儿化音），具体来讲，就是 r 不论作辅音（比如 red），还是作元音（比如说 four），r 都发音。与之相反的是 non-rhotic accent（非儿化音），这种发音风格是只发辅音 r，不发元音 r。英国人和部分美东地区以及小部分南方地区,都是属于非儿化音,美国大部分地区则为儿化音。影视作品中很多剧集虽然把地点设在美东,比如 Friends(六人行)和 Sex and the City(欲望都市),但是这些剧集不能完全反映美东的口音。

3. 美国南部口音

美国南方经济相对落后,民众普遍受教育程度不高,因此长期被美国其他地区的人看不起。南方大部分为农业区,农民被蔑称为 red neck,意思是他们整天在太阳底下晒着,脖子发红。red neck 随后成为美国南方白人的代名词。

美国南方口音的特点就是拖长音,什么元音都拖得老长,而且词与词当中没有停顿,统统连读。再加上南方人爱用鼻音,他们的对话听起来就像两个感冒的人在聊天。

凡是背景设为美国南方的电影,几乎都是清一色的非常容易辨别的南方口音。比较著名的有《阿甘正传》和动画片《山大王》(King of the Hill)。

4. 美国西部口音

西部由于接纳大量移民,因此口音混杂交融。比较突出的是 God 里面的 o 音被拖长为 Gaad,把 leg 发成 layg。

5. 澳洲口音

澳洲最早是英国的殖民地,被用来发配犯人,后来又有大量淘金者涌入。澳洲口音常常省略辅音 h,直接发后面的元音。比如 how 经常发成 ow。澳洲人称朋友为 mate,而且喜欢夸张地发成 myte。于是有一个著名的笑话,说澳洲游客总喜欢缠着导游说:"Where are we going to die?"原文是:"Where are we going today?"澳洲人把 today 念成 to die。

影视作品《海底总动员》(Finding Nemo)里面的鹭鸶、鲨鱼、牙医,都是典型的澳洲音。

6. 以日本和印度为代表的卷舌口音

日本人把 silk 会发音为 siloko。印度人英语口音重、语速快,说起话来满嘴里跑舌头,辅音 r 发颤音,乍听起来很难懂。印度式英语发音的另一个主要特点就是把标准英语中本应该咬舌送气的音 th 简化为 t。而且印度人发的 t 的音,又接近 d 的音,所以印度人自己也拿这个发音特点开玩笑,当他们说 I am thirty. 听上去像 I am dirty. 1968 年美国拍摄的《狂欢宴》(The Party),著名喜剧演员塞勒斯扮演一位倒霉的印度人,满口印度腔英语,一路插科打诨自我解嘲,周旋于美利坚高等白人之华屋盛宴,娄子捅了一个又一个,至今还是美国人模仿印度腔英语的经典。

印度英语是英语大家族里的重要的成员。早在 15 世纪英语就随着英国商人进入了印度,到现在保留了许多现代英语已经很少使用的词汇。比如:Please intimate...(请告知……),或者 You will be intimated shortly. (不久你们就会被告知。)同样的意思,美国人就直截了当地写:Please let us know. 或 You will be informed shortly. 因为印度人口远超过英国人口,以至于已故英国著名作家马尔科姆·蒙格瑞奇(Malcolm Muggeridge)曾经这样说:"世界上最后一个英国绅士没准是印度人。(The last Englishman would be an Indian.)"

除此以外,印度人非常喜欢使用现在进行时,比如:I am understanding it.(我明白。)She is knowing the answer.(她知道答案。)这可不是古苏格兰的语法,而是受了印地语的影响。受印地语影响的常用印度英语还有:Your good name please?(你叫什么名字?)问人家岁数的时候可以用这样委婉的说法:What's your good number? 甚至可以问:When is

your happy birthday?（什么时候生日快乐？）
印度英语发音规律：
WA DIM＝WHAT TIME
I D LIG DOCHANGE DE GALA＝I'D LIKE TO CHANGE THE COLOR
关键点：
p 发 b
t 发 d
k 发 g
r 发 l
没有爆破音和清辅音。

口译笔记理论及技巧（二）

一、创造适合自己的口译笔记系统

在前一个单元讲到，笔记是高级口译的关键。使用笔记，是为了补充大脑短期记忆和耐久力的不足，以保证译文的精确度，并保证其不受讲话人持续时间的影响。每个人的记忆、思维和反应都有各自的特点，最好用的笔记方式是自己发展出来的属于并适合自己的口译笔记系统。另外，笔记越简单，记录就越迅速。但笔记简单了，对短期记忆的要求就相对提高了。所以，笔记多少为最佳，因人而宜，需要摸索出适合于自己的平衡。

以下是几个要点：

1. 少写多画。画线条比写文字快。线条形象，相当于翻译的"半成品"，有助于译员眼看笔记，口出译文。两种情况下应该尽量用线条：

表示动作和动态的词句。比如，以上升的斜线代表"发展"，"增加"，"进步"，"进一步"；以下降的斜线代表"减少"，"下降"，"恶化"等等。

表示因果或前后关系的词句。比如，用一条线代表"因为/所以"，"……之后"，"在……之前"，以体现出上下前后之间的关联关系。

2. 少字多意。养成一个词的笔记不超过一个字的习惯。中文里有大量的词汇是由两个或两个以上的字组成。只要看到其中一个，你的短期记忆就应该能够补齐其余的字，不必多写。比如，"中国"最多写个"中"，"北京"最多写个"北"。英文词也同样处理。"politics"最多写"poli"，"government"最多写"gov"，等等。另外，需要培养笔记与记忆互动，看到一个词能说出几个词，甚至一串词的能力。在有上下文的情况下，这不难。比如，谈中国的近况，听到"改革开放"记一个"改"字，不难从短期记忆中说出原文，听到"British Prime Minister Tony Blair"，记"PM"，也同样能说出原文。

3. 少线多指。通用一小组线条/标记，否则在自己本来熟悉的中英文之外，又编出一套自己不熟悉的文码使用，会导致需要想一想用哪个符号的情况，适得其反。

4. 少横多竖。采取从上往下的阶梯结构记录，尽量少用通常书写时的横向记录。阶梯结构形象地体现出上下文的逻辑结构，简化了译员的思维过程，方便出译文。

5. 快速书写。必须发展自己的汉字快速书写系统。口译笔记完全是自己看，而且只需要几分钟之内能看懂就行。很多汉字笔划减少后,并不影响确认。我这里讲的不是潦草,而是除了实际口译经常不得不潦草之外,花一些时间,把练习中或口译工作中常用的字琢磨一下,看看可以怎样减少笔划,或理顺笔划,一笔成字。

  6. 明确结束。口译中,讲话人说一段,停下来让译员译一段,然后再继续。这样,上一段话和下一段话之间,必须有明确的界限。上一次的结束点,就成了下一次翻译的开始点。其重要性在于,如果笔记是从本子的 1/3 处开始的,下一段话可能写了 2～3 页,翻回来口译时,眼光无法确定这页上面哪一条线或符号是这次翻译内容的开始点,所以需要标明。

  此外,讲一下所需装备。

  建议使用带有活页圈的笔记本。有活页圈才能来回翻倒方便。笔记本大小以自己感觉舒服为准。记完一页,翻过去一页。讲话人收口后,一把抓地全部翻回来,落眼处正是这个段子的开头。然后,译一页,翻过去一页。这段译完后,把翻过去的几页一把压在手掌中。这等于是用手掌把已经翻完的和下一段的笔记清楚分开。这点很重要,否则,很容易出现讲话人收口后,你来回翻找本段首页的难堪局面。

  如果是坐在桌前,笔记本放在桌面上,也是记完一页,翻过去一页。千万不要忘记在讲话人开口说下一段之前,把已经翻完的笔记页压到笔记本下。

  笔建议用按压式的,这样,一手持本,另一手随时都可以掏出笔来,一按就开始记。如果是旋转开盖的笔,则需要两只手操作。如果笔套不紧的,还时不时要掉,很分心。最好带两支笔,免遭墨水用尽之难。

二、口译记录的常用符号

  职业译员的口译记录是用富含意义的精练文字和指称明确的符号作为信息载体的。这些作为信息载体的符号有些具有语言指代性质,有些则属于非语言性质的"纯"符号。一般情况下,译员们只对使用频率很高的词语创造或借鉴使用一些易记易辨的符号加以指代。这些符号通常"不属于某种特定的语言","在各种语言中都是一目了然的"。这样,译员"用一种语言作记录使用这些符号和缩写词,在看记录时,又可毫不费力地用另一种语言把这些符号和缩写词重读出来"。

  口译记录的符号多种多样,根据其来源和创造的方式可大致划分为以下几种类型:

  1. 象形、会意符号

  汉字属于象形文字,具有很强的表意功能,口译记录可以借用单个汉字或某些偏旁部首,然后再混合其他符号来表达一些概念。例如,如果我们用一条横线"—"表示大地,那么"冰"(意为:水淹着地面)这一符号则可以表示"水淹"、"洪灾";而采用类似方法创造的另一个符号"水̄"(意为:水退到地表下)则可以表示"干旱"、"缺水"等。再如,"口"的四条边很容易使人想起"边境"、"疆域",因此在做口译记录时,常用"口"来表示"国家"、"民族"。如果我们再在"口"的上面加上一个人头样的小圆圈"o",这时又可以表示"某国人"。

  2. 标点符号

  标点符号对口译记录很有帮助,因而经常使用。例如,口译记录时问号"?"常用来表示"问题"、"难题"等,因此口译过程中若涉及"台湾问题"时,译员只记作"TW?"即可。其他一些标点符号如"·"可用来表示"观点"、"观念"、"主意"、"论点"等;":"可以表示与"说"有关的概念,如"告诉"、"演讲"、"宣称"、"声明"、"认为"、"赞成"、"抱怨"、"抗议"等。

3. 印刷符号

常用于口译记录的还有一些印刷符号。例如,口译记录时可用"～"表示"前后颠倒"、"颠倒黑白"、"出尔反尔"的意思;用"^"表示"插入"、"干涉"、"介入"、"侵略";而"/"则可表示"删(剔)除"、"取消"。

4. 数学符号

数学运算符号不受语言限制,具有准确、简洁、明了的优点,因而是理想的口译记录符号。例如,"＋"可以表示"增加"、"补充";"－"可以表示"扣除"、"减少";"≈"可以表示"大约"、"几乎";"∴"则可以表示"由于"、"因为"等概念。除了这些符号外,数学符号还有很多,译员都应熟练地掌握。

5. 数字符号

口译时,说话人往往会列举一连串的统计数据来描述经济或社会的运行状况,迅速地记下这些数据是译员的一项重要基本功。一般说来,年代的前2位至前3位数字可以不记,仅以分节号"—"来代替。例如,"1995年至1999年间"可以简单地记作"95-9"。对于较大的数字,我们可以用写在数字右上角的小数字"1"、"2"、"3"来分别表示"千"、"百万"、"十亿"等单位。例如,"85 000"可以记作"85^1","657 000 000"则记作"657^2"。

6. 箭头符号

与其他类型的符号相比,箭头符号直观、明了,因而在口译记录符号系统中占有更重要的地位,使用得更多、更广泛。例如,右指箭头"→"常用来表示"派遣"、"出使"、"出国"、"运往"、"前往"、"到达"、"听命于"、"出口"、"屈服于"、"交给……"、"向……传达"、"导致"等概念;左指箭头"←"则可以表示"来自"、"源于"、"返回"、"收到"等意思;垂直上指箭头"↑"可意指"发射"、"升空"、"起飞"、"增长"、"跳高"、"火山喷发"、"井喷"、"提拔"、"晋升"等;垂直下指箭头"↓"则可意指"下落"、"下沉"、"轰炸"、"跳水"、"压力"、"解职"、"降低"、"减少"、"限制"、"压缩"、"裁减"等意思。此外,斜指向右上方的箭头"↗"和斜指向左下方的箭头"↙",以及同时指向左右两端的箭头"←→"亦可分别指称大量的信息。

7. 否定符号

人们在讲话时总会表明自己赞成什么或反对什么,口译时译员采用合适的符号将它们准确地记录下来非常重要。通常,否定形式用一条贯穿某一概念的斜线"/"表示。例如,"伊朗代表在发言中表示:伊朗不赞成增加石油输出国组织的原油日产量"就可以记作"Ir:/OPEC日产。"如果讲话人对否定形式加以强调,译员可以用贯穿这一概念的双斜线"//"将讲话人的这一观点记录下来。

8. 指示过去、现在和将来的符号

这个问题可以用一个小圆点来解决,小圆点在不同的位置便表示不同的时间概念。例如,如果我们用"Y"表示"今年",那么"去年"则可以记作".Y",而"3年后"便可以记着"3Y."。其他一些时间单位如分、秒、时、日、周、月、世纪等的记录方式都可以如法炮制。至于发生在过去或将来的行为,在动词的左或右方画上一竖线,就可以记录得准确无误。例如,"中国国家主席习近平将于下个月访问美国。"就可以简单地记作:"习访|美 m."。

9. 强调符号

对于比较重要或极重要的信息,在它们的下面画上一条或两条线,就能记录得准确无

误。例如,"俄罗斯坚决反对美国对车臣事务的干涉"这一句话,在口译员的记录本上就变成了:"R 反 USA 车"。至于以缓和或委婉的语气传达的信息,可以用虚线标出。例如,"我感到有点儿冷。"就可以记作:"I 冷"。

10. 缩略词

为了书写或表达的需要,英汉两种语言都大量使用缩略词,这些缩略词一般用于对国名、地名或组织机构名称等的简化,广泛应用于新闻报道、电报、电传之类的文体中。例如,"西班牙"(Spain)、"中国人民政治协商会议"(Chinese People's Political Consultative Conference)和"北美自由贸易区"(North American Free Trade Area)在英语中可分别简化成"Es"、"CPPCC"和"NAFTA"。口译时,译员若能熟练地使用这类缩略词,可以大大节省口译记录的时间,为口译工作带来意想不到的便利。

三、口译记录应注意的问题

语言选择

即席翻译过程中口译员借助符号和文字来记录信息。那么,译员通常应该选用哪一种语言文字做记录呢?一般认为,口译员宜"使用译入语做记录","这已成为一种惯例"。即,外汉互译时,译员若要将汉语讲话翻译成外语,他宜用外文记录;译员若要翻译外语讲话时则适宜用中文记录。这种记录方法能使语际转换在记录阶段即可完成,便于译员在动口说出译文之前就开始着手克服语际转码过程中遇到的种种困难,从而为他接踵而至的口译活动扫除障碍。

然而,口译员记录时可以使用他自己擅长的那种语言,再辅之以少量其他语言。这是因为对于母语为中文的译员来说,他们用中文做记录会写得更快、更顺利一些。事实上,中国译员在做英译中时常常会自觉或不自觉地这么做。当然,由于记录的过程也是一个翻译的过程,译员在中译英时,也应尽可能多用英语文字做记录,力争使双语转换活动在记录阶段就得以完成。总的来说,中国译员的笔记应该汉语、英语并用,以中文为主。在某些特殊情况下,假如用英语或汉语记录都很浪费笔墨或很困难,译员还可以尝试着用更经济、更有效果的第三种语言来记录。

实例解析

讲话原文

Following the 1997 election, in which the Labour Party came to power, the macroeconomic policy framework has been reformed.

第一层次:一个箭头,加 97,再加"选",足以帮助短期记忆,说出译文:"1997 年大选之后"。

第二层次:一个"工"加圆圈,提醒"工"字后面还有话。另外,一条垂直线体现出第二层与第一层有关联。此后一个箭头,再加"权",足以帮助短期记忆,说出译文:"工党上台掌权"。

第三层次:一个"M"加圆圈,提醒"M"字后面还有话。从短期记忆中回顾出"宏观经济框架"。

接着,一条横线体现关联,线后一个"改"字,于是补齐译文:"对宏观经济框架进行了改革"。

最后画圈,带横杆,表示本段讲话到此结束。

备注:使用的4个汉字都经过"理顺",其中2个是一笔成字。

讲话原文

The aim of this reform is to help provide a framework for improved macroeconomic stability and economic growth.

承上启下:一画从上段的"改"字左斜拉下来,接着往右一拐弯。足以从短期记忆中回顾出:"改革的目的"。

第一层次:写一个"框"字。从短期记忆中顺着上文,不难说出:"是为了提供一个框架"。

至此,听到"improved",随之画一条上行箭头,再补一个"M"加圈,提醒"M"字后面还有话。这样就不难说出:"以改善宏观经济稳定"。

若担心"M"不够,则可以加"稳"字,或一条水平横线代表之。

第二层次:此时,已听到"and economic growth",于是在"M"之下写"经"字,或"E"外带上弧线。这就不难说出:"促进经济增长"。

最后画个圈,顺手一横杆,表示本段讲话到此结束。

备注:采用了同传里的断句和变通技巧,在"框架"后断句,"improved"翻作"改善";在"经济增长"前加"促进"两字完句。

讲话原文

I would like to explain the key features of the UK economic policy framework, identify the key institutions, their leaders and their main responsibilities. There are three main institutions.

第一层次:首先写一个理顺过的"我"字,一横杆代表所做之事,写一个"特"字加圈,提醒字后有话。据此不难说出:"我想解释一下"。

第二层次:谁的特点呢,正好是下一层的意思,于是,画垂直线表示关联,写"U"加圈代表英国,接着写"E",如感不够,再加"P"。既然前面已经写过"框"字,回手一条斜线代表之。据此已不难说出:"英国经济政策框架的特点"。

第三层次:此时听到"identify the key...",警觉到这是与上文排比,立刻从"我"画下斜线,线尾接着写"机"加圈,提醒字后有话。据此不难说出:"指出主要机构"。

此时听到"their leaders",顺手一横杆,写"领"字。

此时听到"their main responsibilities",顺手又一横杆,写"责"字。据此不难说出:"他们的领导人,他们的主要职责"。

此时听到"there are three main institutions",顺手画下斜线,写"3"。据此不难说出:"一共有三个主要机构"。

最后画个圈,顺手一横杆,表示本段讲话到此结束。

讲话原文

The first is HM Treasury which is responsible for the overall economic framework and for fiscal policy in particular. It is led by the Chancellor, Gordon Brown who is an elected politician. He is supported by 4 junior ministers.

第一层次:顺手一个"1"带圈(不带圈容易误解)。写"财"带圈表示财政部。据此不难说出:"第一个是财政部"。

第二层次:顺手画垂直线表示关联,写"全"字加圈,提醒字后有话。此时听到"and...",知道是并列关系,一条下斜线,写"P"加圈,提醒字后有话。此时又听到"in particular",在右下角重画两道,表示强调。据此不难说出:"财政部负责整体经济框架,尤其是财政政策"。

第三层次:听到"it is lead by...",顺手一条左斜线,右拐弯,写"大"加圈,写"GB",接着画下斜线连写"选"字。据此不难说出:"财政部由布朗大臣领导,他是当选的政界人士"。

第四层次:听到"he",还是他,顺手从"GB"下端再画一条下斜线,表示支持关系,接着写"4",如不放心再加"部"。据此不难说出:"他由4位次长支持工作"。

最后画个圈,顺手一横杆,表示本段讲话到此结束。

拓 展 阅 读

选文A

On January 30th, FT publishes its interview with Ambassador FU Ying. The Transcript is as following:

Fu Ying(F): First of all, thank you for choosing this restaurant. I read its background, it's very good. When people asked me what is the best English cuisine, I always tell them fish and chips and pudding. Maybe I can have something more to tell them.

Lionel Barber(B): Yes, this restaurant is very British. Well, you have been very helpful and kind during your tenure here. I will never forget the fact that you manage to secure the interview with Premier Wen, which is one of the highlights of my career. I have talked with many people about you and they are very positive about you. They said Madam Fu Ying is the first Ambassador to use wit and charm as a weapon. And you do have a sense of humour and you are quite different from the sort of stereotype Chinese diplomat.

F: I think there are some stereotyped views about the Chinese. A lot of Chinese are witty and humorous. The Chinese are very humorous people. There seems to be a barrier between us. And when I was a student here, I found that I couldn't get all the British jokes either. Probably because I have been a student here for a year and I was in Australia so I am more relaxed and I can get to this side of the barrier and try to see why there is a barrier.

B: Let's get back to this barrier a little bit later. Well, you are leaving at somewhat short notice, will you miss this country?

F: Yeah, very much. I think leaving is probably the most painful part for any ambassador on the post. Coming in, it takes time, but it is relatively easy; when leaving, all the good things would come out and hold you. I will take my last jog in the park, the last beer in the pub, the last walk on Oxford street... I feel sad when I realize it would be the last... but I think I will leave with a very good memory of this country.

B: Let's go back to China as a world power. This is the Martin Wolf piece. China says we don't want to be a hegemony. First question: but no country wants to tell the world they want to be hegemony. The second point is as China's economic interests grow, and its presence overseas expands, would people on the ground, what happens if there is a problem? As in Sudan? China would need to be able to come to the help of its citizens on the ground. So inevitably, China's presence would expand, and there will be a military presence too as China's interests outside its own country grow. Do you accept that piece?

F: No. Deng Xiaoping said many years ago China would never be hegemonic. One day should China become one, the world should stand up against China. This is very deep in our heart. Every diplomat knows that.

B: It would be too late, once you become a hegemony that would be too late for people to stand up.

F: I think your view comes from your history, comes from your belief that there has to be a hegemony in the world. Years ago, I remember, in the 90s there was an American journalist who came to interview me, and his first question was, what do you think if Asian people do not accept China as a leader in Asia. It took me a while to understand this question. I said what makes you think Asia needs a leader, and China wants to be the leader. For me that was because the question was out of blue. China does not have that in our culture, in our political genes. That's number one.

Number two, he said, what work should China do? China should work with the world. China, in Darfur, we have about 400 people as peacekeepers. We send our military force with U.N. U.N. is the basic condition. Even in gulf of Aden and sea outside of Somalia, we send naval ships to protect the ships. That was also after the discussion with the U.N. I think China would not be an occupying force in the world precisely because we suffered from foreign occupation. We don't believe in occupation. We don't believe in sanction. We don't believe in bulling other countries. We don't believe in treating other countries not as equal.

B: I was only quoting Martin Wolf. I didn't say I necessarily agree with that.

F: I know. Martin Wolf has lots of interesting views.

B: He does, he does. But in that sense, there is another reason why he will have lots of articles in Financial Times about G2. I keep talking to people. China has no interest in G2 arrangement because it is not interested in co-managing the world or the rest of the world with America. When you want to manage the world, problems at home... Also, you want to be able to have more scope to pursue your own interests. You don't want to be tied to some G2(arrangement). That's the case in Copenhagen, wasn't it?

F: No, I think you are leading me away from my part. China does not believe in bulling. But we do support international issues being solved through dialogues by the countries concerned. We do believing in finding the consensus. In Copenhagen, for example, every country tried to seek consensus. So there should not be one country to be the headmaster and everybody should follow that instructions. And if EU could do 30%, why would they come with 20%, and then conditioning the other 10% on other countries? Very funny. If you can do 30%, you do 30%. You cannot say I am damaging the world just because you are damaging the world. And China can do 40% or 45%, it's based on our calculation. We can do more if we have better technology. So all countries should do the best. That's negotiation, that's global solution.

What will the world become? It's a very interesting question. As a Chinese diplomat, I start to think more, and feel closed to the global issues now than before, for example. In the past, if G8 or G7 had a meeting, I thought that's thousands miles way. We read the news, that's all. Now China is part of G20. We are in the meeting and are expected to do part of the discussion of solving many global issues. In that sense, global issues are concerning us. That's why I think it is more important for us to solve this barrier as soon as possible. I think the west really needs to change its view of China. They need to have a cooler mind, and more, a kind of open mind. Open it up to differences. China also needs to understand the world better.

译 文

2010年1月30日《金融时报》发表该报专栏"与FT共进午餐"专访傅莹大使文章,以下为这次的采访实录:

傅莹(傅):感谢你选择这家餐馆,我看了背景材料,这里很有英国特色。每次回国有人问我什么是典型的英国菜时,我总说是"鱼和薯条",要不就是圣诞布丁,也许今后我可以推荐更多的英国菜。

巴伯(巴):这家餐馆的确很有英国特色。大使阁下,你任期内总是乐于提供帮助。我不会忘记,你帮忙促成《金融时报》专访温家宝总理,这也是我个人职业生涯的亮点之一。我跟很多人谈起过你,他们对你的评价都很正面,说你是第一位善于发挥智慧和魅力攻势的大使。你有幽默感,与老派的中国外交官不太一样。

傅:我认为外界对中国有不少陈旧观念。实际上,中国人是非常机智、幽默的。也许是因为中西方之间有一些隔阂,我在英国留学的时候,对英式幽默也不能完全体会。但是有了在英国留学一年的经历,又在澳大利亚待过,因此能感受到这种隔阂,并思考个中原因。

巴:我们一会儿再谈隔阂。你即将离任,是否会怀念英国?

傅:当然,我会非常怀念英国。对于任何一个大使来说,告别总是不舍的。履新时需要时间适应,但相对容易;告别时,所有美好的记忆都会涌上心头。我将在公园里最后一次慢跑,在酒吧里最后一次品尝啤酒,在牛津街最后一次散步。我会非常不舍,并带着对这个国家的美好记忆离开。

巴:咱们聊聊成为世界强国的中国吧,这是马丁·沃尔夫文章的话题。中国说不称霸,但第一,没有哪个国家会告诉世界我想称霸。第二,随着中国海外经济利益的拓展和人员流动,发生问题后如何处理?比如在苏丹,中国需要在当地帮助自己的公民。因此随着中国海外存在和利益的延伸,中国军队将不可避免走向海外。你赞同这个观点吗?

傅:不。邓小平早就说过,中国绝不称霸,如果有一天中国称霸,全世界都会站起来反对中国,这深深烙在了我们心里,每个外交官都知道。

巴:当你们成了霸权,别国再站起来就晚啦。

傅:你的看法源自你们的历史,你们相信世界需要霸权。90年代,有个美国记者采访我,他上来就问:"你认为亚洲人民会接受中国成为亚洲领导者吗?"我花了好一会儿去理解这个问题,然后说:"为什么你认为亚洲需要领袖,而且中国想成为领袖呢?这个问题对我来说太突兀啦,中国的文化和政治传统中没有这个概念。"

第二点:中国应该做什么?中国应该与世界合作,中国向达尔富尔派出了近400名维和人员,在亚丁湾和索马里海域由联合国授权派海军保护来往商船。中国无意侵略,因为中国饱受侵略之苦,我们不相信侵略,不相信制裁,不会欺压和歧视他国。

巴:我只是引用马丁·沃尔的话,不是说我完全赞同他。

傅:我明白。马丁·沃尔夫经常有一些有意思的想法。

巴:的确,他在《金融时报》上有不少关于G2的文章。我不同意他的观点,我常常说,中国对G2不感兴趣,对与美国共管世界不感兴趣,不想被G2捆住手脚,希望有更多空间追求自身利益。这在哥本哈根会议上得到很好的印证,对吗?

傅:不,你把我引得跑题啦。中国不相信欺压,但支持相关国家通过对话解决问题,相信能够达成共识。在哥本哈根,各国都努力寻求共识,不应该有哪个国家充当老大,发号施令。如果欧盟能减排30%,为什么只提出20%的目标,然后拿另外的10%和其他国家讨价还价?如果你们能减排30%,就应当减排30%,不能说你排放我也排放。中国提出碳强度减少40%至45%,是经过计算的,如果获得更先进的技术,我们可以做得更好。所有国家都应该尽全力,在这个基础上通过谈判达成全面解决方案。

未来的世界会变成什么样子?这是个非常有意思的问题。作为中国外交官,我思考得很多,感觉比过去更接近国际问题。以前,8国或者7国集团开会,我会觉得离我们很远,也就是当作新闻看看。现在中国是20国集团成员,我们不仅参与会议,而且被期待在解决全球性问题上发挥更大作用。国际问题与我们日益相关,这就是为什么我认为应当尽早消除中西方相互认知上的隔阂,西方确实应该改变对中国的看法和看待中国的方式,需要以更加冷静的头脑、开放的心态包容不同,中国同样需要更好地理解世界。

选文B

About the Earth Day Network with President Kathleen Rogers

Earth Day, celebrated on April 22 each year, marks the anniversary of the birth in 1970 of the modern environmental movement in the United States. The first Earth Day led to the creation of the U.S. Environmental Protection Agency and the passage of the Clean Air, Clean Water and Endangered Species Acts. By April 22, 2000, 5,000 environmental groups around the world were on board, reaching out to hundreds of millions of people in 184 countries. Today more than 1 billion people participate in Earth Day activities, making it the largest secular civic event in the world. The Earth Day Network, founded by the organizers of the first Earth Day, promotes environmental citizenship and year-round action worldwide.

Q: When did Earth Day move from the United States to nations around the world?

Rogers: Earth Day has been global since its inception but became truly global on its 20th anniversary in 1990. That year, a group of environmental leaders asked Dennis Hayes, the organizer of the first Earth Day and chairman of Earth Day 2010, to step up again. This was in the lead up to the 1992 U. N. Earth Summit in Rio and environmental issues were entering the global consciousness. That year, Denis and the Earth Day Network mobilized 200 million people in 141 countries.

Q: Describe some of your major international programs and activities.

Rogers: First, let me say that the State Department has been absolutely essential in helping Earth Day Network plan our programs abroad. Some of the biggest Earth Day events this year are taking place in India and China, where we are collaborating directly with the U. S. embassies in Delhi and Beijing and with four or five consulates in each country. In India, the American Cultural Centers across the country will host Earth Day events, and in China the State Department is using materials from our Education Department to teach university students about environmental issues and the history of Earth Day.

We have also partnered with the Kingdom of Morocco to organize events surrounding the presentation of their National Charter for Environment and Sustainable Development. Morocco is the first African, Muslim and Arab nation to commit, at the highest levels of government, to carry out a national event in honor of the 40th anniversary of Earth Day.

We also have events planned with partners in Buenos Aires, Kolkata, Barcelona and Tokyo, to name a few. Earth Day remains truly global!

Q: What's next for the Earth Day Network?

Rogers: Earth Day Network plans to build on the connections we have made this year, to deepen and broaden the scope of our activities and the mission of Earth Day. For instance, our Global Day of Conversation program has strengthened our relationship with 290 mayors and locally elected officials in more than 39 countries. We are working with more than 1,500 NGOs worldwide on climate change issues and building partnerships in many countries to create green schools. We are finishing up plans for a global conference on women and climate to be held in Washington. We are also planting 1 million trees around the world in partnership with James Cameron's film Avatar and Twentieth Century Fox Home Entertainment, and this vast undertaking will endure well after Earth Day. Domestically, we will continue to push for comprehensive legislation to confront climate change and to lay the foundation for a green economy.

We are extremely excited to see what we as an organization, and we as a global movement, can all accomplish in the next 40 years.

译 文

"地球日网络"总裁罗杰斯访谈

每年4月22日的"地球日"(Earth Day)是1970年在美国诞生的现代环保活动纪念日。第一个地球日催生了美国环境保护署(U. S. Environmental Protection Agency),《洁净空气法》(Clean Air Act)、《洁净水法》(Clean Water Act)和《濒临灭绝动植物保护法》(Endangered Species Act)等一系列法案也相继出台。至2000年4月22日止,全世界已有5 000个环保组织开展工作,深入184个国家的亿万民众。今天,有10多亿人民参加与地球日有关的活动,使地球日成为全世界最大的非宗教公民活动。由第一个地球日组织者创办的"地球日网络"(The Earth Day Network)组织正在为提高全世界民众的环保意识和常年举办的活动积极奔走。

问:地球日什么时候开始从美国走向世界各国?

罗杰斯:地球日从成立伊始就面向全球,但在1990年第20个纪念日起成为名符其实的全球性活动。一群环保工作领导人在1990年敦请第一个地球日的组织者和2010年地球日的主席丹尼斯·海斯(Dennis Hayes)带领大家重整旗鼓。这股势头于1992年在巴西里约热内卢召开的"地球峰会"(Earth Summit)(联合国环境与发展会议(United Nations Conference on Environment and Development))上得到继续,环保问题逐渐成为全球共识。丹尼斯与"地球日网络"组织在那一年动员了141个国家的2亿人民参加活动。

问:请给我们介绍一些你们主办的主要国际性项目和主题活动。

罗杰斯:首先,我得告诉大家,国务院为帮助"地球日网络"规划我们的国际项目发挥了绝对关键的作用,今年有几个规模最大的"地球日"活动在印度和中国举行。我们在那两个国家与美国驻德里(Delhi)和北京(Beijing)大使馆及四五个领事馆直接进行协作。在印度,遍布各地的美国文化中心(American Cultural Centers)将主持"地球日"主题活动;在中国,国务院采用我们教育部的材料向大学生们宣讲环保和"地球日"的由来。

我们还与摩洛哥王国(Kingdom of Morocco)结成伙伴,以介绍他们的"国家环境与可持续发展宪章"(National Charter for Environment and Sustainable Development)为中心组织各种活动。摩洛哥是在政府最高一级承诺开展纪念"地球日"成立40周年活动的第一个非洲国家,也是第一个举行该项活动的穆斯林和阿拉伯国家。

我们还与在布宜诺斯艾利斯(Buenos Aires)、加尔各答(Kolkata)、巴塞罗那(Barcelona)和东京(Tokyo)等地的合作伙伴规划了各项主题活动,其他的就不一一列举了。"地球日"仍然是名符其实的全球性纪念日!

问:"地球日网络"下一步的计划是什么?

罗杰斯:"地球日网络"计划继续发展我们今年所建立的与各方的联系,深化并扩展"地球日"的使命以及我们各项活动的范围。例如,我们的"全球对话日"(Global Day of Conversation)项目已经加强了我们与超过39个国家中的290位市长和当地民选官员的关系;我们正与全世界1500个非政府组织(NGO)就气候变化问题进行合作,并与许多国家建立伙伴关系以创建绿色学校;一个将于华盛顿召开的世界妇女与气候会议的计划工作已进入最后阶段;我们还正在与詹姆斯·卡梅隆(James Cameron)导演的巨片《阿凡达》

(Avatar)和20世纪福克斯家庭娱乐公司(Twentieth Century Fox Home Entertainment)合作,在全世界种植一百万棵树,这个宏大的事业将在"地球日"以后很长时间里继续进行;在美国国内,我们将继续推动全面立法,以应对气候变化,并为绿色经济奠定基础。

  作为一个组织、一个全球性的运动,展望在未来的40年中我们将能达成的伟业,我们无比兴奋。

第五单元 饮食文化
（Catering Culture）

单元要点

本单元共分五个层次，分别是：中国驻英国大使刘晓明在英国筷子俱乐部的演讲汉译英一篇；美国正式晚餐的礼仪文化英译汉一篇；中文菜单英译的几个原则；翻译的语言转换理论；拓展阅读（汉译英、英译汉各一篇）。第一、二部分提供饮食文化口译的例文及其翻译和重难点评析；第三、四部分主要是相关口译理论与技能的介绍；第五部分的拓展阅读中，提供汉、英原文和参考译文。

理论难点提示

1. 中文菜单英译的几个原则。
2. 翻译的语言转换理论。

选文A

中国驻英国大使刘晓明在英国筷子俱乐部的演讲
2010年10月19日，伦敦皇家学会

尊敬的童海珍主席，
女士们，先生们，朋友们：

我和我夫人很高兴首次参加筷子俱乐部的活动。我今年初来到英国不久，就听说有"筷子俱乐部"这么别具一格的民间组织，在推崇中华美食，宣传中国文化，促进中英了解。因此，一直期待着有时间与大家见面交流。我也特别喜欢"筷子俱乐部"这个可谓"形神兼备"的名字：一是俱乐部活动形式上多借用聚餐安排演讲和交流；二是筷子作为餐具，尽管平常简单，但许多学者认为这是东方智慧的体现。

我今天的演讲就想从筷子谈起。关于筷子的起源，文献中最早提到筷子的使用者是三千多年前的商纣王，当时他使用"象牙箸"。我个人比较倾向这么一种说法，中国的先民最初以树枝或细竹从陶锅中夹取热食，慢慢筷子就产生了。这情形就仿佛我们今天吃四川火锅，徒手不能，刀叉也不便，只能是借助筷子帮忙。

三千多年来，中国人为什么保留了使用筷子的习惯，我认为这与中国长期的农耕文明和饮食结构有关。中国人的饮食一直以谷物等种植物为主，即使食肉，也一直按孔子所说："食不厌精，脍不厌细。"因此，餐桌上一双细细的筷子足矣。可见，使用筷子是中国的经济、历史和文化等多种因素决定的。

我由此想起有这么一句听来富有哲理的话，这个世界上没有什么是最好的，只有适合自己的才是最好的。筷子是这样,社会制度、经济发展模式也是这样。

我想说的第二点是,筷子与刀叉并非水火不容,只是代表着两种不同的文化。

为什么西方人使用刀叉吃饭呢?这个问题我并没有考证过。但是直觉告诉我,当你面对盘子里的一大块牛排时,筷子尽管不能说完全没用,但肯定比不上使用刀叉的那份优雅。这是由于中西方饮食结构、食物制作方法不同,因而体现在餐具上的区别。但无论使用何种餐具,都不会妨碍我们享用本民族的美食。广而言之,只要东西方国家根据自身国情选择政治制度和经济模式,也就不会妨碍我们享用发展的盛宴。

中国的社会制度、经济发展模式与西方不同,这是不争的事实,但并不影响中西方的和平共存、共享繁荣。正如阳光因七色而斑斓,世界因多样而美丽。从人类历史上看,正是不同文明之间的相互接触和吸纳,才导致了新观念的萌芽,才产生了新思想的火花。

第三点,既会用筷子,又会用刀叉,世界将会更加和谐。

我高兴地看到,今天,到中餐馆就餐并使用筷子的外国人越来越多,同时许多中国人拿起刀叉吃顿西餐也轻松平常。中国古训说:"民以食为天。"人类学家、美籍华人张光直先生亦曾直言:"达到一个文化核心的最佳途径之一就是通过它的肚子。"

处理好中西方关系,相互了解和尊重是关键。我一直认为,中国对西方的了解比西方对中国的了解,要多得多。这主要是因为,近现代一百多年来,中国一直在虚心地学习西方。今天,中国的孩子从小学一年级开始就学习英文。而西方有些人总是丢不掉"文化优越论",总认为自己的政治、经济、社会制度和文化高人一等,视自己的价值观为普世价值观,总想把别人的文化变成自己的"亚文化"。他们不愿也不想正视中国的变化,对中国的发展和进步总是感到不适应、不舒服,总想把这种情绪发泄出来,不断给中国制造困难和麻烦,唯恐中国不乱。我确信,这些人不代表西方社会的主流,他们阻止不了东西方相互学习、共谋发展的大趋势,更阻挡不了中国人民前进的步伐。

我认为,实现文明和平共存、共同进步,需要承认不同文明的平等地位,要以开放、包容的态度对待其他文明,要相互理解、相互尊重和相互学习。因此,中国主张"和而不同",主张"求同存异",主张"取长补短",主张"和谐世界"。和谐世界,这是充满东方智慧的词汇,同时这也是最符合世界根本利益的思想。

朋友们,

我来英国后,曾对在英华人华侨说,英国的中餐在欧洲做得最为地道。其实,我还有后面半句话没有说,那就是,英国人用筷子在欧洲也最为熟练。我发现,在中餐馆里,很少有英国人用刀叉的。

中英关系是当今世界很重要的一组大国关系,我有时认为,中英关系就好比一双筷子。

第一,筷子是没有长短、不分左右的,中英关系也是平等的,那意味着两国关系就应当建立在互相尊重、平等对话的基础上,就应当加强战略互信,妥善处理分歧。

第二,筷子使用起来讲究协调、配合,中英关系也需要加强合作。今天的中英关系,早已超出了双边范畴,具有全球性和战略性。中英关系要想发展得好,双方一方面要加强在双边经济、教育、文化等各领域的务实合作,扩大利益基础,造福两国人民;另一方面应当在国际事务中携手合作,同舟共济,共同致力于促进世界的和平、稳定和繁荣。

第三,筷子不只是用来夹食物的,关键是要把食物提起来送到嘴里,中英关系也不能满足于现状,要不断提升发展。过去十多年,中英关系取得了长足发展,两国建立了全面战略伙伴关系。今年5月英国联合政府执政以后,致力于发展"更紧密的英中关系"。中方也高度重视发展中英关系,愿与英方共同努力,推动中英关系朝着友好合作、互利共赢的方向不断迈进。下个月,卡梅伦首相即将对中国进行首次正式访问,这是中英关系发展的一个重要机遇,必将对双边关系起到进一步提升作用。

朋友们,

今天是星期二,在1993年的一个星期二,一个名叫"中国星期二"的团体在杜伦大学成立了,当时成员只有数十人。今天,"中国星期二"有了新的名字——"筷子俱乐部",其注册会员也增加到500多人。借此机会,我要祝贺筷子俱乐部17岁生日快乐!我也衷心地希望"筷子俱乐部"不断成长,在促进中英了解和友谊方面发挥更大作用。

谢谢大家。

重难点评析

1. "我今年初来到英国不久,就听说有'筷子俱乐部'这么别具一格的民间组织,在推崇中华美食,宣传中国文化,促进中英了解。"译者将这个句子分译成了两句话。在第二句中将"推崇中华美食,宣传中国文化,促进中英了解"译为定语后置,结构更加的紧凑。"I got to know the 'Chopsticks Club' soon after arriving in London. It is a unique non-governmental organisation committed to promoting Chinese food and culture in Britain and increasing mutual understanding between the two countries.""be committed to"译为"致力于"。

2. "我也特别喜欢'筷子俱乐部'这个可谓'形神兼备'的名字",由于后文的两个方面是对"形神兼备"的具体解释,因此这里采用了意译"as 'Chopsticks' for us are much more than just something we use every day for eating"。

3. "关于筷子的起源,文献中最早提到筷子的使用者是三千多年前的商纣王,当时他使用'象牙箸'。"译文采用了主谓的换译,将"商纣王"译成了从句的主语,将"其使用'象牙箸'"译成了一个定语从句,从而使得译文结构紧凑:One story has it that King Zhou of the Shang Dynasty over 3,000 years ago was the first user of chopsticks, which were made of ivories.

4. "我个人比较倾向这么一种说法,中国的先民最初以树枝或细竹从陶锅中夹取热食,慢慢筷子就产生了。"译为"I tend to believe that chopsticks came about when ancient Chinese used tree branches or thin bamboo splits to pick up hot food from ceramic pots.""产生,发生"译为"come about",例如:Tell me how the accident came about.

5. "食不厌精,脍不厌细。"意译为"Eat no rice except when it is the finest and no meat except when finely minced."

6. "可见,使用筷子是中国的经济、历史和文化等多种因素决定的。"采用了倒译"So it seems that economic, historical and cultural factors have all contributed to the continued use of chopsticks."

7. "筷子是这样,社会制度、经济发展模式也是这样。"采用了倒译法"Apart from chopsticks, this may well apply to other things, such as a country's social system or model of economic growth."

8. "并非水火不容"译为"rather than being incompatible/irreconcilable/contradictory"。

9. "但无论使用何种餐具,都不会妨碍我们享用本民族的美食。广而言之,只要东西方国家根据自身国情选择政治制度和经济模式,也就不会妨碍我们享用发展的盛宴。"说话人的本意是进行类比,因此在译文中采用了相同的句式进行意译,"Anyway, whatever dining utensils we choose to use, as long as they serve us well, we would be able to enjoy our different national cuisine. In a broader context, whatever political systems and economic models countries adopt, as long as the systems and models serve them well, they would be able to enjoy the feast of development."

10. "从人类历史上看,正是不同文明之间的相互接触和吸纳,才导致了新观念的萌芽,才产生了新思想的火花。""新观念的萌芽,新思想的火花"是说话人所用的比喻,译文联系上文采用了意译,"Throughout history, dialogue and mutual learning between civilisations have always been a source of new ideas and progress."

11. "民以食为天。"译为"Food is the paramount want of the people."

12. "达到一个文化核心的最佳途径之一就是通过它的肚子",这个比喻采用了直译 "one of the best channels to reach the heart of a culture is through its stomach",非常形象,易于理解,言简意赅。

13. "总想把别人的文化变成自己的'亚文化'",采用了意译"expecting others to adapt their own cultures according to Western culture"。若是直译的话可以译为"expecting to convert others' cultures into sub-cultures of Western culture"。

14. "和而不同"译为"harmony but not uniformity";"求同存异"译为"seeking common ground and putting aside differences";"取长补短"译为"drawing on the strong points of others to make up for one's weak points"。

15. "其实,我还有后面半句话没有说",根据上下文及英语的表达习惯采用了意译 "And I must add that..."。

16. "中英关系也不能满足于现状,要不断提升发展。"译文采用倒译,使用短语 instead of 连接前后两部分,"Similarly, we should seek to upgrade our relations instead of resting on past progress."

17. "中方也高度重视发展中英关系",译为"We also give the same priority to our relations with the UK"或"We also attach great importance to our relations with the UK"。

18. "今天是星期二,在 1993 年的一个星期二,……",为了突出"1993 年的星期二"和现今的对比,译文采用了强调句的句式,"It is Tuesday today and it was on a Tuesday in 1993 that..."。

译文

Speech by H. E. Ambassador Liu Xiaoming at the Chopsticks Club
19 October 2010, Royal Society, London

Ms H-J Colston,
Ladies and Gentlemen,

Friends from the Chopsticks Club,

It is a great pleasure for me and my wife to attend our first event with the Chopsticks Club. I got to know the "Chopsticks Club" soon after arriving in London. It is a unique non-governmental organisation committed to promoting Chinese food and culture in Britain and increasing mutual understanding between the two countries. And I have been looking forward to this opportunity to meet you. I like the name of your club, as "Chopsticks" for us are much more than just something we use every day for eating. I was glad to know that you have a good tradition of networking over delicious food, as chopsticks are also believed by many scholars to embody oriental wisdom.

Let me start my speech with the origin of chopsticks. One story has it that King Zhou of the Shang Dynasty over 3,000 years ago was the first user of chopsticks, which were made of ivories. Personally, I tend to believe that chopsticks came about when ancient Chinese used tree branches or thin bamboo splits to pick up hot food from ceramic pots. Those of you who tried Sichuan hotpot would know that you could never take food from the hotpot with hand or a knife and fork; chopsticks seem to be the only practical choice.

The 3,000-year tradition of using chopsticks has a lot to do with our farming culture and eating habit. This meant that our diet has included grain as its mainstay, with meat being sliced or shredded. As Confucius said, "Eat no rice except when it is the finest and no meat except when finely minced." So it seems that economic, historical and cultural factors have all contributed to the continued use of chopsticks.

I remember a saying that makes sense to me: "Nothing is better than what suits one best." Apart from chopsticks, this may well apply to other things, such as a country's social system or model of economic growth.

Chopsticks and knives and forks, rather than being incompatible, are just symbols of two different cultures.

Although I have not done any research on why Westerners use knives and forks, experience has taught me that if you have a large piece of steak in front of you, you had better use knife and fork, which would be much more elegant and effective than chopsticks. This is a reflection of our different ways of cooking and dietary structure. Anyway, whatever dining utensils we choose to use, as long as they serve us well, we would be able to enjoy our different national cuisine. In a broader context, whatever political systems and economic models countries adopt, as long as the systems and models serve them well, they would be able to enjoy the feast of development.

China has a different social system and economic model from the West. But this does not mean that China and the West are not capable of living in peace with each other and sharing prosperity. Sunshine is made up of seven colours, and our world is beautiful for its diversity. Throughout history, dialogue and mutual learning between civilisations have always been a source of new ideas and progress.

When every Chinese is able to use a knife and fork, and every Westerner can use chopsticks, our world will be a better place.

I noticed with pleasure that more and more foreigners are eating in Chinese restaurants with chopsticks. And many Chinese now seem to be at ease using knife and fork. As an ancient Chinese saying goes, "Food is the paramount want of the people." Mr Zhang Guangzhi, a Chinese American anthropologist, pointed out that "one of the best channels to reach the heart of a culture is through its stomach".

Mutual understanding and mutual respect are the key to a better East-West relationship, and my impression is that China knows more about the West than the other way round. This is because China has been learning from the West for over a century. Today Chinese children start to learn English in the first year at primary school. Some people in the West, on the other hand, have been preoccupied by a sense of cultural superiority, believing that the West has the best political, economic, social and cultural system. They also tend to regard their own values as universal, expecting others to adapt their own cultures according to Western culture. Some people are reluctant to see the changes in China and feel uneasy about the development and progress of China. Some go so far as to attempt to create problems or even chaos for China. I'm sure they do not represent the mainstream in the West. They can in no way prevent China and the West from learning from each other and engaging each other in the general trend of common development. Nor can they obstruct the Chinese people's progress.

I believe that peaceful coexistence between cultures requires a sense of equality and an open and accommodating approach based on mutual understanding and respect. That is why China stands for the principles of "harmony but not uniformity", "seeking common ground and putting aside differences" and "drawing on the strong points of others to make up for one's weak points". This is also why China stands for building a harmonious world. We believe this term of harmony is full of oriental wisdom and best serves the fundamental interests of our world.

Dear friends,

I told the Chinese community here that the UK has the best Chinese food in Europe. And I must add that the British are probably best at using chopsticks in Europe as well, as I have discovered that people here seldom use knives and forks when eating in a Chinese restaurant.

When it comes to describing the China-UK relationship, I think we can also use the chopsticks analogy.

Firstly, the two chopsticks are of equal length, just as China and the UK are equals in our relationship. This means that we should hold dialogues on an equal footing and with mutual respect enhance mutual trust on strategic issues and properly handle differences.

Secondly, just as it takes coordination of your fingers to use chopsticks properly, it takes cooperation for our relationship to grow stronger. Our relations have gone beyond being bilateral and become more global and strategic. A better relationship also calls for strengthened cooperation in areas such as the economy, education and culture, along with wider common interests in international affairs and a shared commitment to world peace, stability and prosperity.

Thirdly, the most important function of chopsticks is not only to pick up food, but to bring food to your mouth. Similarly, we should seek to upgrade our relations instead of resting on past progress. China-UK relations have come a long way in the past decade and a comprehensive strategic partnership has been established. Since the British coalition government took office in May, it has been committed to developing "closer engagement" with China. We also give the same priority to our relations with the UK to ensure we achieve friendly and mutually beneficial cooperation. Prime Minister David Cameron's first official visit to China next month will be an important opportunity for elevating China-UK relations to a new high. We will work closely with the British colleagues to make the visit a great success.

Dear friends,

It is Tuesday today and it was on a Tuesday in 1993 that a group called "China Tuesdays" was founded with several dozens members. Today with a new name "Chopsticks Club", the membership has increased to more than 500. So, may I take this opportunity to congratulate the "Chopsticks Club" on its 17th birthday. And I wish you continued growth in strength and hope you will contribute more to the mutual understanding and friendship between our two countries!

Thank you.

选文B

A Talk about the Formal Dinner in the USA

Good morning, everyone!

It's my great pleasure to give you a talk about American culture. My topic tonight is about the formal dinner in the United States.

For a "truly formal dinner", we used to have all guests sit at one long U-shaped table covered with a white damask cloth. You know, this arrangement made conversation difficult and required a very lengthy dinner room. Now people begin to use round tables for eight or ten. And as for the centerpiece decoration on the table, the hostess's own imagination should come into full play. A pretty setting of the table for guests helps make the food better and taste better. It makes the guests feel that an effort has been made on their behalf.

However, there are two elements of the formal dinner that have not changed over the years. One is the use of a butler and waiters for serving, and the other is the necessity for a chef who can produce a fabulous meal of five courses — usually a soup, fish, meat or fowl, salad and cheese, and dessert. At a formal dinner, we usually have a white wine, red wine and champagne served with the meal(sometimes sherry first, too). The way the food served is extremely important at a formal dinner. The platters must all be garnished beautifully, so that the guests will admire each one as a work of art, not just the serving of a dish. For example, the butter might be rolled into balls or carved into flowers. The vegetables and desserts are served in imaginative ways. I notice that in China, you, too, have many beautifully-carved figures out of carrots or turnips.

If you are invited to a formal dinner, make sure that you do not sit at a wrong table. There are two ways of handling the seating logistics at a formal dinner. In one, after each man has given his coat to the butler or maid, he receives a small envelope with his name on it. Inside is a card bearing the name of his dinner partner. These envelopes with cards are kept on a tray in the front hall, alphabetized for easy finding. Now that we have round tables more often, the more popular way is for there to be an envelope for each guest, placed on the hall table in alphabetical order. As each guest arrives, he or she takes the envelope and finds inside a card with the proper table number written on it. There is no need to find one's dinner partner.

At a large formal dinner there should be a table chart shown to each guest as he arrives. The butler either holds the chart in his hand, or, if there are several round tables, the guests look at all the table charts on the hall table. When the party begins, the host and hostess should be near the entrance to the living room, so that they will be able to greet each arriving guest. They should see to it that newcomers are introduced to everyone through the cocktail hour.

Finally, I would say something about leaving. First, how to leave the table before the eating is finished. If you suddenly feel ill, or have an urgent need to go to the bathroom, no apologies are necessary. You may just say to the hostess, "Please excuse me for a moment," and depart. You need to make no explanations when you return. Secondly, how to leave the formal dinner. Except for some very good reason discussed previously with the hostess, no guest should leave after a formal dinner in a private home until the guest or guests of honor have departed. At formal public dinners guests who must leave early go quietly either before the speeches begin or between them, never while a guest of honor is speaking or while a national anthem is being played. Those who must leave, leave by the nearest exit without stopping to talk or bid farewell to guests encountered en route, except to bow briefly.

Well, I can't tell you all about the formal dinner within such a short time. Anyhow, if there is any chance of being invited, just ask people beforehand and be observant at the dinner, you won't be very wrong.

Thanks for your attention.

重难点评析

1. "…we used to have all guests sit…"句子中的"used to"表示"过去常常",在译成

汉语时应该使用增译法加上"在过去"。

2. "Now people begin to use round tables for eight or ten."句中"round tables for eight or ten"译为"八至十人的圆桌",而且增译了"能坐",在翻译时往往要根据语言习惯适当增译或减译。

3. "At a formal dinner, we usually have a white wine, red wine..."句中"white wine, red wine"译为"白/红葡萄酒"。中国的白酒度数很高,一般都在 35 度以上,英语中把酒精含量在 14% 以上的称为烈酒,英文是 spirits 或 liquor,如威士忌、杜松子酒、雪利酒、白兰地等。

4. "The vegetables and desserts are served in imaginative ways."译为"蔬菜和点心可以做得别出心裁。" imaginative 意为"充满想象力的",译为"别出心裁",更符合中文的习惯。

5. "They should see to it that newcomers are introduced to everyone through the cocktail hour."译为"确保在喝开胃酒这段时间内把每一位新来的客人介绍给大家。"原文中的被动句 newcomers are introduced to everyone 用汉语里常用的"把"字句译出来,符合汉语的习惯。"see to it"意为"确保"。

6. "how to leave the table before the eating is finished",若是按原文直译成"在吃完之前",不如译为"在用餐过程中"。由于全文介绍的是正式宴会,译文也用较正式的用语,如"用餐""餐桌"。在翻译过程中译者要注意各种场合所使用的文体。

7. "Those who must leave, leave by the nearest exit..."译文中没有将前面部分"那些一定要离开的人"译出,因为上下文已经很清楚,译出来就多余了。

8. "I can't tell you all about the formal dinner..."句中的 all 原意为"所有的东西",这里译为"方方面面",符合汉语的习惯。

译 文

美国的正式晚餐

各位,晚上好!

很高兴有机会和大家谈美国文化。今晚演讲的题目是美国的正式宴会。

过去,在"非常正式的宴会"上,常常是所有的客人围着一张长长的 U 型桌而坐,桌上铺有白色锦缎台布。大家知道,这样相互交谈就比较困难,而且餐厅也要很长。现在人们开始用能坐八至十人的圆桌。至于餐桌中央的装饰品,女主人可以充分施展自己的想象力。漂亮的餐桌布置可以给餐桌上的食物添色加味,让客人感受到主人为此付出的心血。

不过,正式宴会有两点多年来始终没有改变,一是司膳管理员和服务员,二是一位能烹饪五道精美菜肴的厨师:汤、鱼、肉或家禽、色拉与奶酪,以及甜点。正式宴会上使用的饮料一般是白葡萄酒、红葡萄酒和香槟酒(有时也有先喝雪利酒的)。正式宴会上,如何上菜是极为重要的。盘子必须擦得很亮,客人们会把它们当作艺术品欣赏,而不仅仅当作盛菜的盘子。黄油可以卷成球状或刻成花状。蔬菜和点心可以做得别出心裁。我注意到,在中国,你们也把胡萝卜和萝卜雕成许多漂亮的形状。

如果你被邀请参加正式宴会,切忌坐错座位。正式宴会坐席的安排有两种。一种是这样的:男宾脱下外套交给司膳总管或女侍后,他会拿到一只写有他名字的小信封,信封里有一张卡片,上面写着他的宴会搭档的名字。这些信封都放在前厅的一只托盘里,以字母顺序排列,找起来比较方便。由于现在更多地使用小圆桌,所以另外一种更流行的办法是:在大厅桌上为每位客人准备一只信封,信封按照字母顺序排列。客人到达后,他们可以按信封里写的桌号找到座位,因而没有必要知道自己的搭档是谁。

在大型正式宴会上,客人到达后会看到一张座位平面图,司膳总管可以把座位平面图拿在手里。如果有好几张圆餐桌,客人们则可以去大厅桌上查看所有的座位平面图。宴会开始时,男主人和女主人应站在起居室的门口,这样可以向每一位到来的客人打招呼,确保在喝开胃酒这段时间内把每一位新来的客人介绍给大家。

最后,我想谈谈如何离开。首先谈谈在用餐过程中如何离开餐桌。如果你突然感到不舒服,或急于要上洗手间,你不必道歉,在离开前你只需向女主人说一声:"对不起,我离开一下。"回到座位上时,也不必作任何解释。我再谈谈如何离开正式宴会。在私人家里举办正式宴会时,客人们必须等主宾告别离去后才能动身,除非事先与女主人说好因有特殊理由才能提前离去。在正式公共宴会上,必须提前离开的客人总是在演说之前或演说间隙悄悄离去,但不能在主宾演说时或奏国歌时走开。离开时,通常从最近的出口出去,在路上碰到别的客人,也只是朝他们点点头,不应停下来与之交谈或说"再见"。

在这么短的时间里,我无法谈及关于正式宴会的方方面面。不过,如果你受到邀请的话,只要事先问问别人,并在宴会上多留神,就不会出大错的。

谢谢大家。

中文菜单英文翻译的原则

餐饮专业英语主要包括日常会话用语、烹饪技术用语和中餐英文菜单等等,而这其中尤以中餐英文菜单用得最为普遍。

要将中餐菜单翻译成英文,就先得了解中餐菜名的构成及命名方法。中餐菜名通常由原料名称、烹制方法、菜肴的色香味形器、菜肴的创始人或发源地等构成。这种反映菜肴内容和特色的命名方法叫做写实性命名法,此外还有反映菜肴深刻含义的写意性命名法。

由于汉语和英语的差异很大,我们在把中餐菜名由中文译成英文的时候,应该采用写实性命名法,尽量将菜肴的原料、烹制方法、菜肴的味、形等翻译出来,以便让客人一目了然。为了让大家更好地掌握将中餐菜名译成英文的技巧,翻译过程中应掌握如下几个原则:

一、以主料为主、配料为辅的翻译原则

1. 菜肴的主料和配料

主料(名称/形状)＋with＋配料

如:白灵菇扣鸭掌 Mushrooms with Duck Webs

2. 菜肴的主料和配汁

主料＋with/in＋汤汁(Sauce)

如:冰梅凉瓜 Bitter Melon in Plum Sauce

二、以烹制方法为主、原料为辅的翻译原则

1. 菜肴的做法和主料

做法(动词过去分词)＋主料(名称/形状)

如：火爆腰花 Sautéed Pig Kidney

2. 菜肴的做法、主料和配料

做法（动词过去分词）+主料（名称/形状）+配料

如：地瓜烧肉 Stewed Diced Pork and Sweet Potatoes

3. 菜肴的做法、主料和汤汁

做法（动词过去分词）+主料（名称/形状）+with/in+汤汁

如：京酱肉丝 Sautéed Shredded Pork in Sweet Bean Sauce

三、以形状、口感为主，原料为辅的翻译原则

1. 菜肴形状或口感以及主配料

形状/口感+主料

如：玉兔馒头 Rabbit-Shaped Mantou
　　脆皮鸡 Crispy Chicken

2. 菜肴的做法、形状或口感、做法以及主配料

做法（动词过去分词）+形状/口感+主料+配料

如：小炒黑山羊 Sautéed Sliced Lamb with Pepper and Parsley

四、以人名、地名为主，原料为辅的翻译原则

1. 菜肴的创始人（发源地）和主料

人名（地名）+主料

如：麻婆豆腐 Mapo Tofu（Sautéed Tofu in Hot and Spicy Sauce）
　　广东点心 Cantonese Dim Sum

2. 介绍菜肴的创始人（发源地）、主配料及做法

做法（动词过去式）+主辅料+人名/地名+Style

如：北京炒肝 Stewed Liver, Beijing Style
　　北京炸酱面 Noodles with Soy Bean Paste, Beijing Style

五、体现中国餐饮文化，使用汉语拼音命名或音译的翻译原则

1. 具有中国特色且被外国人接受的传统食品，本着推广汉语及中国餐饮文化的原则，使用汉语拼音。

如：饺子 Jiaozi
　　包子 Baozi
　　馒头 Mantou
　　花卷 Huajuan
　　烧卖 Shaomai

2. 具有中国特色且被外国人接受的，使用地方语言拼写或音译拼写的菜名，仍保留其拼写方式。

如：豆腐 Tofu
　　宫保鸡丁 Kung Pao Chicken
　　杂碎 Chop Suey
　　馄饨 Wonton

3. 中文菜肴名称无法体现其做法及主配料的,使用汉语拼音,并在后标注英文注释。

如:佛跳墙 Fotiaoqiang — Steamed Abalone with Shark's Fin and Fish Maw in Broth
锅贴 Guotie(Pan-Fried Dumplings)
窝头 Wotou(Steamed Corn Bun)
蒸饺 Steamed Jiaozi(Steamed Dumplings)
油条 Youtiao(Deep-Fried Dough Sticks)
汤圆 Tangyuan(Glutinous Rice Balls)
咕噜肉 Gulaorou(Sweet and Sour Pork)
粽子 Zongzi(Glutinous Rice Wrapped in Bamboo Leaves)
元宵 Yuanxiao(Glutinous Rice Balls for Lantern Festival)
驴打滚儿 Lǘdagunr — (Glutinous Rice Rolls Stuffed with Red Bean Paste)
艾窝窝 Aiwowo(Steamed Rice Cakes with Sweet Stuffing)
豆汁儿 Douzhir(Fermented Bean Drink)

六、可数名词单复数使用原则

菜单中的可数名词基本使用复数,但在整道菜中只有一件或太细碎无法数清的用单数。

如:蔬菜面 Noodles with Vegetables
葱爆羊肉 Sautéed Lamb Slices with Scallion

七、介词 in 和 with 在汤汁、配料中的用法

1. 如主料是浸在汤汁或配料中时,使用 in 连接。

如:豉汁牛仔骨 Steamed Beef Ribs in Black Bean Sauce

2. 如汤汁或蘸料和主料是分开的,或是后浇在主菜上的,则用 with 连接。

如:海鲜乌冬汤面 Japanese Noodle Soup with Seafood

八、酒类的译法原则

进口酒类的英文名称仍使用其原英文译法,国产酒类以其注册的英文为准,如酒类本身没有英文名称的则使用其中文名称的汉语拼音。

由此可见,中餐菜名的英译方法是灵活多变的。至于我们在翻译中最终采用哪种方法,则可根据各人的习惯和具体情况确定。不过根据笔者的经验,只要掌握了第一种以主料开头的翻译方法,对其他种类的翻译方法便可以触类旁通,我们只需根据文中所列出的翻译原则相应作一些交换就行了。

翻译的语言转换理论

1. 英汉两种语言的特征对比

美国的著名语言学家、翻译家尤金·A·奈达(Eugene A. Nida)在《译意》(Translating Meaning)中指出,汉语和英语在语言学上最重要的区别就是形合与意合的对比(contrast between hypotaxis and parataxis)。

英语形合(hypotaxis):语言组织主要靠语言本身的语法手段,即句子内部的连接或句子间的连接采用句法手段(syntactic devices)或词汇手段(lexical devices)。英语重"形合",语句各成分的相互结合常用适当的连接词语或各种语言连接手段,以表示其结构关系。英语是"显性连接"。

汉语意合(parataxis):语言组织主要靠语言本身的语义手段,即句子内部的连接或句子间的连接采用语义手段(semantic connection)。汉语重"意合",句中各成分之间或句子之间的结合多依靠语义的贯通,少用连接语,所以句法结构形式短小精悍。汉语是"隐性连接"。

让我们来看一个中文例子:

一只青蛙一张嘴,两只眼睛四条腿。

本句中"一张嘴""两只眼睛"和"四条腿"之间存在并列关系,而它们又同"青蛙"之间存在从属关系,表达的实际意义为"一只青蛙(有)一张嘴、两只眼睛(和)四条腿",汉语中即使省略"有""和"两字,仍然能依靠语义的贯通表达清楚句子内部的逻辑关系和实际意思。而如果用英语说这个句子,则必须要通过语法连接将意思和逻辑关系表现出来:A frog has a mouth, two eyes and four legs.

再看一个英文例子:

The boy had his breakfast and went off to school.

本句中"his"跟"The boy"前后照应、相互攀连,"and"将两个承接的动作衔接起来,是英文形合的手段。如果翻译时过于拘泥于原文的"形合",译文会显得冗余累赘和拘谨("男孩吃过他的早饭,然后上学去了"),而汉语只要说"男孩吃过早饭上学去了"即可,两个连贯的动作显得很紧凑,说出的话一气呵成。

让我们再看一句温家宝总理同美国总统布什在奥运期间会谈时的讲话:

我在美国队进入会场的时候看到你穿上西装站起来向他们招手。

本句中文语句连贯,一气呵成,形如流水,是典型的中文流水句。而译为英文时却要大量使用连接词进行前后勾连,才能符合英文的语法规则:

When the U.S. team marched into the stadium I saw that you put back your coat and your suit and then you stood up and cheered for your team.

小结:

汉译英时:先分析汉语句子的功能、意义,以及隐含的逻辑关系,译成英语时再确定句子的结构、形式,适当借助关联词语连接。

英译汉时:先分析英语句子的结构、形式,再确定它的功能、意义。译成汉语时在意义上体现逻辑关系,在形式上尽量简洁明了,省略冗余词语。

掌握了英汉两种语言的本质特征,就可以很好地理解它们之间的更多区别之处:

(1) 英语"客观",汉语"主观"

英语:强调客体思维,表述客观,经常见到用非人称作主语,用被动式语态的情况也很多。

汉语:侧重主体思维,以人的主观作为出发点,常用具体的人称作主语,或省略主语,常采用主动式语态。

英译汉时:可以将无生命词作主语的句子(包括 It is…,There be… 等)变成有生命词作主语的句子,尽量使用主动结构。

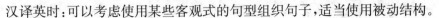

汉译英时:可以考虑使用某些客观式的句型组织句子,适当使用被动结构。
(2) 英语"直接",汉语"委婉"
英语:"结论+事实"
　　　It is my great honor to...
汉语:"事实+结论"
　　　……我深感荣幸。
(3) 英语"主语",汉语"主题"
英语以"主语"引导句子:主语起语法作用,但不一定是此句的主题。
汉语以"主题"引导句子:主题即话题,起语义作用。
英译汉时:确定英语句子中的主语是否可以当作汉语中的主题,如果不合适,即重新按汉语习惯调整或增添主语。
汉译英时:确定汉语句子中的主题词是否可以当作英语中的主语,如果不合适,即重新按英语习惯选择或增添主语。
(4) 英语"重心在前",汉语"重心在后"
英语:中心词+修饰限定的短语(或从句);主句+从句
汉语:修饰限定的短语+中心词;从句+主句
英译汉时:将英语中起修饰限定的内容提前,将中心词或主句放后,省略关联词。
汉译英时:将汉语里的中心词或主句提前,将起修饰限定的内容放后,用关联词连接。
(5) 英语"主要以动词充当谓语",汉语"多种成分充当谓语"
英语句子:主要是"主语+谓语动词"的结构。
汉语句子:名词、形容词等都可充当谓语。
英译汉时:可以将动词转换为名词或形容词。
汉译英时:通常要增加助动词,或是将名词或形容词直接转换为动词形态。

2. **语言转换的原则**
(1) 在内容上力求准确,符合原语的真实意思。
(2) 在形式上做到通顺,符合目的语的语言习惯。

3. **语言重组技巧**
(1) 转换(conversion):包括词性转换、句型转换和语态转换。词性转换,如英语中的名词和介词译成汉语时可以变为动词,汉语中的某些动词译成英语时可以变成名词或介词。句型转换,指将句中成分的语序进行调整,例如中心词与修饰限定词的位置调整。例:
　　我代表市委市政府…… On behalf of...(动词变介词短语)
　　He is a good speaker. 他擅长演讲。(形容词变动词)
(2) 释义(paraphrasing):摆脱源语句式,以符合目的语习惯的表达将原意表述出来。
(3) 增补与省略(addition & omission):增补是指将发言者未能表达的意思说出来,或面对非专业人士听众将某些术语或习语进行额外解释;而省略是指将重复冗余的信息或啰嗦的话省略。增补和省略不意味着自由发挥,而是为了更好地将原文的实际意思用符合目的语习惯的表达口译出来,要做到增减词不增减意。
(4) 拆分与合并(segmentation & combination):长句的拆分和短句的合并。
(5) 顺句驱动(parallelism):顺句驱动是指把句子按照与源语相同的语序或表达方式译

成目标语。它是同声传译中最重要的语言转换技巧,在交替传译中也经常使用。

例:联合国秘书长潘基文在南京大学演讲开场白:

I am delighted to be here on this beautiful campus at one of the world's oldest centers of learning.

很高兴能来到这里,来到这个美丽的校园,这是世界最古老的学府之一。

4. 语言转换的训练

(1) 专项技巧训练:转换、释义、增补省略、拆分合并、顺句驱动等专项技巧练习。

(2) 笔译比较训练:有参考译文的材料(句子、段落、文章)自己先译,然后对比参考译文分析学习;无参考译文的材料进行试译,然后交给老师批改点评。

(3) 视译训练:通览全文,然后根据每句里的关键词提示将全句的意思按照自己的理解用目的语说出来。

(4) 口译训练:在口译模拟训练中侧重对语言转换这一环节的重视,将自己的译文同参考译文进行比较分析、归纳总结。

拓展阅读

选文A

如果某人说"我喜欢中国菜",这种说法似乎过于简单了。其实并不存在所谓的"中国菜"这一简单的概念。确切的说法应该是喜欢某一种菜系,或者喜欢某一地区的中国菜。像中国这样幅员辽阔、历史悠久而又复杂的国家,千百年来必然会形成具有鲜明地方烹饪特色的区域性菜系或帮菜。这种不可避免的差异是由地理位置、气候条件、交通状况、人口迁移、海外文化影响等因素所决定的。

虽然中国究竟有多少种地方菜系并无定论,但是有关人士认为,中国有鲁菜、川菜、粤菜和淮扬菜等四大地方菜系。福建—台湾菜通常被列为第五种地方菜系。必须指出,这种区域划分并无严格的地理界线。例如,北京菜虽属鲁菜,却也融入了一些川菜的特色,并受到蒙古菜的影响。又如,淮扬菜系的范围,覆盖了人口居住密集的整个长江三角洲地区,汇集了无锡、苏州、上海和杭州等菜式。一般来说,各地的菜式都有讲究新鲜、用料精选、做工细腻之特点。而全国各地的地方风味小吃以及少数民族风味餐,则数以千计,甚至难以计数。

由于地方菜系之间存在着频频交覆现象,以及相互借鉴的情况,人们因而认为,区分地方菜系最为简便的方法是按菜的知名度,而不是按菜的烹调风格或口味进行辨别。

中国四大菜系大致可按以下这些特点区分:

鲁菜通常较咸,汁色普遍较浅。鲁菜注重选料,精于刀工,善于炊技。作为我国北方菜系的代表,鲁菜烹饪技术广泛运用于明清两代的宫廷菜。

川菜选料范围大,调味及炊技变化多样。据统计,川菜的品种在五千种以上。川菜最大的特点是口味重,以麻辣著称。

最难归类的粤菜强调轻炒浅煮,选料似乎不受限制。粤菜源于明清,在发展过程中不仅吸收借鉴了中国北方烹调和西餐烹调的精华,同时也保持了自己的传统特色。

淮扬菜是以江苏境内的扬州、南京、苏州等地的地方菜式为基础之大成。淮扬菜注重选料的原汁原味，在菜的装饰上讲究形态的艺术性和颜色的鲜艳性。淮扬菜实际上糅合了南北菜系之精华。

也有人以八个字来归纳这四大菜系的口味特点，即"南淡北咸，东甜西辣"。

译文

If you hear someone say "I love Chinese food", he or she is taking too much for granted. As a matter of fact, there is no such a simple thing as the so-called "Chinese food". A more accurate statement in this instance should be such that expresses one's preference for a particular Chinese cuisine or a particular regional way of cooking. With a territory as large and a history as long and complex as China's, it is inevitable that distinct regional differences in cuisine have evolved over the course of centuries. Numerous factors are involved in this inevitable distinction: geography, climate, transportation, migration, influence from overseas cultures, etc.

Although there is no agreement on the precise number of Chinese regional cuisines, those concerned with such matters agree that the four principal culinary regions are Shandong, Sichuan, Canton and Yangzhou, with Fujian-Taiwan most commonly listed as a fifth. It should be pointed out that these designations are not hard and fast geographical boundaries. Beijing food, for instance, falls within the realm of Shandong cooking, but includes some Sichuan dishes and Mongolian-influenced specialties, while the cuisine of the entire densely populated Yangtze River delta area, including Wuxi, Suzhou, Shanghai, and Hangzhou dishes, falls under the category of Yangzhou cuisine. Generally speaking, the many types of cuisine across China invariably emphasize freshness and tenderness of the food, cooked with carefully chosen materials and fine craftsmanship. All over China, local delicacies and foods unique to various ethnic groups are in number of several thousands, or simply numerous.

The frequent overlapping and borrowing that take place among the regional cuisine lead one to the conclusion that they are most conveniently distinguished by their famous dishes, rather than by any prevailing style or taste.

The four major cuisine traditions in China can be roughly distinguished by these generalities:

Shandong cuisine is generally salty, with a prevalence of light-colored sauces. The dishes feature choice of materials, adept technique in slicing and perfect cooking skills. Shandong cuisine is representative of northern China's cooking and its technique has been widely absorbed by the imperial dishes of the Ming and Qing dynasties.

Sichuan cuisine features a wide range of materials, various seasonings and different cooking techniques. Statistics show that the number of Sichuan dishes has surpassed 5,000. With a rich variety of strong flavors, Sichuan food is famous for its numerous varieties of delicacies, dominated by peppery and chili flavors and best known for being spicy-hot.

Cantonese cuisine, the hardest to categorize, emphasizes light cooking with seemingly limitless range of ingredients. Cantonese cuisine took shape in the Ming and Qing dynasties. In the process of its development, it has borrowed the culinary essence of Northern China and of the Western-style food, while maintaining its traditional local flavor.

Yangzhou cuisine bases itself largely on the three local cooking styles of Yangzhou, Nanjing and Suzhou, all within Jiangsu Province. While emphasizing the original flavor of well-chosen materials, it features carefully selected ingredients. Also, the artistic shape and bright colors of the dishes add more ornamental value. Yangzhou cuisine is essentially a combination of the best elements of northern and southern cooking.

According to some others, the characteristic flavors of China's four cuisines can be summed up in the following expression: "The light southern(Canton) cuisine, and the salty northern(Shandong) cuisine; the sweet eastern(Yangzhou) cuisine, and the spicy western(Sichuan) cuisine."

选文B

Remarks at the Chinese New Year Food & Culture Festival
by the Ambassador H. E. Mr. Zhang Yan
January 31, 2010

Distinguished guests,

Excellencies,

Ladies and Gentlemen,

After 10 more days, Chinese people are going to celebrate the Chinese lunar new year, the Year of Tiger. We are very happy and honoured to have so many friends come to joint us in this Chinese New Year Food & Culture Festival and share the festivity with us. Allow me to extend my warm welcome and new year greetings to all of you.

The Year of Tiger is a very lucky year. In China, tiger stands for being courageous, energetic and very capable. I wish the Year of Tiger will bring every body good luck.

2010 is a very important year for China. Chinese people after a very successful year of 2009, will continue to work hard to build their country into a moderately prosperous society in an all-aspects way, and make their fresh contribution to the world peace and development. This year, China will host the World Expo in Shanghai from May to October and the 16th Asian Games in Guangzhou in November. More than 240 countries, regions and international organizations will participate in the Shanghai Expo. This makes it the largest ever in the world expo history. With the theme of "Better City, Better Life", all countries, including India, will exhibit their latest achievement in science and technology especially in green life and environment-friendly technology. I hope all friends, including Indian friends, will have chance to visit this spectacular event.

2010 is also an auspicious year for China-India relation. Two countries are going to celebrate the 60th anniversary of the establishment of diplomatic relation. China Festival and India Festival will be held respectively. We are also busily preparing the state visit by Indian President to China. I am sure those activities will further promote the people to people exchanges and strengthen the bilateral cooperation. I am confident with your gracious support, we will further advance China-India Strategic Cooperative Partnership and open a new chapter in China-India relation.

Dear friends,

Today's gathering is part of the celebration for the 60th anniversary and it will warm up the China Festival in India. We have prepared lots of Chinese delicacies. There are typical dishes representing various branches of Chinese cuisine. My staff and their spouses have also prepared some fantastic culture shows. They are not dancers and models, but better than professional dancers and models. I hope you will enjoy both the Chinese food and the performances.

Finally, as Chinese custom goes, I would like to wish everybody good health, good luck and big wealth in the new year!

Thank you!

译文

在"中国新年食品文化节"开幕式的致辞

中国驻印度大使　张　炎

2010年1月31日

各位来宾，

女士们，先生们，

再过十多天，中国人民将庆祝农历新年——虎年。我们很高兴也很荣幸有这么多朋友来参加这个"中国新年食品文化节"的开幕式，和我们同欢。请允许我向你们表示热烈的欢迎并致以新年的问候。

虎年是一个非常幸运的年份。在中国，虎代表勇气、活力以及能力。我祝各位虎年都交好运。

2010年对中国是一个非常重要的年份，送走成就辉煌的2009，中国人民将继续致力于全面建设小康社会，为世界的和平与发展作出新贡献。今年5月至10月，中国将在上海举办世博会，11月在广州召开第16届亚运会。届时，240个国家和地区以及国际组织将参展世博会，是世博历史上最大规模的一次盛会。以"城市让生活更美好"为主题，所有参展方，包括印度，将展示最新科技，特别是绿色生活和环境友好型技术。我希望包括印度朋友在内的所有人都能有机会参加这一盛事。

2010年是中印关系发展不平凡的一年。两国将庆祝建交60周年,将互相在对方国家举办"中国节"和"印度节"。我们也在积极筹备印度总统对中国的国事访问。我相信这些活动将进一步促进两国人民之间的理解和友谊,深化双边关系的发展。我也相信在你们的大力支持下,我们将会进一步加强中印战略伙伴关系,谱写中印关系的新篇章。

各位朋友,

今天的活动是庆祝建交60周年的开始,也是为"中国节"的到来预热。我们准备了许多道中国菜肴,包括了不同菜系的特色菜。我的同事和配偶们也准备了一些精彩的文化表演。他们虽然不是舞蹈家和模特,但比专业舞者和模特还专业。希望大家一起享受我们的中国美食和表演。

最后,按中国的习俗,祝大家新年身体健康,运气亨通,财源广进!

谢谢!

第六单元　外交政策
（Foreign Policy）

单元要点

本单元共分五个层次,分别是:外交政策汉译英一篇;外文政策英译汉一篇;听辨与解析;重译法;拓展阅读(汉译英、英译汉各一篇)。第一、二部分提供外交政策口译的例文及其翻译和重难点评析;第三、四部分主要是相关口译理论与技能的介绍;第五部分的拓展阅读中,提供汉、英原文和参考译文。

理论难点提示

1. 听辨与解析。
2. 重译法。

选文A

尊敬的各位使节,
女士们、先生们:

国际形势正在发生复杂而深刻的变化。和平与发展仍然是当今时代的主题。维护和平、促进发展,是各国人民共同的强烈愿望。但是,国际关系中不确定、不稳定因素有所增加,各种传统和非传统安全问题相互交织。和平问题没有解决,发展问题更加严重。解决当今世界面临的各种紧迫问题和长远问题,需要世界各国坚持不懈的努力,需要加强国际间的友好合作。和平共处五项原则作为指导国际关系的准则,具有重大的现实意义,应该得到认真遵循和切实履行。

我们应该坚定不移地维护国家主权平等。国家主权是国家独立的根本标志,是国家利益的集中体现和可靠保障。随着经济全球化和新科技革命的发展,国家间的相互联系和相互依存日益加深,但这并不意味着可以忽视和削弱国家主权的地位与作用。必须实行国际关系民主化,任何国家都无权把自己的意志强加于人,以任何借口损害和剥夺别国的主权,不尊重别国主权,以大欺小,以强凌弱,推行霸权主义和强权政治,实践证明是行不通的。

我们应该尊重和维护世界文明的多样性。各国文明的多样性,是人类社会的基本特征,也是推动世界文明进步的重要动力。当今世界拥有60亿人口,200多个国家和地区,2 500多个民族,5 000多种语言。各个国家和地区,无论是历史传统、宗教信仰和文化背景,还是社会制度、价值观念和发展程度,往往存在这样那样的差异,整个人类文明也因此而交相辉映、多姿多彩。这种文明的多样性是在历史长河中形成的,并将长期存在下去。中国古代思想家孔子曾说过:"万物并育而不相害,道并行而不悖。"我们应该充分尊重各国文明的多样性,而不应人为歧视或贬低他国文明;应该鼓励各种文明在对话交流中相互借鉴、取长补短,而不应相互隔绝和相互排斥;应该倡导各种文明在相互包容、求同存异中共同发展,而不应强求一律、强加于人。

我们应该在平等互利基础上促进各国经济的共同发展。经济领域的平等互利,就是要尊重各国的经济自主权,平等参与,公平竞争,互利共赢。解决发展问题,首先要靠发展中国家的自身努力,同时发达国家也应负起责任,在开放市场、扩大贸易、增加援助、减免债务等方面进一步采取切实措施。国际经济规则的制定和修改,应尊重和体现发展中国家的权益,而一经制定就要共同遵守。面对新科技革命的迅猛发展,应积极推动技术转让和科技合作,使各国能够分享人类科技进步的成果。

我们应该通过对话与协作维护世界的和平与安全。历史表明,以军事联盟为基础、以加强军备为手段的旧安全观,无助于保障国际安全。动辄诉诸武力或以武力相威胁,就会影响乃至破坏世界的和平与安宁。必须坚决摒弃冷战思维,牢固树立以互信、互利、平等、协作为核心的新安全观。要防范和打击一切形式的恐怖主义,并努力消除产生恐怖主义的根源。对核武器扩散、毒品泛滥和其他跨国犯罪等非传统安全威胁,应在国际法原则基础上,通过加强国际合作加以有效应对。对于艾滋病蔓延、生态恶化等威胁人类健康与生存的全球性问题,应本着对子孙后代负责的态度,加大国际合作防治的力度。

中国社会主义现代化建设道路是一条和平发展的道路。这条道路,就是利用世界和平的有利时机实现自身发展,又以自身的发展更好地维护和促进世界和平;就是在积极参与经济全球化和区域合作的同时,主要依靠自己的力量和改革创新来实现发展;就是坚持对外开放,在平等互利的基础上,积极发展同世界各国的合作;就是聚精会神搞建设,一心一意谋发展,长期维护和平的国际环境和良好的周边环境;就是永远不称霸,永远做维护世界和平和促进共同发展的坚定力量。

我们坚持走和平发展的道路,坚定不移地高举和平、发展、合作的旗帜,一如既往地奉行独立自主的和平外交政策,坚持在和平共处五项原则基础上与世界各国友好相处。

我们将坚定维护国家主权和领土完整,决不允许别人干涉中国内政,同时尊重别国的主权和领土完整。我们将继续推动世界多极化、国际关系民主化和发展模式多样化,促进经济全球化朝着有利于各国共同繁荣的方向发展,积极倡导多边主义和新安全观,反对霸权主义和强权政治,反对一切形式的恐怖主义,推动建立和平稳定、公正合理的国际新秩序。我们将在平等互利基础上扩大对外开放,广泛深入开展对外经济技术合作。我们将深化与发展中国家的互利合作,维护与发展中国家的共同利益,积极探索新形势下开展南南合作的有效途径。坚持与邻为善、以邻为伴的方针,继续推进睦邻、安邻、富邻的政策,加强与周边国家的友好合作关系,深化区域合作。进一步发展同发达国家的关系,努力扩大共同利益的汇合点,妥善处理分歧。我们将积极参与国际多边外交活动,维护加强联合国及安理会的权威与主导作用,在国际和地区组织中做出建设性的努力。我们将全面加强经济外交和对外文化交流,积极维护我国公民在海外的生命安全和合法权益。

要和平、求发展、促合作,已成为人心所向、奔腾不息的时代潮流。中国政府和中国人民愿与世界人民一道,共同为维护和促进人类的和平、发展与进步事业而不懈努力。

谢谢大家。

重难点评析

1. 国际形势正在发生复杂而深刻的变化。这里所讲的"变化"是一系列持续不断的变化,所以用复数表示,译为"complex and profound changes"。译文用了 undergoing 一词,能更好地表达原文的含义。

2. 维护和平、促进发展,是各国人民共同的强烈愿望。"各国人民"有多种译法,"people of all lands"既可表示各国人民,也可表示各地区人民。

3. 国际关系中不确定、不稳定因素有所增加,"有所增加"可以译为"on the increase",也可译为"on the rise"。

4. 和平问题没有解决,发展问题更加严重。不必将问题都译成 question,甚至可以不译,如参考译文所示:While peace is yet to be achieved, development has become an even more aggravated issue.

5. 和平共处五项原则作为指导国际关系的基本原则,具有重大的现实意义,应该得到认真遵循和切实履行。和平共处五项原则首先由中(国)、印(度)、缅(甸)三国政府于1954年一起倡导,是广大国家认同的指导国与国关系的基本原则,其内容包括:①互相尊重主权与领土完整;②互不侵犯;③互不干涉内政;④平等互利;⑤和平共处译为"mutual respect for sovereignty and territorial integrity, non-aggression, non-interference in the internal affairs of other countries, equality and mutual benefit and peaceful coexistence"。将"具有重大的现实意义"译为"remain highly relevant"显得较为简洁。

6. 以大欺小,以强凌弱,推行霸权主义和强权政治,实践证明是行不通的。"以大欺小,以强凌弱"两个短语合译成一个短语"bullying the small and the weak by dint of one's size and power",符合翻译"简明原则"。

7. 这种文明的多样性是在历史长河中形成的,并将长期存在下去。文明的多样性是地球文明的本质,所以用"stay with us into the future",可表明"将长期存在下去"的意义。

8. 中国古代思想家孔子曾说过:"万物并育而不相害,道并行而不悖。"引语翻译几乎是每个议员都会遇到的难题,需要不断学习和积累。

9. 我们应该充分尊重各国文明的多样性,而不应人为歧视或贬低他国文明;应该鼓励各种文明在对话交流中相互借鉴、取长补短,而不应相互隔绝和相互排斥;应该倡导各种文明在相互包容、求同存异中共同发展,而不应强求一律、强加于人。此句含三个"应该……而不应……",可将此句对应地译为含三个"instead of . . . , we should. . ."结构的句子。

10. 动辄诉诸武力或以武力相威胁,就会影响乃至破坏世界的和平与安宁。"动辄诉诸武力"意指"一有情况就使用武力","动辄"为讲明什么情况,所以译作"resorting to use or threat of force at every turn"。

11. 反对一切形式的恐怖主义,"一切形式"是指"一切表现形式",即"in all its manifestations"。

12. 推动建立和平稳定、公正合理的国际新秩序。英语属后置式定语的语言,因而将前置式定语"和平稳定、公正合理的"译为"a new international order that is peaceful, stable, fair and equitable",这符合英语的表达习惯。

译 文

Distinguished Diplomatic Envoys,
Ladies and Gentlemen,

  The international situation is undergoing complex and profound changes. Peace and development remain the themes of our times. As more secured peace and greater development is the common aspiration of the people of all lands. However, factors of uncertainty and instability in international relations are on the increase, as the various traditional and non-traditional security threats are interwoven. While peace is yet to be achieved, development has become an even more aggravated issue. Finding answers to the multiple problems facing the world, immediate and long-term, requires the persistent efforts of all countries and their strengthened friendship and cooperation. The Five Principles of Peaceful Coexistence, as the basic norms governing international relations, remain highly relevant and should be observed with all seriousness and implemented in real earnest.

  We should firmly uphold the principle of sovereign equality. Sovereignty is the birthmark of any independent state, the crystallization of its national interests and the best safeguard of all it holds dear. The increasing interaction and interdependence among countries, thanks to the surging economic globalization and technological revolution, does not mean that the status and role of sovereignty can in any way be neglected or weakened. It is imperative to have greater democracy in international relations. No country has the right to impose its will on others, nor can it undermine or deny other countries' sovereignty under whatever excuse. Facts have proven that such practices as disregarding others', sovereignty, bullying the small and the weak by dint of one's size and power and pursuing hegemony and power politics would not get anywhere.

  We should respect and maintain the diversity of the world's civilizations. The diverse civilizations are a hallmark of human society and an important driving force behind human progress. Our world today has over 6 billion inhabitants living in more than 200 countries and regions. They break down into 2,500 ethnic groups and speak more than 5,000 different languages. Be it historical tradition, faith and culture, or social system, values and level of development, those countries or regions are often different from one another. It is these differences that make our planet dazzling, colorful and bustling with life. Such diversity is a legacy of history and will stay with us into the future. The ancient Chinese thinker Confucius once said, "All living creatures grow together without harming one another; ways run parallel without interfering with one another. "Instead of harboring bias against or deliberately belittling other civilizations, we should give full respect to the diversity of civilizations. Instead of shutting each other out in mutual exclusion, we should encourage dialogue and exchange between civilizations so that they can learn from each other in mutual emulation. Instead of demanding uniformity and imposing one's will on others, we should promote common development of all civilizations in the course of mutual tolerance and seeking agreement while shelving differences.

We should promote common development of the world's economics on the basis of equality and mutual benefit. In applying the principle of equality and mutual benefit to the economic realm, we should respect the right of all countries to make independent economic decisions, their equal right to participate in competition on a level playing field, and their access to mutual benefit and economic success. Finding an answer to development, first and foremost, requires the efforts of the developing countries themselves. But the developed countries must also live up to their share of responsibilities, by taking further steps in opening up their markets, expanding trade, increasing aid programs, and reducing and forgiving debts. In formulating or revising international economic rules, it is necessary to respect and reflect the rights and interests of the developing world. Once made, the rules must be faithfully observed by all parties. In the face of rapid technological revolution, it is necessary to facilitate technological transfer and cooperation so that all nations can share the benefits of scientific advances.

We should maintain peace and security through dialog and cooperation. History shows that the old security concept centered on military alliances and arms build-ups did poorly to keep the world safe. Resorting to use or threat of force at every turn can only impede, even jeopardize peace and tranquility in the world. The Cold War mentality must be done away with in favor of a new security concept featuring mutual trust, mutual benefit, equality and cooperation. While we stand on guard against and strike hard on terrorism in all forms and manifestations, it is essential to remove the root causes that breed the menace. With respect to weapons proliferation, drug trafficking, trans-boundary crimes and other non-traditional security threats, it is necessary to take on them with strengthened international cooperation consistent with the principles of international law. In the face of such global concerns as HIV/AIDS, environmental degradation and other threats to human health and survival, it is necessary to step up a globalized approach bearing in mind a keen sense of responsibility for the welfare of future generations.

The road of China's socialist modernization drive is a road of peaceful development. China's intentions in taking this road are to take advantage of favorable conditions presented by world peace to develop itself and better safeguard and promote world peace through its development. China bases its development mainly on its own resources and its own restructuring and innovation efforts, while also taking an active part in economic globalization and regional cooperation. We will continue the process of opening up and promote cooperation with all other countries on the basis of equality and mutual benefit, focus on construction, concentrate on development and work to preserve a long-term peaceful international environment and an excellent neighboring environment. We will never seek hegemony and will always remain a staunch force safeguarding world peace and promoting common development.

In taking the road of peaceful development, we unswervingly hold high the banner of peace, development and cooperation, always follow an independent foreign policy of peace, and maintain friendly relations with all other countries on the basis of the Five Principles of Peaceful Coexistence.

We will firmly safeguard national sovereignty and territorial integrity, tolerating no one to interfere in our internal affairs. At the same time, we will respect the sovereignty and territorial integrity of others. We will continue to promote world multipolarization, democracy in international relations and diversity in development models, and encourage the progress of economic globalization in a direction conductive to the common prosperity of all nations. We will vigorously advocate multilateralism and a new concept of security and oppose hegemony, power politics, and terrorism in all its manifestations. We will work for a new international order that is peaceful, stable, fair and equitable. We will open still wider to the outside world on the basis of equality and mutual benefit, while engaging in economic and technical cooperation with other countries with greater scope and depth. We will promote mutually beneficial cooperation with developing countries, safeguard the common interests we share with them, and actively explore ways for effective South-South cooperation under the new circumstances. We will adhere to our policy of building friendship and partnership with neighboring countries and creating an amicable, secure and prosperous neighborhood, strengthen friendly relations and cooperation with our neighboring countries and facilitate regional cooperation. We will strengthen relations with developed countries, strive to expand areas of common interests and deal with differences appropriately. We will actively participate in international and multilateral diplomacy, safeguard and strengthen the authority and leading role of the United Nations and the UN Security Council, and work constructively in international and regional organizations. We will intensify economic diplomacy and expand cultural exchanges with other countries. We will vigorously protect the lives and legitimate rights and interests of Chinese nationals living abroad.

Aspiring for peace, development and cooperation has become the popular will and the irresistible tide of the times. The Chinese government and people stand ready to work unremittingly with the people of all other nations to safeguard and promote the cause of world peace, development and progress.

Thank you.

选文B

Ladies and Gentlemen,

It's my pleasure this morning to outline the most important instruments of modern American foreign policy, namely, diplomacy, the United Nations, the international monetary structure, economic aid, collective security, and military deterrence. An understanding of these instruments, I believe, will help you further understand the conduct of American foreign policy.

The utmost purpose of American foreign policy is to defend national sovereignty and national interests. In light of the history and development of American values, diplomacy has been regarded as the most important instrument to which all other instruments must be subordinated. Its purpose is to promote national values or interests by peaceful means. However, diplomacy, by its very nature, is often overshadowed by spectacular international events, dramatic initiatives and meetings among heads of states. Worse still, traditional American distrust of diplomacy continues today, albeit in weaker form. Impatience with or downright distrust of diplomacy has been built not only into all the other instruments of foreign policy but also into the modern presidential system itself. Due to the time limit, I'm not going to talk about this problem in any extensive way.

The utility of the United Nations to the United States as an instrument of foreign policy can too easily be underestimated. Over the years since its founding in 1945, the United Nations has been more or less a servant of American interests. The most spectacular examples were the official UN authorization and sponsorship of intervention in the "troubled spots" of the world with an international peacekeeping force. Consider this fact: The United States provides an average quarter of the UN budget. Many Americans feel the United Nations does not give good value for the investment. But many evaluation of the United Nations must take into account the purpose for which the United States sought to create it: power without diplomacy. In many cases, a victory of the United Nations is a victory of the United States. In recent years, however, with the growing position of China and some other countries in international diplomacy, the United States can no longer control UN decisions as it did before. But the United Nations will continue to function as a useful instrument of American foreign policy.

The World Bank was set up to finance long-term capital. Leading nations took on the obligation of contributing funds to enable the World Bank to make loans to capital-hungry countries. The U. S. quota has been about one-third of the total. The IMF (the International Monetary Fund) was set up to provide for the shorten-term flow of money and lend dollars to needy member countries to help them overcome temporary trade deficits. The United States also has a big role in financing the IMF.

American commitment to rebuilding war-torn countries came as early as its commitment to the postwar international monetary structure. Enacting American foreign aid constitutes part of the American foreign policy. During the last fifty years, the geographic emphasis of American economic aid shifted from assisting the reconstruction and recovery of western Europe, to Southeast Asia, and then to what became known as the Third World. Many critics have argued that foreign aid is really aid for the minority political and economic elites, not for the people. A much more important critique is that American foreign economic assistance has failed to contribute fully to American interests because its administration is often put outside the State Department.

The United States gives great importance to regional collective security agreement. This country has entered a number of collective security treaties, both multilateral and bilateral. A typical example is the North Atlantic Treaty Organization (NATO). Americans realize that the United States cannot meet its world obligation through the United Nations and economic structures alone. There is a need for military alliance with other countries for national and world security. Consequently, the United States has consistently devoted at least 6 percent of its gross domestic national product to defense.

Military deterrence was a product of the U. S. -Soviet confrontation since the end of the World War II, when the traditional American strategy of "demobilization in peace and remobilization in war" was broken. However, the size of the defense budget has not been central to the consideration of deterrence as an instrument of foreign policy. What is important is the advanced military technology, which is regarded by most congressmen as the primary deterrence in the world.

Although Republicans and Democrats look at the world somewhat differently, and although each president has tried to impose a distinctive flavor of his on foreign policy, they have all made use of these basic instruments. They all understand that power plus diplomacy is the best solution to the problem of controlling conflict among the distrustful nations of the world.

重难点评析

1. It's my pleasure this morning to outline the most important instruments of modern American foreign policy, namely, diplomacy, the United Nations, the international monetary structure, economic aid, collective security, and military deterrence. 我们可以将这里的"diplomacy"译作"外交方法"、"外交手段"、"外交途径"、"外交策略"等。"collective security"意指"共同安保"或"共同防范",指的是美国与其他国家结成军事同盟。

2. An understanding of these instruments, I believe, will help you further understand the conduct of American foreign policy. 所谓的"conduct"是指美国外交政策的"实施"或"操作"。

3. However, diplomacy, by its very nature, is often overshadowed by spectacular international events, dramatic initiatives and meetings among heads of states. "diplomacy, by its very nature"主要是指"外交斡旋"这些活动,也可以译成"外交手段"。当出现突发事件时,外交手段的作用被"overshadow"了,即"显示不出其魅力"或"相形见绌"了。

4. Impatience with or downright distrust of diplomacy has been built... into the modern presidential system itself. 这句话的言下之意是:美国总统对外交活动及其作用的态度受到选举的影响,竞选时的承诺可能在当选后被忘却了。

5. Due to the time limit, I'm not going to talk about this problem in any extensive way. "extensive way"即广泛讨论,用今天比较流行的汉语来说,是"展开讨论"。

6. Many Americans feel the United Nations does not give good value for the investment. 这句话有两层意思:一层意思是美国人不希望将这么多的钱用于国际事务;另

第六单元 外交政策(Foreign Policy)

一层意思是美国人对联合国的回报不满。将句子直译可以同时保存这两层意思。

7. American commitment to rebuilding war-torn countries came as early as its commitment to the postwar international monetary structure. 注意"structure"的不同释义,这里的"international monetary structure"是指"国际货币组织"。

8. ... because its administration is often put outside the State Department. 美国同样存在部门"各自为政"的现象,虽然外交工作由国务院负责,但涉及经济援助时,许多援助工作的具体操作则由农业、卫生、财政等部门承担。

9. ... the traditional American strategy of "demobilization in peace and remobilization in war" was broken. 美国在建国后的一百年间一直实行"平时民兵、战时军队"的国防战略。

10. ... they have all made use of these basic instruments. 这篇讲话最后一段提到的"these basic instruments"是指"上述六种手段",所以译文应以添词法予以表明。

译文

女士们,先生们:

今天上午我很高兴向各位简单介绍一下现代美国外交政策中最重要的工具,即外交手段、联合王国、国际货币组织、经济援助、共同安保和军事威慑。我认为,了解美国外交政策的这些工具将有助于各位进一步了解美国外交政策的表现。

美国外交政策的最高宗旨是维护国家主权和利益。从美国价值观的历史和发展角度来看,外交手段被视为最重要的外交工具,其他工具都必须服从于外交手段。外交手段的目的在于通过和平方法强化美国的价值和国家利益。然而,由于外交手段受到自身特征的制约,一些不寻常的国际事件、戏剧性的主动行动以及国家元首的峰会等,常常导致外交手段的作用黯然失色。更糟糕的是,美国对外交手段不信任的传统仍在延续,只是形式上不那么强烈而已。对采用外交手段的不耐烦或彻底不信任的态度,不仅已渗透到美国外交政策的其他工具中去,而且也影响到现在总统体制。由于时间关系,我对这个问题就不展开讨论了。

美国利用联合国作为其外交政策的工具很容易被低估。联合国自1945年成立以来,或多或少地成为了美国利益的服务工具。最典型的事例是,在联合国正式授权或操办下,国际维和部队可以对世界上的"麻烦"地区进行干预。你得考虑这样一个事实:美国给联合国提供的经费占了联合国预算的1/4。许多美国人认为,联合国没有对这种投资予以良好的回报。但是,对联合国的任何评价都必须考虑到美国所追求的目的,即不使用外交手段的力量。很多事例表明,联合国的胜利就是美国的胜利。然而,由于中国以及其他一些国家近年来国家外交地位的提高,美国再也无法像以前那样控制联合国的决策。当然,联合国作为美国外交政策的有效工具,将继续发挥这样的作用。

世界银行的建立是为了提供长期资本。强国承担了提供资本的义务,以便世界银行可以向资本紧缺的国家贷款。美国的配额占世界银行的总资本的1/3。国际货币基金组织(IMF)的建立是为了向所需资金的成员国提供短期贷款,帮助这些国家解决暂时的贸易赤字问题。美国在向世界货币基金组织提供资金方面也同样起着重要作用。

美国在致力于建立战后国际货币组织的同时,又致力于帮助遭受战争破坏的国家重建家园的工作。实施美国对外援助是美国外交政策的一个组成部分。在过去的50年里,美国经济援助的地域重心由援助西欧的重建转为援助东南亚,后又转为所谓的第三世界。许多批评人士认为,对外援助事实上是对一小部分政治上层人物和经济上层人物的援助,不是对普通老百姓的援助。另一种更为重要的批评是,美国对外经济援助未能充分发挥有助于美国利益的作用,因为外援的实施常常不是在国务院范围内进行的。

美国重视签订地区性共同安保协定。美国已加入一系列共同安保条约,有多边的,也有双边的。一个典型的例子就是北大西洋公约组织(北约)。美国人意识到,美国不能单单依靠联合国和经济组织来负担其世界责任。国家安全和世界安全需要美国与其他国家结成联盟。为此,美国在国防上投入的资金一直占其国民生产总值的6%以上。

军事威慑是二战后美苏对抗的产物。二战结束后,美国打破了"和平时期遣散军队、战争时期重组军队"的传统政策。然而,防卫预算的大小对于是否将威慑视为外交政策的一种手段并不重要,重要的是先进的军事技术。大部分国会议员都将先进的军事技术视为世界上最重要的威慑力量。

虽然共和党人和民主党人看待世界的方法有所不同,虽然每届总统都试图将自己与众不同的个人特色强加于外交政策,但是他们无不利用上述六种基本外交手段。他们都明白,强权加外交是控制世界上互不信任的国家之间冲突的最佳良方。

听辨与解析

听辨与解析是整个口译过程的第一步,也是关键而艰难的一步。口译的认知过程要求译者在很短的时间内实现工作内容的高效化与准确化。如果以每分钟150个单词的语速计算,4分钟的讲话要使用近600个词。人脑的短时记忆能力很难将这600个字词过耳不忘,储存人脑,但人脑能够将这600个字词进行分析、整合、提炼,进而储存其所构成的言语信息。在这个过程中,译员的听力并不总是"万无一失"的,种种听力障碍与问题往往难以避免。

总体来说,听力的障碍主要体现在以下几个方面:①连续、弱读、失去爆破、重音转移等超音段方面的语音困难;②口音与方言障碍,如英国英语、美国英语、非洲英语、澳洲英语、其他英联邦国家以及非说英语国家人士所讲的英语;③来自源语本身的困难,如逻辑混乱、语法不清、语篇表达较为随意、掺和与主题无关的内容;④专有话题的术语与内容上的理解困难;⑤源语语篇的语体理解困难;⑥文化差异造成的理解困难。

1. 词义理解错误

口译的理解是在语篇中完成的,具体的词义取决于上下文所提供的语境。因此,如何依据语篇的背景信息和源语说话人的演讲意图来确定词语的正确含义,就成为译员要面临的一大挑战,而由此产生的词义理解错误也比比皆是。如:

The brisk pickup of business in abortion industry has greatly alarmed many people.

industry一词的意思可为"工业",也可为"勤勉,刻苦",此外,它还有"行业、企业"等意思。在这句话中,该词则对应着"行业"的意思,应理解为"堕胎行当的生意兴隆使许多人大为震惊"。

He put forward some new ideas to challenge the interest of all concerned.

在这句话中,challenge并非常用的"向……挑战"的意思,而表示"引起"的意思,如果译

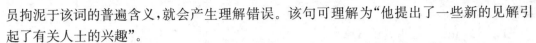

员拘泥于该词的普遍含义,就会产生理解错误。该句可理解为"他提出了一些新的见解引起了有关人士的兴趣"。

再以 credit 一词为例,在如下 7 个句子中都有 credit 这个词,但其词义各有不同,听解时尤要注意:

He got all the credit for the discovery. 他由于这项发现而获得这种好评。

The availability of cheap long-term credit would help small business. 低息长期贷款可以扶持小型企业。

They sold grain on credit during time of famine. 饥荒季节,他们则赊销粮食。

How much do I have to my credit? 我的银行户头上还有多少存款?

They cannot obtain credit at all in the trade. 他们的生意信誉已经荡然无存。

They have opened the covering credit with the Bank of China, London. 他们已从伦敦中国银行开立了有关的信用证。

2. 成语和谚语等文化差异形成的理解错误

成语和谚语是社会语言和文化在历史中的积淀,在口译场合中,源语说话人对成语和谚语的使用,往往使表达言简意赅,形象生动。译员如果对该民族的历史、文化和风俗等知识了解不够,就会碰到理解困难,造成错误。

John can be relied on. He eats no fish and plays the game.

如果此句被理解为"约翰是可靠的,他不吃鱼,还玩游戏",则明显译员未能参透 eat no fish 和 play the game 的含义。在英国历史上,宗教斗争十分惨烈,旧教规定斋日只许吃鱼,新教推翻了旧政之后,教徒拒绝斋日吃鱼,以示效忠新教,因此 eat no fish 就表示"忠诚"的意思。play the game 则表示"规规矩矩地比赛",可引申为"为人正直"。该句正确译文为"约翰是个靠得住的人,他既忠诚又正直"。对源语成语和谚语理解不到位就很容易产生误译。再如:

John likes to pat himself on the back. 约翰喜欢自吹。(不宜理解为:约翰喜欢捶自己的背。)

There was never a night or a problem that could defeat sunrise or hope. 黑夜不能阻止日出,难题无法抹杀希望。(不宜理解为:黑夜或难题无法击败日出或希望。)

除习语、谚语之外,文化差异而造成的困难比比皆是,词语的情感色彩差异也往往令译员在理解中出现偏差。如 aggressive 一词在汉语中常被译为"侵略的,攻击性的",这是因为中国文化总是以谦虚内敛为美德,行事锋芒毕露,咄咄逼人者往往遭人诟病;而在英语文化中该词所体现的内涵甚至有褒扬之意,可以理解为"有进取心的,积极的"。译员听取该词时,则要特别关注其所附带的文化色彩,加以甄别,如 aggressive policy 可以理解为"侵略政策"或"咄咄逼人的政策",aggressive war 可译为"侵略战争",而 John was an aggressive guy, who did his job well. 则要理解为"约翰是一个很有上进心的小伙子,他的工作很出色"。

3. 专业知识匮乏而造成的理解错误

口译往往涉及面极广,政治、经济、历史、地理、文学、科技、外贸、法律、娱乐等各方面无所不包。译员如未能掌握有关专业知识,口译时就会非驴非马,让人费解。如 partial shipment 在涉及物流的会议中,专指"分批装运",因此该词不可理解为"部分转运"或"部分运输"。再如：

He was found guilty of murder.

There is no right of appeal against the decision.

在事涉法律的口译中，find 并不是常见的"发现"的意思，而是指"裁决，判决"；appeal 也并非常见的"呼吁"的意思，而是指"上诉"。因此，这两句的正确理解应分别是"经裁决，他犯有谋杀罪"和"关于这项裁决，没有上诉权"。

再看一句以外交为主题的口译现场中的话：

We would like to build a color-blind society where all men can have equal educational opportunity. 我们要建立一个无种族歧视的社会，让人人都能获得平等的教育权利。

此句中的关键词 color-blind 不是指"色盲"，而是带有一定的政治色彩，应相应理解为"无种族歧视"的意思。

那么，译员应该如何建立起有效的学习模式，消除口译过程中的障碍与困难，切实培养敏锐、强大的听辨能力呢？

事实上，听力理解包括从载有源语信息的声波传入译员的耳朵到译员辨认出单词，最后做出判断，在脑中形成源语所表达的思想内容或概念的全过程。丹尼尔·吉尔（Daniel Gile）专门就口译的理解过程提出过了一个理解模式：

$$C=KL+ELK+A$$

即理解（Comprehension）= 语言知识（Knowledge for the Language）+ 言外知识（Extra-Linguistic Knowledge）+ 分析（Analysis）

根据这一模式的要求，译员在口译开始之前，就应已具备充分的语言知识和非语言知识，即必须具备扎实的语言基本功和广博的知识面。扎实的语言基本功主要是指译员敏锐流畅的听说能力。译员必须在平时多留意英语的多种口音、方言和变体，注意总结各自特点规律，熟悉和了解源语的词、语法、句型结构和各种习惯用法，这样才能保证正确的理解。其次，译员广博的知识面，尤其是口译现场所要求的专业知识也是必不可少的。因主题知识或百科知识的缺陷而出现无解或误解的现象屡见不鲜。再者，在步入会场之前，译员必须对该口译任务的性质、时间、地点、内容及相关背景知识等有充分的了解，在一切了然于胸的情况下进行口译，可以大大提高听觉感知的敏锐度、反应力、自信心和准确性。另外，口译的工作现场肃穆紧张，译员需要做好充分的心理准备，时时准备好承受现场的紧张气氛和压力。译员在整个口译的过程中，集中精力，积极地分析、吸收、反馈信息，保证听辨在最大可能的限度内高效地实现。

根据这一模式的要求，源语说话人开始说话时，译员必须就其言语的思路，按照话语意图、逻辑、情感、意群等话语线索，逐步推进，始终把握话语要旨。在整个口译过程中，译者要始终保持精神高度集中，不断地积极思考，在稍纵即逝的语流中搜寻主要信息，即能够预测所译内容，达到听辨理解与讲话人同步。换言之，口译中听辨解析的要旨就是要整体把握，综合理解，善于预测，抓住关键词和标记信息。具体而言，译员必须：①了解说话人的话语目的，把握源语语篇的整体思路和布局；②利用已有信息和语境因素，预测新信息；③把握语音、语调、节奏等信息的变化，借此把握其中表述的语义细微差异；④把握源语表达的逻辑主线，尤其是对英语主谓轴心结构的核心句进行辨析时，依照语言的线性，依次对英语长句的各个部分进行切分和理解;⑤过滤语篇中的冗余材料或与主题无关的语料等,抓紧关键信息。

听取源语时,译员如果遭遇到陌生的单词或短语,不必惊慌。在很多场合,译员无法将源语说话人的每一个单词明白获取,例如下句:

I don't think that the advisory committee is the appropriate forum for discussion of this point. What is important is that the groundwork be done in the technical working parties, in order to prepare the basis for a decision in the executive committee.

即使无法识得 forum 或者 groundwork 这两个词,但这并不阻碍译员对整句话的理解:①顾问委员会不是讨论该事的适当场所;②技术层需将问题提交管理委员会。从此例可看出,口译听力的要旨是要关注言语的逻辑、意图、意群等,而并非是孤立的单个字词。

而当译员面对不同文体时,听力所要关注的焦点也各为不同。如遇到礼仪性文体的发言时,译员的听力要点是要注意讲话人的感情、态度、观点、立场以及语言的主要特色,因为该类文体的发言多用来传达感情,表示态度、立场,如庆典、仪式的讲话等;遇到信息性文体的发言时,译员的听力要点是要注意 what, where, when, who, how 和 why 等问题,因为该文体的特点是信息较密集,如新闻、述评等;遇到描写性文体的发言时,译员的听力要点以人物刻画、情节发展为主,充分利用形象思维在头脑中形成画面,不但便于理解,且利于记忆,因为该类发言的特点往往是以人物、事件、经历、情节为主,按发生的先后顺序、时空关系展开;而遇到论证性文体的发言时,译员的听力要点是要把握论点、论据、主要实例和推理方式,因为该类文体特点是逻辑推理为主,论点突出,层次清楚,通过论据与实例说明某种观点。

在整个听辨解析过程中,译员尤其注重对"抓住关键词语"、"关注话语标记词"、"掌握话语预测能力"、"借助冗余现象"等具体技巧的领会与运用。

(1) 抓住关键词语

听力理解中的关键词语,指的是那些包含大量信息的词语,这些信息往往构成全句乃至全篇理解的关键。译员把握住这些词语,往往就可以对其指示的上下文了然于胸。这些表达信息的关键词语都是篇段中的实意词语,即名词、动词、形容词和副词,而源语说话人在表述这些词语时,往往会着重语气、语调,放慢语速。译员可根据语篇的内容信息和说话人的表述特征来进行分析、判断,以把握整个听解篇章的要旨,并做到承上启下、成竹在胸。例如:

The Irish tourism industry is now well accustomed to the vagaries of the international marketplace and it has proven very adept at responding to the challenges.

在这段话中,Irish tourism, international marketplace, challenges 是关键词语。抓住这几个关键词语,该段落的意思就一目了然。再看一个段落:

As you all know, marketing is risky business at the best of times. It requires the best information and intelligence available. It also needs the application of sound commercial judgment. The element of risk can be minimized but, as well all know, never eliminated.

在这段话中,marketing, risky, information, intelligence, sound commercial judgment, minimize, eliminate 的词性为名词、形容词和动词,这些实意词语构成了该小段的主体信息,理解好这几个词,也就抓住了这段话的精髓,该篇段的理解也就迎刃而解。

(2) 关注话语标记词

任何一篇口译发言绝不仅仅由一系列离散、独立的句子构成,相反,这些句子彼此之间存在着无法割裂的逻辑关系,相互联系,相互关照,相互印证,从而决定整篇发言的意义。当译员理解一篇话语时,首先要识别各种观点,其次要分析这些观点之间的逻辑关系。而表现种种逻辑关系、能够使译员就此展开语篇推理的语词就是话语标记词,既包括诸如 moreover, so far, because 等单个语词,也包括如 you know, you see, I mean 等语用表达式。

在源语的实际运用中,这些话语标记词往往扮演十分重要的角色。它们可以维系一篇讲话的逻辑,或是赋予一篇讲话更丰富的生命。经验不足的译员往往认为这些词语与讯息的内容没有直接的关系,所以容易忽视它们,结果导致口译传达缺乏连贯性,话语支离破碎。

具体而言,这些话语标记词体现了语篇内部的衔接和连贯,暗示了说话人对话语内容的态度和情感,从而辅助说话人构建语篇。可将其分为若干类,如:表示时间顺序的 in the first place, next, previously, secondly, after that 等;表示强调的 the point you must remember is, I'd like to emphasize, as we all know, as you know 等;表示举例的 for example, for instance 等;表示因果的 so, therefore, thus 等;表示递进的 moreover, furthermore, what's more 等。

在经验丰富的译员眼里,这些话语标记词就像引路标识,指引译员顺利到达目的地。在自然讲话或采访中,这些词语并不凸显,这就需要译员有意识地培养自己对这些语篇标记词的敏感度。

如 as we all know, as you know, as is known to all,这些标记词虽无法像关键词一样构成话语的基本内容,对话语的内容也无法产生实质的影响,但是它们却是话语中的评论性标记,说明即将出现的话语内容是说话者和听话者都十分熟悉的。请看下例:

The stock response in times like these, as we all know, would be for non-statutory services to be the first to suffer, the first for cuts and in line for savings. I'm sure that is a real pressure colleagues are facing at the moment.

as we all know 所暗示的就是大家都知晓的信息。选择这一标记词即强调或突出即将说出的内容,译员听到这个词,就对下文要听到的信息有所准备。

再以美国总统奥巴马在国会两院联席会议上演讲的一句话为例:

I know that for many Americans watching right now, the state of our economy is a concern that rises above all others. And rightly so.

and 一般被认为是上下句的连接词,在语法上使得前后句构成并列关系,但在此处,作为话语标记词,它则不仅仅是单纯地表连贯和衔接的连接词。and 一词一方面发挥了并列连词的语法作用,同时又肯定了前文信息,即前面说的 I know that for many Americans watching right now, the state of our economy is a concern that rises above all others.(我知道,对于现在正在看电视的许多美国人而言,没有什么比我们的经济状况更令人担心的了。)这一事实的肯定才引出了后文 And rightly so.(事实正是如此。)译员在听到 and 一词后,就会对后文的逻辑关系有所准备,即会预期说话人对前述内容表示肯定。

优秀的口译员对语言的话语标记有充分的敏感和认知,能据此控制、处理并很好地消化,进而有条不紊地整合、分析源语说话人的信息。

(3) 掌握话语预测能力

口译听力理解中的预测能力是指译员在听完讲话人的全部话语之前，能够依托一定的交际场合和背景，根据相关语法知识和主题知识判断、推理说话人之后要表达的含义。预测并不是纯粹的主观臆断，而是一种有理有据的逻辑推理。正确应用预测策略可以大大降低译员所要承受的听力负担。该策略主要可以用于两方面，即语言系预测和非语言系预测。前者针对语义而言，后者针对源语讲话人要表达的思想和信息而论。

语言系预测就是译员根据语言规律与规则，如短语搭配、句子之间表示逻辑关系的连接词等来预测说话人下一步所要表达的意思。比如在英语里，介词后面接代词或名词的概率很高，而接另一个介词或动词的概率则很低。这种规律可以帮助人们对在特定语境中的词义进行预测。下面将从短语搭配和连接词两个方面稍加阐述。

短语搭配因为其规律性为口译，尤其是同声传译提供了难得的听力预测机会。如听到 difference/relations 等词时，译员很自然会预测到其后会出现限定成分，如 between...and...。这时，译员应注意等待，等到后面信息出现再开始口译，不然句子容易破碎。再如当听到 importance, significance, necessity, confidence 等表示属性的抽象名词时，译员应预测到后面必然会出现限定成分（通常是介宾短语）来完成表述的实际意义。例如：

Both governments have expressed their mutual confidence in the importance of diplomatic and friendly relations and wished to work together in helping to consolidate international peace and security as well as peaceful co-existence.

显然，其中的 confidence 与 importance 是抽象名词，不能表现"信心"与"重要性"的实质性信息，难以达到交际目的。因此，译员应该预测到其后通常会紧跟限定成分，等待介宾结构的出现，以充分的心理期待来完成之后的听力过程。

前文论述到话语标记词的时候，已略微提到这些功能词汇可以帮助译员较为准确地进行句子之间以及段落之间的预测。如在听到下面这句话时：

He was found innocent in the court, that is to say, the court could not convict him legally.

that is to say 这个词对话题内容不构成任何影响，可是却传达了明确的信息给译员，即前文所述内容将在后文得到重复，借这个标记词的功能，译者能良好地预测出之后话语内容将进一步确认前文。

再如当听到 however 时，译员可预测到其后的信息与先前信息必然相反，因此只要抓住了先前信息，借助于 however 生成的预测，译员可以相对从容地边听边转为译入语。例如：

During his graduation speech at the University of Notre Dame, President Barack Obama pushed embryonic stem cell research for juvenile diabetes. However, Obama ignored how research scientists have already had tremendous success using adult stem cells.

在这句话中，前后两句话间是一种转向的关系，这样的话语标记词也让译员有充分的准备去接受后文，从而更好地从整体上把握讲话人拟传递的信息。

预测策略应用的另一方面是非语言系预测。它主要指译员对源语讲话人"在某一特定语境或情况下可能做出的各种反应或说话方式"的预测，即对讲话人要表达的思想的预测，而非准确无误地预测讲话人的具体措辞。非语言系预测既包括译员的译前预测,又包括在口译过程中所做的预测。

口译活动是一种目的性很强的现场言语交际活动,其主题往往事先给定,会议内容、会议话语都与主题紧密联系,这意味着在当时语境中许多因素是特定的,这些因素可以有效地调动储存在译员大脑里与主题相关的知识,缩小了大脑对信息记忆的时间,激活相关信息储备与知识图式,为译员提供了大量可帮助其预测下文的信息。

例如,2009年5月21日英国驻华大使欧·威廉爵士(Sir William Geoffrey Ehrman)访问中国政法大学,并对在座师生发表了讲话。发言人的身份为驻华大使,发言的对象群体是中国政法大学的学生,在这一特定的语境中,译员在大使讲话前就可预测到以下内容:①法律在英国的重要性;②中英双边关系;③法律对中英双边关系的意义;④对中国学生的美好祝愿与期望。

从这个例子可以看出,非语言系预测要求译员具有认知和推理能力,会议的背景信息,如讲话人的身份、听众身份以及主题可以作为译员预测的依据,从而对整个演讲进行把握。

再以亚太区葡萄酒及烈酒展览会的开幕致辞为例。香港作为主办方,在开幕发言中,必然会说到香港作为主办方十分荣幸、十分感谢各位的列席,非常欢迎各位的光临等等。该致辞开篇如下:

It is my great pleasure to join you for the opening ceremony of this year's Vinexpo.

A warm welcome to you all, specially to those who have traveled from overseas to be here.

I am delighted that Hong Kong has been chosen to host the Vinexpo Asis-Pacific for a third time. This year's event promises to be the bigger and best so far.

Your presence is a huge vote of confidence for Hong Kong in hosting this important event, and strengthens our commitment to become a centre for trading in wine in Asia.

而在其后的发言中,该发言人谈到了亚太区域的酒业现状,整体经济形势,对该行业的预期与期望,对各同行合作的展望等等。各项内容的陈述都应与译员的事先预期相差无几,这样的话,译员在整体听解的过程中就能做到从容不迫。

不善于用预测技能的译员很难在口译中做好听力准备,因为在口译过程中要是等到全部信息接收以后再进行翻译,译员的压力就会非常大,尤其在同声传译中,即使口译能够进行下去,也是断断续续,听众很难接收到完整的信息。

事实上,发生在口译听力过程中的预测是语言系预测和非语言系预测综合作用的结果。译员可以利用语言知识、语境惯例、交际场合和交际对象的背景知识来预测发言人在以下的发言过程中将要表达的信息,从而为译员的顺利准确表达做铺垫。

(4) 借助冗余现象

冗余是所有言语中存在的普遍现象。在口译的源语发言中没有冗余是不可能的,即便是构思严谨、出口成章的人也不可避免地要说一些多余的话,尤其是语义上的冗余,即意思的重复。说话人把同一个意思用不同的方式说一遍以上,有时甚至多遍,个中原因是多方面的,比如讲话人为使听者注意某些要点,有意识或无意识地重复。这一现象为译员在听解过程中提供了不可多得的宝贵机会。请看下面一段话:

第六单元 外交政策(Foreign Policy)

Liverpool's year as European Capital of Culture has changed the terms of the debate — bringing in an £800 million boost to the regional economy. 3.5 million visitors put £176 million into the visitor economy.

Culture did more than bring visitors to Liverpool though. *It transformed the way that the rest of the country thinks about Liverpool and how the people of Liverpool feel about the city and themselves.*

One of the myths that was demolished was that world-class cultural events could not be successfully staged outside London, that the big names and the visitors would simply not travel to places like Liverpool.

Liverpool shows us what is possible, and a fitting legacy, I think, would be to repeat that success on a regular basis through a program of British Cities of Culture up and running as soon as possible.

I'm delighted with the positive reaction to the proposal the Phil Redmond made and the interest there was from cities around the country to meet with *Phil to learn from Liverpool's success and express interest in the ideal.*

I believe we can do much much more to unlock the creative potential of towns and cities up and down the country and expect the City of Culture to shrine spotlight on each individual city that wins the award. *But the experience from Liverpool is that benefits flow out across the whole region and on to the national cultural landscape.*

斜体部分用不同的文字讲述了同样一个思想,那就是利物浦的欧洲文化之都活动取得了巨大的成就。说话人积极颂扬了利物浦在文化方面取得的成绩,而这种冗余不断地加深了听众的印象,也给了译员充分的空间,游刃有余地利用自己的语言知识去理解与翻译。

事实上,冗余是语言的血肉所在,没有冗余的发言,言语中只充满了精而又精的所谓要旨词,语言就会成为干瘪的概念骨架,无生动性可言,而且必然会导致意义不明或残缺。有了冗余部分,译员也多了一些自由度,听解的过程会更为从容,译出的语言也会显得通顺流畅。

以上讲述了听力理解过程中四个重要的技巧。事实上,口译中的听力理解过程是个不断分析综合的过程。针对讲话语段,译员要不断进行语音听辨、语义和篇章分析、意义推断和综合、存储记忆、预测下文等。译员的语音听辨不是断开的、毫无关系的单独音节或词汇的简单拼凑,而是连续性的言语链,要对话语意义有整体明确的把握。与此同时,译员还要进行话语的语义和篇章分析。源语话语主体和语境、译员的个人经历和社会经验等理解因素对语义和语篇意义起某种智力加工、整合作用,先前的语言和语言外知识是理解整个篇章的基础,随着语流不断输入,译者不断获得信息,形成整体语篇意义。简而言之,口译听力理解的对象是讲话语段的整体语篇意义,而不是流连或困惑于某个单词或句子的听力理解。

总之,语篇中的一个个句子、一个个段落、一个个意思并不是孤立的而是由某种特定的逻辑关系连接起来的有机整体。这就要求译员要有很好的语言功底和很好的语感,在听力理解的过程中把握句子的结构框架、上下文的逻辑关系以及发言的大体脉络和走向,从而很好地进行信息整合、分析、判断和推理,并将发言人的话语流利地翻译出来。

重 译 法

这一节要讲的重译法,有的著家亦称之为重复法等。repetition 既然在翻译中被称为一种技巧,自然就不是一般所说的不必要的重复,而是一种必不可少的方法。可以这样确定它的定义:在翻译中有时为了忠实于原文,不得不重复某些词语,否则就不能忠实表达原文的意思。这样反复使用某些词语的翻译的方法就叫重译法。

一般说来,重译法有如下三个作用:一是为了明确;二是为了强调;三是为了生动。

一、为了使疑问明确或强调重要内容,就要设法消除任何可能出现的误解。要消除这些误解,在某些文体中,要少用代词而重复使用名词。譬如下面的译例,在译文中要重复使用用"日本"等名词而尽量避免使用代词"它"。因为这段文字引自一涉及中国、前苏联和日本三国关系的条约,引文中的 both contracting parties 指 China 和 the Soviet Union,所谈指示关系重大,如果用"它"太多,那么"它"代表 China 和 Japan 呢,还是代表 the Soviet Union 呢?不同的人会有不同的理解,因此翻译下句中代词 it 时应重译其前面的名词。

"Both contracting parties undertake jointly to adopt all necessary measures as their disposal for the purpose of preventing the resumption of aggression and violation of peace on the part of Japan or any other state which would collaborate with Japan directly or indirectly in act of aggression. In the event of one of the contracting parties being attacked by Japan or any other state allied with it and thus being involved in a state of war, the other contracting party will immediately render military and other assistance with all means at its disposal."

"缔约国双方保证共同尽力采取一切必要的措施,以期制止日本或其他直接或间接在侵略行为上与日本勾结的任何国家之重新侵略与破坏和平。一旦缔约国的一方受到日本或与日本同盟的任何国家之侵袭,而处于战争状态时,缔约国的另一方应立即尽其全力给予军事及其他援助。"

二、为了明确,有时需要重复宾语。在英语中,一句话里两个动词共用一个宾语,宾语只在第二个动词之后出现一次。而在汉语中,这样的宾语要在每个动词后分别出现,定语后的名词亦如此。如:

1. We have to analyze and solve problems.

我们要分析问题,解决问题。

2. Let us revise our safety and sanitary regulations.

我们来修改安全规则和卫生规则吧。

3. Aristocratic and democratic tendencies in a nation often show themselves in its speech.

民族的贵族倾向和民主倾向常在其言语中表现出来。

三、英语常用省略,但为了明确,也为了强调某些内容,在汉语中常常要将省去的部分重译出来。如:

1. I have fulfilled my assigned work ahead of schedule, so has he.

我已提前完成了交给我的工作,他也提前完成了交给他的工作。

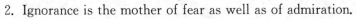

2. Ignorance is the mother of fear as well as of admiration.

无知是恐惧的根源,也是敬佩的根源。

3. The use of atomic weapons is a clear violation of international law—in particular of the Geneva Convention.

使用原子武器显然违反国际法,特别违反日内瓦公约。

4. At that time many people could not read or write.

当时,许多人不会读书,也不会写字。

5. They forget the democratic centralism which subordinates the minority to the majority, the lower level to the higher level, the part to the whole, and the whole Party to the Central Committee.

他们忘记了少数服从多数,下级服从上级,局部服从全体,全党服从中央的民主集中制。

6. But we still have defects, and very big ones.

但是我们还是有缺点的,而且还有很大的缺点。

四、被定语从句修饰的名词有时在英译汉中要重复。

We have advocated the principle of peaceful coexistence, which is now growing more and more popular among the nations of Asia and Africa.

我们提倡和平共处的原则,这个原则目前在亚非各国越来越得人心了。

五、在汉译英时,往往还有下面两种情况:一是汉语重复,英译时也重复;二是根据两种语言各自的习惯用法,以不同的表达方式进行重复,这种重复通常是为了传达原文的生动性。

1. 这种人闹什么东西呢？闹名誉,闹地位,闹出风头。

What are they after? They are after name, after position, and they want to cut smart figures.

2. 大(家庭)有大(家庭)的难处。

A large family has its difficulties.

3. 车辚辚,马萧萧,行人弓箭各在腰。

Chariots rumble and roll; horses whinny and neigh.

Footmen at their girdle bows and arrows display.

4. 帝城春欲暮,喧喧车马度。

In the Royal city spring is almost over;

Tinkle, tinkle — the coaches and horsemen pass.

5. 白杨何萧萧,松柏夹广路。

The white aspens, how they murmur, murmur;

Pines and cypresses flank the broad paths.

6. 天苍苍,野茫茫,风吹草地见牛羊。

The sky is blue, blue;

And the steppe wide, wide;

Over grass that the wind has battered low;

Sheep and oxen roam.

7. 寻寻觅觅,冷冷清清,凄凄惨惨戚戚。乍暖还寒时候,最难将息。

Seek, seek; search, search;

Cold, cold; bare, bare;

Grief, grief; cruel, cruel; grief, grief.

Now warm, then like the autumn cold again,

How hard to calm the heart.

8. 忙忙九派流中国,沉沉一线穿南北。

Wide, wide flow the nine streams through the land,

Dark, dark threads the line from south to north.

9. 行行重行行,与君生别离。

On and on, always on and on,

Away from you, parted by a life-parting.

10. 这几件旧衣服和些旧家什,当的当了,卖的卖了。

Our old clothes and few sticks of furniture have been pawned or sold.

11. 胜也罢,败也罢,我们要打到底。

Victory or defeat, we shall fight to the bitter end.

12. 我们死也好,活也好,一定要忠于祖国。

Live or die, we shall be loyal to our motherland.

13. 悲莫悲兮生别离,乐莫乐兮新相知。

Nothing is sadder than to part for ever;

Nothing is happier than to contract a new acquaintance.

14. 一个个面面相觑,都软倒了。

Each stared speechless at the other, and all fell feebly to the ground.

15. 桃花谢了春红,太匆匆。

The flowering trees have lost their spring hues, all too soon!

16. 谁知盘中餐,粒粒皆辛苦。

Who knows that every grain in the bowl,

Is the fruit of so much pain and toil?

17. 夜夜长留半被,待君魂梦归来。

Night after night I ever keep for him the half of my quilt,

in expectation of his spirit coming back to me in a dream.

18. 青青河边草,郁郁园中柳。

Green grows the grass upon the bank,

The willow shoots are long and lank.

19. 梯田渐渐稀,村舍遥遥对。

Ridges of fields grow few and far between,

While far away some cottages are seen.

20. 舟遥遥以轻扬,风飘飘而吹衣。

Lightly floats and drifts the boat, and gently flows and flaps my gown.
21. 春眠不觉晓,处处闻啼鸟。
In spring we sleep a sleep that knows no dawn,
And everywhere the songs of birds resound.
22. 一个蚊子哼哼哼,两个苍蝇嗡嗡嗡。
A mosquito hums and hums,
Two flies drone and drone.

以上22个译例之原文绝大多数源自中国古典文学,因多为名句,故每一句原文均可找出多种译法,只供讨论翻译技巧时参考。

与汉译英的情况相似,英译汉时有时也要根据各自的习惯用法进行重复。

如:

1. Gentlemen may cry, peace, peace — but there is no peace.
先生们尽管可以高呼和平,和平——但是依然没有和平。
2. If you didn't succeed at first, try, try, try again.
起初不成功,可以一试再试。
3. What we want, first and foremost, is to learn, to learn and to learn.
我们首先需要的是学习、学习、再学习。
4. Scrooge went to bed again, and thought and thought and thought it over and over.
司克罗琪又上床去,左思右想,想个不休。
5. Nels had it all written out neatly.
纳尔斯把它写得清清楚楚。

拓展阅读

选文A

女士们、先生们:

我愿借此机会来回顾一下中美关系,并对中美关系的未来作出展望。中美关系可以说是"历经风雨,不断向前发展"。

中美建交前,两国关系曾经有一段众所周知的不幸历史。如今,中美共同致力于发展中美建设性合作关系,两国领导人通过访问、国际场合会晤、热线电话、书信等方式就双边关系和共同关心的重大国际问题和地区问题保持着密切联系和沟通。

建交之初,中美之间没有任何政府间合作协议。如今,两国政府合作协议已超过30个。双边贸易额在1978年只有9.9亿美元,相互投资为零。去年双边贸易额达1 696.2亿美元。美在华实际投资累计已达500亿美元,一些中国企业也开始落户美国。

中美曾经几近隔绝。如今,双方人员往来每年超过百万人次,平均每天有3 000多人飞越太平洋。中美航班现在每周54次,到2010年将达到249次。

26年来,世界形势发生了深刻变化。人类走出了冷战对抗的阴霾,求和平、谋发展、促合作成为不可阻挡的历史潮流。世界各国利益交织,相互依存加深。同时,世界上仍存在着不少不稳定、不安全因素,恐怖主义、大规模杀伤性武器扩散、毒品走私、疾病传播等全球性问题日益突出。

在此背景下,中美之间的共同利益不但没有减少,反而增加了;中美之间的合作基础不但没有削弱,反而加强了;中美之间的重要性不但没有降低,反而更加突出了。

去年11月,胡锦涛主席和布什总统在智利圣地亚哥会晤,一致同意进一步推进中美建设性合作关系,加强两国在双边领域和重要国际和地区问题上的对话与合作。这为新世纪中美关系的发展指明了方向。今年,胡锦涛主席和布什总统将实现互访。两国元首成功互访,将为中美建设性合作关系的进一步发展注入新的动力。

目前,中美双方在经贸、反恐、执法、防扩散等领域以及朝鲜半岛核问题、联合国改革等问题上的协调与合作富有成效。过几天,中美还将在北京举行首次战略对话。我坚信,中美两国加强在国际和地区事务中的协调和合作,既符合双方的根本利益,也是世界和平与发展的需要。

中美关系在面临新的发展机遇的同时,也面临一些挑战。我们应该登高望远,看清中美关系的主流和时代的潮流,把握大局,着眼未来,扩大共识,发展合作。

26年前,中美领导人以非凡的勇气,实现了两国关系正常化。26年后的今天,我们需要同样的勇气,努力推进新世纪中美建设性合作关系,更好地造福于两国人民和世界人民。

作为世界上最大的发展中国家和最大的发达国家,中美对世界和平与安全负有重要责任。

反恐斗争直接关乎中美和世界人民的安全。中美已经在外交、执法、情报、金融等领域进行了卓有成效的反恐合作。中方愿本着双向互利原则继续与美方加强反恐合作。

中国政府坚决反对大规模杀伤性武器扩散、不断完善出口管制法规体系,加强执法,并积极参与国际防扩散合作。我们愿在相互尊重和信任的基础上与美方加强防扩散合作。

中方支持联合国改革,认为改革是全方位和多领域的,重点推动解决发展问题、落实千年发展目标。改革方案应由全体会员国民主协商,达成广泛一致。同时,各项改革措施也必须有利于维护联合国的权威和效率。我们愿与包括美方在内的有关各方加强磋商,引导改革朝着正确的方向发展。

中美同处亚太地区,维护地区和平、促进共同繁荣符合我们的共同利益。双方在朝鲜半岛核问题上和亚太经合组织、东盟地区论坛等多边机制内进行了良好的合作。在半岛核问题上,中方一向主张坚持实现半岛无核化,坚持对话和平解决的大方向,坚持维护半岛和平稳定。

台湾问题事关中国的主权和领土完整,是中国的核心利益。妥善处理台湾问题,是中美关系稳定发展的关键。

"和平统一、一国两制"是我们的基本方针。今年3月,胡锦涛主席就新形势下发展两岸关系提出了四点建议。我们愿以最大诚意,尽最大努力争取和平统一的前景,但绝不容忍"台湾独立",绝不允许任何人以任何方式将台湾从中国分割出去。

反对和遏制"台独"、维护台海和平稳定符合了中美两国的共同利益。我们赞赏布什总统和美国政府多次重申坚持一个中国政策。遵守中美三个联合公报、反对"台独"。希望美方切实履行承诺,与中方一道反对和遏制"台独",维护台海和平稳定和中美共同利益。

女士们、先生们,让我们立足当前,放眼未来,从战略的高度审视和处理中美关系,认真落实两国领导人达成的共识,坚持中美三个联合公报的指导原则,牢牢把握两国共同利益,加强对话、交流与合作,努力消除误解,妥善处理分歧,推动中美建设性合作关系不断向前发展。

谢谢大家。

译 文

Ladies and Gentlemen:

I'd like to take this opportunity to review Sino-U. S. relations and outline their future development. Sino-U. S. relations, so to speak, have moved ahead steadily amid twists and turns.

As you all know, relations between China and the United States had had a rather unfortunate experience before the establishment of diplomatic ties. Today the two countries work closely together to promote a constructive and cooperative relationship. Through exchange of visits, meetings at international gatherings, hotline conversations and correspondence, the leaders of our two countries have stayed in touch with each other on bilateral relations and major international or regional issues of mutual interest.

In the early days of Sino-U. S. diplomatic relations, there was no intergovernmental cooperation agreement to speak of. Today the number of such agreement has exceeded 30. Bilateral trade in 1978 was only $990 million and mutual investment, zero. Last year, Sino-U. S. trade reached $169.62 billion. U. S. government in China has added up to $50 billion in paid-in value and some Chinese enterprises are starting U. S.-based businesses.

China and the United States, once almost completely cut off from each other are seeing more than one million of their people traveling every year with over 3,000 people flying over the Pacific every day. Right now the two countries are served by 54 flights a week and the number is expected to reach 249 by 2010.

Over the 26 years, the world has undergone profound changes. Humanity has moved out of the dark shadow cast by the Cold War standoff, with peace, development and cooperation emerging as the irresistible trend of history. With their interests interwearing, countries have become increasingly interdependent. In the meantime, many factors of instability and insecurity remain, such as terrorism, proliferation of weapons of mass destruction, drug trafficking, spread of deadly diseases and other outstanding global problems.

Against such a backdrop, Sino-U. S. common interest has increased rather than decreased; the foundation of their cooperation has solidified rather than weakened; and the importance of the relationship has become more pronounced rather than curtailed.

During their summit meeting in Santiago, Chile last November, President Hu Jintao and President Bush agreed to further the constructive and cooperative relations between the two countries and step up their dialogue and cooperation in bilateral ties and on important international and regional issues. What they did amounted to charting a direction for Sino-U. S. relations in the 21st century. This year, the two presidents will exchange visits. The successful exchange of visits between the two heads of state, I am sure, will inject fresh impetus for further headway in our constructive and cooperative relationship.

The two countries have now carried out fruitful coordination and cooperation in the economy, trade, counter-terrorism, law enforcement, non-proliferation, as well as on the Korean nuclear issue and the UN reform. In a few days, China and the United States will hold their first strategic dialogue in Beijing. I firmly believe that stronger Sino-U. S. coordination and cooperation in regional and international affairs will serve not only the fundamental interests of the two countries, but also world peace and development.

While enjoying the new opportunities for development, Sino-U. S. relations are also faced certain challenges. We should stand high to get a commanding view, recognize the mainstream of the relationship and the trend of the times, keep the overall picture and the future in mind and work to broaden consensus and promote cooperation.

Twenty-six years ago, our leaders displayed extraordinary courage and brought the normalization process to fruition. Today, we need the same courage to push our constructive and cooperative relations in the new century in the interest of our two peoples and the people all over the world.

As the world's largest developing country and the largest developed country, China and the United States shoulder an important responsibility for peace and security in the world.

The counter-terrorism war has a direct bearing on the security of the Chinese, Americans and the people around the world. China and the United States have conducted fruitful counter-terrorism cooperation in the past in such fields as diplomacy, law enforcement, intelligence and financing. China is ready to continue such cooperation with the United State on the basis of reciprocity and mutual benefit.

Firmly opposed to proliferation of weapons of mass destruction, the Chinese Government has worked continuously to improve its legal regime of export control, beef up law enforcement and participate in international non-proliferation cooperation. We are ready to enhance such cooperation with the United States on the basis of mutual respect and mutual trust.

China supports UN-reform and believes that such reform should be all-dimensional and wide-ranging, with emphasis on the settlement of the development issue and implementation of the Millennium Development Goals. All reform programs should be discussed democratically by the entire membership with a view to reaching broadly-based consensus. All reform measures must also help strengthen the authority and efficiency of the UN. We are ready to set up consultation with the relevant parties including the United States to help move UN reform in the right direction.

Both located in the Asia-Pacific, China and the United States share a common stake in maintaining peace and common prosperity in the region. The two sides have enjoyed sound cooperation on the Korean nuclear issue and worked productively within such multilateral mechanisms as APEC and ASEAN Regional Forum. With respect to the Korean nuclear issue, China consistently stands for a nuclear-weapon-free Korea Peninsula, the direction of a peaceful solution through dialogue and maintenance of peace and stability on the peninsula.

The Taiwan issue is China's core interest as it bears on the country's sovereignty and territorial integrity. An appropriate handling of the question, therefore, is the key to stable and growing relationship between China and the United States.

"Peaceful reunification" and "one country, two systems" remains our basic policy. In March, President Hu Jintao made a four-point proposal on the development of cross-strait relations under the new situation. We are ready to do our utmost with maximum sincerity to secure the prospect of a peaceful reunification. But we will never put up with "Taiwan independence", nor will we allow any one to make Taiwan secede from China by any means.

Opposing and checking "Taiwan independence" and maintaining peace and stability in the strait serve the common interests of both China and the United States. We appreciate repeated statements by President Bush and the U.S. Government that the United States will commit to the one China policy, abide by the three joint communiqués and oppose "Taiwan independence" so as to preserve our common interests of seeing a peaceful and stable Taiwan Strait.

Ladies and Gentlemen, let us get grounded on the current situation and take a long view with a strategic vision when looking at and handling Sino-U.S. relations. Let us earnestly act on the agreement reached by our state leaders, keep faith with the principles of the three joint communiqués, focus ourselves on our common interests with strengthened dialogue, exchanges and cooperation, remove misunderstanding and properly address the differences, thus moving forward the constructive and cooperative relations between the two countries.

Thank you.

选文B

British trade with China has doubled over the last five years alone. This growth is faster than any other G8 countrry. Britain is the largest European investor here. Culturally our links are also strong. More students from China study in the UK than from any other country, and partnerships between our schools are growing. We have just launched the UK-China Partners in Science Campaign to strengthen our scientific links.

The partnership between our two countries is important not just for what it brings both of us, but also for the common work which Britain and China can do together in the world. For example, there is a wider message in the global response to the tragedy of tsunami. It is that people around the world feel that the interdependence of nations, so long talked about by statesmen, is today more than ever a concrete reality.

This reality is also a challenge to which governments must respond. The first part of the challenge is economic — finding the determination not to seek shelter from the global market, but to exploit the opportunities that it offers. In Britain, we have been determined to meet that challenge. And thanks to our open and flexible approach, and the investment that we are making in skills and innovations, Britain is now Europe's most successful large economy, and experiencing our longest unbroken period of economic growth on record.

The challenge of responding to global competition is also one that China has embraced. And the results are simply staggering. The world has never before seen growth on the scale that China is producing. It is turning this country into a central player in the global economy and lifting millions of people out of poverty.

This is the rise of China that many predicted. But as it is happening, I think one fundamental thing has changed. Where some years ago the world may have worried about the rise of China, now it welcomes this as truly an opportunity for us all.

The second challenge posed by globalization is one for our foreign policy — the need to act globally to promote safety and prosperity at home and in the world. As China's prosperity has grown, so too has its stake in global security and global prosperity. It is a crucial partner in the fight against proliferation and in international efforts to combat terrorism. China's contribution to UN peacekeeping missions is growing, and I greatly welcome President Hu's recent commitment to increase that contribution further.

Meanwhile China is embracing more fully globally-accepted rules and standards. I particularly applaud China's ratification of the International Covenant on Economic, Social and Cultural Rights.

The partnership between our two nations is strengthening, but there is more that we can and should do together to strengthen further our growing global partnership. I would like today to suggest three areas on which we should focus that effort. They are in pursuing reform of the United Nations, working for a better future for Africa, and tackling climate change.

As permanent members of the UN Security Council, both Britain and China base our foreign policy on the maintenance of a strong and effective international system. But we both too think that the United Nations, designed 60 years ago, needs reform to meet the challenges of the new century. Many of those challenges are very different from those faced by those who drafted the Chapter in 1945— from terrorism to AIDS, from the environment to weapons' proliferation.

But we both recognize that reform certainly does not mean tearing up the UN Chapter and starting again; neither we nor other nation favors such an approach. The Millennium

Review Summit should set the direction for the way ahead on United Nations reform. In the preparation for that summit, I hope that Britain and China can continue and indeed enhance our productive dialogue on this issue of such importance to us both.

The second issue on which I suggest we can deepen our cooperation is Africa. Britain has made Africa a priority of our work as Presidency of the G8 in the coming year. And I Would like China and Britain to work together on this as close partners.

Both our countries already have strong links with the continent. We share our experiences of work on poverty reduction, and have opened a dialogue on our cooperation in Africa. Africa will require an even greater investment of aid than it receives today if it is to meet its goals for development. But it is also crucial that we set the conditions that allow the people of Africa to build a better future for themselves.

Alongside its own position China now presides over the G20 group of developing nations. And Britain has assumed the Presidency of the G8 and will, from July, take on that of European Union. That makes us both crucial players in the issues of the world trade negotiations.

The third issue that I want to highlight is tackling the threat from climate change.

I want to deal first with two misconceptions. The first is that climate change is a threat that matters mainly to environmentalists. In fact it matters to everyone. Climate change is a potential source of conflict over scarce natural resources, and of the displacement of millions of people from their land, with all the instability that would provoke. Climate change is an economic threat too: Swiss Re, the world's second-largest reinsurer, has estimated the insurance costs at an extra $265 billion per year by 2010.

The second misconception about climate change is that there is a necessary trade-off between limiting global warming on the one hand, and promoting economic growth on the other. In fact, as those figures from Swiss Re demonstrate, inaction on climate will have an enormous cost of its own. And, as we mitigate the efforts of climate change, we also have to work to ensure access to the secure and affordable energy supplies that our economies need, both from traditional and from more innovative sources. There are especially exciting opportunities for that here in China. If I may say so, China has a great opportunity to lead the way in building clean-energy technology, with all the environmental and economic benefits that it offers.

Britain and China have shared commitment to meeting the challenges posed by globalization — and to exploiting its opportunities. Of course we won't always agree. But there is an enormous amount of work for us to do together. I am confident that there will be markedly a growing and strengthened global partnership between Britain and China in the process of globalization.

译 文

英中两国贸易仅在过去五年就翻了一番,八国集团成员中没有谁能超过。英国是目前欧洲在华的最大投资国。我们两国在文化方面的联系也十分密切。在英国的中国留学生超过了世界上其他任何一个国家,两国教育机构的合作也在加强。前不久我们推出了"英中科技伙伴计划"以推动彼此间的科技联系。

英中伙伴关系的重要性并不仅仅局限于它能够给我们两国带来什么好处,其意义还在于我们两国可以就一些共同问题开展国际合作。例如,全球对于前不久发生的海啸灾难所作出的反应传达了一种超出事件本身的信息,这就使世界各地的人们深切地感受到,多少年来一直停留在政治家口中的国家间依赖性问题,比以往任何时候都更为清楚地摆在我们的面前。

这种现实也是各国政府必须回应的挑战。挑战首先表现在经济方面,即痛下决心利用全球市场提供的机会,而不是在全球市场中寻求保护。英国已下定决心迎接挑战。我国得益于开放和灵活的政策,得益于对技术和开发的投入,已成为欧洲最成功的大型经济体,并正经历着有史以来持续时间最长的不间断的经济增长。

中国也积极应对全球竞争的挑战,其结果是翻天覆地的变化。中国经济增长规模之大,为人类有史以来前所未有。积极参与全球竞争使中国在世界经济舞台上扮演了核心人物的角色,数以百计的中国人也因此脱贫。

这就是很多人曾经预言过的中国崛起。但是随着中国的日益崛起,我认为人们的看法也随之发生了根本的转变。几年前,其他国家还可能为中国的崛起而忧心忡忡,但时至今日,世界各国欢迎中国的崛起,他们认为这种崛起为大家带来真正的机会。

全球化带来的第二种挑战是我们的外交政策——它要求我们以全球性的行动来促进本国和世界的安全与繁荣。随着中国的日益繁荣,它在全球安全和繁荣中的作用也在加大。中国在防止核扩散以及国际反恐行动中起着举足轻重的作用。中国对联合国维和行动的参与度也在加大,我们非常欢迎胡锦涛主席最近关于中国将进一步加大参与的承诺。

同时,中国正在更全面地接受国际通行规则和标准。我尤其欢迎中国通过了《经济、社会和文化权利国际公约》。

虽然我们两国的伙伴关系在不断加强,但是对于促进我们在国际上合作,英中双方可以而且应该做出更多的努力。今天,我想提出三个我认为双方应当加强合作的领域,它们是促进联合国改革的问题、造福于非洲的问题,以及对付气候变化的问题。

作为联合国安理会的常任理事国,英中两国的外交政策都着眼于维护一个强大而有效的国际体系。我们双方都认为60年前规划建立起来的联合国必须进行改革以适应新世纪的挑战。这些挑战,无论是恐怖主义还是艾滋病,无论是环境保护还是武器扩散,都与联合国宪章制定时的1945年所面临的问题有很大的不同。

但是我们双方都认为,联合国改革并不意味着要抛弃联合国宪章而改弦更张。无论是我们两国还是其他什么国家都不赞同这样做。将要举行的千年评议峰会应该为联合国改革预先确定发展方向。在峰会的准备过程中,我希望英中双方能继续就此重要议题加强建设性对话。

第二个领域是非洲问题。作为8国集团明年的主席国,英国已经将非洲列为工作的重中之重。我希望中国和英国在这个问题上密切合作。

英中两国都和非洲大陆有着紧密的联系。我们在脱贫方面有共同经历,我们也在非洲合作问题上展开了对话。非洲若要实现其发展目标,应该得到比今天获得的大得多的援助。但同样不可缺的是,我们应该创造条件帮助非洲人民,使他们为自己创造一个更美好的未来。

中国除了自身的地位之外,现在还是发展中国家20国集团的主席国。英国也已接任8国集团主席国身份,并将从7月开始担任欧盟主席国。这些变化使我们两国在推动世界贸易谈判成功中起着关键作用。

我想强调的第三个合作领域是应对气候变化的威胁。

我首先要澄清两种错误观念。第一种观点认为,气候变化主要是环保主义者关心的问题。其实,气候变化问题与每个人都有关系。气候变化是引发争夺稀缺资源冲突的潜在根源,可能造成数百万人流离失所,引发由此产生的一切不稳定因素。气候变化也是一种经济威胁:据世界第二大保险商瑞士再保险公司预计,2010年气候变化保险支出将增长2 650亿美元。

第二种错误观点是,阻止全球气候变暖与促进经济发展必然是两者去其一,不能两全其美。实际上瑞士再保险公司所提供的数据表明,置气候变化于不顾会造成巨大的经济损失。我们在努力减低气候变化造成的影响的同时,必须确保我们的经济能够获得所需的既安全又支付得起的能源供应,包括使用传统和非传统能源采集渠道。中国在这方面的前景十分看好。据我看,中国在开发清洁能源技术方面很有希望领导世界潮流,中国也将从环保和经济两方面获益。

英中两国已经共同承诺迎接全球化带来的挑战,充分挖掘全球化带来的种种机遇。当然我们也会有分歧,但是我们有大量的工作需要共同完成。我相信英中两国之间的全球伙伴关系一定会在全球化的进程中得到进一步的发展和强化。

第七单元　商务谈判
(Business Negotiation)

单元要点

本单元共分五个层次,分别是:如何做成功的销售员汉译英一篇;商务谈判英译汉一篇;英汉双语的衔接和连贯;词序调整法;拓展阅读(汉译英、英译汉各一篇)。第一、二部分提供关于如何做成功的销售员和商务谈判口译的例文及其翻译和重难点评析;第三、四部分主要是相关口译理论与技能的介绍;第五部分的拓展阅读中,提供汉、英原文和参考译文。

理论难点提示

1. 英语和汉语的衔接和连贯。
2. 词序调整法。

选文A

如何做成功的销售员

女士们、先生们:

下午好! 今天我想谈一谈在我们这一行,也就是办公家具行业,一个优秀的推销员应该具备的素质。你们知道,各国经济已经从短缺期进入剩余期。现在的商品交易量比历史上任何时候都要大。当下的市场为买方市场,消费者要求的是服务而不是强行推销。那我们怎样才能与众不同呢? 当然,答案要在我们的推销员的素质和服务质量里面去找。我们公司在世界各地有着成千上万的优秀推销员,而你们作为我们在这个地区的新鲜血液,也将成为我们该地区分部中最为重要的一员。

我们作为推销员的首要任务是什么呢? 为客户服务。你们一定注意到了我没有使用"向顾客推销"这个说法,因为我们所做的事情远远不止于"推销"。通过"咨询性销售",我们帮助顾客做一个很明智的决定。我们的手段是同顾客平等对话,在这个过程中我们了解信息,同时提供信息。咨询性的推销员不会以居高临下的方式和顾客讲话,不会去主宰他们。相反,他们通过双向的交流,去了解消费者的需求。询问顾客很有必要,不然你怎么真正了解他们的要求? 在销售一套办公用品的时候,我们销售的远远不止于一些家具。我们销售的可能是一种新的形象。顾客想让人一走进他们的办公室就能认可他们的能力。办公室必须体现出主人想要的一种成功的氛围。

咨询性销售强调的是信息的供给和协商,而不是要让顾客适应我们的思维方式。有了信息的交流,有了对客户需求的反应,我们就取得了顾客的信任。现在的客户对自己要购买的东西,要有更多的、更全面的了解才行。这就意味着,优秀的推销员必须了解自己的产品。在这间展室里面,我们只有为数不多的几种款式,你们必须对这些款式非常熟悉。而且,你们还要知道我们都有哪些选择,有什么颜色,送货要花多长时间,以及最终的花费会有多少等。你们不可能是万事通,什么都懂。那是不可能的。但是,你们每个人都要尽可能地去了解,而且身边要有产品目录和产品介绍,不知道就去查阅。

对顾客、对自己要诚实。如果你自己了解自己的产品,那你就不会不诚实。要真心诚意地去帮助顾客购买自己中意的产品。顾客满意了,我们就成功了一半。满意的顾客会对我们的公司产生信任感,是我们最好的活广告,因为他们会在朋友和同事那里给我们做宣传。

优秀的推销员在销售的过程中总是很有计划。咨询性销售是一个有计划的过程,可以清楚地分为四步:

了解顾客需求;

帮助顾客选择合适的产品;

表明这样才能满足他们的需求;

顾客购买后,要让他们确信货物会准时、完好无损地送达,并保证他们对货物完全满意。

同时,一位优秀的推销员讲求职业道德。你们应该自始至终以顾客需求为中心。职业推销员总是把顾客的利益放在首位。你们必须诚心诚意地去了解并去满足顾客的需求。不要刻意去夸大顾客购买自己产品会得到的利益。产品销售之后,回访顾客也很重要,这样可以创造友情,保证顾客真的对自己购买的产品称心如意。

最后,一位优秀的推销员明白他们有可能不经意就破坏了自己的销售形象。你们因此要为自己和自己的产品树立恰当的形象。不要穿会给人留下错误印象的衣服。讲话不应太快,也不能太慢,更不能震耳欲聋。握手时坚定有力,会表达出你的力量和诚意。微笑会让顾客敞开心扉,讲出他们对所需产品的真实想法。最后一点是,要充满自信。有自信心的销售员能提高销售量。有了自信,成功就不远了。

谢谢大家!

重难点评析

1. 你们知道,各国经济已经从短缺期进入剩余期。译为"You see, economics have moved from a period of scarcity to one of abundance.""进入"一词可直接翻译为"move from... to..."或者enter"。例如:"enter a new phase/move to a new stage"译为"进入一个新的阶段"。

2. 当下的市场为买方市场,消费者要求的是服务而不是强行推销。译为"It's a buyer's market and the buyer demands service rather than hard sell."汉语的"而不是"经常可以翻译为"rather than"或者"instead of"。例如:Rather than criticizing his wife, he tried to find out if there was something wrong. 他试图去了解到底出了什么问题,而不是去批评他的妻子。

3. 你们一定注意到了我没有使用"向顾客推销"这个说法,因为我们所做的事情远远不止于"推销"。译为"You must have noticed that I don't say sell to the customer, because we are doing far more than just selling."英语里修饰形容词比较级,常用much, far, a great deal, a lot等。例如:An agent has to do much/far more than selling a product in an

area. 代理的工作远远不止于在一个地区销售一种产品。下文"在销售一套办公用品的时候,我们销售的远远不止于一些家具"一句也可以如法炮制,翻译为:In selling new office equipment we are selling far/much more than pieces of furniture.

4. 顾客满意了,我们就成功了一半。译为"Half the battle is customer satisfaction." "half the battle",意思是"接近成功/胜利"。例如:If you can get an interview, that's half the battle. 得到了面试的机会,你就接近成功了。

5. 满意的顾客会对我们的公司产生信任感,是我们最好的活广告,因为他们会在朋友和同事那里给我们做宣传。"A satisfied customer develops company loyalty and provides our best advertising, because they tell their friends and colleagues about our business."汉语"我们最好的活广告"翻译为"our best advertising",也能表达汉语句子的思想,没有必要在"活"字上面做文章。

6. 同时,一位优秀的推销员讲求职业道德。"Good sales people are also ethical in the sales."汉语词"职业道德"的英文是"professional ethics"。例如,His professional ethics are suspect, but he is within the law. 他的职业道德令人怀疑,但他并没有违法。但是,"讲求职业道德"完全可以翻译为 be ethical。可见在翻译的过程中,我们要 translate the meaning,而不能拘泥于词和句子。这一点在口译中更为重要。

7. 你们应该自始至终以顾客需求为中心。译为"You should always concentrate on the customer's needs." "以……为中心"可以用动词"concentrate/focus(one's attention) on"。例如:We must concentrate/focus our attention on the quality rather than quantity of the products. 我们必须把重心放在产品的质量,而不是数量上。

8. 最后,一位优秀的推销员明白他们有可能不经意就破坏了自己的销售形象。译为"Finally, a good sales person is conscious of the fragile nature of their sales image."我们这样的翻译完全是根据意义翻译,而没有拘泥于文字。如果按照文字把这句翻译为"A good sales person understands what they would harm/tarnish their sales image easily."就显得更有主观性,而 the fragile nature of their sales image 则体现出销售形象的脆弱性。

9. 微笑会让顾客敞开心扉,讲出他们对所需产品的真实想法。译为"Smiling encourages the customer to tell you what they really want."汉语句子中的"敞开心扉"和后面"讲出他们对所需产品的真实想法"其实所指相同,因此在英文中翻译为"tell you what they really want"就能表达原句的含义。

译 文

How to Become Good Sales People

Ladies and Gentlemen:

Good afternoon! Today I thought we'd talk about the qualities good sales people in our line of business, office equipment, must have. You see, economies have moved from a period of scarcity to one of abundance. There are more goods being sold today than any time in history. It's a buyer's market and the buyer demands service rather than hard sell. How can you be different? The answer is, of course, in the quality of our sales people and the service we offer. We have thousands of good sales people in other parts of the world, and you, as our new sales people, will be the most important element in our branch in this region.

What is the most important thing we must do? Serve the customer. You must have noticed that I don't say sell to the customer, because we are doing far more than just selling. Through consultative selling we are helping the customer towards making an intelligent decision. We do this by establishing a balanced dialogue with the customer during which we ask for information and give it. The consultative sales person does not try to dominate the customer with high-pressure sales talk. Instead, the buyer's needs are identified through two-way communication. It is necessary to ask questions in order to find out what the buyer's needs really are. In selling new office equipment we're selling far more than pieces of furniture. We may be selling a new image to the buyer. The customer wants people who step into the office to feel confident in their ability. The office must reflect the success that the customer wants to project to the public.

Consultative selling puts the emphasis on information giving and negotiation rather than on trying to make the customer fit into our way of thinking instead. By exchanging information and responding to their needs we create customer trust. The customer today is asking for more and better information about the things they purchase. This means that good sales people must know the products that they have on sale. In this new showroom we have only a few models on display. You must know all about them. In addition, you should know what choices we can supply, what colors we can supply things in, how long it will take to deliver items and what the final cost will be. You can't know everything. That's not possible. However, each of you should know as much as you can and should have the brochures and catalogues available to look up anything you don't know.

Be honest with the customer and yourself. If you really know what you are selling, then you can be honest about it. Be sincere in your desire to help the customer towards buying what they want. Half the battle is customer satisfaction. A satisfied customer develops company loyalty and provides our best advertising, because they tell their friends and colleagues about our business.

Good sales people plan their approach to selling. Consultative selling is a planned process with four clearly defined phases:

Discovering the customer's needs;

Helping the customer select the right products;

Showing how this satisfies their requirements;

Serving the customer after the sale by ensuring that goods are delivered on time and in good condition and that the customer is happy with their purchase.

Good sales people are also ethical in their sales. You should always concentrate on the customer's needs. A professional sales person puts the customer's interests first. You must make a genuine attempt to discover the customer's needs and fulfill them. Don't exaggerate the benefits that will be gained from buying our products. After-sales follow-up is important in creating goodwill and ensuring that the customer is really satisfied with what they have bought.

Finally, a good sales person is conscious of the fragile nature of their sales image. Try to create right image for yourself and the product. Do not dress in clothes that would create the wrong impression. Avoid speaking too fast or too slowly, and never too loudly. A good firm handshake communicates your strength and honesty. Smiling encourages the customer to tell you what they really want. Last of all, be confident. A confident sales person creates sales. Be confident and you will be successful.

Thank you.

选文B

Negotiation is something that we do all the time and is not only used for business purposes. For example, we use it in our social lives perhaps for deciding a time to meet, or where to go on a rainy day. Negotiation is usually considered as a compromise to settle an argument or issue to benefit ourselves as much as possible. Communication is always the link that will be used to negotiate the issue/argument whether it is face-to-face, on the telephone or in writing. Remember, negotiation is not always between two people: it can involve several members from two parties. There are many reasons why you may want to negotiate and there are several ways to approach it. The following is a few things that you may want to consider. If your reason for negotiation is seen as "beating" the opposition, it is known as "distributive negotiation". This way, you must be prepared to use persuasive tactics and you may not end up with maximum benefit.

This is because your agreement is not being directed to a certain compromise and both parties are looking for a different outcome. Should you feel your negotiation is much more "friendly" with both parties aiming to reach agreement, it is known as "integrative negotiation". This way usually brings an outcome where you will both benefit highly. Negotiation, in a business context, can be used for selling, purchasing, staff (e.g. Contracts), borrowing (e.g. Loans) and transaction, along with anything else that you feel are applicable for your business.

Before you decide to negotiate, it is a good idea to prepare. What is it exactly that you want to negotiate? Set out your objectives (e.g. I want more time to pay off the loan). You have to take into account how it will benefit the other party by offering some sort of reward or incentive (explained later). What is involved (money, sales, time, conditions, discounts, terms, etc.)? Know your extremes: how much extra can you afford to give to settle an agreement? Although you are not aiming to give out the maximum, it is worth knowing so that you will not go out of your limits. Know what your opposition is trying to achieve by their negotiation. This is useful information that could be used to your benefit and may well be used to reach a final agreement. Consider what is valuable to your business, not the costs. You may end up losing something in the negotiation that is more valuable to your business than money. It could be reliable client or your company reputation.

It is important that you approach the other party directly to make an appointment to negotiate, should it be in person, writing or by phone (not through a phone operator, receptionist, assistant, etc.), as this will allow you to set the agenda in advance, and improve the prospects of the other party preparing sufficiently enough to make a decision on the day. Try to be fairly open about your reason for contact or they may lose interest instantly and not follow up the appointment. Save all your comments for the actual appointment — don't give away anything that will give them a chance to prepare too thoroughly: it's not war, but it is business! So, it's time to negotiate and you've prepared well. What else must you have? Two things: confidence and power. Your power will come from your ability to influence. For example, you may be the buyer (but not always a strong position), or have something that the other party wants, or you may be able to give an intention to penalize if the other party fails to meet the agreement (as is the way with construction). As briefly mentioned above, you may be able to give a reward or an incentive. For example, you may be selling kitchen knives and as part of the package you are giving a knife sharpener and a strong unit away free as an incentive.

It is always important that you keep the negotiation in your control: this can mean within your price range, your delivery time or your profit margin. If you fail to do so, you will end up on the wrong side of the agreement, and with nothing more out of the deal other than maintaining trading relationships. When negotiating, aim as high as you feel necessary in order to gain the best deal for yourself. The other party may bring this down but it is a good tactic, as it is always easier to play down than to gain. Make sure that you remain flexible throughout the negotiation in case the opposition decides to change the direction of the agreement (they may want different incentives or even change their objectives). This is where your preparation comes to good use: knowing your limits and the other party's needs. If you're a quick thinker, then you've got an advantage. You'll need to turn it around quickly if things start to against you without putting your objectives at risk. Confidence comes from knowing your business, your product, what it's worth, and being able to communicate this well to the other party: these people are almost impossible to get the better of, as some of you will know only too well.

重难点评析

1. "Negotiation is something that we do all the time…"该句是定语从句，在"something"之后紧跟 that 引导的定语从句来修饰"negotiation"。

2. "If your reason for negotiation is seen as 'beating' the opposition, it is known as 'distributive negotiation'."译为：如果谈判的目的是要"打败"对手，那这种谈判就叫做"分配式谈判"。该句是 if 引导的条件状语从句。"be seen as"原意是"被看成"，但是在该句翻

译中需要联系上下文,直接翻译成"是"。

3. "This way, you must be prepared to use persuasive tactics and you may not end up with maximum benefit."译为"这种方式必须采用说服性策略,而且最终有可能得不到利益的最大化。"该句中的两个"you"均未翻译出来。"end up with"译为"以……而告终"。

4. "Should you feel your negotiation is much more 'friendly' with both parties aiming to reach agreement, it is known as 'integrative negotiation'."译为:如果你觉得双方都试图达成协议,谈判显得十分"友好",这样的谈判就叫做"整合式谈判"。该句以"should"置于句首,实际表达条件"如果……"。"integrative negotiation"翻译成"整合式谈判"。

5. "This way usually brings an outcome where you will both benefit highly."译为"这种方式通常能给双方带来双赢的结果。"该句是一个限制性定语从句,用"where"来引导从句修饰"outcome"。

6. "Negotiation, in a business context, can be used for selling, purchasing, staff(e. g. Contracts), borrowing(e. g. Loans) and transaction, along with anything else that you feel are applicable for your business."译为"在商务环境下的谈判行为,可以用于销售、采购、员工(如合同协议)、借入(如借贷)和交易,还有其他所有你认为适用的商务环节。"该句有一个插入语"in a business context",翻译时要放在句首,翻译成"在商务环境下"。"along with"是一个副词词组,"一起,一道"的意思。"anything else"后的定语从句仅能由 that 引导。

7. "Set out your objectives(e. g. I want more time to pay off the loan.)"译为"应先设定你的目标(例如,我希望争取到更多的时间来还贷)。""set out"的意思很多,如"出发,开始"、"装饰,陈列"、"宣布,陈述"、"种植,移植"等等。在本句中,翻译成"设定"。

8. "You have to take into account how it will benefit the other party by offering some sort of reward or incentive(explained later)."译为"接下来,考虑如果给予一些报酬或者激励措施,对方会得到怎样的好处(稍后再进行阐述)。"该句中的词组"take into account"为"考虑,重视"的含义,后面跟的是"how…"所引导的宾语从句。

9. "What is involved(money, sales, time, conditions, discounts, terms, etc.)? Know your extremes: how much extra can you afford to give to settle an agreement? Although you are not aiming to give out the maximum, it is worth knowing so that you will not go out of your limits."译为"谈判涉及哪些方面(金钱、销售、时间、条件、折扣、条款等)? 了解自己的底线:为了达成协议,你能给得起多少额外的让步? 即使你不准备做出最大限度的让步,但是清楚自己的底线也是必要的,这样你在日后的谈判中就不会超越底线。"该句中的"involved"本意为"卷入",翻译成"涉及"。"extreme"既可以用作形容词,也可以用作名词。此处为名词,意为"极端",翻译成"底线"。"Although…"引导的是一个让步状语从句。

10. "…as this will allow you to set the agenda in advance, and improve the prospects of the other party preparing sufficiently enough to make a decision on the day."译为"因为这样一来,你就能提前设定好议程,并让对方充分准备从而能在预定的日期做出决定。"该句是 as 引导的原因状语从句。"set the agenda"翻译成"设定好议程"。"preparing sufficiently enough to make a decision on the day"是现在分词短语作伴随状语来修饰"the

other party"。

11. "... you may be able to give an intention to penalize if the other party fails to meet the agreement(as is the way with construction)."译为"又或者在对方不能达成协议要求的情况下,你能表现出惩罚的意图(像建筑工程一样)。""penalize"为动词,意思是"惩罚"。

12. "... and with nothing more out of the deal other than maintaining trading relationships."译为"如果你掌控不了,最终的协议就对你不利,除了维持贸易关系以外,你不会从交易中得到任何好处。"该句重点是"nothing more A other than B"短语,翻译成"除了B以外,不能得到A"。

译 文

　　谈判是一种我们总在进行的活动,它并不仅限于商务用途。例如,我们也许会用它来决定见面的时间,或者下雨天该去哪儿。谈判通常被视为一种妥协手段来处理争端或问题,从而尽可能使双方都受惠。无论是采取面对面、打电话还是书面的形式,沟通总是被用作对问题/争端进行谈判的纽带。请记住,谈判不总是发生在两个人之间:它可能涉及双方的好几个成员。你想通过谈判来解决问题的原因有很多,要达到目的的方式也有好几个。下面的几个方式可供参考。如果谈判的目的是要"打败"对手,那这种谈判就叫做"分配式谈判"。这种方式必须采用说服性策略,而且最终有可能得不到利益的最大化。

　　这是因为双方达成的协议并没有导向某种妥协,双方所期待的结果也不一样。如果你觉得双方都试图达成协议,谈判显得十分"友好",这样的谈判就叫做"整合式谈判"。这种方式通常能给双方带来双赢的结果。在商务环境下的谈判行为,可以用于销售、采购、员工(如合同协议)、借入(如借贷)和交易,还有其他所有你认为适用的商务环节。

　　在决定谈判之前,最好先进行准备。首先要清楚谈判的确切目标是什么? 设定你的目标(例如,我希望争取到更多的时间来还贷)。接下来,考虑如果给予一些报酬或者激励措施,对方会得到怎样的好处(稍后再进行阐述)。谈判涉及哪些方面(金钱、销售、时间、条件、折扣、条款等)? 了解自己的底线:为了达成协议,你能给得起多少额外的让步? 即使你不准备做出最大限度的让步,但是清楚自己的底线也是必要的,这样你在日后的谈判中就不会超越底线。还要了解对方试图从谈判中得到什么。这是一个很有用的信息,既有利于争取你自身的利益,也有利于达成最终的协议。你需要考虑什么对你的企业来说是有价值的,当然这不是指金钱。因为在谈判中,你有可能最终失去对你的企业来说比金钱更有价值的东西。它可能是一个可靠的客户,或是你企业的信誉。

　　直接通过见面、书面或打电话(不应经过电话接线员、前台、助理等转述)的方式与对方接触来做一个谈判的预约是很重要的,因为这样一来,你就能提前设定好议程,并让对方充分准备从而能在预定的日期做出决定。而且要把你们为什么联系的原因说明白,否则对方会立刻失去兴趣,或者不遵守约定。在实际的预约过程中,保留你所有的意见——不要透露可以使对方有机会做过于充分的准备的任何信息;这虽然不是战场,但也是商场! 再接下来就是谈判了,而你已经做了充分准备。除此之外,你还必须具备什么呢? 两样东西:自信和强势。你的强势来自你施加影响的能力。例如,你可能是买家(但不总处在上风),或者你拥有对方想要的东西,又或者在对方不能达成协议要求的情况下,你能表现出惩罚的意图(像建筑工程一样)。前面已经简单地提到过,你需要给予对方一些报酬或者激励。例如,你在销售厨房刀具,作为一种促销手段,你可能会附赠磨刀器和储刀盒,和刀具一并打包销售。

把谈判掌控在自己的手中是一条金科玉律:这可能意味着谈判会在你的价格幅度以内、交货期限以前或保证在最小利润以上进行。如果你掌控不了,最终的协议就对你不利,除了维持贸易关系以外,你不会从交易中得到任何好处。在谈判中,为了获取对你最有利的结果,你应该在必要的范围内把目标定高。对方可能会降低这个目标,这也是一个很好的策略,因为降低总比获取容易。在整个谈判过程中,你必须确保留有余地,以防对方决定改变协议的方向(他们可能想要不同的激励措施,甚至改变初衷)。这时候,你的准备就派上用场了:你了解自身的底线和对方的需求。如果你才思够敏捷,就能拿下主动权。如果事情开始朝着对你不利的方向发展,你就需要在保证原定目标不受威胁的前提下迅速地把局面扭转过来。自信,来自对自己企业、产品和其价值的了解,并能在这些方面与对方很好地沟通:只要你们之中能有人非常清楚这些情况,对方是几乎不可能占上风的。

英汉双语的衔接和连贯

1. 英语的衔接和连贯

衔接是语篇表层的结构形式之间的语义关系,反映的是句子表层结构的连接是否合理,各句承前启后是否恰当,是表层关系网络在篇章中连接词语的各种表达手段。衔接通常由一些连接词来完成。各语言间的衔接手段各有异同。而连贯则是表层之下的概念关系网络,是从概念出发,看各部分间的逻辑关系以及内容的组织结构是否合理。前者以篇章的形式得到体现,后者则借助篇章的形式加以体现。

Halliday 把衔接分为语法衔接(grammatical cohesion)和词汇衔接(lexical cohesion)两大类。常见的语法衔接手段主要有照应(reference)、替代(substitution)、省略(ellipsis)和连接(conjunction);常见的词汇衔接有重复(repetition),同义/反义(synonym/antonym)和上下义(hyponymy)等。这些衔接方式为我们提供了直接的、显著地语言线索,具有相当的提示作用,有利于语篇的产生和理解,是建立语篇连贯的重要手段之一。

(1) 语法衔接

语法学里"语法"指任何自然语言中字、词、句的组成逻辑和结构规则。语法衔接指利用某些语法手段,如动词时态、代词的语法形式及照应(reference)、替代(substitution)、省略(ellipsis)、连接(conjuncture)等,达到衔接上下文的目的。比如,用 he 指代前文提到过的 taxi driver,即为"照应"。下面两句话分别用了"省略"和"替代"的衔接手段。

The younger child was outgoing, the elder much more reserved. (省略)

I dropped the chocolate ice-cream. That's the only one I had. (替代)

此外,所谓"连接"手段就是用时态连接词(after/first)、因果连接词(because)、转折连接词(but)、附加连接词(further)和语篇标记(now, well, after all)等起到衔接作用。

(2) 词汇衔接

词汇衔接指通过词汇选择在篇章中建立一个贯穿篇章的链条,从而建立篇章的连接性。英语词汇衔接关系有两种:复现(reiteration)和同现(collocation)。复现关系指的是某一词以原词(repetition)、同义词、近义词(synonym)、上下义词(hyponymy)、概括词(generic term)或其他形式重复出现在语篇中,语篇中的句子通过这种复现关系达到了相互衔接。同现关系指的是词汇共同出现的倾向性(co-occurrence tendency),包括反义关系(antonym)、互补关系等。口译中一系列相关联的词汇(lexical set)激活口译员大脑里的图式(schema),有助于理解。

He got lots of presents from his friends and family. All the gifts were wrapped up in colored paper.（presents 和 gifts 为同义词的复现）

Mary is a good waitress, but she is a bad hostess.（good 和 bad 为反义词的同现）

（3）英译汉时衔接切换手段

以上对英语衔接的介绍旨在着重说明英汉口译时衔接手段切换的特点。英译汉时衔接切换手段主要有再现(reproduction)和省略(omission)。如:

These terrorist acts shatter steel, but they cannot dent the steel of American resolve.
这些恐怖行径破坏了钢铁大厦,却不能摧毁美国人民的钢铁意志。（再现）

None of us will ever forget this day, yet we go forward to defend our freedom and all that is good and just in our world.

没有人会忘记这一天,我们会继续捍卫自由,捍卫这个世界上所有美好正义的东西。（省略）

第二个译例中 yet 和 and 表示"补充"和"递进",使原文语法结构整饬,但译文为了符合汉语习惯,省略了这两个关联词的汉译,使译文更紧凑自然。

（4）英语衔接词

从口译听辨的角度,熟悉以下衔接词能使口译员快速理解源语,选择合适的笔记符号并准确表达译语。

① 表示时间关系的衔接词

first, in the past, since then, thereafter, lately, later, meanwhile, at last, etc.

② 表示空间关系的衔接词

beyond, above, under, nearby, outside, in here, across, close to, on(to) the left (right), ahead of, in front of, from, adjacent to, against, around, at the bottom, before, behind, below, beneath, between, close at hand, far, farther, in the center of, in the distance, in the middle of, near to, next to, on the opposite side, opposite to, on top of, over, up, etc.

③ 表示解释的衔接词

now, in addition, for, in this case, furthermore, in fact, that is to say, etc.

④ 表示强调的衔接词

indeed, certainly, above all, surely, most important, etc.

⑤ 表示举例的衔接词

for example, for instance, for one thing, for another, to illustrate, one example is, to begin with, first, second, furthermore, besides, in addition, moreover, finally, in conclusion, also, a case in point, as an illustration, incidentally, namely, that is, etc.

⑥ 表示递进或补充的衔接词

in addition, furthermore, also, moreover, yet, besides, again, what's more, another, etc.

⑦ 表示列举和顺序的衔接词

first, second, third, afterward(s), meanwhile, thereafter, last, finally, eventually, to begin with, in the first place, etc.

⑧ 用以表示比较和对比的衔接词

like, likewise, unlike, similarly, in the same way, on the other hand, compare with, by comparison, in contrast to, on the contrary, but, despite, yet, instead, while, whereas, however, nevertheless, although, even though, conversely, different from, equally important, in spite of, in the same manner, still, etc.

⑨ 表示让步的衔接词

although, nevertheless, of course, after all, still, yet, etc.

⑩ 表示因果关系的衔接词

because, since, as, seeing that, the reason why..., because of, on account of, due to, so, thus, hence, therefore, accordingly, consequently, so that, as a result of, in consequence of, result in, result from, lead to, so... as to, owing to, to have an effect on, for the reason, in this way, etc.

⑪ 表示总结的衔接词

to sum up, finally, in conclusion, at last, in short, in a word, in the long run, in summary, on the whole, as has noted, etc.

⑫ 表示类别的衔接词

to divide... into, to classify... into, to group... into, to fall into classes, there are... kinds(types, groups, classes, categories, sorts) of, according to, in terms of, depending on, at the level of, etc.

2. 汉语中的衔接和连贯

口译活动中源语的衔接和连贯自然由发言人拿捏，了解和掌握英语源语衔接和连贯的特点有助于译员理解和把握源语意思，为迅速转译为母语做准备。但是，在中国等亚洲口译市场，口译员除了按照国际惯例把外语译为自己的母语之外，还需要把母语译为外语。本单元另一个侧重点是汉译英的衔接和连贯切换问题。口译培训中初学者常见的问题是英译汉时自己听不懂英文；汉译英时老外听不懂自己，译语逻辑连贯性差。这主要是因为汉语和英语在语法和结构上差异很大造成的。在完整的语篇中，英语语篇的衔接手段差不多是汉语衔接手段的两倍。汉语语篇大多通过句意之间的逻辑联系和语义联系来连贯篇章。

研究表明，意合语言如汉语，常常是把片语、分句、句子放在一起，很少用连接词，即使用，也是用"和、但是、或者"这一类的连接词，最小限度地使用或不使用表示从属关系的词连接句子。在具体的译例中我们还发现因为发言人口误或表达习惯所导致的关联词误用的现象。这都需要口译员对汉英关联词的切换具有高度敏感性和熟练的转换技能。汉英口译中，正确使用逻辑连接词是实现话语连贯的重要途径。逻辑连接词的口译能力与口译质量成正比，逻辑连接词处理得当会提高口译质量。

(1) 汉语逻辑连贯表达法

汉语中明确表示逻辑连贯的词语及与之对应的英文表达法有：

① 表示原因。
由于,因为:as, because (of), since, owing to, on account of, by reason, due to, for
② 表示结果。
因此,所以,以致,结果:so, therefore, consequently, so that, as a result
③ 表示条件/让步。
假如,即使,只有,只要,假设:if, even if, in the event of, in case of, in that case, only if, on condition that, as long as, provided that, assuming that, providing that
④ 表示转折。
但是,仍然:but, still, however, yet
⑤ 表示对比。
尽管,另一方面,相反:though, although, nevertheless, on the other hand, while, in turn, on the contrary
⑥ 表示顺序。
和,接着,然后,同时:and, then, now, in the meantime, meanwhile, thereupon, whereupon
⑦ 表示历史对比。
回顾过去,展望未来:looking back, reflecting on, in the future

(2) 汉译英时衔接切换手段

汉译英时衔接切换的手段主要有四种类型:再现(reproduction)、增加(addition)、替换(substitution)和省略(omission)。汉语重意合,属于高语境文本,所以汉译英衔接转换是一个从隐性衔接到显性衔接的过程,"增加"占主导地位。例如:

如果大家坐下来,按照国际惯例谈一谈嘛,用资产重组的办法,用注资的办法,用债券改股权的办法,这个问题可以解决啊,你的债务可以得到偿还,它也不用破产了嘛。

If everyone can sit down and have a talk according to international practice, for instance, to recapitalize the firm, to instill fresh capital into it, to swap debt into equity, then the problem can be settled. The debt can be repaid and there will be no need for the firm concerned to apply for bankruptcy.

原文中出现了"你"和"它",其实都是指"该公司",译员替换了衔接手段,使译语更通畅明晰。

江泽民主席非常重视这个问题,多次阐明科教兴国的重要性。但是,我们为什么贯彻得不好呢? 没有钱,钱到哪里去了呢? 第一,我们政府机关庞大,吃饭财政,把钱都吃光了。

President Jiang Zemin attaches great importance to this issue and has repeatedly emphasized on the importance of science and education to China's development. But why hasn't this been implemented well? Because there is no money. Where has all the money gone? We have, you know, currently a very unyielding government organization and government institutions, so we call, it's like an eating finance or eating budget. That is to say, a large proportion of the budget have been ear-marked for paying the salaries of the government functionaries, so all the money has been eaten up.

该例中增加了 that is to say,是为了向外国记者说明极富中国特色的概念"吃饭财政"。

当时有各种各样的建议。比方说,中国的人民币应该贬值以促进出口,也有另外一个主意,应该把国有资产卖了,就可以渡过这次危机。

At that time, we had various proposals before us. Some suggested that we should devalue RMB to give a boost to export. Some other suggested that we simply sell the state assets to help us get over the difficulty.

译例中"比方说"被省略,由平行的两个 suggest 表达出来,使译语更明确。

1997年亚洲发生了金融危机,中国也面临着很大的困难,一个是出口的大幅下降。1997年中国出口增加了20%,1998年出口零增长甚至是负增长。

The Asian financial crisis broke out in 1997 and presented China with lots of difficulties. For instance, China's export suffered a drastic decline. In 1997, China's export grew by 20% over the previous year. However in 1998 China's export suffered zero growth or even negative growth.

译例中增加了 for instance 以列举中国受到亚洲金融危机的影响;增加了 however 以突显危机后中国出口的显著差异。

我在中学的时候就学了 Merchants of Venice,当时翻译叫做《一磅肉》。这个剧本,《威尼斯商人》这个剧本里面,讲了那个商人 Shylock 借给 Antonio 三千块钱,但这个契约讲了,三个月如果你不还的话呢,我就要在你身上任何一个地方割下一磅肉。

In my middle school, I read the Merchants of Venice written by Shakespeare, and that was translated as One Pound of Flesh in Chinese. According to the script, that is the Merchants of venice, Shylock lent 3,000 to Antonio. According to the contract they signed, if Antonio failed to repay the money in three months, then Shylock had the right to cut one pound of flesh from any part of Antonio's body.

译例中省略了原文中的"但",因为表示转折的意味并不强,只是继续描述契约对违约的处置而已。

3. 其他

下面再结合英语中的主谓一致、前后一致等规则看看英语口译中的衔接连贯问题。在英语句子中,谓语受主语支配,其动词必须和主语在人称和数上保持一致。主谓一致又分为语法形式一致、概念一致(逻辑意义一致)和毗邻一致(谓语动词的单复数形式和紧邻于其前的主语一致)。这些属于英汉两种工作语言熟练能力(proficiency)的问题,在此仅以更多译例佐以说明。

Days after Mexico suspended public activities to reduce the spread of A/H1N1 flue, the country is reporting a leveling off in the rate of new infections.

墨西哥停止了公众活动以减少甲型 H1N1 流感的传播,几天后当局报告的新增感染病例开始减少。

In the United States, the number of confirmed influenza cases continues to rise, but most flu sufferers report relatively mild symptoms, and only one death has been recorded.

美国新确诊的流感病例数量继续上升,但多数感染者症状相对较轻,并且只有一个死亡病例。

Sustained high economic growth in China over more than two decades has been a phenomenon that has engaged the interest of analysts all over the world. You are the fastest growing economy in the world and the second largest in purchasing power parity. China has a grand plan for the future economic growth, but in view of China's past record and its enterprise, it would not be surprising if these are achieved within your defined scheduled time frames. China's achievements have truly been remarkable.

中国二十多年来持续的经济高增长现象引起了世界分析师们的高度兴趣。贵国是全球发展最快的经济体,购买力高居世界第二。中国对未来经济增长有着宏伟的计划,但鉴于中国过去的发展实力和干劲,在既定的时间内大成目标是不足为奇的。中国取得的成绩是令人赞叹的。

The EPA began operating in 1970. But officials say the agency probably got its true start in 1962. That is when an American scientist published an important book called "Silent Spring". The book created a nonviolent revolution in American thought.

美国环保署于1970年开始正式运作,但是官员们称早在1962年该机构可能就开始工作了。当时一位美国科学家出版了一本名为《寂寞的春天》的重要著作,这本书引发了一场非暴力的美国思维革命。

The EPA can point to progress against a number of environmental threats. For example, it has set new requirements for chemical factories. It has taken action to prevent the rain from being polluted by chemicals. It has almost completely removed lead from the air. And half of the nation's worst waste areas have been cleaned up.

环保署在应对一些重大环境威胁上取得了不小的成绩。比如,它为化工厂指定了新的要求,采取措施防止降雨被化学物质污染,它几乎已经完全消除了空气中的铅。此外,全国近半污染最严重的区域已被清理干净。

词序调整法

词序调整法的英语inversion一词,不能译成"倒译"、"倒译法"或"颠倒词序"之类,否则容易与语法中的"倒装"概念相混淆。inversion作为一种翻译技巧,其意思为:翻译时对词序作必要或必不可少的改变,并不是纯粹地颠倒词序或倒装。

某些语言家说的九种倒装,是语法概念,是指同一种语言内的倒装情况,有其各自独特的语言构成方式。这些情况与方式和它们被译成另一种语言后的语言构成形式并非完全相同。试对照每种倒装例句的英文及其译文:

1. Interrogative inversion(疑问倒装):What did you do yesterday?(你昨天干什么了?)

2. Imperative inversion(命令倒装):"Speak you," said Mr. Black,"speak you, good fellow!"(布莱克先生命令道:"说,说吧!伙计!")

3. Exclamatory inversion(惊叹倒装):How dreadful is this place!(这地方好可怕呀!)

4. Hypothetical inversion(假设倒装):Had you come yesterday, you could have seen him here.(要是昨天来了,你就会在这里看到他的。)

5. Balance inversion(平衡倒装):Through a gap came an elaborately described ray. (从一个空洞中透出一束精心设计的光线。)

6. Link inversion(衔接倒装):On this depends the whole argument.(整个争论都以此为论据。)

7. Signpost inversion(点题倒装):By strategy is meant something wider.(战略的意义比较广。)

8. Negative inversion(否定倒装):Not a word did he say.(他只字未说。)

9. Metrical inversion(韵律倒装):在诗行中常用此倒装。如:As pants the hart for cooling streams.(在一般散文或小说中的正常语序中这行诗应为:As the hart pants for cooling streams. 意思为:因为公鹿喜欢清凉的小溪。)

上述9条可说明:语法倒装一般是指主语与谓语或与谓语的一部分颠倒位置,而翻译中的 inversion 是指译文与原文相比,词序发生了变化,故译为"词序调整法"。

词序调整在英汉互译中的运用是非常普遍的,不管是短语的翻译,或是句子的翻译,都是如此。

一、短语翻译

1. Miss Fang 方小姐

2. Mr. Steveson 史蒂文森先生

3. Room 911 911房间

4. Page 15 第15页

5. April 17th,2003 2003年4月17日

6. The Central Committee of the Communist Party of China 中国共产党中央委员会

7. tough-minded 意志坚强的

8. heart-warming 暖人心的

9. well-conducted 行为端正的

10. ill-tempered 脾气不好的

11. East China 华东

12. northeast 东北

13. southwest 西南

14. north, south, east and west 东西南北

15. Mr Zhang,
Protocol Department,
Ministry of Foreign Affairs
外交部礼宾司张先生

16. Major-General Mohammed Khan,
The First Brigade,
The Sixth Division,
Pakistan Army
巴基斯坦陆军第六师第一旅穆罕默德·汗少将

17. (The tea-party was given by) Mr. Smith, senior correspondent of The Times, London.

(这个茶会是由)伦敦《泰晤士报》的高级记者史密斯先生(举行的)。

18. every student of the class 班上每一个学生(不能译成"每个学生的班"或"每个班上的同学")

19. all Party resolutions 党的一切决议(绝对不能译成:一切党的决议)

二、句子翻译

1. They were sons of the men who had left their homes and taken to the mountains with their broad swords by their sides.

他们都是那些抛妻别子、身带大刀进入深山的好汉们的后代。

2. Accounts are given of huge mountains sinking, of former plains seen heaved aloft, of fires flashing out amid the ruin.

大山沉陷,平原隆起,火焰喷射,周围是一片废墟,这些都有记载。

3. He came yesterday.

他昨天来的。(或:昨天他来了。)

4. He drinks half a bottle of beer with each of his meals.

每餐他都要喝半瓶啤酒。

5. He is not happy, though he is rich.

他虽富有,但不幸福。

6. Will you kindly express through your column my keen appreciation of the action of the British government in effecting my release from the Chinese Legation?

本人(指孙中山——编者)承蒙贵国政府之援助,得自中国公使馆获释,拟借贵报一角,敬伸感激之情,不知可邀俞允否?

7. "What does Mr. Darcy mean," said she to Charlott, "by listening to my conversation with Colonel Forster?"

"戴锡先生听我跟福斯塔上校谈话,"她对查乐蒂说,"这究竟是什么意思?"

8. The ladies encouraged the combatants not only by clapping their hands and waving their veils and kerchiefs, but even by exclaiming "Brave lance! Good sword!" when any successful thrust or blow took place under their observation.

贵妇们看见刺中或打中时,不只是鼓掌、挥动头纱和手帕,甚至高声喊叫:"好枪法!好刀法!"这样地来鼓舞比武的英雄。

9. Draw, if you be man, Gregory, remember thy smashing blow.

是汉子就拔出剑来,葛雷古利,别忘了你的杀手锏。

10. The day was just breaking when we were about to start; as I sat thinking of her, came struggling up the coach side, through the mingled day and night Uriah's head.

天将破晓,我们就要动身了,我坐在车上正想着她,忽然当昼夜混沌未分之际,从马车的旁边钻进尤莉亚的头来。(人有词序调整)

11. There are many wonderful stories to tell about the places I visited and the people

I met.

我访问了一些地方,遇到了不少人,要谈起来,奇妙的事可多着呢。

12. We ate to our hearts' content at her home last Sunday.

我们上星期天在她家尽情地吃了一顿。

13. Professor Tong is working with two of his new assistants in the laboratory at the moment.

童教授正在实验室和他的两个新助手一道工作。

14. Never have we seen so bright a future before us!

我们从来没见过这样光明的道路!

15. It was a keen disappointment that I had to postpone the visit which I had intended to pay to China in January.

我原打算在今年一月访问中国,后来又不得不予以推迟,这使得我深感失望。

16. I was all the more delighted when, as a result of the initiative of your Government, it proved possible to reinstate the visit so quickly.

由于贵国政府的提议,才得以这样快地重新实现访问,这使我感到特别高兴。

17. 只有听党中央指挥,调动一切积极因素,中国人民才能全面建设小康社会。

Only by following the instructions of the Party Central Committee, and mobilizing all positive factors, can Chinese people build a well-off society in an all-round way.

18. 这所大学现有计算机科学、高能物理、激光、地球物理、遥感技术、遗传工程六个专业。

This university has six faculties, namely, Computer Science, High Energy Physics, Laser, Geo-physics, Remote Sensing and Genetic Engineering.

拓展阅读

选文 A

女士们、先生们:

我们已经注意到一种崭新而又令人兴奋的信息经济形态的出现,这种经济形态是以网络技术为驱动力的。我所要说的是,计算机因特网正在改变商务运作的模式,促进一种被称之为新信息经济的形态的形成。这种深刻变化所带来的一个直接结果是商务交易的简化。

以我本人最近购车一事为例,首先我上网找到一个因特网站,上面列有不同车种及其性能和价格,既有批发又有零售。所有的市场调查我都自己做了。然后我去一家汽车商行询价。整个交易用不了30分钟便完成了。没有激烈的无休止的讨价还价,既简易又方便。我了解了车的行情,走进车行时已是一个懂行的买主了。

问题不在于这些事情有无发生,问题在于现在所发生的这一切与我们200年来已习以为常的事相比是否具有重要意义。

得益于技术进步的美国经济正在发生一些重大的变化。我们的身边的确出现了一些新鲜事。我们能够使经济在快速增长的同时,免受通货膨胀之苦,这种未导致通货膨胀的经济增长其速度之快是我们以往不可想象的。当然,负面的情况并非不存在。新经济并不意味着我们将永远摆脱新一轮的衰退;新经济并不意味着我们会免于落入通货紧缩的旋涡;新经济并不意味着通货膨胀已寿终正寝;新经济并不意味着股价能在高位上昂首屹立,不会出现新的熊市。没有人能够保证我们的玫瑰花园永不凋谢。

我认为随着新信息经济的出现,错位、波动、不稳定等现象也会随之而来。但是我感到由于生产率的提高,经济仍有可能持续增长,而且不会引发通货膨胀,我们会有更多的就业机会,得到更高的工资。

电子商务的出现给公司经理人员带来了巨大而又激动人心的挑战。因特网商务即刻打开了全球性的更有效率的市场。

我会问许多人,请他们告诉我还有哪些地方因特网商务没有给那里的市场带来更大的效率。作为消费者我们已经从因特网商务中获益。当然,也有一些公司因此而受到伤害,这是事情的另一面。

不管怎样,因特网将改变公司的经营方法。那些不愿正视因特网商务现实的公司是不会成为市场赢家的。

译文

Ladies and Gentlemen,

We're aware of an emergence of a new and exciting mode of information economy driven by network technology. What I want to say is that the computer Internet is transforming business operation patterns and contributing to what is called the new information economy. An immediate consequence of this profound change is the simplification of business transaction.

Take, for example, the way that I recently bought my car. First I went on an Internet site listing cars, their features and their prices, both wholesale and retail. I did all my research. And then I went to an auto dealership and asked for this particular price. The transaction lasted less tan 30 minutes. No hassle. Easy. Simple. I was informed. I went in. I was an informed buyer.

It's not that none of these things are happening. It's the importance of these things compared to what we have been used to for the last 200 years.

Thanks to technology something very important is happening to the U. S. economy. Something new and different is happening around us. We are able to grow faster without triggering inflation than we thought possible. Of course, there's the down side. The new economy does not mean we will never have another recession or even a deflationary spiral. It does not mean inflation is dead. It does not mean stock prices will stay at their lofty levels or that there will never be another bear market. Nobody is promising you a rose garden.

I anticipate dislocation, volatility and uncertainty accompanying the emergence of the new information economy. But because of what I view as higher productivity, I see the possibility of sustained economic growth without the threat of inflation, more jobs and higher wages.

The emergence of electronic business has created enormous and exciting challenges for business managers. Internet commerce immediately opens global and more efficient markets.

I would challenge many people to tell me where it has not brought about greater efficiency in markets. We as consumers have benefited from that. Of course, there are companies that have been hurt by that, which is the other side of the story.

In any case, the Internet will transform the way companies do business. And those companies that do not address that issue will not be the market winners.

选文B

Sole Agency

Mr. Wang: I've been looking forward to meeting you in Shanghai, Mr. Smith.

Mr. Smith: Me too. It's been almost a year since I saw you last time in the States. That's a great year for both of us and you are now one of the most important dealers of our products in Asia. We have been doing business with each other for four years and we have built up trust and a strong working relationship. By the way, please call me Bill.

Mr. Wang: You're right, Mr. Smi... er... Bill. Total sales on the four models were U.S. $200,000 last year, through our agent. And this is more than twenty per cent of your sales in Asia, if our estimate is right. And... as you know, our local offices in Beijing, Shanghai, and Tianjin opened for business in the past several months, and they're gaining market.

Mr. Smith: I understand you're coming to the request to act as our agent in China, which you made in one of the recent emails to us. Our opinions, you know, have been positive. But... but for research shows most of your sales are made in Shanghai. Of course we have noticed your work in other parts of China.

Mr. Wang: You're right, but we're happy with the sales. It's a new product, you know. How could you do better? I'm sure our sales this year will greatly exceed those of last year, as our networks in other parts will help. Our reports indicate a great deal of interest in the products there, especially in cities that have a higher average proportion of people in the higher income brackets.

Mr. Smith: I know the Chinese market has great potential. We all know the size of population has always been an important factor for any product. That means you have a lot to do; it's not easy to persuade customers to switch to a new product.

Mr. Wang: You're absolutely right. But what we have is the experience with the products in Shanghai. Among other things, we know what works with Chinese people. I mean, we have the local knowledge. Once we sign the sole agency agreement which covers the whole China, we can do a substantial job and push your products vigorously, to make the customers believe the products are what they really need.

Mr. Smith: Your analysis is quite convincing, and I'm sure an active, experienced agent is able to develop a successful regional business. But as an agent, your orders must be big enough. Furthermore, we need to know your sales volume during the past three years, your plans for promoting the products, and the possible annual turnover.

Mr. Wang: We'll submit a detailed proposal to you. Right now I can tell you for sure that we could double the annual turnover as your agent in China.

Mr. Smith: I hope your sales will increase sharply.

Mr. Wang: You won't be disappointed if we have your full technical and marketing support. Now, I'd like to come to the matter of commission. What is the rate for a period of two years?

Mr. Smith: Our usual practice is 10 per cent. And as you know commissions depend on the quantity of goods ordered. You get a higher rate if you order a bigger quantity.

Mr. Wang: I feel 10 per cent is really out of the question. Surely you will agree that a big advertising campaign will be needed to pave the way in the new areas for the products. As you indicated just now, a lot of initial work has to be done to draw business away from other manufacturers. I think you should take advertising expenses into account. The training adds to the expenses too. What I have in mind is 15 per cent.

Mr. Smith: That's too much for us. To tell you the truth, we're taking the initial work into consideration. Tell you what, the best I can do is 12 per cent for one year if your sales reach $400,000.

Mr. Wang: That's a good idea. If it works we'll discuss it again for the next year.

Mr. Smith: And, I must make it clear that as our agent you shouldn't sell similar products from other manufacturers.

Mr. Wang: Certainly not without your prior approval.

Mr. Smith: Major issues seem to be set. I will bring in a sample contract tomorrow. If you like, we can sign it then.

译文

独家代理王先生:我一直期待着在上海与您会面,史密斯先生。

史密斯先生:我也一样。从上次我们在美国会面,快一年了吧? 这一年对我们双方来说,都是一个丰年呀。你们现在已成为我们在亚洲的最大代理商之一。我们合作已有四年,已经建立起相互信任和良好的工作关系。顺便说一下,叫我比尔就行。

王先生:你说得对,史密斯先……嗯……比尔。我们四种产品的销售总额去年已经达到 20 万美元。如果我们的估算正确的话,这已经占到你们产品在亚洲销量的百分之二十多。嗯……你知道,我们在北京、上海和天津的办事处在过去几个月已经开张,而且已经有了市场。

史密斯先生:我明白,你想谈在中国独家代理我们产品的问题。这个问题你在最近的电子邮件中也提到过。我们对此也一直持积极态度,但……但是我们发现你们的主要销售还局限于上海。当然,我们已经注意到你们在其他地区的行动。

王先生:不错,但是我们对销售额还是很满意的。毕竟是新产品嘛,要求太高也不现实。我相信我们今年的销售成绩会比去年高出很多,因为我们在其他地区的销售网络会发挥作用。我们做过调查,那些地区的消费者对我们的产品很感兴趣,特别是在城市,因为城市里高收入人群的比例较高。

史密斯先生:我知道中国的市场很有潜力。我们都知道对任何产品而言,人口因素都很重要。但这也意味着你们要做大量的工作。要让顾客放弃自己熟悉的产品,转而购买一种新的产品,并不容易。

王先生:你说得很对。但是,我们的得力武器是在上海销售你们的产品的经验。还有,我们很了解中国人。我的意思是,我们对本地很了解。一旦我们签了在中国独家代理协议,我们就可以做大量工作,大力推广你们的产品,让消费者相信他们真的需要你们的产品。

史密斯先生:你的分析很有说服力。我相信积极进取、富有经验的代理在这个地方会取得很大的成功。但是,做我们的代理,要有相当大的订货量。还有,我们要了解你们过去三年里的销售额,你们的推广计划,以及你们可能的年销售量。

王先生:我们会给你们提交一份详尽的计划书。不过现在我可以肯定地告诉你们,要是我们成为你们的中国代理,年销售量会翻一倍。

史密斯先生:我们希望你们的销售额会有大幅度增长。

王先生:只要你们提供全力的技术和市场支持,我们不会令你们失望的。现在,我想谈谈佣金问题。一份两年的代理期,佣金是多少?

史密斯先生:我们的佣金一般是百分之十。你也知道,佣金的大小是由订货量的大小决定的。订货量越大,佣金就会越高。

王先生:我觉得百分之十是不行的。你肯定知道,为了打开局面,在上海以外的地区我们得做大规模的广告宣传。你刚才也说到,为了从其他厂家抢生意,要做大量的前期工作。你们必须把广告费用考虑在内。另外,我们还得培训不少销售人员。我感觉佣金要达到百分之十五才行。

史密斯先生:那太高了。说实话,我们已经把前期的工作计算在内了。那这样吧,如果年销售额达到40万美元,我们最多给百分之十二。

王先生:这个想法不错。如果行的话,我们再讨论下一年的佣金。

史密斯先生:还有,我得说清楚,作为我们的代理,你们不可以销售其他厂家的类似产品。

王先生:当然不会,除非得到你们事先同意。

史密斯先生:主要的事情看上去已经解决了。那明天我带一份合同草案来。如果你们认为可以,我们就当场签约吧。

第八单元　新闻发布会
（Press Conference）

单元要点

本单元共分五个层次，分别是：政府工作报告汉译英一篇；告别演说英译汉一篇；倍数表示法；分译法；拓展阅读（汉译英，英译汉各一篇）。第一、二部分提供政府工作报告和告别演说的新闻发布会的口译例文及其翻译和重难点评析；第三、四部分主要是相关口译理论与技能的介绍；第五部分的拓展阅读中，提供汉、英原文和参考译文。

理论难点提示

1. 倍数表示法。
2. 分译法。

选文A

社会主义现代化事业的成就

各位代表，现在，我向大家做下列政府工作报告，请予以审议，并请对报告提出意见。

2005年，我国社会主义现代化事业取得了显著成就。

（一）经济平稳较快发展。2005全年国内生产总值达到18.23万亿元，比上年增长9.9％；政府的收入突破3万亿元，比上年增加5 232亿元；消费价格指数总水平上涨1.8％。国民经济呈现增长较快、效益较好、价格稳定的良好局面。

（二）改革开放迈出重大步伐。一些重点领域和关键环节的改革取得了新突破；进出口贸易总额达到1.42万亿美元，增长23.2％；实际利用外商直接投资603亿美元；到2005年末，国家外汇储备达到8 189亿美元。

（三）社会事业取得新进步。科技、教育、文化、卫生、体育等事业全面发展。神舟六号载人航天飞行圆满成功，标志着我国在一些重要科技领域达到世界先进水平。

（四）人民生活进一步改善。城镇新增就业人口970万；城镇居民人均可支配收入达到10 493元，农村居民人均可支配纯收入达到3 255元，扣除价格因素，分别增长9.6％和6.2％。我国在全面建设小康社会道路上迈出了新的坚实步伐。

一年来，我们以科学发展观统领经济社会发展全局，主要做了以下几方面工作：

（一）着力解决经济运行中的突出问题。继续搞好宏观调控，坚持区别对待、有保有压的原则，综合运用财税、货币、土地政策等手段，控制了固定资产投资的过快增长，遏制了房地产投资过快增长和房价过快上涨的势头。进一步增加农业、能源、交通、社会事业等薄弱环节投入，促进协调发展，增强发展后劲。加强经济运行调节，继续缓解煤、电、油供应紧张的压力,缓解运输负载过重的压力,保障了经济平稳较快增长。

(二)积极推进经济结构调整和经济增长方式转变。继续加强"三农"工作。28个省、自治区和直辖市全部免征了农业税,全国取消了牧业税。增加了对种粮农民的补贴和对产粮大县及财政困难县实行转移支付,对部分粮食主产区的重点粮食品种制定了最低收购价政策,多渠道增加农民收入。农业综合生产能力得到加强,粮食稳定增产和农民持续增收,为经济平稳较快发展和社会稳定奠定了基础。

在产业结构调整方面,制定和实施了涉及能源、重要原材料和装备制造等的行业发展规划和产业政策,提出了促进流通业发展的政策和相关措施,引导和支持了重点行业的健康发展。

为推进经济增长方式转变,突出抓了能源、资源节约和环境保护,提出了建设资源节约型社会、发展循环经济的任务和政策措施,启动了178项节能、节水和资源综合利用等重大项目。加强了矿产开发、土地利用和城乡规划管理。去年投入国债资金152亿元,主要用于资助一些重点生态工程,如淮河、太湖等流域和其他河流湖泊的污染防治,天然林保护,退耕还林、还草,防沙、治沙等重点生态工程。深入开展环保专项治理,解决了一些危害群众健康的环境问题。

(三)深化经济体制改革和推进对外开放。农村综合改革试点继续推进。国有商业银行股份制改革和农村信用社改革取得了重要进展,上市公司实行股权分置改革稳步推进,完善人民币汇率机制改革顺利实施。国有企业建立现代企业制度步伐加快。中央财政安排了219亿元支持116户国有企业实施政策性关闭破产,企业分离办社会职能工作继续进行。制定并实施了鼓励、支持和引导非公有制经济发展的政策措施。一些重点领域和关键环节的改革,取得了突破性进展。

我们积极应对对外开放中出现的新情况、新问题。我们调整了出口退税、关税和加工贸易政策,优化对外贸易结构。完善了出口退税机制。稳步推进了服务业对外开放竞争。全面部署了加入世界贸易组织后过渡期的各项工作。

(四)加快发展各项社会事业。2005年中央财政用于科技、教育、卫生、文化等方面的支出1 168亿元,比上年增长了18.3%;国家为这些方面投入了国债建设资金95.4亿元。

在科技方面,加强了国家创新体系、完善了基础研究和基础设施建设的工作。集成电路芯片设计开发、第三代移动通信、高性能复合材料、高档数控机床研制等重大科技项目取得重要进展。在国务院领导下,组织和动员各方面的相关力量,经过两年多的深入研究和广泛论证,最终制定出了《国家中长期科学和技术发展规划纲要》。

在看到成绩的同时,我们也清醒地认识到,国家经济和社会生活中的困难和问题还不少。一些长期积累的和深层次的矛盾尚未根本解决,又出现了一些不容忽视的新问题。

一是粮食增产和农民增收难度加大。当前粮价走低和农业生产资料价格上涨的压力都不小,影响农民增加收入和种粮积极性。而且,耕地总面积不断减少,农业综合生产能力不强,粮食安全存在隐患。

二是固定资产投资增幅仍然偏高。有些行业投资增长过快,新开工项目偏多,投资结构不合理,投资反弹的压力比较大。

三是部分行业过度投资的不良后果开始显现。产能过剩问题日趋突出,相关产品价格下跌,库存上升,企业利润减少,亏损增加,潜在的金融风险正在加大。

四是涉及群众切身利益的不少问题还没有得到很好解决。看病难、看病贵和上学难、上学贵等问题突出,公众对此反映比较强烈;在一些方面,如土地征用、房屋拆迁、库区移民、企业改制、环境保护等方面,还存在一些违反法规和政策而损害群众权益的问题。

五是安全生产形势严峻。煤矿、交通等重特大事故频繁发生,给人民群众生命财产造成严重损失。

我们还认识到,各级政府工作中存在不少缺点和不足。政府职能转变滞后,一些工作落实不够,办事效率不高,形式主义、做表面文章的现象还比较突出,一些政府工作人员弄虚作假、奢侈浪费,甚至贪污腐败。

我们要进一步增强使命感和紧迫感,发扬成绩,改进工作,以更加昂扬的斗志、更加奋发有为的精神状态、更加扎实的工作作风,努力把政府各项工作做得更好,绝不辜负人民的厚望和国家的重托。

重难点评析

1. "社会主义现代化事业的成就"译为"achievements of the socialist construction"。"成就"一般用"achievements",表示巨大的成果。"construction"一词有"建设"的含义,强调社会主义现代化事业的建设过程。

2. "请予以审议"译为"for your deliberation and approval"。"审议"有审查、讨论和批准的意思。因此选用"deliberation"一词,表示"仔细考虑,深思熟虑"。例如,"be taken into deliberation"意思是"被审议"。

3. "消费价格指数"译为"the consumer price index"。"index"的复数为"indexes"或"indices",该词的意思丰富,有"索引,指标,标准,指针等"含义。例如,"the cost of living index"意为"生活消费指数"。

4. "良好局面"译为"was in good shape"。"shape"原意是"形状,形态,样子",也有"情况,状态"的意思。例如,"in good financial shape"译为"经济情况好"。

5. "重点领域和关键环节"译为"major fields and key sectors"。注意"重点"选用"major","环节"译为"sector"。"sector"的原意是"扇形,两脚规",也有"部分,成分,部门"的意思。此处为"环节"之意。

6. "实际利用外商直接投资"译为"the actually-used foreign direct investment"。"实际利用"在此处用了一个合成词"actually-used"作为形容词来修饰,使得该翻译言简意赅。

7. "区别对待、有保有压"译为"taking different approaches to different situations and encouraging the growth of some economic sectors while discouraging the expansion of other economic sectors"。该处的翻译采用的是意译,即对中文进行解释说明。否则仅从字面上翻译,很难懂。

8. "综合运用财税、货币、土地政策等手段"译为"comprehensively used means such as fiscal and tax, monetary and land policies"。该处的翻译需注意两点:"综合运用"译为"comprehensively used";"手段"译为"means"。

9. "遏制了房地产投资过快增长和房价过快上涨的势头"译为"curbed the overheated growth in real estate investment, and curbed the ballooning in housing prices"。"遏制"译为"curb"比较恰当。"curb"原意是"给马装上勒马链,勒住马",现引申为"控制,抑止,遏制"

的意思。"过快上涨"一词用"ballooning"翻译非常形象,表示上涨的速度就像升空的气球一样。

10. "加强'三农'工作"译为"intensified the work regarding 'agriculture, rural areas and farmers'"。此处的翻译采用的是意译,即详细解释了三农的含义,它们是"农业,农村,农民"。

11. "天然林保护,退耕还林、还草,防沙、治沙"译为"protecting virgin forests, returning farmland to forests or grassland, and preventing and controlling desertification"。此处的翻译仍然采用的是意译法。何为"退耕还林、还草"?通过进一步解释,即将农田变回以前的森林和草地,意思便一清二楚。

12. "土地征用、房屋拆迁、库存移民、企业改制"译为"the land expropriation, housing demolition and resident relocation, relocation of people from reservoir areas, corporate restructuring"。注意此处的翻译中,将汉语的动词"征用"、"拆迁"、"移民"和"改制"全部都用名词性英语来表达,如"expropriation","demolition","relocation","restructuring"。

译 文

Achievements of the Socialist Construction

Fellow Deputies,

Now I would like to present to you the following report on the work of the government for your deliberation and approval. And I hope to ask you to present your comments and suggestions on my report.

In 2005, remarkable achievements were made in our socialist modernization.

First of all, the economic growth was fast and steady. The yearly GDP reached 18.23 trillion yuan in 2005, and there was an increase of 9.9% over the previous year. The government revenue exceeded 3 trillion yuan, and there was 523.2 billion yuan more than the previous year. The consumer price index rose by 1.8%. The national economy was in good shape that was characterized by faster growth, better economic returns and more stable prices.

Second, major steps were taken in the reform and opening up. Breakthroughs were achieved in the reform of some major fields and key sectors. China's import and export volume totaled US＄1.42 trillion, and there was an increase of 23.3% over the previous year. The actually-used foreign direct investment reached US＄60.3 billion. By the end of 2005, the country's foreign exchange reserves had amounted to US＄818.9 billion.

Third, progress was made in social undertakings. Science and technology, education, culture, health, sports and other undertakings have developed in an all-round way. The success of the Shenzhou VI manned spaceflight shows that China has reached world-class levels in some important fields of science and technology.

And fourth, people's lives improved further. A new population of 9.7 million in urban areas entered the workforce. The per capita net disposable income of people in urban areas rose to 10,493 yuan, and the per capita net income of people in rural areas grew to 3,255 yuan. After deducting the effect of rises in prices(inflation), there was still an increase of 9.6% and an increase of 6.2% respectively. China took another new and solid step forward on the road of building a moderately prosperous society in all respects.

Last year, we guided China's overall economic and social development with a scientific outlook on development, and mainly carried out the following tasks:

1. Focusing on solving the major problems in economic operation. We continued to do a good job of macroeconomic regulation, stuck to the principles of taking different approaches to different situations and encouraging the growth of some economic sectors while discouraging the expansion of other economic sectors. We comprehensively used means such as fiscal and tax, monetary and land policies, and curbed the overheated growth in fixed asset investment, and curbed the overheated growth in real estate investment, and curbed the ballooning in housing prices. We further increased investment in weak sectors such as agriculture, energy, transport, and social undertaking to promote balanced development and provide a pushing force for further development. We strengthened the regulation in economic operation and continued to reduce the pressure on tight supplies of coal, electricity, and petroleum, and reduce the pressure on the overloaded transportation system. And we ensured the fast yet steady growth in national economy.

2. Actively promoting the adjustment of economic restructure and the transformation of the pattern of economic growth. We further intensified the work regarding "agriculture, rural areas and farmers". In 28 provinces, autonomous regions and municipalities directly under the central government, we cancelled the agricultural tax and the livestock tax throughout the country. We increased subsidies to grain producers and conducted transfer payment to major grain-producing countries and financially poor countries. We set the floor purchase prices for key grains in some major grain-producing areas, and increased rural incomes through a variety of channels. The overall production capacity in agriculture improved, the grain production increased in a stable manner, and the incomes of farmers increased continuously. All these have provided a solid foundation for fast and steady economic development and social stability.

In the adjustment of industrial restructure, we formulated and implemented development programs and industrial policies regarding industries such as energy, important raw materials, and equipment manufacturing. We advanced policies and relevant measures to promote the development of the wholesale and retail industry. We guided and supported the sound development of these major industries.

In order to push forward the change in the pattern of economic growth, we paid particular attention to the conservation of energy and resource, and to the protection of environment. We laid out tasks, policies and measures for building a resource-conserving society and developing a circular economy. We launched 178 major projects that aim at saving energy and water and aiming at comprehensively utilizing resources. We strengthened the management of mineral exploration, land use, and urban and rural planning. Last year, we allocated 15.2 billion yuan from the sale of treasury bonds to finance mainly key ecological projects, such as preventing and controlling the pollution in the basins of the Huai River, Tai Lake and other rivers and lakes, protecting virgin forests, returning farmland to forests or grassland, and preventing and controlling desertification. We launched special and large-scale projects on solving some environmental problems that were endangering people's health.

3. Deepening the reform in economic restructure and promoting the policy of opening up to the outside world. We pushed forward the experimental trial on the comprehensive reform in rural areas. Significant progress was made in the reform that state-owned commercial banks introduce a shareholding system, and in the reform of rural credit cooperatives. Steady progress was made in the reform that listed companies introduce the shareholder structure. The reform was carried out smoothly in perfecting the mechanism for the Renminbi exchange rate. State-owned enterprises quicken their steps in introducing a modern corporate structure. The central government allocated a total of 21.9 billion yuan to subsidize 116 state-owned enterprises to implement the policy-based closure and bankruptcy. We continued our work of freeing enterprises from their obligation to operate social undertakings. We made and carried out policies and measures to encourage, support and guide the growth of the economy of non-public sectors. In some major fields and key sectors, breakthroughs were made in progress.

We actively dealt with new situations and new issues appearing in the process of opening up to the outside world. We adjusted policies regarding export rebates, tariffs and the processing trade, and downsized the structure of foreign trade. The export rebate mechanism was improved. Steady progress was made in opening the service industry to foreign competition. Overall arrangements were made for various kinds of work during the transition period after China's entry into the WTO.

4. Accelerating the development of various social programs. In 2005, the central government spent 116.8 billion yuan on areas such as science and technology, education, health and culture, and this was an increase of 18.3% over the previous year. And in promoting these areas, the government allocated 9.54 billion yuan by the sale of treasury bonds.

In terms of science and technology, we further strengthened the work of building a national innovation system, and improved the work on basic research and infrastructure construction. The design and development of integrated circuit chips, the development of third-generation mobile communications, high-performance composite materials, and high-grade digitally-controlled machine tools and of many others are major projects in science and technology, and they have all progressed considerably. Under the leadership of the State Council, we organized and mobilized the strength of all the parties concerned, and after two years of in-depth research and extensive proof, we finally formulated the "Outline of the National Long-and Medium-Term Program for Scientific and Technological Development".

When seeing successes, we clearly realize at the same time that there are still many difficulties and problems in the national economic and social activities. There are some long-standing and deep-seated contradictions that have not been fundamentally solved. And a number of new problems have appeared that we should not neglect.

First, it has become even more difficult to the grain production to increase and difficult for farmers to increase their incomes. At present, the grain prices are going downward and the prices of agricultural production materials are going upward, and these two kinds of pressure are big enough. They affect negatively the increase in earnings of farmers, and discourage the enthusiasm of farmers for growing grain. Moreover, the total area of usable farmland continues to decrease, and the overall agricultural production capacity is weak. There is a hidden threat to the nation's food security.

Second, the fixed asset investment is still increasing too fast. In some industries investments increase too quickly, and too many projects have been launched. There is irrationality in investment structure, and there is significant pressure for a rebound in investment.

Third, in some industries, the negative consequences of overheated investment start to be apparent. The problem of excess production capacity is getting increasingly worse. The prices of some relevant goods start to drop and inventories begin to increase. Profits of enterprises decrease, and losses of these enterprises increase. Potential financial risks are becoming bigger.

Fourth, quite a few problems regarding the vital interests of the people have not been solved satisfactorily. For example, the problem is still apparent that it is both difficult and costly to get medical treatment and receive an education, and there is a comparatively strong negative reaction to these types of problems in public. In some areas, such as the land expropriation, housing demolition and resident relocation, relocation of people from reservoir areas, corporate restructuring, and environmental protection, there are still some cases of violating regulations and policies, and some cases of jeopardizing the rights and interests of people.

Fifth, the situation in production safety is much severe. Major coalmine and traffic accidents keep occurring, and have caused serious loss of life and property.

We have also realized that there are still quite a few defects and shortcomings in the work of governments at all levels. The work of transforming government function is behind schedule; some tasks have not been adequately carried out, and efficiency is low. The problem of formalism and going through the motions is still serious. Some government working staffs have been involved in fraud, extravagant and wasteful practices, and even corruption.

We must further heighten our senses of mission and urgency. We should further develop our achievements, and improve our work. And we should boost our morale even more, be more in the spirit of working hard for accomplishment, foster a much practical working style, and try our best to do a much better job of all government work. We will never fail to live up to people's sincere expectations and the great trust the country has placed in us.

选文B

Farewell Speech

My fellow citizens, tonight is my last opportunity to speak to you from the Oval Office as your president.

I am profoundly grateful to you for twice giving me the honor to serve, to work for you and with you to prepare our nation for the 21st century. And I'm grateful to Vice President Gore, to my Cabinet Secretaries, and to all those who have served with me for the last eight years.

This has been a time of dramatic transformation, and you have risen to every new challenge. You have made our social fabric stronger, our families healthier and safer, our people more prosperous.

You, the American people, have made our passage into the global information age, an era of great American renewal.

In all the work I have done as president, every decision I have made, every executive action I have taken, every bill I have proposed and signed, I've tried to give all Americans the tools and conditions to build the future of our dreams, in a good society, with a strong economy, a cleaner environment, and a freer, safer, more prosperous world.

I have steered my course by our enduring values. Opportunity for all. Responsibility from all. A community for all Americans. I have sought to give America a new kind of government, smaller, more modern, more effective, full of ideas and policies appropriate to this new time, always putting people first, always focusing on the future.

Working together, America has done well. Our economy is breaking records, with more than 22 million new jobs, the lowest unemployment in 30 years, the highest home ownership ever, the longest expansion in history.

Our families and communities are stronger. Thirty-five million Americans have used the family leave law. Eight million have moved off welfare. Crime is at a 25-year low. Over 10 million Americans receive more college aid, and more people than ever are going to college. Our schools are better-higher standards, greater accountability and larger investments have brought higher test scores, and higher graduation rates.

More than three million children have health insurance now, and more than 7 million Americans have been lifted out of poverty. Incomes are rising across the board. Our air and water are cleaner. Our food and drinking water are safer. And more of our precious land has been preserved, in the continental United States, than at any time in 100 years.

America has been a force for peace and prosperity in every corner of the globe.

I'm very grateful to be able to turn over the reins of leadership to a new president, with America in such a strong position to meet the challenges of the future. Tonight, I want to leave you with three thoughts about our future.

First, America must maintain our record of fiscal responsibility. Through our last four budgets, we've turned record deficits to record surpluses, and we've been able to pay down $600 billion of our national debt, on track to be debt free by the end of the decade for the first time since 1835.

Staying on that course will bring lower interest rates, greater prosperity and the opportunity to meet our big challenges. If we choose wisely, we can pay down the debt, deal with the retirement of the baby boomers, invest more in our future and provide tax relief.

Second, because the world is more connected every day in every way, America's security and prosperity require us to continue to lead in the world. At this remarkable moment in history, more people live in freedom than ever before. Our alliances are stronger than ever. People all around the world look to America to be a force for peace and prosperity, freedom and security. The global economy is giving more of our own people, and billions around the world, the chance to work and live and raise their families with dignity.

But the forces of integration that have created these good opportunities also make us more subject to global forces of destruction, to terrorism, organized crime and nacro-trafficking, the spread of deadly weapons and disease, the degradation of the global environment.

The expansion of trade hasn't fully closed the gap between those of us who live on the cutting edge of the global economy and the billions around the world who live on the knife's edge of survival. This global gap requires more than compassion. It requires action. Global poverty is a powder keg that could be ignited by our indifference.

In his first inaugural address, Thomas Jefferson warned of entangling alliances. But in our times, America cannot and must not disentangle itself from the world. If we want the world to embody our shared values, then we must assume a shared responsibility.

If the wars of the 20th century, especially the recent ones in Kosovo and Bosnia, have taught us anything, it is that we achieve our aims by defending our values and leading the forces of freedom and peace. We must embrace boldly and resolutely that duty to lead, to stand with our allies in word and deed, and to put a human face on the global economy so that expanded trade benefits all people in all nations, lifting lives and hopes all across the world.

Third, we must remember that America cannot lead in the world unless here at home we weave the threads of our coat of many colors into the fabric of one America. As we become ever more diverse, we must work harder to unite around our common values and our common humanity.

We must work harder to overcome our differences. In our hearts and in our laws, we must treat all our people with fairness and dignity, regardless of their race, religion, gender or sexual orientation and regardless of when they arrived in our country, always moving toward the more perfect union of our founders' dreams.

Hillary, Chelsea and I join all Americans in wishing our very best to the next president, George W. Bush, to his family and his administration in meeting these challenges and in leading freedom's march in this new century.

As for me, I'll leave the presidency more idealistic, more full of hope than the day I arrived and more confident than ever that America's best days lie ahead.

My days in this office are nearly through, but my days of service, I hope, are not. In the years ahead, I will never hold a position higher or more sacred than that of president of the United States. But, there is no title I will wear more proudly than that of citizen.

Thank you. God bless you, and God bless America.

重难点评析

1. "moved off welfare"译为"从社保之中解脱出来"。"move off"的原意是"离去,走掉",此处引申译为"从……中解脱出来"。

2. "greater accountability and larger investments have brought higher test scores, and higher graduation rates"译为"巨大的责任感,更多的投资提高了学生的考试成绩,提高了学生的毕业率"。此句中的"greater accountability and larger investments"译为"巨大的责任感,更多的投资",其中的两个形容词"巨大的"、"更多的"选词比较恰当、贴切。同时,该句的核心动词是"bring",表示"带来",但是翻译时译为"提高"更加合适。

3. "turned record deficits to record surpluses"译为"把破纪录的财政赤字转变为破纪录的盈余"。此处的"record"为名词作形容词,修饰其后的名词"deficits"和"surpluses"。

4. "pay down"意思是"偿还"。其另外还有"用现金支付"和"分期付款购物时先支付部分贷款"的意思。

5. "on track to be debt free"译为"在向使国家变成无债务国的方向前进"。"on track to"是"在轨道上"的意思,"be free"译为"免除"。

6. "deal with the retirement of the baby boomers, invest more in our future and provide tax relief"译为"解决二战后出生的大批人群的退休问题,对未来进行更多的投资,减轻税收"。其中"baby boomers"译为"二战后出生的大批人"。"relief"的意思很多,如"免除,宽慰,救济,援救,换班"等等,此处为"减轻"的意思。

7. "the gap between those of us who live on the cutting edge of the global economy and the billions around the world who live on the knife's edge of survival"译为"缩小处于全球经济顺境中的我们同处于生存逆境之中的数十亿人们间的差距"。该句中"the cutting edge"原意是"利刃",此处引申为"顺境"。"the knief's edge"原意为"锐利的刀刃",引申为

"生存逆境"。

8. "a powder keg that could be ignited by our indifference"译为"一个火药桶,可能会被我们的漠不关心所点燃"。"keg"指小桶,容量通常在三十加仑以下。

9. "embody our shared values, then we must assume a shared responsibility"译为"拥有我们所共有的价值观念,那么我们就必须共同承担一种义不容辞的责任"。"embody"的意思有三个:"体现","包含"和"使精神肉体化"。此处译为"包含,拥有"。"assume"的意思有四个,如"假定","承担","采取"和"装出",此处取"承担"的含义。

10. "embrace boldly and resolutely that duty to lead"译为"勇敢地、坚定地承担起这一统帅的责任"。"embrace"词义相当多,基本含义是"拥抱",此处引申为"承担"。"boldly"和"resolutely"这两个副词译为"勇敢地"和"坚定地"修饰"embrace"。

11. "unless here at home we weave the threads of our coat of many colors into the fabric of one America"译为"除非在这里,在美国国内,我们用各自外衣中的五彩缤纷的纱线编织成一件美国所共有的服饰"。在该句的翻译中,"here"指的是美国国内,所以要强调,添上"在美国国内"。"weave… into…"译为"将……编织成……"。

12. "wear more proudly than that of citizen"译为"比起其他美国公民来,会更加具有自豪感"。"wear"的意思很多,如"穿着,呈现,耗损,使厌烦,消失"等等,此处指"面容呈现出自豪感"。

译 文

告别演说

同胞们,

今晚是我最后一次有机会,作为你们的总统,在白宫椭圆形办公室里向你们做演讲。

我从心底深处十分感谢你们给予我两次机会,荣幸地为你们服务,为你们工作,并和你们一起为我们的国家进入21世纪而做出准备。我十分感谢戈尔副总统,十分感谢我的内阁部长们,十分感谢所有在过去的8年中与我一起共事的同事们。

这个时代一直是个极具变革的年代,你们已经奋起迎接新的挑战。你们使得我们的社会组织更加强大,使得我们的家庭变得更加健康和安全,使得我们的人民更加富有。

同胞们,全体的美国人,我们已经进入了全球信息化时代,一个美国复兴的伟大时代。

作为总统,在我所做的一切之中——我所做出的每一个决定,我所执行的每一个行政命令,我所提议、签署的每一项法令——我都在努力为全体美国人提供工具和创造条件,来实现我们所梦想的未来:生活在一个美好的社会之中,具有强大的经济,拥有清洁的环境,生活在一个更为自由、更为安全、更为繁荣的世界之中。

借助我们永恒的价值观念,我驾驭了我的航程。机会属于我们所有的人。责任之心来自我们所有的人:我们要建造一个属于全体美国人的大家庭。我一直在努力探索为美国创建一个新型的政府:它更小,更现代化,更加有效率,充满了适应新时代的创意和政策,永远把人民放在首位,永远寄希望于未来。

我们一起工作,美国取得了斐然的成就。我们的经济在打破一个又一个的记录,我们创造出了2 200万个新的工作岗位,我们的失业率达到30年来最低点,房屋的产权拥有率为历史最高,我们的经济繁荣持续期为历史最长。

我们的家庭、我们的社区变得更加强大。3 500万美国人享受到了"家庭休假法案"给予的权利。800万人从社保之中解脱出来,犯罪率为25年来最低的。1 000多万的美国人享受到更多数额的入学贷款,比以往更多的人将能接受大学教育。我们学校变得更好,水平更高,巨大的责任感,更多的投资提高了学生的考试成绩,提高了学生的毕业比率。

如今,已有300多万美国儿童在享受着医疗保险,700多万美国人已经摆脱了贫困。收入全面提高。我们的空气和水质更加清洁,我们的食品和饮用水更加安全,我们更多的珍惜土地资源得到了保护,这在美国大陆上,在近百年中,绝无仅有。

美国在全世界已经成为一种维护和平,促进繁荣的力量。

我此时感到万分的高兴,我能够将领导权连同美国一并交给一位新任的总统——美国如今具有强大的优势,能够面临未来的各种挑战。今晚,我希望大家能够从以下三点来思考我们的未来。

第一,美国必须要保持对财政负责的良好记录。通过以往四个财政年度的努力,我已经把破纪录的财政赤字变为破纪录的盈余。我们已经能够偿还6 000亿美元的国债。我们正在向10年内使国家变成无债务国的方向前进。这将是自1835年以来的第一次。

只要坚持这条道路,我们的利率就会变得更低,就会有更大的繁荣,就会有更多的机遇迎接各种重大的挑战。如果我们能够做出明智的选择,我们就能以现金偿还债务,就能解决好二战后出生的大批人群的退休问题,就能对未来进行更多的投资,就能减轻税收。

第二,鉴于整个世界的联系日益紧密,为了美国的安全与繁荣,我们应该继续引导世界。在此历史的特别时刻,更多的美国人民享有前所未有的自由。我们的盟国更加强大,前所未有。全世界的人民都期望美国能成为一种维护和平,促进繁荣、自由和安全的力量。全球经济正在给予美国民众一种机遇,正在给全世界数十亿人民一种机遇,这一机遇就是工作、生活、提升家庭尊严。

但是,这种融合的力量一方面为我们创造出了良好的机遇,另一方面也使我们更加易于受到全球破坏性力量的威胁,受到恐怖主义的威胁,受到有组织犯罪和麻醉毒品非法交易的威胁,受到致命性武器扩散和疾病传播的威胁,受到全球环境恶化的威胁。

贸易的不断扩大并没有缩小处于全球经济顺境中的我们同处于生存逆境之中的数十亿人们之间的差距。要缩短这种差异仅仅靠同情和怜悯是不够的,需要实际行动。全球性的贫穷是一个火药桶,可能会被我们的漠不关心所点燃。

托马斯·杰斐逊在他的首次就职演说中就告诫我们要紧密这种联盟。在我们这个时代,美国不能,也不可能使自己脱离这个世界。如果我们想让全世界都拥有我们所共有的价值观念,那么我们就必须共同承担起一种义不容辞的责任。

如果20世纪的历次战争,尤其是新近在科索沃和波斯尼亚爆发的战争,能够让我们得到某种教训的话,那么这种教训就是,我们能实现我们的目标,方法是捍卫我们的价值观念,统帅自由和和平的力量。我们必须勇敢地、坚定地承担起这一统帅的责任,在语言、行动两方面都与我们的同盟者们站在一起,赋予全球经济以一种人本观念,以便使贸易能够不断发展,施惠所有国家的所有人们,提高全世界的生活水平,提升全世界的希望。

第三,我们必须牢记,美国无法统领全世界,除非在这里,在美国国内,我们用各自外衣中的五彩缤纷的纱线编织成一件美国所共有的服饰。随着我们社会变得日益多元化,我们必须更加努力,在我们共同的价值观念和共有的博爱的旗帜下,团结起来。

我们必须加倍努力,克服我们所面临的各种困难。于情于法,我们都必须要公正地对待我们的人民,使他们获得尊严。不论他们的民族背景如何,不论他们的宗教信仰如何,不论他们的性别或性别倾向如何,也不论他们何时来到我们这个国家,我们都必须时刻继续前进,为建立一个尽善尽美的美利坚合众国,实现缔造者们的梦想而奋斗。

希拉里、切尔西和我都愿意与全体美国人民一起,向下任总统乔治·布什表示最为美好的祝愿,最衷心地祝愿他的家人,最衷心地祝愿他的政府,这一政府在新的世纪中要引领自由的大旗阔步前进。

就我而言,在即将离开总统职位时,比起我初次到来时,我充满了更多的理想,充满了更多的希望,更加坚信,美国的盛世就在眼前。

我的任期就要结束,但我希望我的服务期永远不会结束。在未来的岁月里,我再也不会身居一个能比美国总统更高、更为神圣的职位了。但没有一个职位,比身为美国公民更令我自豪。

谢谢你们!愿上帝保佑你们!愿上帝保佑美国!

倍数表示法

倍数翻译是一个很容易出错的问题,这是因为英汉两种语言均有众多的倍数表示法,很容易让人混淆。此外,我国翻译界本身对如何进行倍数翻译也是众说纷纭,莫衷一是。倍数翻译最根本的问题是要搞清楚是否包括基数。汉语有一些句式包括基数,也有一些句式不包括基数,而英语则都包括基数。例如:

  a. A is twice as tall as B.
  b. A is twice taller than B.

这两种句式所表达的含义是一样的,也就是说,如果 B 是 1 的话,那么,A 就是 2。两个句子都应译成"A 的身高是 B 的两倍"。第一句话翻译起来一般不会有什么问题,但翻译第二句话却必须小心,因为如果把它译成"A 比 B 高两倍",那么按汉语的表达习惯,A 就会被错误地理解为 3 倍。

汉语表示倍数的基本句式或表达法有以下五种(句中"n"指倍数):

  1."甲的大小是乙的 n 倍"   (包括基数)
  2."甲已增加到乙的 n 倍"   (包括基数)
  3."甲比乙(形容词或副词)"   (不包括基数)
  4."甲比乙增加了 n 倍"   (不包括基数)
  5."甲比乙翻了 n 番"   (不包括基数)

英语表示倍数的基本句式或表达法有以下五种:

  1. n＋times＋as＋形容词或副词＋as   (包括基数)
  2. n＋times＋形容词或副词的比较＋than   (包括基数)
  3. n＋times＋the(或 its, that of 等)＋名词   (包括基数)
  4. 动词(increase/grow/multiply 等)＋(by)＋n＋times (包括基数)
  5. 动词(double/triple/quadruple 等)＋the＋名词   (包括基数)

无论是汉语还是英语,同一个倍数都有不同的表示法。

1. 表示"甲是乙的两倍"

英语用 twice as... as, twice the number/size/length of, as... again as, to increase by 100%,以及 double 来表示。例如:

(1) 他们今年的产量是去年的两倍。/他们的产量比去年增加了一倍。/他们今年的产量比去年翻了一番。

　　a. Their output this year is twice as much as what it was last year.

　　b. Their output this year is twice the amount of what it was last year.

　　c. Their output this year is as much again as what it was last year.

　　d. Their output this year is double what it was last year.

　　e. Their output this year has doubled, compared with what it was last year.

　　f. Their output this year has increased by 100% over last year.

(2) 这辆车是那辆车的两倍价钱。/这辆车比那辆车贵一倍。

　　a. This car is twice as costly as that one.

　　b. This car is twice the cost of that one.

　　c. This car is as costly again as that one.

2. 表示"甲是乙的三倍"

英语用 thrice/three times as... as, thrice/three times the number of, to increase by 200%,以及 triple/treble 表示。例如:

(1) 这幢楼是那幢楼的三倍高。/这幢楼比那幢楼高两倍。

　　a. This building is thrice/three times as tall as that one.

　　b. This building is thrice/three times the height of that one.

(2) 这条公路是那条公路的三倍长。/这条公路比那条公路长两倍。

　　a. This highway is thrice/three times as long as that one.

　　b. The lenghth of this highway is thrice/three times the lenghth of that one.

(3) 我国今年的出口额是去年的三倍。/我国今年的出口额比去年增长了两倍。/我国今年的出口额比去年增长了百分之二百。

　　a. Our export this year is thrice/three times as much as what it was last year.

　　b. Our export this year is thrice/three times what it was last year.

　　c. Our export this year is triple/treble what it was last year.

　　d. Our export this year has tripled/trebled, compared with what it was last year.

　　e. Our export this year has increased by 200% over last year.

3. 表示"甲是乙的四倍"

表示四倍,英语用 four times/fourfold,以及 quadruple 和 to increase by 300%。表示四倍以上,依次类推。例如:

(1) 到2000年,我国的国民生产总值将是1980年的四倍。/到2000年,我国的国民生产总值将在1980年的基础上达到翻两番。/到2000年,我国的国民生产总值将比1980年增加三倍。

　　a. By 2000, our GNP will have been four times/fourfold as much as it was in 1980.

b. By 2000, our GNP in 1980 will have been quadruple.
　　c. By 2000, our GNP will have increased by 300% over 1980.
　（2）我们现在的工资是十年前的五倍。/我们现在的工资比十年前增加了四倍。
　　a. Our salaries are now five times/fivefold as many as what they were ten years ago.
　　b. Our salaries are now five times/fivefold those ten years ago.
　　c. Our salaries have increased by 400% over ten years ago.
　（3）我国要养活的人口是那个国家的7.5倍。
　　We have to feed 7.5-fold(seven point five fold) the number of people in that country.
　（4）这家商店出售的商品的价格是其他商店的3倍。
　　a. Goods sold in this shop are 3 times as costly as in other shops.
　　b. This shop sells goods at a price 3 times as high as that in other shops.
　（5）改革开放以来,到中国来的游客成倍增长。
　　Since the beginning of reform and opening up, the number of foreign visitors to China has doubled and redoubled.

　　为了避免出错,同时也是为了照顾语感和避免麻烦,在口译倍数时原则上应选用能顾及原文整数的译法,以免在把英文的倍数减去一倍后使20倍、100倍、300倍等整数变成29倍、99倍、299倍等等。其次,英语表示减少时也用倍数,而汉语一般不能用倍数来表示减少的概念,因此在遇到表示倍数减少的概念时,汉语通常要转换成百分数。为了方便口译时迅速换算,我们不妨记住下面两个固定公式:
　　1. 表示净减数时为:减少了$(n-1)/n$
　　2. 包括基数成分(表示剩下)时为:减少到$1/n$
　　公式中的n代表英语原文中所说的减少倍数。

分 译 法

　　分译法主要用于长句的翻译。为了使译文忠实、易懂,有时不得不把一个长句译成两句或更多的句子。Division作为一种翻译的技巧,它除了指句子分译外,还包括某些词语意义的分译。
　　一、单词分译:提起分译法这一技巧,一般都指句子分译,很少有著家谈及单词分译。伍华民曾发表一篇文章,题为《文学翻译中的单词分译》,现摘引其有关部分(略有删改)。
　　（一）单词词义分译:英语有些单词的语义呈综合型,即一个词内集合了几个语义成分。译成汉语时,不易找到合适的对等词,很难将其词义一下全部表达出来。这种情况下,汉译可采用分析型,即"扩展"型的方法分译原语,将其语义成分分布到几个不同的词语上。例如:
　　... that little pink-faced chit Amelia with not half any sense, has ten thousand pounds and an establishment secure,...
　　……爱米丽亚那粉红脸儿的小不点儿,还没有我一半懂事,倒有一万镑财产,住宅、家具、奴仆一应俱全……
　　（二）单词搭配分译:英语中有些词语间的搭配关系颇有特点,汉译时要打破原文的结

构,按照汉语习惯,将有关单词分别译出。例如:

... she treated that lady with every demonstration of cool respect...

……她对那位夫人不冷不热,不错规矩……

... she had such a kindly, smiling, tender, gentle, generous heart of her own, ...

……她心地厚道,性格温柔可疼,气量又大,为人又乐观……(heart 一词被分译成"心地"、"性格"、"气量"和"为人"四个词,再与它前面的五个形容词搭配。)

(三)灵活对等分译:英语中有些单词,如果按其在句中的位置机械地译成汉语,往往意义不够明确。遇到这类情况,应采用灵活对等分译,不拘泥于形式的对应,尽量使读者对译文的反应等值于对原文的反应。例如:

Thus it was that our little romantic friend formed visions of the future for herself...

我们的小朋友一脑袋幻想,憧憬着美丽的将来……

如果逐字译成"我们的浪漫的小朋友憧憬着未来……"并不能算错,但意思却不甚明了,因为"浪漫"一词在汉语中的含义较多。此处为"想入非非",所以拆译成"一脑袋幻想"较为明确,既突出了人物的性格,又避免了翻译腔。

(四)突出语言重点:有时逐字翻译虽然也能文从字顺,但却不如分译能传达句内所含的语意重点。例如:

... there was in the old library at Queen's Crawley a considerable provision of works of light literature of the last century, both in the French and English languages...

……在女王的克劳莱大厦的书房里,有不少18世纪的文学作品,有英文的,也有法文的,都是些轻松的读物……

(五)修辞需要词语分译:有时将单词分译只是为了达到某种修辞效果,如:

And in their further disputes she always returned to this point, "Get me a situation — we hate each other, and I am ready to go."

从此以后他们每拌一次嘴,她就回到老题目,说道:"给我找个事情,反正咱们你恨我我嫌你,我愿意走。"

一个 hate 分译成"恨"与"嫌"两个字,使得译笔生动,读者似乎如见其人,如闻其声。又如:

Not that the parting speech caused Amelia to philosophize, or that it aimed her in any way with a calmness, the result of argument, ...

倒并不是(平克顿小姐的)临别赠言使爱米丽亚想得通丢得开,因此心平气和,镇静下来……

此处将"philosophize"分译作"想得通"、"丢得开",将"calmness"分译作"心平气和"、"镇静下来",说明译者真正吃透原文,摆脱了字典释义的束缚,使用恰当的译文语言再现了原文的特色,并做到了结构匀称,声调和谐,保持了原文的神韵与丰姿。

二、句子分译:这是分译法的主要内容。下面叙述句子分译法的几种常见情况。所谓一长句可分译成几句中的"句子"的含义是什么呢?此处所谓的"句子"不在于结尾处用句号,而在于有无主谓结构。一般来说,含有一个主谓结构的语言部分就是一个句子。

(一)含定语从句的句子:除少数情况外,这类从句都是长句。在英汉互译时,如能将定语从句译成前置定语,则尽量避免其他译法;如译成前置定语不合适,则按其他方法翻译,

一般是分译成另外一个独立的句子或另一种从句,如状语从句等。如:

1. "Well, there's never anything happened in my family I'm ashamed of."

"嘿,我家可从来没出现过见不得人的事。"(译成前置定语。)

2. I am going to see my grandmother, who was ill in bed, to take her some butter and eggs and a fresh-baked cake that my mother has made for her.

我去看病在床上的祖母,给她带些奶油、鸡蛋和妈妈刚刚烤好的蛋糕。(译法同上)

3. Elizabeth was determined to make no effort for conversation with a woman, who was now more than usually insolent and disagreeable.

伊莉莎白不肯再和这样一个女人说话,这个女人现在异常无礼,十分令人反感。(定语从句译成另外一句。)

4. It's in line with the Charter, which recognizes the value of regional efforts to solve problems and settle disputes.

它符合宪章精神,因为宪章承认由地区进行排难解纷的作用。(定语从句译成状语从句。)

5. ... so my chances of getting to revolutionary China are pretty slim, although I have not given up my efforts to get a passport that will enable us to visit the countries of Socialism.

……因此,我到革命的中国来的希望相当小了,虽然我并没有放弃努力来争取一张护照,以便访问社会主义国家。(定语从句译成状语。)

6. They tried to stamp out the revolt, which spread all the more furiously throughout the country.

他们企图扑灭反抗,结果反抗愈来愈猛,遍及全国。(定语从句译成状语。)

7. In a dispute between two states with which one is friendly, try not to get involved.

当两国发生争端时,如与两国都友好,第三国则力避卷入。(定语从句译成状语。)

8. However great the joy with which he welcomed a new discovery in some theoretical science whose practical application perhaps it was as yet quite impossible to envisage, he experienced quite another kind of joy when the discovery involved immediate revolutionary changes in industry, and in historical development in general.

任何一门理论科学中的每一个新发现,即使它的实际应用甚至还无法预见,都使他(马克思)感到由衷地喜悦,但是当有了立即会对工业、对一般历史发展产生革命影响的发现的时候,他的喜悦就完全不同了。(定语从句译成状语。)

9. The cook turned pale, and asked the housemaid to shut the door, who asked Brittle, who asked the tinker, who pretended not to hear.

厨子的脸发起白来,要使唤丫头把门关上,丫头叫布立特尔去,布立特尔叫补锅匠去,补锅匠却装着没听见。(这个长句中有三个定语从句,如果不这样分成几个等立成分来译,那么译出来的句子不一定会让人看得懂。把这一长句分成五个分句,意思既明确又忠实于原文。)

10. He dropped the mattress against the rough wooden fence which had replaced the iron bars taken up for war efforts, and wiped his brow.

他把褥垫扔下,靠着木栅栏(原来是铁栏杆,为了支援战争而换成木头的了),擦了擦额头。(有时候,同一句中的定语从句前后两个动作紧接发生,为了使这两个动作仍显得紧凑,翻译时可将原文中的定语从句的译文置于括号中。)

11. It(The People's Republic of China) must be created by the blood and the work of all of us who believe in the future, who believe in man and his glorious man-made destiny.

伟大的中华人民共和国必须用我们大家的鲜血和工作来缔造。我们这些人相信未来,相信人们,相信人们能够掌握自己的命运——光辉灿烂的命运。(同位语从句译成了单独的句子。)

12. But as the song surged up in increasing loudness, even the most timid lost their fear and joined in, and all the things that King had said at the meeting in the ball-room, things that they hadn't believed or had only half-believed, became suddenly and powerfully ture.

但是当歌声越来越响的时候,连那些最胆小的人也没有什么恐惧了,他们也跟着唱起来,金在舞厅里开会时所说的一切,那些他们曾经不相信或半信半疑的话,忽然很有力地变成是真的了。(定语从句译成一般的前置定语,整个的译文能按原文顺序翻译出来而又忠实、清楚,当然就不必采取别的分译方法。)

13. He had a set of little tools and saws of various sizes manufactured by himself. With the aid of these, Issac contrived to make many curious articles, at which he worked with so much skill, that he seemed to have been born with a saw or chisel in his hand.

艾萨克有一套自制的小工具和各种尺寸的锯子。由于这些工具,加之手很巧,他制造出许多罕见的东西,好像他天生就是用锯子或凿子似的。(分译这两句较长的英文句子时,要重新安排词序,译成若干短句。)

14. They remarked now he took a different seat from that which he usually occupied when he chose to attend divine worship.

他往常做礼拜的时候,总坐在固定的座位上,可是那天他们发现他不坐老位置了。(此句使用了逆序分译法,较好地传达了原文的意思。)

15. He visited many places, in all of which he was received with the usual enthusiasm which attended his arduous labors.

他访问了许多地方,到处受到热情的欢迎。他的艰苦努力是经常受到热情欢迎的。(此句原文中有两个定语从句,将这样一个英文长句分译成两个独立的句子,意思显得很清楚。)

16. Intellectually emancipated at a time when women of good family were not encouraged to do anything more ambitious than dabble in the arts, she became the editor of a review entitled Correspondence des Families in which she was bold enough to publish essays by the revolutionary socialist Jules Valles.

当时,有教养的人家对于女子至多不过让她们对艺术稍有涉猎,并不鼓励她们去做比此更有抱负的事情。但她不受旧思想的约束,担任了一家叫《家庭通讯》杂志的编辑。她在这个刊物上大胆地发表了革命社会主义者 朱尔·瓦莱斯的文章。(一个英文长句译成三句汉语。)

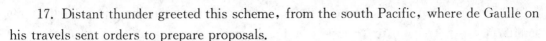

17. Distant thunder greeted this scheme, from the south Pacific, where de Gaulle on his travels sent orders to prepare proposals.

当时远在南太平洋地区旅行的戴高乐听到这个计划,大发雷霆,下令提出新的方案。(打散原文的结构,重新组合译文,把译文分成几个小部分,读来流畅顺口。)

18. Perhaps, after all, there was no enigma about him, except in the minds of lesser men who found it hard to conceive such tenacity of purpose.

关于他的谜,也许根本就不存在。所谓谜者,只是那些不及他的人对他那样坚忍不拔的意志感到不可思议而已。(一句译成两句。)

(二) 其他长句的某些翻译规则

1. 一个长句包含作者的多步逻辑推理,英译汉时可用分译法。如:

Thus it happened that when the new factories that were springing up required labor, tens of thousands of homeless and hungry agricultural workers, with their wives and children, were forced into the cities in search of work, any work, under any condition, that would keep them alive.

于是,就出现了这样的情况:正当新办的工厂纷纷成立、需要劳动力的时候,成千上万无家可归、饥肠辘辘的从事农业的劳动者,携妻带儿,被迫流入城市;他们要活干,不管什么活儿,不讲什么条件,只要不让他们饿死就行。

这段译文把原作者的逻辑推理表达得一清二楚:新工厂要求廉价劳动力并容易得到,是因为大批农民破产,流往城市,急于找工作。

2. 宾语的修饰成分太长时亦需分译。如:

The Prime Minister added, "We are now once again regarded by other states as a power whose judgment can be trusted and whose promises can be relied on."

首相说:"我们这个大国的判断是可以相信的,我们这个大国的诺言是可以信赖的;现在,其他国家又把我们当作这样的大国了。"

3. 当状语太长而硬译成一句变得不容易读或不容易理解时,应该分译。如:

A report of the proposed compromise plan came from a reliable source only a few hours after the president's special envoy, Mr. X, emerged from his fifth secret session with the Egyptian Foreign Minister and told newsmen "A solution is in sight."

关于折中方案的消息是一位可靠人士传出来的。在这个消息传出之前不过几个小时,总统的特使某先生在与埃及外长进行第五次秘密会谈之后,曾对记者说"解决方案现已在望"。

4. 一个长句的从句实际上起过渡或承上启下的作用,即是说此从句可以帮助长句的前一部分向后一部分过渡,这时要分译。例如:

This suggestion was made today by the influential New York Times which predicted a "change of topic" at the forthcoming meeting, with emphasis shifting from armament limitation to human rights...

这个建议是有影响的《纽约时报》今天提出来的。该报预言,即将举行的会议"议题会有改变",侧重点会由武器限制问题转到人权问题……

5. 一长句提及多个方面内容,可以在分译中重译原文的某个关键性词语。如:

"The Civil War, lasting four years and costing at least a million lives, civilian and military, was the most extensive war ever fought on the soil of the New World, a war that proved to the planters in a revolutionary way that human beings in America could no longer be bought or sold, worked and killed at will to serve the profit of parasitic landowners."

美国的南北战争历时四年之久,夺去了至少一百万军民的生命,是在新大陆(新世界)进行过的规模最大的一次战争,据此战争以革命的方式使种植园主认识到:在美国,再也不能为了寄生的土地所有者的利益而把人任意买卖、任意驱使、任意杀害了。

(三)典型长句英汉对照:英语长句很多。英语中一个句号前最多能有多少词,在浩如烟海的文献中无法弄清楚,但含有上百个词的英文长句是不难找到的。下面列出四个长句及其译文。第一句引自 The Life and Opinions of Tristram Shandy;第二句引自 David Copperfield;第三句引自 The Adventures of Huckleberry Finn;第四句引自 Speech at the Graveside of Karl Marx。

1. I wish either my father or my mother, or indeed both of them, as they were in duty both equally bound to it, had minded what they were about when they begot me; had they duly considered how much depended upon what they were then doing;— that not only the production of a rational being was concerned in it, but that possibly the happy formation and temperature of his body, perhaps his genius and the very cast of his mind;— and, for aught they knew to the contrary, even the fortunes of his whole house might take their turn from the humorous and dispositions which were then uppermost;— had they duly weighed and considered all this, and proceeded accordingly, I am verily persuaded I should have made a quite different figure in the world, from that in which the reader is likely to see me. (145 words)

2. The rest is all a more or less incoherent dream... Of Miss Lavinia, who acts as a semiauxiliary bridesmaid, being the first to cry, and of her doing homage(as I take it) to the memory of Pidger, in sobs; of Miss Clarissa applying a smelling-bottle; of Agnes taking care of Dora; of my aunt endeavoring to represent herself as a model of sternness, with tears rolling down her face; of little Dora trembling very much, and making her responses in faint whispers. (这一例实为一介词短语)(75 words)

3. ... And load up the cabin with rats and snakes and so on, for company for Jim; and then you kept Tom here so long with the butter in his hat that you come near spoiling the whole business, because the men came before we were out of the cabin, and we had to resh, and they heard us and let drive at us, and I got my share, and we dodged out of the path and let them go by, and when the dogs came they weren't interested in us, but went for the most noise, and we got our canoe, and made for the raft, and was all safe, and Jim was a free man, and we done it all by ourselves, and wasn't it bully, Aunty! (128 words)

4. Just as Darwin discovered the law of development of organic nature, so Marx discovered the law of development of human history: the simple fact, hitherto concealed by an overgrowth of ideology, that mankind must first of all eat, drink, have shelter and

clothing, before it can pursue politics, science, art, religion, etc.; that therefore the production of the immediate material means of subsistence and consequently the degree of economic development attained by a given people or during a given epoch from the foundation upon which the state institutions, the legal conceptions, art, and even the ideas on religion, of the people concerned have been evolved, and in the light of which they must, therefore, be explained, instead of vice versa, as had hitherto been the case. (126 words)

译文

1. 我希望我的父亲或是母亲，不，我的双亲，因为他们两人同样地对此都有义务，当他们生我的时候，曾注意到他们所做的事；如果他们适当地想过，他们当时所做的事，是有何等大的影响，那不单是产生一个有理性的人，而且身体适合的形成和要素的配合，也许他的天赋及其心灵的典型都产生出来；而由于那时他们最强烈的性情和意向，恐怕要甚至改变他们全家的命运；如果他们适当地仔细考虑过这一切，因而照着进行的话，我确信我早成为与读者诸君此后可能见到的我，完全两样的一个人物了吧。（钱歌川《翻译的基本知识》）

2. 其余的情况，只是一场或多或少不相连属的大梦。……莱薇妮亚小姐怎样好像是半个助理伴娘，怎样头一个哭起来；她怎样对于故去的皮治先生唏嘘致敬（这是我的想法）；珂萝莉莎小姐怎样拿出闻药来闻；爱格尼怎样照顾朵萝；我姨婆怎样表面上装作是铁石心肠的模范，眼泪却止不住地从脸上滚滚往下直流；朵萝怎样浑身抖得厉害，应答的时候，怎样有气无力、声音低微：所有这种情况，对于我，也只是一场大梦。（张谷若译）

3. ……还在小屋里装满了老鼠、长虫等等，为的是给吉姆做伴。后来你把汤姆留在这儿那么老半天，他帽子里那块黄油化了，差一点儿就把整个事情弄糟了，因为那些人没等我们从小屋里爬出来就来了，因此我们不得不拼命往前冲，他们听见我们的响声，就对着我们开枪，于是就挨了这一下，可是我们马上闪到一旁，把他们都让过去了，那些狗赶到我们跟前，对我们并不感兴趣，光知道对着那些热闹的地方跑，我们就找着我们的小船，朝着我们的木筏划去，我们都平安无事，吉姆有了自由，决不再当奴隶。这些事从头到尾都是我们自己干的，姨妈，这不是棒极了吗！（张万里译）

4. 正像达尔文发现有机界的发展规律一样，马克思发现了人类历史的发展规律，即历来为纷繁芜杂的意识形态所掩盖着的一个简单事实：人们首先必须吃、喝、住、穿，然后才能从事政治、科学、艺术、宗教等等；所以，直接的物质生活资料的生产，从而一个民族或一个时代的一定的经济发展阶段，便构成基础。人们的国家设施、法的观点、艺术以至宗教观念，就是从这个基础上发展起来的，因而，也必须由这个基础来解释，而不是像过去那样做得相反。（《在马克思墓前的讲话》）

（四）汉语长句英译的分译

和英译汉的情形差不多，汉语长句英译也可使用分译法。如果留心读读五卷《毛泽东选集》英译本，便会发现大量分译的例子。

汉译英的分译也可以总结出不少规则，常见的有如下五种：

1. 如果长句以一表示判断或小结的从句结尾，可使用分译法。例如：

这些国家的共产党和进步党派，正促使它们的政府和我们做生意，以至建立外交关系，这是善意的,这就是援助。

The Communist Parties and progressive groups in these countries are urging their governments to establish trade and even diplomatic relations with us. This is goodwill. This is help.

2. 如果汉语句子较长,其中有语气或话题的转折,为了使英译文明确,可进行分译。例如:

蒋介石说,中国过去没有内战,只有剿匪;不管叫什么吧,总之要发动反人民的内战。

Chiang Kai-shek says there has never been any "civil war" in China, only "bandit suppression". Whatever he likes to call it, the fact is he wants to start a civil war against the people.

3. 如果汉语长句中含有反问句(或反诘句)或感叹号,英译时通常要分译。例如:

① 不和中国的人民民主专政的当局好好地打交道,却要干这些混账工作,而且公开地发表出来,丢脸!丢脸。

Instead of dealing with the authorities of the Chinese people's democratic dictatorship in the proper way, Acheson and his like are doing filthy work, and, what is more, they have openly published it. What a loss of face! What a loss of face!

② 蒋介石说要建国,今后就是建什么国的斗争,是建立一个无产阶级领导的人民大众的新民主主义国家呢,还是建立一个大地主大资产阶级专政的半殖民地半封建的国家呢?

Chiang Kai-shek talks about "building the country". From now on the struggle will be to build what sort of country. To build a new-democratic country of the broad massed under the leadership of the proletariat? Or to build a semi-colonial and semi-feudal country under the dictatorship of the big landlords and the big bourgeoisie?

4. 如果汉语长句中含有从一般到具体或从具体到一般的过渡,英译时应分译。例如:

这一点现在就必须向党内讲明白,务必使同志们继续地保持谦虚、谨慎、不骄、不躁的作风,务必使同志们继续地保持艰苦奋斗的作风。

This must be made clear now in the Party. The comrades must be taught to remain modest, prudent and free from arrogance and rashness in their style of work. The comrades must be taught to preserve the style of plain living and hard struggle.

5. 如果汉语长句中含有几个平行的子句,各讲一个方面的内容,英译时最好分译。例如:

我军的现代化,就是要有一支强大的陆军空军海军,要有现代化的武器装备,包括导弹和核武器,要严格训练,要按实战要求苦练过硬的杀敌本领,熟练掌握使用现代化武器装备的新技术,以及随之而来的新战术。

Our army's modernization calls for powerful ground, air and naval forces and modern arms and equipment, including guided missiles and nuclear weapons; it calls for rigorous and hard training to develop the ability to wipe out the enemy as required in actual combat; it calls for mastery of the new techniques involved in handling modern arms and equipment and of the new tactics entailed.

拓展阅读

选文A

在第十一届全国人民代表大会第三次会议上的政府工作报告

国务院总理　温家宝

2010年3月5日

各位代表，

现在，我代表国务院向大会作政府工作报告，请予审议，并请全国政协各位委员提出意见。

一、2009年工作回顾

2009年是新世纪以来我国经济发展最为困难的一年。去年这个时候，国际金融危机还在扩散蔓延，世界经济深度衰退，我国经济受到严重冲击，出口大幅下降，不少企业经营困难，有的甚至停产倒闭，失业人员大量增加，农民工大批返乡，经济增速陡然下滑。在异常困难的情况下，全国各族人民在中国共产党的坚强领导下，坚定信心，迎难而上，顽强拼搏，从容应对国际金融危机冲击，在世界率先实现经济回升向好，改革开放和社会主义现代化建设取得新的重大成就。国内生产总值达到33.5万亿元，比上年增长8.7%；财政收入6.85万亿元，增长11.7%；粮食产量5.31亿吨，再创历史新高，实现连续6年增产；城镇新增就业1 102万人；城镇居民人均可支配收入17 175元，农村居民人均纯收入5 153元，实际增长9.8%和8.5%。我国在全面建设小康社会道路上又迈出坚实的一步。实践再次证明，任何艰难险阻都挡不住中华民族伟大复兴的历史进程。

过去的一年，极不平凡，令人振奋。我们隆重庆祝新中国成立60周年。抚今追昔，伟大祖国的辉煌成就极大地激发了全国人民的自信心和自豪感，极大地增强了中华民族的向心力和凝聚力，极大地提升了我国的国际地位和影响力，必将激励我们在中国特色社会主义道路上继续奋勇前进。

一年来，我们主要做了以下工作：

（一）加强和改善宏观调控，促进经济平稳较快发展。我们实行积极的财政政策和适度宽松的货币政策，全面实施并不断完善应对国际金融危机的一揽子计划。大规模增加财政支出和实行结构性减税，保持货币信贷快速增长，提高货币政策的可持续性，扩大直接融资规模，满足经济社会发展的资金需求，有效扩大了内需，很快扭转了经济增速下滑趋势。

着力扩大居民消费。我们鼓励消费的政策领域之宽、力度之大、受惠面之广前所未有。中央财政投入资金450亿元，补贴家电汽车摩托车下乡、汽车家电以旧换新和农机具购置。减半征收小排量汽车购置税，减免住房交易相关税收，支持自住性住房消费。全年汽车销售1 364万辆，增长46.2%；商品房销售9.37亿平方米，增长42.1%；社会消费品零售总额实际增长16.9%，消费对经济增长的拉动作用明显增强。

促进投资快速增长。我们发挥政府投资"四两拨千斤"的作用，引导带动社会投资。实施两年新增4万亿元的投资计划。2009年中央政府公共投资9 243亿元，比上年预算增加5 038亿元，其中，保障性住房、农村民生工程、社会事业投资占44%，自主创新、结构调整、节能减排和生态建设占16%,重大基础设施建设占23%,灾后恢复重建占14%。全社会固定资产投资增长30.1%,投资结构进一步优化。投资快速增长有效弥补了外需下降的缺口,加强了薄弱环节,为经济社会长远发展奠定了坚实的基础。

我们加快推进汶川地震灾后恢复重建,重灾区已完成投资6 545亿元,占规划总投资的65.5%。国家的大力支持,全国人民的无私援助,灾区群众的艰苦奋斗,使遭受重大创伤的灾区呈现出崭新面貌。一座座新城拔地而起,一个个村庄焕发出蓬勃生机。这充分体现了中华民族的无疆大爱,有力彰显了社会主义制度的无比优越。

(二)大力调整经济结构,夯实长远发展基础。我们把保增长与调结构紧密结合起来,加快解决制约经济发展的结构性矛盾。

"三农"工作进一步加强。中央财政用于"三农"的支出7 253亿元,增长21.8%。大幅度提高粮食最低收购价。启动实施全国新增千亿斤粮食生产能力建设规划。继续改善农村生产生活条件,农村饮水安全工程使6 069万农民受益,新增510万沼气用户,新建和改造农村公路38万公里、农村电网线路26.6万公里,又有80万户农村危房得到改造,9.2万户游牧民实现了定居。我们加大扶贫力度,贫困地区的生产生活条件得到明显改善。

产业结构调整力度加大。制定并实施十大重点产业调整振兴规划。鼓励企业加快技术改造,安排200亿元技改专项资金支持4 441个技改项目。重点行业兼并重组取得新进展。下大力气抑制部分行业产能过剩和重复建设,关停小火电机组2 617万千瓦,淘汰落后的炼钢产能1 691万吨、炼铁产能2 113万吨、水泥产能7 416万吨、焦炭产能1 809万吨。加快实施国家科技重大专项,中央财政用于科技的支出1 512亿元,增长30%。积极支持自主创新产品推广应用,清洁能源、第三代移动通信等一批新兴产业快速发展。大力加强基础设施建设,新建铁路投入运营5 557公里,高速公路新建通车4 719公里,城市轨道交通建设加快,新建、改扩建民用机场35个;新增发电装机8 970万千瓦,西气东输二线西段工程实现供气,南水北调工程建设加快推进,6 183座病险水库除险加固工程开工建设。

节能减排和环境保护扎实推进。安排预算内资金,支持重点节能工程、循环经济等项目2 983个;实施节能产品惠民工程,推广节能空调500多万台、高效照明灯具1.5亿只。继续推进林业重点生态工程建设,完成造林8 827万亩,森林覆盖率达到20.36%。综合治理水土流失面积4.8万平方公里。加强"三河三湖"等重点流域水污染防治和工业废水废气废渣治理。"十一五"前四年累计单位国内生产总值能耗下降14.38%,化学需氧量、二氧化硫排放量分别下降9.66%和13.14%。积极开展应对气候变化工作,明确提出2020年我国控制温室气体排放行动目标和政策措施。气象预报预警和地震监测工作得到加强,灾害防御能力不断提升。

区域协调发展迈出新步伐。深入实施区域发展总体战略,制定若干区域发展重大规划和政策。中西部和东北地区加快开放开发,积极承接产业转移,发展基础不断夯实;东部地区加快结构和自主创新,经济发展活力增强。区域发展呈现布局改善、结构优化、协调性提高的良好态势。

(三)坚持深化改革开放,不断完善有利于科学发展的体制机制。我们把深化改革开放作为应对国际金融危机的强大动力,努力消除体制障碍,不断提高对外开放水平。

重点领域和关键环节改革加快推进。增值税转型全面实施。成品油价格和税费改革顺利推进,新的成品油价格形成机制规范运行。国家开发银行商业化转型和农业银行股份制改革扎实推进,跨境贸易人民币结算试点启动实施。创业板正式推出,为自主创新及其他成长型创业企业开辟了新的融资渠道。地方政府机构改革有序开展,事业单位分类改革试点稳步进行。集体林权制度改革全面推开,15亿亩林地确权到户,占全国集体林地面积的60%,这是继土地家庭承包之后我国农村经营制度的又一重大变革。

开放型经济水平不断提高。出台一系列稳定外需的政策措施,采取符合国际惯例的方式支持出口企业,完成短期出口信用保险承保900亿美元,安排421亿美元大型成套设备出口融资保险。鼓励增加进口。去年下半年开始进出口降幅明显收窄,国际市场份额得到巩固,全年进出口总额2.2万亿美元。扭转利用外资下降局面,全年实际利用外商直接投资900亿美元。企业"走出去"逆势上扬,非金融类对外直接投资和对外工程承包营业额分别达433亿美元和777亿美元。积极参与国际宏观经济政策对话协调和经贸金融合作,在共同应对国际金融危机中发挥了建设性作用。

(四)着力改善民生,加快发展社会事业。在应对国际金融危机的困难情况下,我们更加注重保障和改善民生,切实解决人民群众最关心、最直接、最现实的利益问题。

实施更加积极的就业政策。强化政府促进就业的责任。中央财政安排就业专项资金426亿元,比上年增长59%。实施困难企业缓缴社会保险费或降低部分费率、再就业税收减免及提供相关补贴等政策,鼓励企业稳定和增加就业。开展系列就业服务活动,多渠道开辟公益性就业岗位,促进高校毕业生到基层就业、应征入伍和到企事业单位就业见习。全年组织2 100万城乡劳动者参加职业培训。这些措施促进了就业的基本稳定。

加快完善社会保障体系。普遍建立养老保险省级统筹制度,出台包括农民工在内的城镇企业职工养老保险关系转移接续办法。在320个县开展新型农村社会养老保险试点,推动我国社会保障制度建设迈出历史性步伐。中央财政安排社会保障资金2 906亿元,比上年增长16.6%。企业退休人员基本养老金连续5年增加,去年又人均提高10%。农村五保户供养水平、优抚对象抚恤补助标准、城乡低保对象保障水平都有新的提高。中央财政安排保障性安居工程补助资金551亿元,比上年增长2倍。新建、改扩建各类保障性住房200万套,棚户区改造解决住房130万套。全国社会保障基金积累6 927亿元,比上年增长44.2%。社会保障体系得到加强。

进一步促进教育公平。大幅度增加全国教育支出,其中中央财政支出1 981亿元,比上年增长23.6%。全面落实城乡义务教育政策,中央下达农村义务教育经费666亿元,提前一年实现农村中小学生人均公用经费500元和300元的目标。实行义务教育阶段教师绩效工资制度。中等职业学校农村家庭经济困难学生和涉农专业学生免学费政策开始实施。国家助学制度不断完善,资助学生2 871万人,基本保障了困难家庭的孩子不因贫困而失学。

稳步推进医药卫生事业改革发展。组织实施医药卫生体制改革。中央财政医疗卫生支出1 277亿元,比上年增长49.5%。城镇职工和城镇居民基本医疗保险参保4.01亿人,新型农村合作医疗制度覆盖8.3亿人。中央财政安排429亿元,解决关闭破产国有企业退休人员医疗保险问题。基本药物制度在30%的基层医疗卫生机构实施。中央财政支持建设了一批县级医院、乡镇中心卫生院和社区卫生服务中心。启动实施扩大乙肝疫苗接种等重大公共卫生服务专项。加强食品、药品安全专项整治。面对突如其来的甲型H1N1流感疫情,我们依法科学有序地开展防控工作,有效保障了人民群众生命安全,维护了社会正常秩序。

在国际金融危机严重冲击、世界经济负增长的背景下,我国取得这样的成绩极为不易。这是以胡锦涛同志为总书记的党中央统揽全局、正确领导的结果,是全党全军全国各族人民和衷共济、团结奋斗的结果。在这里,我代表国务院,向全国各族人民,各民主党派、各人民团体和各界人士,表示诚挚的感谢!向香港特别行政区同胞、澳门特别行政区同胞、台湾同胞和海外侨胞,表示诚挚的感谢!向关心和支持中国现代化建设的各国政府、国际组织和各国朋友,表示诚挚的感谢!

一年来,我们认真贯彻落实科学发展观,积极应对国际金融危机,全面做好政府工作,有以下几点体会:必须坚持运用市场机制和宏观调控两种手段,在坚持市场经济改革方向、发挥市场配置资源基础性作用、激发市场活力的同时,充分发挥我国社会主义制度决策高效、组织有力、集中力量办大事的优势。必须坚持处理好短期和长期两方面关系,注重远近结合、标本兼治,既克服短期困难、解决突出矛盾,又加强重点领域和薄弱环节,为长远发展奠定基础。必须坚持统筹国内国际两个大局,把扩大内需作为长期战略方针,坚定不移地实行互利共赢的开放战略,加快形成内需外需协调拉动经济增长的格局。必须坚持发展经济与改善民生、维护社会公平正义的内在统一,围绕改善民生谋发展,把改善民生作为经济发展的出发点、落脚点和持久动力,着眼维护公平正义,让全体人民共享改革发展成果,促进社会和谐稳定。必须坚持发挥中央和地方两个积极性,既强调统一思想、顾全大局,又鼓励因地制宜、探索创新,形成共克时艰的强大合力。这些经验对我们坚持中国特色社会主义道路,提高驾驭社会主义市场经济能力,推进现代化进程,具有重要而深远的意义。

译文

REPORT ON THE WORK OF THE GOVERNMENT
— Delivered at the Third Session of the Eleventh National People's Congress
on March 5, 2010
Wen Jiabao
Premier of the State Council

Fellow Deputies,

On behalf of the State Council, I now present to you my report on the work of the government for your deliberation and approval. I also invite the members of the National Committee of the Chinese People's Political Consultative Conference (CPPCC) to provide comments and suggestions.

I. Review of Work in 2009

The year 2009 was the most difficult year for our country's economic development since the beginning of the new century. This time last year the global financial crisis was still spreading, and the world economy was in a deep recession. Our economy was severely affected; our exports decreased significantly; a large number of enterprises had operating difficulties, and some even suspended production or closed down; the number of unemployed people increased significantly; many migrant workers had to return to their home villages; and the pace of our economic growth suddenly slowed down. In these unusually difficult circumstances, the people of all our ethnic groups fortified their confidence, tackled difficulties head on, worked tenaciously, and responded calmly to the impact of the global financial crisis under the firm leadership of the Communist Party of China(CPC). Our economy was the first in the world to have made a turnaround, and we made major new achievements in reform and opening up as well as socialist modernization. GDP reached 33.5 trillion yuan, an increase of 8.7% over the previous year(here and below). Fiscal revenue was 6.85 trillion yuan, up 11.7%. Grain production was 531 million tons, a new record and an increase for the sixth consecutive year. A total of 11.02 million urban jobs were created. The per capita disposable income of urban residents was 17,175 yuan, and the net per capita income of rural residents was 5,153 yuan, up 9.8% and 8.5% respectively in real terms. We took another steady step along the path of building a moderately prosperous society in all respects. Events again proved that no difficulties or obstacles can impede the course of the great rejuvenation of the Chinese nation.

The past year was truly extraordinary and inspiring. We held a grand celebration of the 60th anniversary of the founding of New China. The outstanding achievements we made in that time have greatly boosted the confidence and pride of the people, strengthened the cohesiveness of the Chinese nation, and raised China's international standing and influence. All this definitely encourages us to continue to forge ahead on the path of socialism with Chinese characteristics.

Over the last year, we mainly undertook the following work.

1. Strengthening and improving macro-control and promoting steady and rapid economic development. We carried out a proactive fiscal policy and a moderately easy monetary policy. We comprehensively implemented and constantly improved the package plan for addressing the global financial crisis. We significantly increased government spending, implemented structural tax reductions, rapidly increased supplies of money and credit, made our monetary policy more sustainable, and increased the amount of direct financing. We thus ensured funding for economic and social development, effectively boosted domestic demand, and quickly reversed the slowdown in economic growth.

We vigorously expanded consumer spending. Our policies to encourage consumption covered more areas, were stronger and benefited more people than ever before. The central government provided 45 billion yuan in subsidies for rural residents to purchase home appliances and motor vehicles, including motorbikes. Part of the subsidies also supported trading-in old home appliances for new ones and purchasing agricultural machinery and tools. We halved the purchase tax on small-displacement automobiles. We reduced or exempted taxes on buying and selling homes to support the purchase of homes to be used as their owners' residences. Throughout the year 13.64 million motor vehicles were sold, an increase of 46.2%; commodity housing sales amounted to 937 million square meters, up 42.1%; and total retail sales of consumer goods increased 16.9% in real terms. Consumption played a much bigger role in fueling economic growth.

We promoted rapid growth in investment. We guided and stimulated non-government investment by means of well-leveraged government investment. We implemented a plan to invest an additional 4 trillion yuan over two years. In 2009, the central government's public investment was 924.3 billion yuan, 503.8 billion yuan more than the previous year's budget. Of this, 44% was invested in low-income housing, projects to improve the wellbeing of rural residents, and social programs; 16% in independent innovation, restructuring, energy conservation, emission reductions, and ecological improvement; 23% in major infrastructure projects; and 14% in post-Wenchuan earthquake recovery and reconstruction. Fixed asset investment increased 30.1% nationwide. We further improved the investment structure. Rapid investment growth effectively compensated for the shortfall created by shrinking external demand, strengthened weak links, and laid a solid foundation for long-term economic and social development.

We accelerated the post-Wenchuan earthquake recovery and reconstruction work. We have already invested 654.5 billion yuan, 65.5% of the total planned investment, in the worst hit areas. Thanks to the government's strong support, the selfless assistance of people throughout the country, and the hard work of residents of the earthquake area, the badly damaged areas have taken on a brand-new appearance, with new towns rising straight out of the ground, and villages brimming with vitality. All this fully reflects the boundless love of the Chinese nation and powerfully demonstrates the incomparable superiority of the socialist system.

2. Vigorously carrying out economic restructuring, and shoring up the foundation for long-term development. We closely integrated sustaining economic growth with economic restructuring, and moved more quickly to resolve structural problems limiting economic development.

We further strengthened the work related to agriculture, rural areas, and farmers. The central government used 725.3 billion yuan to support agriculture, rural areas, and farmers, an increase of 21.8%. We raised the minimum grain purchase prices by a large margin. We began implementation of the plan to increase grain production capacity by 50 million tons nationwide. We continued to improve living and working conditions in rural areas. We implemented rural drinking water safety projects that benefited 60.69 million people, increased the number of methane gas users by 5.1 million, built and upgraded 380,000 kilometers of roads and 266,000 kilometers of electric power lines and renovated 800,000 dilapidated houses in the countryside, and helped build permanent housing for 92,000 nomadic families. We also intensified our efforts to fight poverty. As a result, working and living conditions notably improved in poverty-stricken areas.

We intensified industrial restructuring. We formulated and implemented a plan for restructuring and invigorating ten key industries. We encouraged enterprises to accelerate technological upgrading, and provided 20 billion yuan to support 4,441 technological upgrading projects. Further progress was made in mergers and reorganization in key industries. We made great efforts to restrict excess production capacity and redundant development in some industries. We closed down 26.17 million kilowatts of small thermal power stations, and eliminated backward facilities with total production 16.91 million tons in the steelmaking industry, 21.13 million tons in the iron-smelting, 74.16 million tons in the cement industry, and 18.09 million tons in the coke industry. We accelerated the implementation of major national science and technology projects, and spent 151.2 billion yuan of central government funds on science and technology, an increase of 30%. We vigorously supported the widespread use of domestically innovated products, and the development of emerging industries such as clean energy and third-generation mobile communications. We vigorously strengthened infrastructure development; put 5,557 kilometers of newly built railway lines into operation; opened 4,719 kilometers of new expressways to traffic, accelerated urban rail development; and built, renovated or expanded 35 civil airports. We increased the installed power-generating capacity by 89.7 million kilowatts, began supplying gas through the western section of the second line of the project for shipping natural gas from west to east, accelerated construction on the South-to-North Water Diversion Project, and began reinforcing 6,183 dangerous reservoirs.

We made solid progress in conserving energy, reducing emissions and protecting the environment. We supported 2,983 key energy conservation and recycling projects through budgetary investment. We implemented a project to promote energy-efficient products for the benefit of the people, putting into use more than 5 million energy-saving air-conditioners and 150 million energy-efficient light bulbs. We continued to develop key ecological projects in the forestry industry, and completed the afforestation of 5.88 million hectares, thereby raising the percentage of land covered by forest to 20.36%. Through combined measures, we brought soil erosion on 48,000 square kilometers of land under control. We strengthened the prevention and treatment of water pollution in the key watersheds of the Huai, Hai, and Liao rivers and Tai, Chao, and Dianchi lakes, and improved the control of waste water, gases and residues from industry. Over the first four years of the Eleventh Five-Year Plan period, energy consumption per unit of GDP fell 14.38%, and chemical oxygen demand and sulfur dioxide emissions decreased 9.66% and 13.14% respectively. We made vigorous efforts to respond to climate change, and set forth our country's targets, policies and measures for controlling greenhouse gas emissions by 2020. We improved our weather forecasting and early warning, as well as earthquake monitoring, and constantly improved our disaster prevention and protection capabilities.

We took new steps in balancing development between regions. We thoroughly implemented the overall strategy for regional development; and formulated several major regional development plans and policies. The central and western regions and northeast

China accelerated opening up and development, welcomed industries relocated from other parts of the country, and continuously strengthened their foundation for development. The eastern region accelerated restructuring and independent innovation, and the vitality of its economic development increased. A favorable situation emerged in which regional development was better distributed, structured and coordinated.

3. Steadfastly deepening reform and opening up, and constantly improving institutions and mechanisms conducive to developing scientifically. We deepened reform and opening up to respond more powerfully to the global financial crisis, worked hard to remove institutional obstacles and continued to open wider to the outside world.

We accelerated reform in key areas and links. We comprehensively carried out VAT reform. The reform of the prices of refined oil products and taxes and fees on them was implemented smoothly, and a new mechanism for pricing them worked well. We made solid progress in commercializing the China Development Bank and introducing the joint stock system in the Agricultural Bank of China, and launched a pilot project to use the renminbi as the settlement currency for cross-border trade. The ChiNext stock market was officially launched, which opened a new financing channel for enterprises based on independent innovation and other growth enterprises. We proceeded with the reform of local government departments in an orderly manner, and steadily carried out a trial of reforming institutions by type. We comprehensively launched the reform of tenure in collective forests. We devolved tenure in 1,500 million hectares of forest land to rural households, equaling 60% of the country's total area of collective forests. This is another major reform of China's rural operation system, and follows in the footsteps of the household land contract responsibility system.

We constantly raised the level of the open economy. We introduced policies and measures to stabilize foreign demand, adopted methods that conform to international practices to support export companies, completed the issuance of short-term export credit insurance worth US$ 90 billion, and arranged $42.1 billion of export financing insurance for complete sets of large equipment. We encouraged increases in imports. Since the second half of last year, falls in imports and exports have clearly eased, and we have consolidated our share of international markets. Last year imports and exports totaled $2.2 trillion. We reversed the decline in utilized foreign investment, and actual utilized foreign direct investment amounted to $90 billion for the entire year. More enterprises "went global" in spite of the adverse situation; non-financial outward direct investment amounted to $43.3 billion, and receipts from overseas project contracting operations reached $77.7 billion. We actively participated in international macroeconomic policy dialogue and coordination as well as economic, trade and financial cooperation, and played a constructive role in the joint response to the global financial crisis.

4. Striving to improve people's wellbeing and accelerating the development of social programs. In the difficult circumstances of responding to the global financial crisis, we

gave greater priority to ensuring and improving people's wellbeing and effectively solved the most practical problems of the greatest and most direct concern to the people.

We implemented a more active employment policy. We increased the responsibility of the government for stimulating employment. The central government allocated 42.6 billion yuan in special employment funds, an increase of 59%. For distressed enterprises, we postponed and in some cases reduced their payment of social security contributions. We also reduced or exempted reemployment tax and provided related subsidies to encourage enterprises to maintain or increase their levels of employment. We launched a series of employment service activities, created public-service jobs through multiple channels, and encouraged college graduates to take jobs at the primary level, enlist in the army, or join enterprises and institutions as interns. We provided job training for 21 million urban and rural workers. These measures helped bring about basic employment stability.

We accelerated improvements in the social security system. We established a nationwide pension planning system at the provincial level, and introduced a method for transferring pension accounts for workers of urban enterprises, some of whom are rural migrant workers. We launched a pilot project for a new rural pension insurance system in 320 counties — a historic step forward in the development of China's social security system. The central government allocated 290.6 billion yuan in social security funds, an increase of 16.6%. Pensions for enterprise retirees increased for the fifth consecutive year and registered another 10% rise per person. We provided better care for childless and infirm rural residents receiving guarantees of food, clothing, medical care, housing and burial expenses. We increased subsidies for entitled groups and subsistence allowances for both urban and rural recipients. The central government used 55.1 billion yuan to develop low-income housing projects, a two-fold increase over the previous year. We built, renovated or expanded 2 million low-income housing units of various types, and renovated or built 1.3 million housing units in run-down areas. Nationwide, social security funds reached 692.7 billion yuan, an increase of 44.2%. We strengthened the social security system.

We made education more equitable. We increased education spending nationwide significantly, including central government spending of 198.1 billion yuan, an increase of 23.6%. We comprehensively implemented the urban and rural compulsory education policy, spent 66.6 billion yuan of central government funds on rural compulsory education, and reached the target of raising public spending for rural secondary and primary school students to an average of 500 yuan and 300 yuan per student respectively a year ahead of schedule. We implemented a performance-based pay system for compulsory education teachers. We started to implement the policy of free tuition for rural students attending secondary vocational schools whose families have financial difficulties and students in such schools who are studying agriculture-related majors. We constantly improved the national student financial aid system, which benefited 28.71 million students and basically ensured that no children from poor families were denied schooling due to financial difficulties.

We made steady progress in the reform and development of the pharmaceutical and healthcare fields. We organized the implementation of the reform of the pharmaceutical and healthcare systems. The central government spent 127.7 billion yuan on medical and health care, an increase of 49.5%. A total of 401 million urban workers and non-working urban residents subscribed to basic medical insurance; and coverage of the new type of rural cooperative medical care system reached 830 million people. The central government allocated 42.9 billion yuan to solve the problem of medical insurance for retired workers from closed and bankrupt state-owned enterprises. The basic drug system has been implemented in 30% of primary-level medical and health care institutions. Central government funds were used to support the construction of a number of county-level hospitals, town and township central hospitals, and community health service centers. We launched major public health service projects, including one to increase vaccinations against hepatitis B. We intensified special campaigns for food and drug safety. Faced with the sudden outbreak of influenza A (H1N1), we carried out scientific and orderly prevention and control work in accordance with the law, and thereby effectively protected people's lives and maintained normal order in society.

It was not at all easy for our country to make all these achievements against the backdrop of the severe impact of the global financial crisis and the negative growth of the world economy. They were the result of the overall planning and correct leadership of the Party Central Committee with Comrade Hu Jintao as General Secretary as well as the concerted and strenuous efforts of the whole Party, the entire army, and the people of all of our ethnic groups. On behalf of the State Council, I hereby express our sincere gratitude to the people of all of our ethnic groups and to the democratic parties, mass organizations, and people from all sectors of society. I also express our sincere thanks to our compatriots in the Hong Kong and Macao special administrative regions, in Taiwan, and overseas, as well as to foreign governments, international organizations, and friends in other countries that take an interest in and support China's modernization.

In the course of the past year, as we conscientiously applied the Scientific Outlook on Development; vigorously responded to the global financial crisis and completed all of our government work, we came to the following conclusions: We must continue to make use of both market mechanisms and macro-control, that is, at the same time as we keep our reforms oriented toward a market economy, let market forces play their basic role in allocating resources, and stimulate the market's vitality, we must make best use of the socialist system's advantages, which enable us to make decisions efficiently, organize effectively, and concentrate resources to accomplish large undertakings. We must balance long-and short-term interests, take into account long-and short-term needs, and address both the symptoms and root causes of problems. We must overcome short-term difficulties and solve major problems as well as strengthen key areas and weak links in order to lay a foundation for long-term development. We must continue to consider domestic and international situations, make it a long-term strategic policy to boost domestic demand, adhere to the win-win strategy of opening up, and quickly formulate a pattern in which domestic demand and foreign demand drive economic growth in concert. We must always remember that developing the economy is inseparable from improving people's wellbeing and safeguarding social fairness and justice; make improving people's wellbeing the focus of development, and the starting point, goal, and lasting driving force of economic development; strive to safeguard fairness and justice; ensure that all of the people share in the fruits of reform and development; and promote social harmony and stability. We must give free rein to the initiative of both the central and local authorities. While stressing unity of thinking and keeping overall interests in mind, we also need to encourage everyone to proceed in light of local conditions and make explorations and innovations, in order to form a powerful, concerted force for overcoming present difficulties. All of these experiences are of vital and profound significance for keeping to the path of socialism with Chinese characteristics, improving our ability to run the socialist market economy, and pushing ahead the process of modernization.

Remarks of President Barack Obama in State of the Union Address

Washington, D. C.

January 25, 2011

Mr. Speaker, Mr. Vice President, Members of Congress, distinguished guests, and fellow Americans:

Tonight I want to begin by congratulating the men and women of the 112th Congress, as well as your new Speaker, John Boehner. And as we mark this occasion, we are also mindful of the empty chair in this Chamber, and pray for the health of our colleague — and our friend — Gabby Giffords.

It's no secret that those of us here tonight have had our differences over the last two years. The debates have been contentious; we have fought fiercely for our beliefs. And that's a good thing. That's what a robust democracy demands. That's what helps set us apart as a nation.

But there's a reason the tragedy in Tucson gave us pause. Amid all the noise and passions and rancor of our public debate, Tucson reminded us that no matter who we are or where we come from, each of us is a part of something greater — something more consequential than party or political preference.

We are part of the American family. We believe that in a country where every race and faith and point of view can be found, we are still bound together as one people; that we share common hopes and a common creed; that the dreams of a little girl in Tucson are not so different than those of our own children, and that they all deserve the chance to be fulfilled.

That, too, is what sets us apart as a nation.

Now, by itself, this simple recognition won't usher in a new era of cooperation. What comes of this moment is up to us. What comes of this moment will be determined not by whether we can sit together tonight, but whether we can work together tomorrow.

I believe we can. I believe we must. That's what the people who sent us here expect of us. With their votes, they've determined that governing will now be a shared responsibility between parties. New laws will only pass with support from Democrats and Republicans. We will move forward together, or not at all — for the challenges we face are bigger than party, and bigger than politics.

At stake right now is not who wins the next election — after all, we just had an election. At stake is whether new jobs and industries take root in this country, or somewhere else. It's whether the hard work and industry of our people is rewarded. It's whether we sustain the leadership that has made America not just a place on a map, but a light to the world.

We are poised for progress. Two years after the worst recession most of us have ever known, the stock market has come roaring back. Corporate profits are up. The economy is growing again.

But we have never measured progress by these yardsticks alone. We measure progress by the success of our people. By the jobs they can find and the quality of life those jobs offer. By the prospects of a small business owner who dreams of turning a good idea into a thriving enterprise. By the opportunities for a better life that we pass on to our children.

That's the project the American people want us to work on. Together.

We did that in December. Thanks to the tax cuts we passed, Americans' paychecks are a little bigger today. Every business can write off the full cost of the new investments they make this year. These steps, taken by Democrats and Republicans, will grow the economy and add to the more than one million private sector jobs created last year.

But we have more work to do. The steps we've taken over the last two years may have broken the back of this recession — but to win the future, we'll need to take on challenges that have been decades in the making.

Many people watching tonight can probably remember a time when finding a good job meant showing up at a nearby factory or a business downtown. You didn't always need a degree, and your competition was pretty much limited to your neighbors. If you worked hard, chances are you'd have a job for life, with a decent paycheck, good benefits, and the occasional promotion. Maybe you'd even have the pride of seeing your kids work at the same company.

That world has changed. And for many, the change has been painful. I've seen it in the shuttered windows of once booming factories, and the vacant storefronts of once busy Main Streets. I've heard it in the frustrations of Americans who've seen their paychecks dwindle or their jobs disappear — proud men and women who feel like the rules have been changed in the middle of the game.

They're right. The rules have changed. In a single generation, revolutions in technology have transformed the way we live, work and do business. Steel mills that once needed 1,000 workers can now do the same work with 100. Today, just about any company can set up shop, hire workers, and sell their products wherever there's an Internet connection.

Meanwhile, nations like China and India realized that with some changes of their own, they could compete in this new world. And so they started educating their children earlier and longer, with greater emphasis on math and science. They're investing in research and new technologies. Just recently, China became home to the world's largest private solar research facility, and the world's fastest computer.

So yes, the world has changed. The competition for jobs is real. But this shouldn't discourage us. It should challenge us. Remember — for all the hits we've taken these last few years, for all the naysayers predicting our decline, America still has the largest, most prosperous economy in the world. No workers are more productive than ours. No country has more successful companies, or grants more patents to inventors and entrepreneurs. We are home to the world's best colleges and universities, where more students come to study than any other place on Earth.

What's more, we are the first nation to be founded for the sake of an idea — the idea that each of us deserves the chance to shape our own destiny. That is why centuries of pioneers and immigrants have risked everything to come here. It's why our students don't just memorize equations, but answer questions like "What do you think of that idea? What would you change about the world? What do you want to be when you grow up?"

The future is ours to win. But to get there, we can't just stand still. As Robert Kennedy told us, "The future is not a gift. It is an achievement."Sustaining the American Dream has never been about standing pat. It has required each generation to sacrifice, and struggle, and meet the demands of a new age.

Now it's our turn. We know what it takes to compete for the jobs and industries of our time. We need to out-innovate, out-educate, and out-build the rest of the world. We have to make America the best place on Earth to do business. We need to take responsibility for our deficit, and reform our government. That's how our people will prosper. That's how we'll win the future. And tonight, I'd like to talk about how we get there.

The first step in winning the future is encouraging American innovation.

None of us can predict with certainty what the next big industry will be, or where the new jobs will come from. Thirty years ago, we couldn't know that something called the

Internet would lead to an economic revolution. What we can do — what America does better than anyone — is spark the creativity and imagination of our people. We are the nation that put cars in driveways and computers in offices; the nation of Edison and the Wright brothers; of Google and Facebook. In America, innovation doesn't just change our lives. It's how we make a living.

Our free enterprise system is what drives innovation. But because it's not always profitable for companies to invest in basic research, throughout history our government has provided cutting-edge scientists and inventors with the support that they need. That's what planted the seeds for the Internet. That's what helped make possible things like computer chips and GPS.

Just think of all the good jobs — from manufacturing to retail — that have come from those breakthroughs.

Half a century ago, when the Soviets beat us into space with the launch of a satellite called Sputnik, we had no idea how we'd beat them to the moon. The science wasn't there yet. NASA didn't even exist. But after investing in better research and education, we didn't just surpass the Soviets; we unleashed a wave of innovation that created new industries and millions of new jobs.

This is our generation's Sputnik moment. Two years ago, I said that we needed to reach a level of research and development we haven't seen since the height of the Space Race. In a few weeks, I will be sending a budget to Congress that helps us meet that goal. We'll invest in biomedical research, information technology, and especially clean energy technology — an investment that will strengthen our security, protect our planet, and create countless new jobs for our people.

Already, we are seeing the promise of renewable energy. Robert and Gary Allen are brothers who run a small Michigan roofing company. After September 11th, they volunteered their best roofers to help repair the Pentagon. But half of their factory went unused, and the recession hit them hard.

Today, with the help of a government loan, that empty space is being used to manufacture solar shingles that are being sold all across the country. In Robert's words, "We reinvented ourselves."

That's what Americans have done for over two hundred years: reinvented ourselves. And to spur on more success stories like the Allen Brothers, we've begun to reinvent our energy policy. We're not just handing out money. We're issuing a challenge. We're telling America's scientists and engineers that if they assemble teams of the best minds in their fields, and focus on the hardest problems in clean energy, we'll fund the Apollo Projects of our time.

At the California Institute of Technology, they're developing a way to turn sunlight and water into fuel for our cars. At Oak Ridge National Laboratory, they're using supercomputers to get a lot more power out of our nuclear facilities. With more research and incentives, we can break our dependence on oil with biofuels, and become the first country to have 1 million electric vehicles on the road by 2015.

We need to get behind this innovation. And to help pay for it, I'm asking Congress to eliminate the billions in taxpayer dollars we currently give to oil companies. I don't know if you've noticed, but they're doing just fine on their own. So instead of subsidizing yesterday's energy, let's invest in tomorrow's.

Now, clean energy breakthroughs will only translate into clean energy jobs if businesses know there will be a market for what they're selling. So tonight, I challenge you to join me in setting a new goal: by 2035, 80% of America's electricity will come from clean energy sources. Some folks want wind and solar. Others want nuclear, clean coal, and natural gas. To meet this goal, we will need them all — and I urge Democrats and Republicans to work together to make it happen.

Maintaining our leadership in research and technology is crucial to America's success. But if we want to win the future — if we want innovation to produce jobs in America and not overseas — then we also have to win the race to educate our kids.

Think about it. Over the next ten years, nearly half of all new jobs will require education that goes beyond a high school degree. And yet, as many as a quarter of our students aren't even finishing high school. The quality of our math and science education lags behind many other nations. America has fallen to 9th in the proportion of young people with a college degree. And so the question is whether all of us — as citizens, and as parents — are willing to do what's necessary to give every child a chance to succeed.

That responsibility begins not in our classrooms, but in our homes and communities. It's family that first instills the love of learning in a child. Only parents can make sure the TV is turned off and homework gets done. We need to teach our kids that it's not just the winner of the Super Bowl who deserves to be celebrated, but the winner of the science fair; that success is not a function of fame or PR, but of hard work and discipline.

Our schools share this responsibility. When a child walks into a classroom, it should be a place of high expectations and high performance. But too many schools don't meet this test. That's why instead of just pouring money into a system that's not working, we launched a competition called Race to the Top. To all fifty states, we said, "If you show us the most innovative plans to improve teacher quality and student achievement, we'll show you the money."

Race to the Top is the most meaningful reform of our public schools in a generation. For less than one percent of what we spend on education each year, it has led over 40 states to raise their standards for teaching and learning. These standards were developed, not by Washington, but by Republican and Democratic governors throughout the country. And Race to the Top should be the approach we follow this year as we replace No Child Left Behind with a law that is more flexible and focused on what's best for our kids.

You see, we know what's possible for our children when reform isn't just a top-down mandate, but the work of local teachers and principals; school boards and communities.

Take a school like Bruce Randolph in Denver. Three years ago, it was rated one of the worst schools in Colorado; located on turf between two rival gangs. But last May, 97% of the seniors received their diploma. Most will be the first in their family to go to college. And after the first year of the school's transformation, the principal who made it possible wiped away tears when a student said, "Thank you, Mrs. Waters, for showing... that we are smart and we can make it."

Let's also remember that after parents, the biggest impact on a child's success comes from the man or woman at the front of the classroom. In South Korea, teachers are known as "nation builders". Here in America, it's time we treated the people who educate our children with the same level of respect. We want to reward good teachers and stop making excuses for bad ones. And over the next ten years, with so many Baby Boomers retiring from our classrooms, we want to prepare 100,000 new teachers in the fields of science, technology, engineering, and math.

In fact, to every young person listening tonight who's contemplating their career choice: If you want to make a difference in the life of our nation; if you want to make a difference in the life of a child — become a teacher. Your country needs you.

Of course, the education race doesn't end with a high school diploma. To compete, higher education must be within reach of every American. That's why we've ended the unwarranted taxpayer subsidies that went to banks, and used the savings to make college affordable for millions of students. And this year, I ask Congress to go further, and make permanent our tuition tax credit — worth $10,000 for four years of college.

Because people need to be able to train for new jobs and careers in today's fast-changing economy, we are also revitalizing America's community colleges. Last month, I saw the promise of these schools at Forsyth Tech in North Carolina. Many of the students there used to work in the surrounding factories that have since left town. One mother of two, a woman named Kathy Proctor, had worked in the furniture industry since she was 18 years old. And she told me she's earning her degree in biotechnology now, at 55 years old, not just because the furniture jobs are gone, but because she wants to inspire her children to pursue their dreams too. As Kathy said, "I hope it tells them to never give up."

If we take these steps — if we raise expectations for every child, and give them the best possible chance at an education, from the day they're born until the last job they take — we will reach the goal I set two years ago: by the end of the decade, America will once again have the highest proportion of college graduates in the world.

One last point about education. Today, there are hundreds of thousands of students excelling in our schools who are not American citizens. Some are the children of undocumented workers, who had nothing to do with the actions of their parents. They grew up as Americans and pledge allegiance to our flag, and yet live every day with the threat of deportation. Others come here from abroad to study in our colleges and universities. But as soon as they obtain advanced degrees, we send them back home to compete against us. It makes no sense.

Now, I strongly believe that we should take on, once and for all, the issue of illegal immigration. I am prepared to work with Republicans and Democrats to protect our borders, enforce our laws and address the millions of undocumented workers who are now living in the shadows. I know that debate will be difficult and take time. But tonight, let's agree to make that effort. And let's stop expelling talented, responsible young people who can staff our research labs, start new businesses, and further enrich this nation.

译 文

奥巴马总统 2011 年国情咨文

2011 年 1 月 25 日

华盛顿特区

众议院议长先生、副总统先生、各位国会议员、尊敬的客人们、同胞们：

今晚我想首先向美国第 112 届国会的男女议员、你们的新议长约翰·博纳表示祝贺。在我们庆祝这一时刻时，我们仍然很清楚一位国会议员的座位是空着的，让我们为我们的同事、我们的朋友加布里埃尔·吉福兹的健康祈祷。

我们今晚出席这一活动的人在过去两年曾存在分歧，这不是秘密。辩论是非常激烈的，我们为我们各自的观点进行了激烈的斗争。这是一件好事，这是强有力的民主所要求的。这种争论帮助美国成为区别于其他国家的民主国家。

但图森市的悲剧给了我们一个停止争论的理由。我们进行的公共辩论引发了噪音、情绪、怨恨。图森的悲剧提醒我们，不管我们是谁、来自何方，我们中的每一个人都是一个更伟大事务的一部分，它比政党或者政治倾向更具必然性。

我们是美国大家庭的组成部分。我们相信，在这个各种种族、信仰、观点并存的国家，我们仍是一个团结在一起的民族。我们拥有共同的希望和信条，图森小女孩的梦想与我们自己孩子的梦想没有什么大的差别，这些梦想都应获得实现的机会。

这也是使我们作为一个国家产生分歧的原因。

现在，简单地认识到这一点本身将不会开启一个合作的新时代。这一时刻所能产生的成果取决于我们。这一时刻所产生的成果将不会由我们是否今晚坐在一起而决定，它将由我们明天是否合作所决定。

我认为我们能够实现合作。我认为我们必须这样。这是那些把我们送到这里的人们所期望的。他们通过他们的选票决定，执政将是两党共同的责任。新的法案只有在获得民主党和共和党议员的支持下才能通过。在面对比党派或者政治更大的挑战面前，我们将一起前行，或者原地不动。

现在的利害不是谁将赢得下次选举，毕竟，我们刚刚举行完一次选举。现在的利害是新的就业机会和新的行业是否会在美国生根或者在其他地方。这事关我们人民的辛劳工作和行业是否能得到回报。这事关我们是否能继续保持领导能力，这种领导能力使美国不只局限于地图上的某一个地方,美国因为这种领导能力而成为世界的灯光。

我们做好了前进的准备。在我们大多数人经历最为糟糕的经济衰退两年后,股市已再次大幅上升。公司赢利在增加。经济在再次增长。

但我们从不只以这些标准来衡量进展。我们以我们人民的成功来评估进展,通过他们所能找到的工作和这些工作所提供的生活质量,通过小企业主把好点子的梦想转变成兴旺发达的企业的前景,通过我们给我们孩子更好生活的机遇。

这是美国人民想让我们从事的事业,美国人民想让我们共同致力于这项事业。

我们去年12月做了这方面的工作。由于我们通过的减税法案,美国人今天收到的支票金额要比过去多。所有的企业都可以把它今年所作投资的全部开支注销。这些由民主党人和共和党人合作采取的措施将使经济增长,增加就业岗位,私人行业去年已创造1百多万个就业岗位。

但我们有更多的工作要做。我们在过去两年所采取的措施可能已克服了经济衰退的主要困难,但是为了赢得未来,我们必须直面应对那些在过去数十年来一直积累起来的挑战。

许多观看今晚演讲的人可能还记得那个找到好工作意味着在附近工厂或者市中心商业区就业的时候。你并不总是需要获得一个学位,你的竞争基本只限于你的邻居。如果你努力工作,你可能会终身拥有这个职位,这个工作会给你带来体面的收入、好的福利,有时还会获得升职。你可能还会拥有看到你的孩子在同一公司工作的自豪感。

世界已发生了变革。对于许多人来说,变革是痛苦的。在曾经一度业务繁忙工厂面临关闭时,我透过百叶窗看到了这种痛苦;在一度繁忙的商业街道空空如也的店门前,我看到了这种痛苦;在那些看到收入不断缩水或者失业美国人的绝望言论中,我听到了这种痛苦。这就好像,在比赛进行到一半时,表现出色而又颇感自豪的运动员发现规则突然改变了。

他们是正确的,规则发生了变化。仅仅用了一代人的时间,技术革命已改变了我们的工作、生活和做生意的方式。一度需要1 000名工人的钢铁厂现在用100名工人就可以完成同样的工作。今天,任何一家公司都可以设立商店、雇佣员工、把产品销售给有互联网连接的所有地方。

与此同时,中国和印度等国已意识到,它们在作出一些变革后将能够在新世界里与其他国家进行竞争。所以,他们开始对他们的孩子进行更早和更长时间的教育,更加重视数学和科学。他们投资于研发和新技术。就在不久之前,中国已拥有世界上最大的私营太阳能研究设施,世界上运行速度最快的计算机。

所以,是的,世界发生了变革。就业岗位的竞争是真实存在的,但这不应当使我们灰心,它应当成为激励我们的动力。请记住,尽管我们在过去几年遭受到了巨大打击,尽管所有的悲观者预言美国在衰落,但美国仍是世界上最大、最繁荣的经济体。我们工人的劳动生产率是最高的,我们的公司是最成功的,我们的投资者和企业家所拥有的专利数是最多的。我们拥有世界上最好的院校和大学,来美国就读的学生超过任何其他国家。

更为重要的是,我们是首个以思想立国的国家,这个思想是我们中的每个人都应当有机会来塑造自己的命运。这就是为什么先驱们和移民们数个世纪以来不惜冒着失去一切的风险来到美国的原因。这就是我们的学生不只是记住方程式,而是会回答"你认为这个想法如何?你想如何改变世界?当你长大后你想成为什么样的人?"等问题。

我们将赢得未来,但为了实现这一点,我们不能原地踏步。正如罗伯特·肯尼迪所说的那样,"未来不是一个礼物,它是一个成就"。维持美国梦从来不是墨守成规。它需要每一代人作出牺牲、斗争,满足新时代的要求。

现在轮到我们这一代人了。我们知道在我们的时代为工作和行业进行竞争需要什么。我们需要在创新、教育和建设方面超越其他国家。我们要使美国成为商业环境最好的国家。我们需要对我们的赤字负责任,对我们的政府进行改革。这就是我们的人民实现繁荣的方法。这就是我们赢得未来的方法。今晚,我想谈谈我们如何做到这些。

赢得未来的首个步骤是鼓励美国人创新。

我们所有人都无法肯定地预言下一个主要行业将是什么行业或者新的就业岗位来自哪里。三十年前,我们不知道一个被称作互联网的东西会引发经济革命。我们所能做的是,争取在这些方面比其他国家的人做得更好,激发美国人民的创造性和想像力。我们是一个将车开到车道上、把计算机放在办公室的国家,是一个拥有爱迪生、莱特兄弟的国家,是一个拥有谷歌和脸谱(Facebook)的国家。在美国,创新不只改变我们的生活,更重要的是,这是我们赖以谋生的方法。

我们的自由企业制度驱动着创新,但是由于公司投资基础研究并不总是有利可图,在历史上,我们的政府向一流的科学家和发明家提供了他们所需要的支持。这些支持种下了互联网的种子,这些支持帮助制造出计算机芯片和全球定位仪这样的东西。

想想所有的好工作,从制造业到零售业都来自这些突破。

半个世纪之前,当苏联人发射一颗名为"伴侣号"的人造卫星从而在太空竞赛领域击败我们时,我们不知道我们如何在登月方面击败他们。那方面的科学当时还不存在,美国宇航局当时甚至都还未组建。但在更好的研究和教育方面投资后,我们不仅超过了苏联人,我们还推动了一系列的创新,这些创新创造了新的行业和数百万个新就业岗位。

这是我们那一代人创造的"伴侣号"走在世界前沿的时刻。我在两年前说过,我们需要将研发拓展到自太空竞赛高峰后再也没有出现过的新层次上。我将在未来几周内向国会提交一份预算案,它将帮助我们实现这一目标。我们将投资于生物医药研究、信息技术,尤其是清洁能源技术,这一投资将会强化我们的安全、保护我们的地球、为我们的人民创造无数新就业岗位。

我们已看到了可再生能源的潜力。罗伯特·阿伦和加里·阿伦是一对在密歇根州经营屋顶公司的兄弟。他们在"9·11"恐怖袭击事件后志愿派出他们最好的装修屋顶的员工来帮助维修五角大楼,但是他们工厂的半个厂区没有开工,经济衰退重创了他们的工厂。

今天,在政府贷款的帮助下,空闲的厂房被用于制造销往全国各地的太阳能电池板。用罗伯特的话说:"我们再造了自己。"

这就是美国人在过去两百多年里一直在做的事情:再造自我。为了推动更多像阿伦兄弟这样的成功故事,我们已开始再造我们的能源政策。我们将不只提供款项,我们还将提供挑战。我们将告诉美国的科学家和工程师,如果他们组建他们领域最好的科学家小组,致力解决清洁能源最困难的问题,我们将向我们时代的"阿波罗项目"提供资金支持。

在加州理工学院,科学家正在寻找一种将太阳光和水转换成汽车燃料的方法。在橡树岭国家实验室,科学家们正在通过超级计算机从我们的核设施中获得更多能量。在进行更多的研究和激励措施后,我们可以用生物燃料来打破我们对石油的依赖,成为在 2015 年前首个拥有一百万电动汽车上路的国家。

我们需要找到创新背后的要素。为了向创新提供经费支持,我将请求国会取消向石油公司所提供的数十亿美元税款补贴。我不知道你是否注意到这一情况,但石油公司自身运营得很不错。所以,与其向昨天的能源业提供补贴,我们不如投资于未来的能源。

现在,清洁能源领域的技术突破只有在业界知道有销售市场的情况下才会转变成清洁能源业的工作岗位。所以,今晚,我想让你们和我一起来制订一个新目标:争取在2035年之前使美国80%的电力供应量来自清洁能源。一些人想要风力和太阳能,其他人想要核电、清洁煤炭和天然气。为了实现这一目标,我们将需要所有这些清洁能源。我呼吁民主党人和共和党人通过合作来实现这一目标。

保持我们在研究和技术领域的领导地位对于美国的成功至关重要。如果我们想拥抱未来,如果我们想让创新在美国而不是海外创造就业岗位,那么我们必须赢得教育我们孩子的竞赛。

思考一下吧,在未来十年,近半数新就业岗位将需要拥有高中以上的教育程度。虽然如此,美国仍有近四分之一的学生甚至未完成中学教育。我们数学和科学的教育质量落后于许多国家。美国年轻人拥有大学学位比例的排行已降至世界第九位。所以问题是,我们所有的人,作为公民,作为父母,是否愿意做那些必要的事情以便让每个孩子都有成功的机会?

这一责任不是从我们的教室内开始,而是从我们的家庭和社区开始。是家庭首先培养了孩子爱好学习的习惯,只有父母在确保关掉电视的情况下,孩子的家庭作业才会完成。我们需要教育我们的孩子,不仅是超级碗比赛的获胜者值得庆祝,那些科学大赛的赢家也应当值得庆祝。成功不是名气或者公共关系所带来的,它是由辛劳的工作和自律造就的。

我们的学校也有责任。当一名儿童步入教室,它就应当是一个被寄以厚望和拥有很高教学能力的地方。但是太多的学校未能达到这一标准。这就是为什么我们没有向不发挥作用的教育系统注入大笔资金的原因,我们启动了一个名为"冲顶赛跑"的竞争。我们对所有50个州说:"如果你们能够向我们展示提高教师质量和学生成就的最具创新力的方案,我们将向你们提供款项。"

"冲顶赛跑"是我们公共学校在十年内所进行的最有意义的改革。它只使用了不到我们每年教育开支的1%的经费,但它已使40多个州提高了教学和学习标准。这些标准不是由华盛顿所决定的,它是由美国各个州的共和党和民主党州长们所决定的。"冲顶赛跑"应当成为我们今年所采取的方法。我们今年将用一个更为灵活、专注于给我们的孩子带来最大益处的法律来取代《不让一个儿童落后法》。

你们应该知道,当改革不仅仅是从上到下的指示时,我们的孩子所能够取得的成绩有多大。改革措施将由当地的教师和校长、校董事会和社区来决定。

以丹佛的布鲁斯·兰多夫学校为例,它在三年前被评为是科罗拉多州最差的学校之一,它位于两个敌对黑帮争夺的地盘内。但在去年五月,该校97%的高三学生获得了毕业证,大多数人将是他们家庭中上大学的第一人。在学校实现转变后的第一年,一位学生的话使这一切成为现实的校长流下了眼泪。这个学生说:"感谢你,威特斯女士,感谢你向我们表明,我们是聪明的,我们能够成功。"

让我们也记住,除了父母之外,对一个孩子成功的最大影响来自站在教室前的男女教师们。在韩国，教师们被称作"国家建造者"。在美国，现在是我们该以同样程度尊重对待那些教育我们孩子的人的时候了。我们应当奖励好教师，停止为糟糕的教师找借口。在未来十年，由于非常多的婴儿潮一代教师将退休，我们将需要准备10万名科学、技术、工程和数学学科教师。

　　事实上，对于今晚收听讲演的、正在考虑职业选择的年轻人，如果你想让我们国家前途有所不同，如果你想让一个孩子的生命有所不同，成为一位教师吧。你的国家需要你。

　　当然，教育竞赛不会止步于高中毕业证。为了竞争，必须让每位美国人都有接受高等教育的机会。这就是我们为什么结束向银行提供没有充分根据的税款补贴，用节省下来的钱来使数百万学生能有能力上大学。我今年将请求国会采取进一步措施，使我们的学费税收抵免永久化，对一个人四年的大学来说，这笔钱相当于1万美元。

　　由于人们需要在今天快速变化的经济领域里接受新工作和职业的培训，我们也将重新使美国的社区学院恢复活力。我上个月看到了北卡罗来纳州福费斯社区技术学院的潜力，学院的许多学生曾在现在已搬离城镇的附近工厂就业。凯西·普罗克托是一位两个孩子的母亲，她18岁就开始在家具业工作。她告诉我，现年55岁的她正在攻读生物技术学位，不只是因为家具业的工作没有了，而是因为她想鼓励她的孩子也追求他们的梦想。凯西说："我希望这将能教会他们永不放弃。"

　　如果我们采取这些措施，如果我们提高对每个孩子的期待值，给他们在教育方面最好的机遇，从他们出生至他们上一次的就业岗位，我们将实现我在两年前确定的目标：在这个十年结束的时候，美国将再度成为拥有大学生比例最高的国家。

　　有关教育的最后一点。今天，我们的学校里有数百万学业优秀的非美国公民。一些人是非法工人的孩子，他们与他们父母的行为没有任何关系。他们是以美国人的身份长大的，宣誓效忠美国，却每天生活在将被驱逐的威胁之下。其他人来自海外，在我们的院校和大学里学习，但他们一旦获得学位，我们就把他们送回国和我们进行竞争。这没有道理。

　　现在，我强烈地认为，我们应当一下子解决非法移民的问题。我做好了与共和党人和民主党人合作以保护我们边境的准备，执行我们的法律，解决数百万生活在阴影之下的非法移民问题。我知道，这方面的辩论将是艰难的，将需要时间。但是今晚，让我们就开始作出努力达成共识。停止驱逐那些有才能、负责任的年轻人，他们可以在我们的实验室工作、创业、给美国带来新的财富。

第九单元　广告宣传
(Advertising and Publicity)

单元要点

本单元共分五个层次，分别是：上海市的宣传汉译英一篇；伦敦市的宣传英译汉一篇；重组与表达；增译法和减译法；拓展阅读（汉译英，英译汉各一篇）。第一、二部分提供上海市和伦敦市的宣传例文及其翻译和重难点评析；第三、四部分主要是相关口译理论与技能的介绍；第五部分的拓展阅读中，提供汉、英原文和参考译文。

理论难点提示

1. 重组与表达。
2. 增译法和减译法。

选文 A

上海的字面意思是"海上之埠"，简称"沪"，别称"申"。上海面积为 6 340 平方公里，占全国总面积的 0.06%，属冲积平原，地势平坦，平均海拔高度为 4 米，最高点大金山海拔 103.4 米，常住居民达 1 700 万。

这是世界上最大的海港城市之一，也是中国最大的工业、商业、金融、航运中心之一。这里有着世界上最快的陆地交通工具——磁悬浮列车和亚洲最高的高塔——东方明珠塔，它们标志着速度和高度。随着经济改革的日益深化，这座昔日被誉为远东金融、经济和贸易中心的城市正在为促进长江三角洲的经济发展起着龙头作用。与此同时，上海以她独特的风韵吸引着数以百万计的海外游客。作为一座国际大都市，上海的国际航班可直达世界上 60 多个城市。

以东方明珠闻名于世的上海是中国通向世界的东大门。早在唐宋时期上海便是中国东部的一座外贸商镇，与日本、朝鲜和东南亚各国之间有着商贸往来。到了清朝乾隆、嘉庆年间，上海成了中国东南部的大都市和海运中心。那时，申城里万商云集，浦江上千帆斗艳，好一派繁荣兴旺的景象！自 20 世纪 50 年代起，上海取代广州，成了中国的外贸中心，直至今日仍保持着这一龙头地位。今天这座著名的国际港市已发展成为中国重要的经济、金融、贸易、航运、科技、信息和文化中心。近年来，以上海浦东为龙头的整体工业快速更新，出现了汽车产业、电子产业、钢铁产业、石油化工及精细化工产业、家用电器产业和生物医药产业 6 大支柱产业。科教兴市、人才强市、打造世界级现代服务业，这些不仅是全市人民的共识，而且正在不断地落实之中。

上海作为中国的一座历史文化名城，有 70 余处国家级和市级重点历史文物保护单位，充分展示了特色鲜明的海派文化。上海是美食家的乐园,全市数以千计的餐馆汇集了全国各大名菜,如鲁菜、川菜、粤菜、淮扬菜、闽菜等,各种风味,一应俱全。世界各地的风味烹调,如法、俄、意、英、德、西、日、韩、印等外邦菜,比比皆是,各领风骚。清真人士和素食者,自有去处,各得其所。享有"万国建筑博览会"之美誉的上海,在外滩和市内各处都有风格各异的建筑物。浦东的世纪公园、上海科技馆、金茂大厦、国际会议中心、东方艺术中心和东方明珠塔,相伴电视塔左右的雄伟的南浦大桥和杨浦大桥,连接浦江双桥的内环线高架交通干道,人民广场上的上海博物馆、上海大剧院和上海城市规划展示馆,使申城旧貌换新颜。上海的地铁、轻轨、高架桥和磁悬浮列车,使上海的交通更为便利快捷。

上海是旅游者的天地。上海有众多的休闲度假胜地,如佘山国家旅游度假区、淀山湖风景区、太阳岛度假区、环球乐园、梦幻世界以及野生动物园。上海每年都要举办多姿多彩的旅游节,其中除夕夜的龙华迎新撞钟活动,春天的龙华庙会、南汇桃花节和国际茶文化节,金秋时节的上海黄浦旅游节和上海桂花节。近年来上海不断涌现诸多新的国际性节庆活动,如上海国际电影节、上海国际艺术节、上海国际服装节、上海国际啤酒节。这些海派气息浓郁而又十分迷人的节庆活动,引来无数海外游客竞相参与。

海派文化是南北文化交汇、东西文化融合的结晶。海纳百川,有容乃大。上海恢弘的气度源自于其充分开放的历史,上海的快速崛起是中国改革开放的成果。

论历史,上海在宋代成镇,元代设县,明代筑城,在中国灿若群星的名城古都中,并不耀眼夺目,远不能比西安、开封、洛阳,近不能比南京、苏州、杭州。但是上海自开埠以来,以超常的速度发展。自改革开放以来,尤其是自 20 世纪 90 年代以来,上海开始了新的腾飞,城市面貌日新月异,在建设现代国际大都市的征途上高歌猛进,其巨大成就,举世瞩目。"两千年看西安,五百年看北京,一百年看上海。"上海已成为现代中国城市的象征。历史曾经厚爱过上海,也委屈过上海,现在又给上海以难得的机遇。"乘骐骥以驰骋兮,来吾道夫先路。"

21 世纪的上海人既是聪明的人,也是精明的人,更是具有大气魄的高明人,具有世界公民的特质,他们热爱工作、热爱学习、热爱生活,努力把上海建设成为一座繁荣、富强、和谐的现代化、国际化和时尚化大都市。

21 世纪的上海成为世界经济、金融、贸易、航运中心已属必然。世界注视着中国,尤其注视着上海。上海这座地球上最具希望的城市之一,竭诚欢迎各国朋友光临。

重难点评析

1. "这座昔日被誉为远东金融中心、经济和贸易中心的城市正在为促进长江三角洲的经济发展起着龙头作用。"其中"被誉为"有多种译法,这里取用"crown"一词比较合适,"crown"可指"皇冠",也可指"代表荣誉和胜利的花冠",作为动词"crown"表示"冠以"、"誉为",既形象又达意。若把"龙头作用"直接译为"dragon head role",不甚了解中国文化的人听之会不知所云。这里所谓的"龙头作用"意指"引导、领头、先锋"等作用,采用意译的方法,如"leading role"可使外人一听便懂其中含义。对"龙头地位"一语的翻译,也以意译为妥,即"leading position"。

2. "东方明珠",若译成"Oriental Bright Pearl",也未尝不可,不过添了"Bright"一词之后,似有画蛇添足之嫌。

3. "清朝乾隆、嘉庆年间",一个朝代中各个皇帝在位期也可译为"period",如 the Qianlong Period of the Qing Dynasty。

4. "打造世界级现代服务业。"其中"世界级"也可译为"world-beating"。"现代服务业"的英译应该是复数,打造的是多种现代服务产业的集聚地,即"strive to build a cluster of modern, world-class/world-beating service industries"。

5. "海派文化",译为"sea culture",犹如在谈论什么海洋世界的"海洋文化",或是一种为美食家所津津乐道的"海鲜饮食文化"。我们所指的"海派文化"专指一种代表着上海地区独特风格的文化传统。

6. 各大名菜:将鲁、川、粤、淮扬、闽等菜译成"cuisine"比之"food"为妥,"cuisine"所指不仅仅是一种"food",而且还表示一种自成体系的"culinary art"。

7. "万国建筑博览会"其中"万国"是一种比喻,实指"各国"、"世界"或"国际",这里可以用"world"或"international"表示。

8. "高架交通干道"其中"高架道路"也可译为"elevated"或"overhead motorway"。环线道路可译为"beltway",如美国"Baltimore"的环城道路就是这么称呼的。

9. "庙会"不可硬性对号入座将其译作"temple meeting"。"庙会"指的是一种定期集市,应译作"temple fair"。

10. "乘骐骥以驰骋兮,来吾道夫先路。"名言锦句、经典诗词的翻译需要平时的学习和知识的积累,口译时可根据上下文采用意译的方法。

11. "21世纪的上海人是聪明的人,也是精明的人,更是具有大气魄的高明人。"其中"聪明"、"精明"和"高明"表示了3种不同的"明"法,译语需要区别对待,可将"聪明"译成"bright"或"intelligent","精明"译成"smart"或"shrewd","高明"译成"wise"或"brilliant"。

译文

Shanghai is literally named as "a port on the sea". For historical reasons, this city has acquired two additional names for short, "Hu" and "Shen". Shanghai occupies a soil deposit plain land of 6,340 square kilometers, 0.06% of China's total territory, with an average altitude of 4 meters above sea level, the 103.4-meter Dajinshan being the summit of the land. About 17 million people register as the city's permanent residents.

Shanghai is one of the world's largest sea ports and among China's biggest industrial, commercial, financial and shipping centers. Here you will see the world's fastest means of land transportation, the maglev train, and the tallest tower in Asia, the Oriental Pearl Tower, marking metaphorically the speed and height of Shanghai. With its deepening economic reform, this city, formerly crowned as the financial, economic and trade hub of the Far East, is playing a leading role in boosting economic development in the Yangtze River Delta. Meanwhile, Shanghai has attracted millions of Chinese and overseas tourists with its unique charm. As an international metropolis, Shanghai provides direct flights to more than 60 cities in the world.

Known to the world as the Oriental Pearl, Shanghai is China's major eastern gate to the outside world. As early as the Tang and Song Dynasties, Shanghai functioned as a foreign trade port in East China and has mercantile ties with Japan, Korea and Southeast Asia. During the reigns of Emperor Qianlong(1736—1796) and Emperor Jiaqing(1796—1821) of the Qing Dynasty, Shanghai turned into a navigation hub and metropolis in southeast China, which attracted numerous merchants and countless ships to the Hiangpu River. What a spectacle of prosperity during that period! In the 1950s, Shanghai replaced Guangzhou as China's foreign trade center and has remained so ever since. Today, this well-known international port has developed into China's important center of economy, finance, trade, shipping, science and technology, information and culture. The last few years have seen a rapid upgrading of Shanghai's industrial sector as a whole, led by Pudong, which is best captured by the emergence of six pillar industries: the automaking industry, the electronics-information industry, the steel-making industry, the petrochemical and fine chemical industry, the home electrical appliances and the bioengineering and pharmaceutical industry. Rejuvenating the city by relying on science and education, invigorating the city by relying on talents and striving to build a cluster of modern, world-class service industries — these have not only become the consensus of the Shanghai people, but also turned from rhetoric to action.

One of the noted historic and cultural cities in China, Shanghai has over 70 sites of historical interests and cultural relics under the protection of the state and the municipal governments, which best represent the distinctive characteristics of Shanghai regional culture. Meanwhile, Shanghai is a cherished paradise for gourmets, who may find themselves frequenting the many thousands of restaurants that serve a complete list of China's major well-known cuisines, such as Shandong, Sichuan, Cantonese, Huai yang, Fujian traditions, to name just a few. In addition, you may easily find your way to those competing foreign food restaurants featuring French, Russian, Italian, British, German, Spanish, Japanese, Korean and Indian cuisines. On top of that, authentic Muslim and vegetarian foods may very well satisfy the palate of those religious enthusiasts and interested individuals. Known as the "Exhibition of the World's Architecture", Shanghai has a complete collection of buildings with different architectural styles along the Bund and elsewhere in the city. The Century Park, Shanghai Science & Technology Museum, the Jinmao Building, the International Convention Center, Dongfang Arts Center and the Oriental Pearl Tower in Pudong, flanked by the magnificent Nanpu and Yangpu bridges, which are connected by the city's elevated inner beltway, the Shanghai Museum, Shanghai Center standing on the People's Square — all these bring the city of Shanghai a brand-new look. The multi-tierred transportation system of subway, light railway, elevated expressway and the maglev train route has contributed to the city's more convenient and efficient traffic.

Shanghai is also a tourist destination that boasts quite a few tourist attractions and holiday resorts, including Sheshan State Holiday Resort, Dianshan Lake Scenic Area, the Sun Island Holiday Resort, the World Garden, the Dreamland and the Wildlife Zoo.

Every year Shanghai hosts a variety of tourist festivals, such as the New Year's Greeting Bell-Striking at the Longhua Temple on the eve of the Chinese New Year, the Longhua Temple Fair, the Peach Blossom Festival in Nanhui District and the International Tea Culture Festival in spring, Shanghai Huangpu Tourist Festival in autumn and Shanghai Sweet Osmanthus Festival. Recent years have witnessed the mushrooming of many new international festivals in Shanghai, such as the Shanghai International Film Festival, the Shanghai International Art Festival, the Shanghai International Costume Festival, and the Shanghai International Beer Festival. These fascinating festivals with distinctive Shanghai regional culture attract numerous participating tourists from both home and abroad.

Shanghai culture is the result of combining the cultures of the south and the north and melting the cultures of the east and west. The sea admits hundreds of rivers for its capacity to hold. Shanghai's great tolerance originates from its history of sufficient opening-up. The rapid rise of Shanghai owes so much to China's reform and opening to the outside world.

In its historical development, Shanghai became a small town in the Song Dynasty, a county in the Yuan Dynasty, a walled city in the Ming Dynasty. Shanghai is by no means a shining star among the numerous bright stars of China's famous ancient cities, comparable with no distant cities like Xi'an, Kaifeng and Luoyang, nor with the near cities like Nanjing, Suzhou and Hangzhou. Shanghai accelerated its development at an unusual speed after it was open to the outside world. Shanghai has started a new round of rapid development since China initiated its reform and opening drive, particularly since the early 1990s. The city is changing and taking on a new look with each passing day, pressing ahead the road of building itself into a modernized international metropolis, with remarkable achievements recognized by the whole world. "Visit Xi'an and you'll know China's history of 2,000 years; visit Beijing and you'll know China's history of 500 years; visit Shanghai and you'll know China's history of 100 years." Shanghai has become the symbol of modern Chinese cities. History has favored but also wronged the city of Shanghai. History now entrusts Shanghai with a rare opportunity of development. "On your steed galloping, and on my road pioneering."

Shanghai people of the 21st century are not only bright, but also smart and above all, wise people with broad vision and great courage, possessing the quality of world citizens. Devoted to their job, keen on acquiring new knowledge, Shanghai people aspire to live a better life; they are striving to build this city into a strong, prosperous and harmonious city, a metropolis that is characteristically modern, international and fashionable.

Shanghai of the 21st century will inevitably assume the role of an international economic, financial, trade and shipping center. The world focuses its attention on China and, in particular, on Shanghai. One of the most promising cities on the planet of the Earth, Shanghai cordially welcomes friends from all over the world.

选文 B

London is the capital of the United Kingdom and chief city of the British Commonwealth. With a population of about 7 million and an area of 1,580 sq km, this vast metropolis is by far the largest city in Europe, a distinction it has maintained since the 17th century. In the 19th century it was the largest and most influential city in the world, the center of a large and prosperous overseas empire. Although it no longer ranks among the world's most populous cities, London is still one of the world's major financial and cultural capitals.

By European standards, London is physically spread out and dispersed, without a predominant focal point. London's metropolitan area is divided into 32 boroughs and the city of London. At the core of this immense urban area is Central London, which includes the city of London, the City of Westminster, and the districts in the West End. The City of London is the traditional heart of the City and stands as its own political unit. The City of Westminster is the seat of the national government. Much of the outer portion of this huge conglomeration of people and activities is made up of low-rise residential development.

The historical center of London is now a relatively small area still known as the City, which covers only 2.6 sq km. This is where London began as a Roman colonial town around AD 50. Today this area is one of the world's leading financial centers. The permanent residential population of the City is now less than 6,000, but 350,000 commute here daily to work. The most prominent landmark of the City is Saint Paul's Cathedral.

The City of Westminster, about two miles from the City of London, emerged as England's political and religious center of power after 11th century. At the heart of Westminster is Westminster Abbey, which has always been closely associated with the monarchy and is used for such state occasions as coronations and royal funerals. Virtually across the street are the Houses of Parliament, officially called the New Palace of Westminster. Farther west is the monarch's permanent residence in London, Buckingham Palace.

To the west and north of London's Trafalgar Square is the West End, which is usually regarded as the center of town because it is London's shopping and entertainment hub. The busiest shopping area is Oxford Street, where famous large department stores are located. Scattered throughout the Soho and Covent Garden sections are foreign restaurants and entertainment attractions, including the Royal Opera House and most of London's major theaters and movie houses. In the northern part of the West End is Bloomsbury, the City's traditional intellectual center, with its concentration of bookshops and houses of writers and academics. Here, too, are the British Museum and the giant complex of the University of London.

The East End of London, in strong contrast to the prosperous West End, has frequently been characterized by slums, poverty, and crime. The East End grew with the spread of industries to the east of the City. It is especially famous as the centre of the clothing industry in London. Petticoat market takes place every Sunday morning and has become one of the beautiful sights of London.

London is one of world's great centers for classical and popular culture. It has enjoyed a reputation for superb theater since the time of Shakespeare in the 16th century. The variety ranges from the majestic Royal National Theatre to the lavish Royal Opera House. The sheer number of symphony orchestras is impressive and includes the London Symphony Orchestra, the Royal Philharmonic Orchestra and the English Chamber Orchestra. Some of the most well-known concert halls in the world, such as the Royal Festival Hall, provide favorable venues for the cornucopia of performances in London.

London itself is a living museum, with more than 2,000 years of history and culture. But it also boasts one of the greatest concentrations of significant museums (more than 100) of any city in the world. The jewel in this cultural crown is the British Museum, with 4 kilometers of the galleries and more than 4 million exhibits. The Victoria and Albert Museum displays an important and varied collection of applied arts. Across the street are the National History Museum with its dinosaurs, and the Science Museum, which includes a renowned section on the history of medicine. The Museum of London effectively introduces visitors to London's history by walking them through successive eras chronologically.

London is a major repository of the greatest Western art and a creative center for contemporary artists. The National Gallery on Trafalgar Square contains Britain's premier art collection, with holdings from every major European art school. Next door is the National Portrait Gallery, with thousands of striking portraits of Britons. The Tate Gallery contains the principal collection of British art and modern international art.

What Londoners do for a living has changed considerably since the city was a commercial and industrial center in the 19th century. Manufacturing has steadily declined and today accounts for less than 10 percent of total employment. The printing and publishing industry is now a leading employer. Far more important is the services sector, which employs 85 percent of London's workforce. This is led by financial and business services. Tourism is another important part of the services sector. London attracts more than 24 million visitors annually, more than half of them from outside the country. Servicing tourists is thought to employ at least 300,000 Londoners.

Although London has suffered some growing pains through its history, we have reasons to be optimistic about its future. We're positive that this old city will continue to be one of the world's great cities in a new spirit of youthful enthusiasm.

 重难点评析

1. London is the chief city of the British Commonwealth：英国女王是英联邦国家形式上的国家元首，伦敦自然成了英联邦国家形式上的首府。

2. a distinction it has maintained since the 17th century：这里所说的"distinction"是指伦敦众多的人口和广阔的地域，这些"特征"一直保持不变。

3. By European standards, London is physically spread out and dispersed：欧洲大陆城市的布局大多表现为小而集中，而伦敦的布局则大而散。

4. London's metropolitan area is divided in 32 boroughs 句中"boroughs"可译为"市镇"。

5. the City's traditional intellectual center：也可译为"一直是伦敦的文化教育中心"。

6. the Royal Philharmonic Orchestra：也有人把"Philharmonic Orchestra"译为"交响乐团"。

7. The printing and publishing industry is now a leading employer. 句中"employer"的基本意义是"雇主"，这里是指"提供就业机会的产业"。

8. Far more important is the services sector 句中"services sector"即"tertiary industry"，故译文可添加"第三产业"。

译　文

伦敦是联合王国的首都，也是英联邦的首府。这个有着约 700 万人口、1 580 平方公里土地的大都市显然是欧洲最大的城市，并自 17 世纪以来一直保持不变。19 世纪的伦敦是世界上最大同时也是最有影响力的城市，它是一个庞大繁荣的海外帝国的中心。今天的伦敦虽然已退出世界人口最多的城市的行列，却依然是世界主要的金融和文化都市之一。

按照欧洲的标准，伦敦可算是一座布局很分散的城市，没有一个占主导地位的中心。伦敦的城区分成 32 个区和伦敦城。在这片辽阔的城区的中央地带是伦敦中心城区，中心城区包括伦敦城、威斯敏斯特城和西区地块三部分。伦敦城是伦敦传统的心脏地区，是伦敦的政治中心。威斯敏斯特城是国家政府的所在地。这座大型城市的外围区域大多为底层的居民住宅区。

历史上的伦敦市中心现在只是一个较小的区域，仍被称之为伦敦城，面积只有 2.6 平方公里。伦敦城形成于大约公元 50 年，当时只是罗马帝国的一座殖民城。现在伦敦城已成为世界主要金融中心。这里的常住居民不足 6 000 人，但是每天来这里上班的城外人约有 35 万之众。这里最显著的地貌标志是圣保罗大教堂。

离伦敦城两英里处是威斯敏斯特城，自 11 世纪以来威斯敏斯特城成了英格兰的政治和宗教的权力中心。威斯敏斯特城的中心耸立着威斯敏斯特教堂，与君主政体的活动有着密切的关系，如加冕礼仪和皇家葬礼这类活动。威斯敏斯特教堂的对面是议会大厦，正式名称为威斯敏斯特新宫。从议会大厦往西是皇家在伦敦的永久性住所白金汉宫。

在伦敦特拉法尔加广场的西北面是伦敦的西区，西区是伦敦的购物与娱乐中心，所以通常被视为伦敦的市中心。最繁华的购物区是著名大百货公司的牛津街。在索霍区和科文特加登地段，外国餐厅和娱乐场所四处可见，例如皇家歌剧院以及伦敦大部分的主要剧院和影院。位于西区北部的布卢姆兹伯里区是伦敦传统的知识中心，集聚着许多书店和文人学者的宅第，大英博物馆和伦敦大学的庞大校区也坐落在这里。

与西区的繁华形成鲜明对比的是伦敦东区，常以平民窟、贫穷和犯罪的形象出现。东区的形成是工业向伦敦城以东地区延伸的产物。这里是伦敦的服装业中心。每星期天上午的裙子巷市场,已成为伦敦的一道亮丽的风景线。

伦敦是世界上古典文化和通俗文化的大中心之一。自16世纪莎士比亚时代起伦敦就一直享有拥有一流剧院的美誉,如宏伟的皇家国家剧院和豪华的皇家歌剧院。伦敦拥有数量众多的交响乐团,如伦敦交响乐团、皇家爱乐乐团和英格兰室内乐团。伦敦有一些世界上最富盛名的音乐厅,如皇家节日厅,为伦敦各类音乐演出提供良好的场所。

虽然有着2 000多年历史和文化的伦敦自身就是一座活生生的博物馆,它却集中了一个庞大的博物馆群,数量超过100个,为世界其他城市所少见。大英博物馆是镶刻在这顶文化皇冠上的一颗宝石,拥有4公里长的展廊和400万余件展品。维多利亚及艾伯特博物馆展出的是不同类型的名贵应用艺术品。街对面是含有恐龙展品的自然历史博物馆,以及有着闻名遐迩的医药发展史馆的科学博物馆。进入伦敦博物馆的参观者可以通过伦敦各个发展阶段的演变来了解这座城市的历史。

伦敦是西方艺术精华的一个主要陈列馆,也是当代画家的创作中心。坐落在特拉法尔加广场上的国家美术馆收藏了英国最重要的美术作品,作品代表着欧洲艺术的每个主要流派。与国家美术馆为邻的是国家人物肖像馆,那里陈列着数以千计的不列颠人逼真的肖像。泰特美术馆除了拥有一大批国内美术作品外,还收藏了许多现代国际美术作品。

自19世纪伦敦城成为工商业中心以来,伦敦人的谋生方式发生了显著的变化。制造业逐步萎缩,今天在伦敦的就业人员中,制造业从业人员所占的比率不足10%。印刷出版业已成为一个吸纳就业者的主要行业。更为重要的行业是服务业(即第三产业),以金融商贸业为龙头,吸纳着伦敦劳动力的85%。服务业的另一重要组成部分是旅游业,每年吸引了2 400万以上的游客,其中一半以上的游客来自国外。据说伦敦有30万人在旅游服务行业就职。

虽然伦敦在历史发展过程中经历了一些成长的烦劳,但是我们有理由对伦敦未来表示乐观。我们相信这座古老的城市将焕发出青春的气息,继续名列世界伟大城市之林。

重组与表达

1. 词序重组

英汉两个民族由于身处的社会、历史、地理、文化、政治经济形态各不相同,形成了迥异的思维方式、思维特征及思维风格,在语言表达模式中英汉两种语言的差别首先反映在词序上。在口译实践中,当源语人所说的句子较长,句式复杂,包含的信息量较大时,译员若要迅速、完整、准确地传达说话人的信息,保证交流的顺畅及质量,就必须经常有效地进行词序重组,处理好句子各个成分词的相互关系。

(1) 对定语的重组

在汉语中,定语大多前置;而在英文中,如果定语为单词,通常放在所修饰的名词前面,如果定语为短语,大多放在所修饰的名词之后。例如:

我们要努力实现"十一五"确定的节能减排目标,使生态环境有一个明显的改善。

在这句话中,有两个定语"十一五"确定的和"节能减排",口译成英语时,宜将这两个定语放在中心名词goal的后面,可译为:We need to work to attain the goal set in the 11th Five-Year-Plan for energy conservation and emission reduction in order to markedly improve the ecological environment.

我们还是第一批向世界粮农组织捐赠3 000万美元投资发展基金的国家。

在这句话中,有两个定语"第一批"和"向世界粮农组织捐赠3 000万美元投资发展基金的"。前一个定语较短,可以用一个单词完成,口译时可以前置,而后一个定语较长,意义较为复杂,则处理为后置更为妥当。可译为:China was among the first batch of countries to contribute 30 million US dollars to the FAO to establish a trust fund.

(2) 对状语的重组

英语中单词做状语修饰动词时,一般放在动词之后,而汉语则多放在动词之前。英语中表示程度的状语在修饰其他状语时既可前置也可后置,而汉语多为前置。英语中短语做状语时放在被修饰的动词之前或之后,汉语则多放在被修饰的动词之前。英语中地点状语多在时间状语之前,多按从小到大的顺序排列;而在汉语中时间状语往往在地点状语之前,多按从大到小的顺序排列。例如:

我们要在结构调整和经济发展方式的转变上有新的突破。

在这句话中,条件状语"在结构调整和经济发展方式的转变"位于谓语"有新的突破"之前,在口译为英语时,宜将它后置,可译为:We need to make new breakthroughs in adjusting the economic structure and changing the model of economic development.

我们免除农业税和农业特产税是立了法的;我们实行免费的九年义务教育是立了法的;我们将要开始实行覆盖城乡的低保制度也要用法制保障。

这个包含三个并列分句的句子中,"免除农业税和农业特产税"、"实行免费的九年义务教育"、"将要开始实行覆盖城乡的低保制度"这三个成分均指我们在这三个方面立法,为前置状语。在口译时,因其所涉含义较为复杂,宜处理为后置状语,以保证含义的完整和准确。可译为:We have legislation on rescinding the agricultural tax and taxes on special agricultural products. We have legislation on nine-year free compulsory education. And we will develop a legal framework for the system of urban and rural basic cost of living allowances to be established.

(3) 对特殊语句的重组

中国实行从紧的货币政策和稳健的财政政策,是从中国的实际出发,主要是固定资产增长过快、货币信贷投放过多、外贸顺差过大。

"固定资产增长过快"、"货币信贷投放过多"、"外贸顺差过大"这三个短语是汉语中惯用的主谓结构,而英语中多以名词性结构为主,所以口译时要适当调整,以免听起来句式破碎、零乱。可译为:China has pursued a tight monetary policy and a prudent fiscal policy in light of its actual condition. The main problems we face now are the excessive investment in fixed assets, excessive money and credit supply, and a large trade surplus.

我们对于印度政府在对待达赖集团策划的所谓"独立"活动所采取的立场和措施表示赞赏。

这句源语是个倒装句式,说话人为表示强调,将宾语"对于印度政府在对待达赖集团策划的所谓'独立'活动所采取的立场和措施"前置,口译时可适当调整,进行重组,可译为:We appreciate the position and measures taken by the Indian government regarding the Tibet independence activities masterminded by Dalai clique.

这个历史遗留的十分复杂的问题,不是一朝一夕能够解决的。但是,只要中印双方都抱有诚意,本着平等相待、互谅互让的原则,我想解决边界问题的谈判会有新的进展。

在这句话中,有多处语序需要调整、重组。"这个"、"历史遗留的"、"十分复杂的",口译时可以将其分别处理,用个别单词即可完成的则前置,而需要短语形式完成的则后置;之后的"一朝一夕"为状语,位于动词"解决"之前,口译时可以后置;整句话:"这个历史遗留的十分复杂的问题,不是一朝一夕能够解决的。"可以使用 it 结构进行重组。在后一句中,"平等相待、互谅互让的原则"拥有两个并列定语,因包含信息量较多,宜处理为后置;而"我想解决边界问题的谈判会有新的进展"可以调整为被动语态,全句可以译为: It is not easy to resolve such a complex issue left from the past and we cannot expect it to be resolved overnight. However, I believe that as long as China and India show sincerity and follow the principles of equality, mutual understanding and mutual accommodation, new progress will be made in the negotiations.

2. 断句与翻译

英语作为"形合"的语言,各种语法手段使得句子不断扩展,句子较长,层次较多,句间组合较为多样。而汉语是"意合"的语言,内在意义衔接紧密自然,而语段结构流散,多散句、松句、紧缩句、流水句等形式。因此,在英汉互译中,往往要求对源语进行必要的断句,化整为零,顺原句次序而译,节省语言结构调整的时间,迅速完成口译任务。

具体而言,"断句"指的就是在口译时,将原句按照适当的意群进行切分,划为合理的、大小不等的、语义相对独立的语流段。而"顺句驱动"指的是在断句之后,自然地、天衣无缝地把断开的句子重新衔接起来,将其内含信息转化为目的语。断句与顺译是口译尤其是同声传译最重要的技巧,是同声传译成功的关键所在。例如:

To the people of poor nations,/we pledge to work alongside you/to make your farms flourish/and let clean waters flow,/to nourish starved bodies/and feed hungry minds.

句中的小斜线标记了各个相对独立的意群,译员在接受到源语信息时,依据意群顺序,顺源句而下,完成口译。要注意的是,对意群的划分和断开并非取决于字词,而是以句中的语流模块为基建。此句可译为:"对于那些贫苦国家的人民,我们发誓将跟你们并肩战斗,让你们的农场繁茂,让洁净的水源流淌,让挨饿的身体获得营养,让饥饿的头脑获得食粮。"从译文可见,原文的语序未做任何大的调整和更变,这样可以很好地保证口译的产出速度。

再看一个例子:

In a global economy/where the most valuable skill you can sell/is your knowledge,/a good education/is no longer just a pathway to opportunity /— it is a pre-requisite.

同样,句中小斜线标记了各个意群,译员遵循意群的次序,顺流而下,进行口译,此句可译为:"在全球化经济时代,你可以出售的最有价值的技能莫过于知识,良好的教育不再仅仅是通往机会之门的台阶,而是先决条件。"

Cultural and scientific contact went from strength to strength/through the nineteenth and early twentieth centuries.

对此句断句可以发现得到两个小分句,处理后可译为:"文化和科学方面的接触日益增多,整个 19 世纪和 20 世纪初都是这样。"

It should be taken as a fact/that the combat against piracy is enjoying greater priority in both developed countries and developing countries/in economy, science and technology, education, and commerce.

这句话较长,各个意群也相对较长,译员在接受信息时,要耐心等待意群内语义完整之后再口译。可译为:"这应该是一个事实,即打击盗版行为在发达和发展中国家都受到更多的重视,经济、科技、教育和商业领域中都是如此。"

It is therefore in the interest of the industrial countries/to adopt structural adjustment policies/that will phase out the uncompetitive production of textile and clothing.

在这个句子中,译员为避免记忆负荷超载,当听到形式主语之后,就应有意识地搭建好主谓结构,再依次传递后面主语的详细内容。可译为:"工业国家有利的是,采取结构调整政策,淘汰没有竞争力的纺织和服装产业。"

以上例证讲述了断句的原则和方法,简而言之,就是依照意群,将长句断成相对独立的小句,译员再对信息重组表达。而断句之后的顺句驱动,就是指译员依照意群次序,顺流而下,不对句序做大的调整和更改。为了实现顺译,译员往往需要灵活的策略和丰富的经验,依照不同的句法特征和表达习惯进行口译。其中重复与改变词性是常用的两个技巧。

(1) 重复

顺译中的重复表现在词语调配、句式安排和篇章结构等方面。译员适当地应用重复技巧,可以解决顺译所带来的表达困难,使表达自然、交流顺畅。看下面一个例子:

We will build the roads and bridges, the electric grids and digital lines that feed our commerce and bind us together.

在这句话中,that 所引导的定语从句如果要顺原句语序,就需要添加代词"它们",重复指代前面意群的相关内容,此句可译为:"我们将建设道路和桥梁、电网和数字网络,它们将为我们的商业活动服务,把我们联系在一起。"再如:

They are still striving for independence 50 years after the Second World War.

和上一句一样,可以选用代词"这样"进行重复,此句可译为:"他们仍在努力争取独立,二战 50 年后还在这样做。"

(2) 改变词性

In a few minutes/the Secretary of State will give us a report/on the latest developments in the Middle East,/about his meetings with leaders in the region /and his efforts for an international peace conference.

在这句话的几个意群中,on the latest developments in the Middle East, about his meetings with leaders in the region and his efforts for an international peace conference 都用来讲述 report 的内容,要做到顺译的话,就必须将 on 和 about 的词性转换为动词,该句可译为:"几分钟后,国务卿将给我们作报告,谈一谈中东的最新发展局势,谈一谈他与地区领导们的会晤,谈一谈他为国际和平会议所做出的努力。"

They agreed that nuclear weapons on the Korean Peninsula would represent a grave threat to regional and international security, and decided that their countries would consult with each other on ways to eliminate this danger.

在这句话中,represent a grave threat to regional and international security 按照汉语习惯,很自然会译为"意味着对地区和国际安全的一个严重威胁",这个译文并没有做到顺应原句语序,其原因就在于拘泥于原文的词性,如果将 a grave threat 的词性改变,就可以做到顺译,此句可译为:"他们认为,朝鲜半岛的核武器严重威胁了地区和国际安全,因此决定要互相磋商,采取措施来消除这一威胁。"

重复与改变词性是顺译的两个常用手段,但并不能解决所有的语言问题。事实上,源语说话人所使用的语言大多句式多样,句意丰富,这就要求译员在不同的语境下灵活应变,积极应对。

下面以不同句式要求来看看顺译策略的实施。

(1) 定语从句

在口译由先行词引导的定语从句中,重复是经常使用的方法。例如:

On the other hand, the United States has large industrial plants capable of producing a variety of goods, such as chemicals and airplanes, which can be sold to nations that need them.

这一句话后半部分的关系代词 which 可译为"这些产品",原文意思没变,只是为了汉语结构上的需要,这样可以避免在汉语中做更多的句式调整。整句可译为:"另外一方面,美国拥有规模庞大的工厂,有能力生产各种产品,例如化学品和飞机,这些产品都可销往需要的国家。"

All delegations which are to speak at the conference tomorrow morning or join in the small group discussions tomorrow afternoon should first sign up with the secretariat.

定语从句要实现顺译,除了使用重复的方法外,还可以转换逻辑关系,比如在这句话中,就可以变原先的定语关系为条件关系,可以顺译为:"任何代表团,如果希望在明天上午的会议中发言,或者参加明天下午的小组讨论,都必须先在秘书处登记。"

Those who opposed the emphasis we place on human rights say that economic development and trade, and greater interchange of people and information, will inevitably lead to democracy and greater respect of human rights.

这个句子的定语从句可采取简略表达的方法,转为简单句处理,既毋需重复,也毋需转换逻辑关系,可译为:"有人反对我们强调人权,他们说经济发展和商业,更多的人际交流,更多的信息交流,都必将产生民主,令人们更为尊重人权。"

(2) 状语从句

The power of the market to generate wealth and expand freedom is unmatched, but this crisis has reminded us that without a watchful eye, the market can spin out of control — and that a nation cannot prosper long when it favors only the prosperous.

在口译后半句 a nation cannot prosper long when it favors only the prosperous 时,通常的做法是调整语序,译为:"当一个国家只青睐富人时,它的繁荣就无法持久。"如果要贯彻顺句的原则,在同传中把握时间,那么就可以将句式的逻辑关系进行转化,转译为:"一个国家要实现持久繁荣,就不能只青睐富人。"全句可以译为:"市场产生财富和扩张自由的能力是无以匹敌的。但这场危机提醒我们,没有有效的监督,市场会失控。一个国家要实现持久繁荣,就不能只青睐富人。"

The economics of the developing countries must be placed on a sustained growth path if the hopes and aspirations of mankind embodied in the Charter are to be fulfilled.

按照一般的表达习惯，这句话会译为："如果要实现联合国宪章中所蕴含的人类的希望与梦想，发展中国家的经济就必须走可持续发展的道路。"这样一来，句序就经过了大调整。如果要符合顺译的要求，就要改变这句话的逻辑，可译为："发展中国家的经济必须走可持续发展的道路，这样联合国宪章中所蕴含的人类的希望与梦想才能实现。"

Before he was hired by the Board in 2008 to take over the job of Mr. Johnson, the president of this ＄30 billion company, he had been a CFO of a large financial company on Wall Street.

在这句由 before 引导的从句中，要实现顺译，就必须对句子的逻辑意义进行灵活的调整。根据经验，在句首出现的时间连词，如 before, after, when, 等等往往先略去不译，之后再根据句意进行适当调整，比如此句中的 before 就可以在后文中再处理，转移为"在这之前"。这句话可译为："2008 年他被董事会任命，接替约翰逊先生的工作，就任这家市值 300 亿美元的公司的总裁，在这之前，他是华尔街一家大型财务公司的财务总监。"再看一个例子：

After we had an extensive discussion with the other group on this important issue, we decided that we should go ahead with the plan and forget about the budget.

这句话是以 after 引导的时间状语从句，口译时，先把从句中的完整句意表达出来，在陈述 after "这之后"，实现两个分句的连接，可译为："我们和另一组就这一重要议题展开了广泛讨论，这之后，我们决定开展该计划，将预算问题搁置一边。"

(3) 被动语态的句式

由于句法、修辞、文体等方面的原因，英语的被动句应用得非常广泛。英语的被动句将动作的执行者置于动词之后，若按照汉语习惯，势必要进行语序调整，为了实现顺译，译员常常应用种种手段将英语被动句进行转换。请看下面例子：

The only way to fully restore America's economic strength is to make the long-term investments that will lead to new jobs, new industries, and a renewed ability to compete with rest of the world. This inflow of the world savings to the United States was largely triggered by the high interest rates prevailing in the American market.

在这句话中，标志被动语态的语言标记是 was largely triggered by，可以将其词性转换为名词，以完成顺译，此句可译为："世界储蓄大量流入美国，其主要原因是美国市场利率居高不小。"再看一个例子：

Liberalization of trade and investment has been influenced by the expansion and intensification of regional integration efforts.

在这句话中，可以将被动句标示词 by 改译为表示原因的词组，expansion and intensification 词性转换为动词，此句可译为："贸易和投资的自由化受到了影响，是因为扩大并加强了区域一体化的努力。"

(4) it 引导的句式

这里的 it 句式，是指英语中非人称代词 it 作为虚指成分的一些用法，如强调句式、形式主语句、形式宾语句等，特别是其中的形式主语句。由 it 构成的形式主语句的显著特点是，it 作为语法主语占据主语位置，之后是谓语，而语句意义上的主语被置于最后。这种句式中的意义主语通常很长，如果要等意义主语传译完之后再译谓语，必然要加大记忆负荷，干扰对后续句子的处理,影响口译效果,在同传翻译中尤为不可行。因此,可以考虑运用多种灵活策略进行必要的调整,依照源语次序进行顺译。例如:

It is essential that the Committee discuss the budget issue at its next meeting with a view to submitting it for approval at the general conference to be held in November.

在这句话的口译中,it is essential 可以融入之后的语义主语部分,使得全句一气呵成,可译为:"委员会有必要在下次会议上讨论预算问题,已将其提交给11月召开的大会审核。"

It is hoped that by providing Chinese students with a better understanding of American perspectives on international trade and investment, they will be better qualified to do business with American businessmen, attorneys, and corporations.

在口译这句话中的 it is hoped 时,可用人称主语替代 it,将引文没有说出来而实际上隐含的"人们"二字说出来,使语句更符合汉语表达习惯,达到顺义的效果。全句可译为:"人们希望通过让中国学生更好地了解美国人对国际贸易和投资的看法,从而使他们更好地与美国的商人、律师和公司做生意。"

针对一些使用频率较高的 it 形式主语句,可以套用惯用的表达方式。如:It is believed that... 可译为"人们(大家)认为……";It is said that... 可译为"据说……";It is reported that... 可译为"据报道……";It is confirmed that... 可译为"据证实……"。要注意的是,英语这种特殊句式,也常常译成汉语的无主句。例如:

It must be pointed out that these islands have always been under Chinese jurisdiction.

这句话就可以处理为:"必须指出,这些岛屿向来归中国管辖。"

It is necessary to guarantee women full equality of rights in social life as a whole.

这句话可译为:"有必要保障妇女充分的平等权,在整个社会中的平等权。"

以上罗列了几种主要句式的口译方法。限于篇幅,只能扼要阐述。口译作为一种挑战性极强的交际活动,发言人、译语听众、母语听众、主题、会场气氛等交际因素彼此制约、相互影响。在具体的语言环境中,往往多种句式、多种语言情况糅杂在一起,译员要达到顺义的要求,就必须灵活运用各种策略,因情而定,因势而变。再看下面几个句子:

The world reaction was one of shock, grief and disbelief following the tragic assassination of Rabin, the Prime Minster of Israel who was one of the architects of the Middle East peace process which was to resolve the century-old conflicts between Israel and Arab countries in this region.

译员在口译这段话时,要进行词性转换,也要重复表达,在准确断句的基础上,完成顺译,全句可译为:"全世界的反应是震惊、悲痛和难以置信,以色列总理拉宾惨遭杀害,拉宾是中东和平进程的缔造者之一,该和平进程旨在解决该地区以色列和阿拉伯各国间长达世纪之久的冲突。"

The renegotiation for a settlement was barred by suspicion, indeed, by the fear of losing part of the country.

这句话中的被动语态需要进行调整,而断句之后,需要添加主语,再对相应的词性进行改变,才能完成顺译,全句可译为:"解决问题的重新谈判受到阻碍,是因为有人怀疑、害怕会丧失部分领土。"

Output increase is not really feasible in this country, which must restructure its entire economy along free-market lines before it can hope to increase output significantly.

　　而这句话的口译需要译员注意转换句式逻辑关系,同时调整词性,可译为:"产量的增长在该国不切实际,该国必须重组经济结构,走自由市场的路线,这样才有希望大幅增长。"

　　No nation can even run a tax system, an airline, a good health system, fight AIDs, or guarantee a clean environment, without the co-operation of others.

　　在否定态的句子中,译者口译时要注意对语气的把握,同时运用其他策略完成顺译。可译为:"任何国家,如果需要运作税收系统、运营航线、建立良好的医疗体系、抗击艾滋病,或保障环境清洁,没有其他国家的合作是做不到的。"

　　3. 归纳概括

　　译员作为文化中介者,其职责在于传达给特定的听众群有意义的信息,而非拘泥于孤立的学问。口译是否成功,取决于译员对讲话信息或内容的转达是否准确,译语风格、口吻和语气是否恰当,口译语言表达是否准确、流畅;同时也取决于译语是否满足听众的期望,重点和非重点、简略程度与听众是否吻合,译语能否产生与源语一致的内容和情感效果。这就要求译员根据听众不同的文化程度、专业知识、价值取向等加以变通,不断做出适当的调整。

　　例如,邀请比尔·盖茨来华演讲,如话题对象是一般听众,那他们的预期和着重点主要落在盖茨的个人奋斗和成功经历之上,对于计算机领域的专业知识与术语可能不在听众关注或理解的范围之内。因此,尽管发言人出于职业习惯会提及专业知识,但译员可根据需要和听众反应进行删减、归纳和概括,确保信息传递的顺畅,以抓住听众的心理。反之,如果听众是业内人士,口译时则需要在某些知识点上展开阐述,对术语的运用也要尽量专业,以确保信息传达的全面和准确。再如,在一段记者对某成功人士的访谈中,该人士在谈及个人奋斗经历时说道:"我当过代课老师、做过推销、卖过保险、开过饭店……"这些具体经历如果与后文没有太多联系与铺垫,口译时可归纳处理为"I once had various working experiences, which paved the way for my latter success"即可。有时译员一味地顺从、忠实,反而会使得译语听起来冗长累赘、逻辑凌乱、观点不鲜明,还不如言简意赅,直接到位。在这种情况下,适当地归纳概括就显得十分必要。简而言之,归纳就是对相对信息的概括性、综合性说明,以使表达自然衔接,保持信息通畅。请看下例:

　　Our two countries have developed good cooperation in such wide areas as politics, commerce, education, culture, defense, science, agriculture, and medicine.

　　这句可译为:"我们两国已在这些领域开展了友好的合作,如政治、商业、教育、文化、国防、等等。"词句的重点含义是两国的友好合作,原句中的许多列举项是为了进一步证明合作开展得十分广泛。译员在口译时不妨进行简要归纳,使用"等"、"等等"、"多"等概括性词语来总结前述信息。这样做既不损害原句主旨含义,同时也能为自己做好充分心理准备,以处理好后续信息。再看一个例子:

　　The total project costs 250,654,315 US dollars.

　　这句可译为:"整个项目耗资为2亿5千多万美元。"数字向来是口译中的难点。大额数字集中出现的话,更是对译员的严峻挑战。译员对数字口译的常见策略是,根据具体口译场景、信息内容、听众要求等,将主体数字准确译出,而省略较小的单位。这种归纳的译法也是权宜之计,如果数字单位并不大,或对上下文意义重大,译员就不可避繁就简,需要尽力准确翻译。

口译中的变通一定要把握好尺度。这在很大程度上取决于译者对译文宗旨和精髓、听众需求和反应的真切理解。译员要把握如源语意图、交际环境和交际反应方面的沟通效果的主要参照值,在"灵活度"的控制上,仔细权衡,审慎判断。

增译法和减译法

一、增译法

什么叫增译法? 我们可以这样确定它的定义:为了使译文忠实地表达原文的意思与风格并使译文合乎表达习惯,必须增加一些词语,这就叫增译法。试仔细对照如下译例看看此技巧应用的一些情况:

1. I am looking forward to the holidays.
我在等待假日的到来。

2. Much of our morality is customary.
我们大部分的道德观念都有习惯性。

3. Courage in excess becomes foolhardiness, affection weakness, thrift avarice.
勇敢过度,即成蛮勇;情感过度,即成溺爱;俭约过度,即成贪婪。

4. Histories make men wise; poets witty; the mathematics subtle; natural philosophy deep; moral grave; logic and rhetoric able to contend.
读史使人明志,读诗使人灵秀,数学使人周密,科学使人深刻,伦理使人庄重,逻辑修辞之学使人善辩。(或:历史使人聪明;诗人使人遐想;数学使人精细;格致使人深沉;伦理使人庄严;逻辑和修辞使人能够争论。)(后一种译文虽然偏古并且有个别欠信之处,但与前一种译文相比,几乎有异曲同工之妙,在译文中都使用了增译法或重译法,反复使用了"使人"这两个字。)

5. Reading makes a full man; conference a ready man; and writing an exact man.
读书使人充实,讨论使人机智,笔记使人准确。

6. We won't retreat, we never have and never will.
我们不后退,我们从来没有后退过,我们将来也决不后退。

7. Paris all truth, Versailles all lies; and that lies vented through the mouth of theirs.
巴黎全是真理,凡尔赛全是谎言,而这种谎言是从梯也尔嘴里发出的。

8. The journey which has brought me to Peking has been a very long one. Long when measured in miles. Long when measured in time.
我来北京的旅途是漫长的。用里程衡量,它是漫长的。用时间衡量,它也是漫长的。

9. Last summer more than 3,000 city welfare employees staged a "work-in" during which they showed up at the office but refused to process cases.
上一个夏天,3 000多名城市福利救济部门的雇员举行了一次"到职罢工"活动,他们人到了办公室,但拒绝审核要求救济的申请。

10. As an Oriental, I cannot but be proud of you.

作为一个东方人,我不得不为你们所取得的历史性成就感到骄傲。

11. I can imagine the almost insuperable obstacles to the unity of a billion-odd people.

我可以想象到要使10亿多人民团结起来将会遇到的几乎不可克服的困难。

12. Theory is something but practice is everything.

理论固然重要,实践尤其重要。

13. Henry Kissinger had slept there before, in July and again in October.

这之前,基辛格在7月和10月两度在那里下榻。

14. Their host carved, poured, served, cut bread, talked, laughed, proposed health.

他们的主人,(又是)割啊,(又是)倒啊,(又是)布菜啊,(又是)切面包啊,(又是)谈啊,(又是)笑啊,(又是)敬酒啊,忙个不停。

15. 没有调查就没有发言权。

He who makes no investigation and study has no right to speak.

16. 没有眼睛向下的兴趣和决心,是一辈子也不会真正懂得中国的事情的。

Unless a person is interested in turning his eyes downward and is determined to do so, he will never in his life really understand things in China.

17. 虚心使人进步,骄傲使人落后。

Modesty helps one to go forward, whereas conceit makes one lag behind.

18. 跑了和尚跑不了庙。

The monk may run away, but the temple can't run away with him.

19. 吃饭防噎,走路防跌。

While eating, take heed that you do not choke; while walking, take heed that you do not fall.

20. 留得青山在,不怕没柴烧。

So long as green hills remain, there will never be a shortage of firewood.

21. 送君千里,终有一别。

Although you may escort a guest a thousand miles, yet the parting must come at last.

22. 小不忍则乱大谋。

If one is not patient in small things, one will never be able to control great ventures.

23. 老同志应支持中青年干部的工作,担负起传、帮、带的任务。

Old veteran cadres should support the young and middle-aged cadres in their work and take upon the task of helping and guiding the latter and passing on experience to them.

24. 我们在生产建设中不仅需要创造更多更好的物质产品,而且需要培育一代又一代的社会主义新人。

In production and construction, we should try not only to turn out more and better material products, but also train successive generations of socialist-minded people of a new type.

25. 谁都知道朝鲜战场是艰苦些。

Every one knows that life on the Korean battle-field was rather hard.

26. 三个臭皮匠,顶个诸葛亮。

Three cobblers with their wits combined equal Zhuge Liang, the master mind.

27. 一个篱笆三个桩,一个好汉三个帮。

A fence needs the support of three stakes, an able fellow needs the help of three other people.

28. 立党为公,还是立党为私,这是无产阶级政党和资产阶级政党的分水岭,是真共产党员和假共产党的试金石。

To build a party for the interests of the vast majority or for the interests of the minority? This is the watershed between proletarian and bourgeois parties and the touchstone for distinguishing true communists from sham.

29. 交出翻译之前,必须读几遍,看看有没有要修改的地方。这样你才能把工作做好。

Before handing in your translation, you have to read it over and over again and see if there is anything in it to be corrected or improved. Only thus can you do your work well.

30. 班门弄斧。

Showing off one's proficiency with the axe before Lu Ban, the master carpenter.

31. 只许州官放火,不许百姓点灯。

The magistrates are free to burn down houses while the common people are forbidden even to light lamps. (or. One man may steal a horse while another may not look over the hedge.)

增词的情况是各种各样的。总的规则是:为了使译文忠于原文,需要增加什么就增加什么。根据以上31例,大致归纳如下:

1. 增译的部分在原文中虽找不出对应的词语,但为了忠实传达原文信息,译文非增补不可(见例1,23,24,25,26,27,28,30)。

2. 增加动词(见例3,4,5,6,7)。

3. 增加名词(见例2,9,16)。

4. 增加主谓结构(见例8)。

5. 增加定语(见例10,11)。

6. 增加状语或副词(见例12,13)。

7. 增加语气助词(见例14)。

8. 增加代词(见例5,22,29)。

9. 增加连词(见例17,18,19,20,21,22,31)。汉译英时,增加连词的情况是常见的,因为英语的连词比汉语使用得多。冠词的情况更是如此。

二、减译法

和其他一切事物一样,翻译也是有增必有减。懂了增译法之后自然也就会懂得什么是减译法。它是增译法的反面:以同一个译例来说,在英译汉中如果用增译法的话,在汉译英中自然就要用减译法了。把第二节中的31个例子倒译的话(即把汉译英改为英译汉或把英译汉改为汉译英),所用的译法就不是增译法而是减译法了。

关于减译法,应该记住这样一条总规则:减译法是指原文中有些词在译文中不译出来,因为译文中虽无其词而已有其意,或者在译文中是不言而喻的;换言之,减译法是删去一些可有可无的,或者有了把嫌累赘或违背译文习惯表达法的词,但减译并不是把原文的某些思想内容删去。

此外,冠词、连词、代词(尤其是人称代词、关系代词)、关系副词,等等,在英语中经常使用,但译成汉语时几乎很少出现,要使译文忠实而地道,减译法就自然必不可少了。例如:

1. A book is useful.

书(是)有用(的)。

2. The earth goes around the sun.

地球绕太阳转。

3. On Sundays we have no school.

礼拜天我们不上学。

4. Mr. Bingley was good-looking and gentleman-like.

宾利先生风度翩翩,彬彬有礼。

5. A wise man will not marry a woman who has attainments but no virtue.

聪明的人是不会娶有才无德的女子为妻的。

6. If you write to him, the response would be absolute silence and void.

你写信给他,总是石沉大海。

7. Sunday is the day when I am least busy.

星期天我最不忙。

8. Could you help me in any way?

你能帮帮我吗?

9. Winter is the best time to study the growth of trees. Although the leaves are gone and the branches are bare, the trees themselves are beautiful.

冬天是研究树木生长的最好的季节,虽然树叶落了,树枝光了,但树木本身却是美丽的。

10. He put his hands into his pockets and then shrugged his shoulders.

他双手插进口袋,然后耸了耸双肩。

11. Anyone who does not recognize this fact is not a materialist.

不承认这个事实,就不是唯物主义者。

12. These developing countries cover vast territories, encompass a large population and abound in natural resources.

这些发展中国家,土地辽阔,人口众多,资源丰富。(或:这些发展中国家地大物博,人口众多。)

13. 我们要培养分析问题、解决问题的能力。

We must cultivate the ability to analyse and solve problems.

14. 要推迟战争的爆发,就要反对那样的绥靖政策,不管军事的、政治的、经济的绥靖,都要反对。

To delay the outbreak of war, it is necessary(or essential) to oppose the policy of appeasement like that, militarily, politically and economically.

15. Everywhere you can find new types of men and objects in New China.
新中国处处可以看到新人、新事物。

16. 他们为国家做的事,比我们所做的多得多。
They have done much more for the state than we have.

17. 郭沫若同志曾说:"中国人民历来是勇于探索、勇于创造、勇于革命的。"
Comrade Guo Moruo once said: "The people of China have always been courageous enough to probe into things, to make inventions and to make revolution."

18. 质子带阳电,电子带阴电,而中子既不带阳电,也不带阴电。
A proton has a positive charge and an electron a negative charge, but a neutron has neither.

19. When it is dark in the east, it is light in the west; when things are dark in the south there is still light in the north.
东方不亮西方亮,黑了南方有北方。

20. It is not entirely right to say that if there is food, let everyone share it.
说有饭大家吃并不完全正确。

21. Eight o'clock found Franz up and dressed.
八点钟,弗兰兹起床穿衣。

22. It is the US that is distorting and perverting the 'Geneva spirit'.
是美国在歪曲颠倒"日内瓦条约"。

23. If you give him an inch, he will take a mile.
得寸进尺。

24. His speech to the Senate was as bald and brief as his address to the soldiers.
他在参议院的发言与对士兵的发言同样单调而简短。

拓展阅读

选文A

女士们、先生们:

今天我要介绍的是"中国的宗教及中国政府的宗教政策"。

中国是个多宗教的国家。主要有佛教、道教、伊斯兰教、天主教和基督教。佛教在中国已有2 000多年的历史。道教发源于中国,已有1 700多年的历史。中国现有道教宫观1 500余座,乾道、坤道2.5万余人。伊斯兰教于公元7世纪传入中国。回族、维吾尔族等10个少数民族中的群众信仰伊斯兰教。这些少数民族总人口约1 800万,现有清真寺3万余座,伊玛目、阿訇4万余人。天主教自公元7世纪起传入中国。中国现有天主教徒约400万人,教职人员约4 000人,教堂、会所4 600余座。基督教于公元19世纪初传入中国。中国现有基督徒1 000万人,教牧传道人员1.8余人,教堂、会所1.2万余座。

在漫长的历史发展中,中国各宗教文化已成为中国传统思想文化的一部分。各宗教都倡导服务社会、造福人群，如佛教的"庄严国土，利乐有情"，天主教、基督教的"荣神益人"，道教的"慈爱和同、济世度人"，伊斯兰教的"两世吉庆"等。

在中国，各宗教地位平等，和谐共处，未发生过宗教纷争；信教的与不信教的公民之间也彼此尊重，团结和睦。这说明宗教受到源远流长的中国传统思想文化中兼容、宽容等精神的影响，也说明中国政府制定和实施了宗教信仰自由政策，建立起了符合国情的政教关系。

中国各宗教团体自主地办理教务，并根据需要开办宗教院校，印刷发行宗教经典，出版宗教刊物，兴办社会公益服务事业。中国与世界许多国家一样，实行宗教与教育分离的原则，在国民教育中，不对学生进行宗教教育。宗教教职人员履行的正常教务活动，在宗教活动场所按宗教习惯或在教徒自己家里进行的一切正常的宗教活动，如拜佛、诵经、礼拜、祈祷、讲经、弥撒、受洗、受戒、封斋、过宗教节日、终傅、追思等，都由宗教组织和教徒自理，受法律保护，任何人不得干涉。

我国宪法规定："中华人民共和国公民有宗教信仰自由。任何国家机关、社会团体和个人不得强迫公民信仰宗教或者不信仰宗教，不得歧视信仰宗教的公民和不信仰宗教的公民。国家保护正常的宗教活动。"国家对各宗教一视同仁，法律保障各教拥有平等的权利。在强调保护宗教自由的同时，也强调保护不信教的自由。人人在法律面前一律平等，公民享有宗教信仰自由权利与承担相应的义务相一致。侵犯公民宗教信仰权利要承担法律责任，无论是否信仰宗教，违反法律规定也要承担法律责任。国家法律的保障，使宗教信仰自由政策具有连续性和稳定性，从而使公民的宗教信仰自由权利得到坚实的保障。

中国对公民宗教信仰自由权利的法律保障，与有关国际文书和公约在这方面的主要内容是一致的。《联合国宪章》、《世界人权宣言》、《经济、社会、文化权利国际公约》、《公民权利和政治权利国际公约》、《联合国消除基于宗教信仰或宗教信仰原因的一切形式的不容忍和歧视宣言》以及《维也纳宣言和行动纲领》中关于"宗教或信仰自由是一项基本人权"、"公民有宗教或信仰的选择自由"等内容在中国法律、法规中都有明确规定，并得到实行。

译 文

Ladies and Gentlemen:

My topic today is "Religions in China and the Chinese Government's Policies on Religions".

China is a country with a great diversity of religious beliefs. The main religions are Buddhism, Taoism, Islam, Catholicism and Protestantism. Buddhism enjoys a history of more than 2,000 years in China. Taoism, native to China, has a history of more than 1,700 years. China now has over 1,500 Taoist temples and more than 25,000 Taoist priests and nuns. Islam was introduced into China in the seventh century. In China there are ten minorities, including the Hui and Uygur, with a total population of 18 million, whose faith is Islam. Their over 30,000-odd mosques are served by 40,000 Imams and Akhunds. Catholicism was introduced into China in the 7th century. At present, China has about four million Catholics, 4,000 priests and more than 4,600 churches and meeting houses. Protestantism was first brought to China in the early 19 centuny with 10 milion Christians and 18,000 clergies, more than 12,000 churches and meeting houses throughout China.

In the course of the country's long history, the various religions in China have become part of the traditional Chinese thinking and culture. The religions all advocate serving society and promoting people's well-being, such as the Buddhist's "honoring the country and benefiting the people", the Catholics and Protestants'"glorifying God and benefiting the people", the Taoists'"being benevolent, peaceful and harmonious, saving the world and benefiting the people", and the Islam's "praying to allah to give great reward in this world and hereafter".

In China all religions have equal status and coexist in harmony. Religious disputes are unknown in China. Religious believers and non-believers respect each other, stay united and have a harmonious relationship. This shows the influence of traditional Chinese thought of compatibility and tolerance, as well as the Chinese government's policy of religious freedom. Therefore, the government established a politico-religious relationship that conforms to China's national conditions.

Religious organizations in China run their own affairs independently and set up religious schools, publish religious classics and periodicals, as well as run social services according to their own needs. As in many other countries, China practices the principle of separating religion from education and religion is not a subject taught in schools of the popular education in China. All normal clerical activities conducted by the clergy and all normal religious activities held either at sites for religious activities or in believers' own homes in accordance with usual religious practices, such as worshipping Buddha, reciting scriptures, going to church, praying, preaching, observing Mass, baptizing, monkhood initiation, fasting, celebrating religious festivals, observing extreme unction, and holding memorial ceremonies, are protected by law as the affairs of religious bodies and the clergy and may not be interfered with.

China's Constitution stipulates, "Citizens of the People's Republic of China enjoy freedom of religious belief. No state organ, public organization or individual may compel citizens to believe in, or not believe in, any religion; nor may they discriminate against citizens who believe in, or do not believe in, any religion. The state protects normal religious activities."In China, the state treats all religions equally and the law protects the equal rights of all religions. While stressing the protection of religious freedom, the law also provides for protection of the freedom not to believe in religions. All are equal before the law. Citizens enjoy the right to religious freedom. On the other hand, they must assume corresponding responsibilities. Violation of such a right entails legal responsibility. Anyone, believer or non-believer will be held accountable if he is found to have broken the law. Protection by law ensures the continuity and stability of the policy of religious freedom. Thus, the rights of citizens to religious freedom will be firmly guaranteed.

The legal protection of citizens' right to the freedom of religious belief in China accords basically with the main contents of the relevant international documents and conventions. Such stipulations as "Freedom of religion or belief is a basic human right" and "People should enjoy freedom of religion or belief", which are documented in *the United Nations Charter*, *the Universal Declaration of Human Rights*, *the International Covenant on Economic*, *Social and Cultural Rights*, *International Convention on Civil and Political Rights*, *the United Nations Declaration on the Elimination of All Forms of Intolerance and of Discrimination Based on Religion or Belief*, and *the Vienna Declaration and Action Program*, are all included in China's laws and legislation in explicit terms and are being put into practice.

选文B

Ladies and Gentlemen:

My topic today is Education in Australia. Each state and territory has its primary and secondary education system. Standards, however, are high and reasonably uniform.

Within each state and territory system there are two main types of school — government and non-government. In government schools, attended by about two thirds of children, tuition is free. About three-quarters of the non-government schools are Catholic. Most non-government schools charges fees. Although the states and territories are responsible for all education, the federal Government provides most funding for higher education. In 1989, it set up a system under which undergraduate and postgraduate students must make a financial contribution toward the cost of their study.

Throughout Australia, schooling is compulsory between the age of six and fifteen years. However, most children begin school earlier than the law requires, usually in pre-schools run by the same organizations that administer the mainstream schools.

Primary schooling lasts six to seven years and the curriculum is similar across the nation. Studies begin with basic language and mathematics, and the fundamentals of inquiry, and social, health and creative skills are taught. Before reaching secondary level, children are learning English, mathematics, elementary science, social studies, music, art, craft and physical education. Optional subjects such as religion, languages and music are common.

Secondary schooling begins at year seven or eight and goes typically to year twelve. More advanced levels of the same subjects are taught, plus technical and commercial ones. The typical secondary school is the co-educational comprehensive or multi-purpose high schools, offering a wide range of subjects. Some states have separate high schools and colleges specializing in technical, agricultural, commercial and other fields. Their curriculums include general academic subjects and practical training.

Major examinations or other formal assessments occur after three to four years of high school and, at this point, most students are old enough to leave the system. Another two years' study is available, however, and many keep going to end — year twelve. In most parts of Australia, certificates are issued at each of these levels, called commonly the School Certificate(at or about year ten) and the higher School Certificate(year twelve). The Higher School Certificate is usually required for university of higher-education college entry.

Post-secondary education in Australia occurs in universities and colleges of technical and further education called TAFEs. Most of Australia's approximately one million TAFE students attend state-administered colleges. The vast majority study part-time. All major skills in a wide range of industrial, commercial, artistic and domestic occupations are covered. Most universities also offer non-degree continuing-education programs.

The entire system is matched by correspondence courses for students prevented by illness, disability or residential isolation from attending schools. There are also "schools of the air", which use two-way radio networks to provide "classroom" experience to students in isolated places. In some states, children living too far from a secondary school to travel daily may live in government founded or subsidized hostels.

Special education services are provided to integrate into classrooms children with disabilities attending special and mainstream schools. They are designed to accommodate the special needs of children with intellectual, physical, sensory, emotional, social or learning disabilities.

There is a nationwide school program designed to increase students' sensitivity to the population's multicultural background and to help ethnic communities maintain their languages and cultures. Students from non-English speaking backgrounds are helped to develop their English to enhance their quality of opportunity in education and participation in society. Educational material developed under federal initiatives is available to schools to meet such language needs.

I'd like to stop here and wish to take your questions.

译 文

女士们,先生们:

我今天的题目是"澳大利亚的教育"。在澳大利亚,各州和各地区都有自己的小学和中学教育制度。但是各地的教育标准是高的,而且相当一致。

在各州和各地区,学校主要分为政府办和民办两大类。约2/3的儿童上政府办的学校,这类学校是免费的。约3/4的民办学校属天主教学校。大多数民办学校都要收取学费。各州和地区对各层次的教育负责,而对高等教育的拨款主要来自联邦政府。联邦政府于1989年规定,不论是本科生还是研究生,都必须负担部分学习费用。

在澳大利亚各地,6岁至15岁的学龄儿童都必须接受义务教育。然而大部分儿童不到法定年龄便上学了,他们通常上那些由主管主流学校的教育机构所办的学龄前儿童学校。

小学教育的学制为6至7年,全国各地的小学有着相同的课程设置,学习内容从基础语言和数学开始,还包括常识、社会知识、卫生常识和创造性技能。在进入中学之前,孩子们需要学习英语、数学、基础科学、社会学、音乐、美术、手工和体育。选修课有宗教、外语和音乐等。

中学教育从第七年或第八年开始,一般延续到第十二年为止。中学的科目与小学的科目基本相同,但难度提高了。此外还增加了一些技术和商业类的课程。典型的中学属男女同校、接受综合性或复合型教育的学校,这类学校所设置的科目较多。有些州还设有专门学习技术、农业、商业或其他知识的中学和专科院校。这类学校的课程设置也包括普通科目,同时也向学生提供实践学习的机会。

主要考试或其他正式学业评定在经过中学学习的 3 至 4 年后举行,这时大多数学生已到可以离校的年龄。当然,学生也可以继续留校学习两年,到第十二年毕业。在澳大利亚的大部分学校,学生在完成每个阶段的学习后都可以得到学校颁发的证书,通常称为"初中证书"(在第十年或临近第十年时颁发)和"高中证书"(在第十二年时颁发)。高中证书通常为大学入学所必备。

中学后的教育,或在大学,或在被称之为"TAFE"的技术进修学院进行。澳大利亚约有 100 万名 TAFE 学生,其中大部分学生在州立学院学习。绝大部分学生为非全日制学生。技术进修学院提供各种主要职业技术培训,职业范围广泛,包括工业、商业、艺术、家政等方面。大部分综合性大学也设有非学位的继续教育课程。

为了满足因疾病、伤残或居住偏远等缘故而无法上学的学生的求学要求,澳大利亚的教育体制有一套与正规教育相匹配的函授课程。另外还有"空中学校",通过双向无线电传播网络向居住在偏远地区的学生提供身临其境的"课堂"教育。有些州,家住远离学校、每日上学不便的中学生可以寄宿在由政府资助或补贴的学生宿舍。

为了使残疾儿童也能在特殊学校或主流学校接受教育,学校配备了相应的特殊教育服务项目,以满足那些在智力、身体、感官、情绪、社交、学习等方面有缺陷的儿童的特殊需要。

由于澳大利亚人民有着各种不同的文化背景,所以全国各所学校都制定了相关的教育计划,以提高学生对这种多种文化共存的状况的认识,帮助少数民族保留自己的语言、保持自己的文化传统。来自非英语国家的学生可以得到帮助,使他们提高自己的英语水平,以便他们在受教育和参与社会活动时享有与其他人同等的机会。为了满足学生提高英语能力的需要,有关人士在联邦政府的积极倡导下编写了一些专门教材。

我先介绍到此,下面请各位提问。

第十单元 医 疗
(Medical Care)

单元要点

本单元共分五个层次,分别是:中国的城镇医药卫生体制改革汉译英一篇;美国医疗保健英译汉一篇;速记;词类转移法;拓展阅读(汉译英,英译汉各一篇)。第一、二部分提供中国卫生体制改革和美国医疗保健的例文及其翻译和重难点评析;第三、四部分主要是相关口译理论与技能的介绍;第五部分的拓展阅读中,提供汉、英原文和参考译文。

理论难点提示

1. 速记。
2. 词类转移法。

选文A

中国的城镇医药卫生体制改革
——国务院新闻办
(2000年5月25日)

最近,国务院办公厅转发了国务院体改办等部门《关于城镇医药卫生体制改革的指导意见》。城镇医药卫生体制改革,是从我国的国情出发,遵循社会主义市场经济原则,与职工医疗保险制度改革相配套,力争在二三年内,初步建立起我国新的城镇医药卫生管理体制和服务体系。改革的目的是:打破垄断,鼓励医药卫生领域形成竞争机制,提高服务质量和效率;通过调整、整顿、优化措施,促进医药卫生事业的健康发展;抑制医药费用的过快增长,减轻社会负担,最终保障广大人民群众享有价格合理、质量优良的医疗服务和药品供应。

几十年来,我国卫生事业取得了很大的成绩,医药卫生总体情况也是好的。但是,现在的医药卫生体制已不能适应形势的发展和要求,也影响了职工医疗保险制度改革的推进。

存在的卫生问题有:

1. 卫生资源配置和结构不合理。我国医疗资源主要集中在大医院,基层服务的卫生资源严重不足。

2. 卫生资源利用效率不高。由于资源配置不合理,造成卫生资源利用率低,运行成本高。加上医疗费用上涨过快,医疗服务需求受到明显抑制。据统计,全国医院医生的日均诊疗人次、日负担住院人次、病床使用率均呈下降趋势。

3. 医疗费用增长过快。1978年到1997年,全国职工医疗费用从27亿元增长到773.7

亿元,增长28倍。在亿元收入中,药费收入比重占医院毛收入的一半以上,少数中小医院高达70%~80%。医疗费用增长过快给国家、用人单位和职工造成了很大的压力和负担。

4. 公立医疗机构在管理和运行上缺乏活力。目前,大多数公立医院还没有真正成为具有自我约束和自我激励机制的事业法人,缺乏根据市场和社会需求调整供给的主动性和自觉性,争创优质服务、参与竞争的意识不足。有的医疗机构医护人员素质不高,管理工作跟不上,冗员多,效率低。

5. 药品监管工作有待加强。药品生产和流通企业存在水平低,结构不合理等问题。目前我国有药品生产企业六千多家,批发企业一万六千多家,零售企业十二万多家,企业经营及产品质量参差不齐,导致市场混乱和无序竞争,造成了药品销售的虚高定价和大回扣促销现象,直接推动了医药费用的过快上涨。此外,社会上假劣药品事件时有发生,迫切需要加强药品监管,加大执法力度。

推进医药卫生体制改革已成为形势发展和保障广大群众权益的迫切要求。城镇医药卫生体制改革的主要内容是:

1. 政府有关部门要转变职能,加强医药卫生行业管理。一是今后卫生行政部门主要应管医院而不是办医院,要运用法律、行政、经济等手段实行卫生行业管理。二是实行医疗机构分类管理,鼓励社会办医,促进医疗机构围绕质量和效率公平竞争;将社会上的医疗机制分为营利性和非营利性两类,非营利性医疗机构在医疗服务体系中占主导地位,享受税收优惠政策,医疗服务执行政府指导价格;营利性医疗机构医疗服务体系放开,依法经营,照章纳税。三是加强对卫生资源配置的调控,调整医疗资源布局,对医疗服务量长期不足的医院采取转型、压缩和撤并等结构调整措施。鼓励组建医疗服务集团。四是继续加强预防保健工作,建立综合性疾病防治、保健体系,指导开展公共卫生、疾病控制和预防保健工作,提供技术咨询并调查处理卫生突发事件。

2. 公立医疗机构要适应社会和广大群众的需要,加快改革的步伐。一是扩大公立医疗机构的运营自主权;二是采用公开竞争、择优聘任为主的多种形式任用医院院长,实行院长任期目标责任制;三是落实医疗技术规范和服务标准,规范医疗行为,保证医疗服务质量;四是加强医疗机构的经济管理,推进医院后勤服务的社会化;五是深化人事和分配制度改革,公开岗位标准,实行双向选择,鼓励员工竞争,员工收入要与技术、服务和贡献挂钩。

3. 逐步推行医药分开核算、分别管理的政策措施,规范医院的经济补偿体制。一是为切断医疗机构和药品营销之间的直接经济利益联系,在逐步规范财政补助方式和调整医疗服务价格的基础上把医院的门诊药房改为药品零售企业,独立核算,照章纳税。各地要选择若干家医院积极进行门诊药房改为药品零售企业的试点。在这一改革措施到位之前,可先对医院药品收入实行收支两条线管理,药品收支结余全部上缴卫生行政部门,纳入财政专户管理,合理返还。社区卫生组织及私人诊所、门诊部除省级卫生、药品监督部门审定的常用和急救用药外,不得从事药品购销活动。二是按照公共财政和分级财政体制的要求,规范对卫生医疗机构的财政补助办法。三是对医疗机构的收入实行总量控制,调整结构。在总量控制幅度内,综合考虑成本、财政补助和药品收入等因素,调整不合理的医疗服务价格,要考虑社区卫生服务组织的特点,促进社区卫生服务组织和中医、名族医学的发展。

4. 整顿药品生产流通秩序,推进药品生产流通体制的改革。一是要加强药品执法监督管理,建立起对药品研制、生产、流通、使用全过程的严格监管体系。二是对药品生产、经营企业按《药品生产质量管理规范》(GMP)和《药品经营质量管理规范》(GSP)进行管理,限期整顿达标,限期过后仍不达标的不许再继续生产和经营。三是试点药品集中招标采购,减少中间环节,促进药品交易方式的公平、公开和公正。集中招标采购成本要让利于患者,减轻社会负担。四是加强药品零售价格管理。对于基本医疗保险用药以及预防用药、必要的儿科用药、垄断经营的特殊药品实行政府定价或政府指导价,有条件的药制定全国统一零售价。对除此以外的其他药品,由企业按照国家规定的作价办法自主定价,实行市场调节。五是逐步实行将零售价格印在药品外包装上的办法,提高透明度,以利于消费者的自我保护。

重难点评析

1. "城镇医药卫生体制改革,是从我国的国情出发,遵循社会主义市场经济原则,与职工医疗保险制度改革相配套……"译为:"health system reform in cities and towns is being carried out in the context of the Chinese situation, in line with the principles of the socialist market economy and in combination with the reform of the health insurance system." 在该句的翻译中,"从我国的国情出发"译为"in the context of Chinese situation","context"的原意是"上下文",此处有"情况"的含义。"遵循……原则"采用"in line with"这一词组,表示"符合"、"跟……一致"。"与……相配套"译为"in combination with",表示"与……相结合"的意思。

2. "改革的目的是:打破垄断,鼓励医药卫生领域形成竞争机制,提高服务质量和效率;通过调整、整顿、优化措施,促进医药卫生事业的健康发展;抑制医药费用的过快增长,减轻社会负担,最终保障广大人民群众享有价格合理、质量优良的医疗服务和药品供应。"翻译成:"The objectives of this reform are: breaking monopoly, encouraging a competition mechanism in the health area and improving the quality and efficiency of medical service; promoting the healthy development of medical and health care through reorientation, reorganization and regrouping; curbing the rapid increase of the costs for medical and health care and lightening the social burden so as to ensure the general public to enjoy quality medical and health care service and drug supply at reasonable prices." 翻译该句时将汉语中的动词,如"打破"、"鼓励"、"提高"、"促进"、"抑制"和"减轻"全部采用英语的动名词形式表达,如"breaking","encouraging","improving","promoting","curbing"和"lightening",使得英语的表达显得清楚、简洁。

3. "几十年来,我国卫生事业取得了很大的成绩,医药卫生总体情况也是好的。"译为"Over the past decades, health care in China has witnessed a great success and the general situation is good." 该句的翻译采用了拟人的方法,即"witness"是"亲眼所见"的意思,栩栩如生地表达出了卫生事业的进步。

4. "但是,现在的医药卫生体制已不能适应形势的发展和要求,也影响了职工医疗保险制度改革的推进。"译为"However, we must realize that the current system of medical and health care is no longer in line with the development and requirements of the situation and hampers the reform of the medical insurance system for workers." 该句的翻译增添了主句"We must realize that…"。同时再次采用"in line with"词组来表达"适应……"。

"hamper"一词生动形象地表达了"影响"。

5. "我国医疗资源主要集中在大医院,基层服务的卫生资源严重不足。"译为"Medical resources in China are concentrated in large hospitals, which has resulted in the serious lack of health care resources for grassroots services."该句仅用一个主句,外加一个非限制性定语从句,表达了导致基层服务的卫生资源严重不足的原因。翻译该句时一定要理清思路,分清主次关系。"基层"用"grassroots"一词很形象。

6. "据统计,全国医院医生的日均诊疗人次、日负担住院人次、病床使用率均呈下降趋势。"译为"Statistics shows that in hospitals throughout the country, the daily average rate of out-patient visits and in-patient cares per doctor, as well as the bed utilization ratio are all on the decline.""医生的日均诊疗人次、日负担住院人次"的翻译要先弄清楚其表达的每一层意思,才能准确译出。"呈下降趋势"用"on the decline"表达,言简意赅。

7. "目前,大多数公立医院还没有真正成为具有自我约束和自我激励机制的事业法人,缺乏根据市场和社会需求调整供给的主动性和自觉性,争创优质服务、参与竞争的意识不足。"译为"Currently, most public hospitals are not yet corporate legal persons with self-controlling and self-stimulating mechanism. They lack the initiative and consciousness to make timely adjustments to their operations in accordance with market and social demands, and the urge to provide quality service and participate in competition."翻译该句时,需要理清楚动作的发出者。例如,"缺乏根据市场和社会需求调整供给的主动性和自觉性,争创优质服务、参与竞争的意识不足。"是谁缺乏?应该是"大多数公立医院",即"they"。所以翻译时,在第二句要增添主语"They"。"意识不足",即"缺乏意识",用"lack the urge"表达。

8. "有的医疗机构医护人员素质不高,管理工作跟不上,冗员多,效率低。"译为"Some medical institutions are overstaffed and operating under low efficiency. Their medical and nursing staff are not sufficiently qualified and their management lags behind."该句的翻译,采用的是意译。

9. "企业经营及产品质量参差不齐,导致市场混乱和无序竞争,造成了药品销售的虚高定价和大回扣促销现象,直接推动了医药费用的过快上涨。此外,社会上假劣药品事件时有发生,迫切需要加强药品监管,加大执法力度。"译为"The difference in management and quality of products in these enterprises results in market chaos and disorderly competition. This has resulted in bubble prices and high commissions in drug promotion, which has directly contributed to the rapid increase of drug costs. Furthermore, incidents of counterfeit and low-quality drugs occur from time to time. There is an urgent need to strengthen drug monitoring and intensify legislation and its implementation."翻译该句时,要考虑"导致"、"造成"和"推动"这几个动词选用什么英语单词或词组表达。另外,采取何种句式?本翻译运用了非限制性定语从句"which has directly contributed to the rapid increase of drug costs",很形象地表达为何医药费用过快上涨。

10. "一是扩大公立医疗机构的运营自主权;二是采用公开竞争、择优聘任为主的多种形式任用医院院长,实行院长任期目标责任制;三是落实医疗技术规范和服务标准,规范医疗行为,保证医疗服务质量;四是加强医疗机构的经济管理,推进医院后勤服务的社会化;

五是深化人事和分配制度改革,公开岗位标准,实行双向选择,鼓励员工竞争,员工收入要与技术、服务和贡献挂钩。"译为"Firstly, the decision-making power of public medical institutions should be enlarged. Secondly, hospital directors should be appointed mainly on the basis of open competition and competitive selection. A term-target responsibility system should be introduced for directors. Thirdly, technical norms and service standards should be implemented and medical practice standardized so as to ensure the quality of medical service. Fourthly, financial management must be strengthened and marketization of logistic services promoted in medical institutions. Finally, the reform of personnel and income distribution system should be intensified. Post description and requirements should be made public, two-way selection adopted, and competition among employees encouraged with income related to their skills, service and contribution."注意:此段落的翻译采用的全是"should"引导的被动语态,显得正式。

译 文

Reform of China's Medical Cares System in Cities and Towns
—the information Office of the State Council
May 25, 2000

Recently the General Office of the State Council transmitted the Guiding Opinion on the Health System Reform in cities and Towns prepared by the System Reform Office of the State Council and other departments. The health system reform in cities and towns is being carried out in the context of the Chinese situation, in line with the principles of the socialist market economy and in combination with the reform of the health insurance system. It is aimed at building up, within two to three years, a basic system for medical and health care management and service in cities and towns.

The objectives of this reform are: breaking monopoly, encouraging a competition mechanism in the health area and improving the quality and efficiency of medical service; promoting the healthy development of medical and health care through reorientation, reorganization and regrouping; curbing the rapid increase of the costs for medical and health care and lightening the social burden so as to ensure the general public to enjoy quality medical and health care service and drug supply at reasonable prices.

Over the past decades, health care in China has witnessed a great success and the general situation is good. However, we must realize that the current system of medical and health care is no longer in line with the development and requirements of the situation and hampers the reform of the medical insurance system for workers.

The existing problems are mainly as follows: (1) Unreasonable distribution and structure of health resources. Medical resources in China are concentrated in large hospitals, which has resulted in the serious lack of health care resources for grassroots services. (2) Low utilization ratio of health care resources. The improper distribution of health care resources results in its low utilization and high costs for operation. Furthermore, the rapid increase of medical costs has doubtlessly restrained the demand for medical services. Statistics shows that in hospitals throughout the country, the daily average rate of out-patient visits and in-patient cares per doctor, as well as the bed utilization ratio are all on the decline. (3)Excessive increase in medical costs. From 1978 to 1997, medical expenditure for workers and employees throughout the country spiraled from RMB 2.7 billion to RMB 77.37 billion, an increase of 28 times. For hospitals, the drug income amounted to more than half of the gross income, and in a few medium-and small-sized hospitals it ran as high as 70%~80%. The high-speed increase in medical costs brought heavy pressure and burdens to both employers and employees. (4) Poor management and operation in public medical institutions. Currently, most public hospitals are not yet corporate legal persons with self-controlling and self-stimulating mechanism. They lack the initiative and consciousness to make timely adjustments to their operations in accordance with market and social demands, and the urge to provide quality service and participate in competition. Some medical institutions are overstaffed and operating under low efficiency. Their medical and nursing staff are not sufficiently qualified and their management lags behind. (5)Insufficient drug supervision and administration. Drug manufacturers and distributors are operating at a low standard, and their structure is not reasonable. China has more than 6,000 drug manufacturing enterprises, more than 16,000 wholesale ones and more than 120,000 retail ones. The difference in management and quality of products in these enterprises results in market chaos and disorderly competition. This has resulted in bubble prices and high commissions in drug promotion, which has directly contributed to the rapid increase of drug costs. Furthermore, incidents of counterfeit and low-quality drugs occur from time to time. There is an urgent need to strengthen drug monitoring and intensify legislation and its implementation.

Promotion of the health system reform is urgently needed in face of the rapid developments in China so as to ensure the rights and benefits of the wide population. Reform of the urban health care system contains mainly the following points:

1. Relevant governmental departments should change their functions so as to strengthen the regulation of the pharmaceutical and health sector. Firstly, health administrations should regulate instead of getting directly involved in hospital operations. Legal, administrative and economic measures should be introduced to regulate the health industry. Secondly, classified regulation should be carried out for medical institutions. Social sectors should be encouraged to run medical institutions to promote fair competition among medical institutions for quality and efficiency. Medical institutions should be classified into profitable and unprofitable ones. Unprofitable ones will occupy a predominant position in the medical service system. They will enjoy preferential tax breaks and will have to follow the guiding prices of the government in their medical service. Profitable ones will have a free hand in setting their medical service prices. They

will run their business according to the law and pay taxes as required by relevant regulations. Thirdly, regulation and control of health care resources should be strengthened and the layout of medical resources adjusted. Hospitals with prolonged insufficient volume of service will be subject to restructuring, including transformation, scale reduction, closedown and merger with other institutions. Establishment of medical service groups will be encouraged. Fourthly a comprehensive system for disease prevention and health care should be established so as to give guidance for public health, disease control and preventive care, as well as to provide technical advice and to investigate and deal with unexpected public health incidents.

2. Public medical institutions should accelerate their reform to meet the needs of the society and the whole population. Firstly, the decision-making power of public medical institutions should be enlarged. Secondly, hospital directors should be appointed mainly on the basis of open competition and competitive selection. A term-target responsibility system should be introduced for directors. Thirdly, technical norms and service standards should be implemented and medical practice standardized so as to ensure the quality of medical service. Fourthly, financial management must be strengthened and marketization of logistic services promoted in medical institutions. Finally, the reform of personnel and income distribution system should be intensified. Post description and requirements should be made public, two-way selection adopted, and competition among employees encouraged with income related to their skills, service and contribution.

3. The policy of separate accounting and management for medical and pharmaceutical income should be gradually adopted, and the mechanism of economic compensation should be standardized. Firstly, direct economic relations between medical institutions and drug distributors will be disconnected. A financial subsidy scheme will be adopted gradually and the prices for medical service adjusted. On this basis pharmacy in the out-patient departments of hospitals will be transformed into drug stores that will have their independent accounting and pay taxes as required. In every area several hospitals will be selected for experiments in substituting pharmacies in out-patient departments for drug stores. Before this measure of reform is implemented, hospital drug incomes and expenditures will be managed separately, namely the balance of payments surplus from drug selling will be turned over to the health administration and kept in a special account for reasonable return. Except drugs for daily and emergency use approved by the provincial health departments or drug supervising authorities, community health organizations, private clinics and out-patient departments are not allowed to engage in drug distribution. Secondly, in accordance with the requirements of a public and classified financial system, a financial subsidy scheme is to be adopted for health and medical institutions. Thirdly, a general control of the total income of medical institutions will be conducted, and its structure adjusted. In the context of the total income control, medical costs, financial subsidies and income from drugs will be considered in a comprehensive

way. The unreasonably low prices of medical service will be adjusted to realize the value of technical work performed by medical personnel. A reasonable number of patients will be diverted to smaller hospitals or community health centers. In the adjustment of the prices of the medical service, the special features of the community health service should be given due consideration so as to stimulate the development of community health service, traditional Chinese medicine and traditional medicine of ethnic minorities.

4. The current drug manufacture and trade order will be reorganized to push the reform of drug manufacturing and trade system. Firstly, supervision and control over law implementation for pharmaceuticals will be strengthened in order to establish a strict control system for the whole process of drug development, manufacture, trade and use. Secondly, enterprises engaged in drug manufacture and trade should be regulated by the Good Manufacture Practice of Drugs (GMP) and the Good Supply Practice(GSP). The set standards must be reached within a specific time, otherwise the production and trade will be discontinued. Thirdly, pilot projects will be launched for mass purchasing of drugs through public bidding so as to reduce the number of intermediate links and facilitate a fair, open and equitable drug trade. The cost reduction achieved in this way will benefit patients and the society in burden alleviation. Fourthly, price regulation will be strengthened in drug retails. Set prices or government-guiding prices will be introduced for pharmaceuticals covered by the basic medical insurance system, as well as drugs for preventive use, essential drugs for children and special monopoly drugs. Unified retail prices across the country will be worked out when feasible. The prices of other pharmaceuticals will be decided by the manufacturers according to state pricing provisions, and regulated by the market. Finally, efforts will be made to print the retail prices on drug packages to raise transparency and to facilitate the self-protection of consumers.

选文B

Studies show about half of Americans lack confidence in health care system. The health care debate in the United States is far from over despite the passage of health care legislation. Others are pushing for a repeal of the health care legislation, and still others put off getting medical help even after a heart attack because they worry about paying for their care.

Americans are just as divided on health care as they were before President Obama's health reform legislation became law.

Protesters in Washington carried signs on Thursday calling for repeal of the legislation. They say it represents runaway spending.

A new Associated Press-GfK poll shows that 50 percent of Americans oppose the new health care law and opposition is strongest among those 64 and older. Many older Americans worry that their care will be affected by cuts in federal payments to hospitals and other providers.

In another survey, this one by Ipsos/Reuters, only 51 percent of Americans thought they could get adequate, affordable health care. The survey included people in 22 nations. Women, adults under the age of 55 and less educated people in all the countries included in the study reported low satisfaction with health care access.

Yet another study showed that Americans without medical insurance, often delay going to a hospital after a heart attack. Dr. Paul Chan was one of the researchers.

"Forty-nine percent of uninsured patients were more likely to wait more than six hours before coming into the hospital and 45 percent of patients with health care insurance but with financial concerns in accessing medical care waited more than six hours before coming into the hospital."

Every minute counts when someone is having a heart attack. This helicopter crew knows that. Doctors say these patients need to get medical care within two hours for the best results. By the time some patients in the study sought help, their hearts were already damaged.

Larry Scott now uses a wheel chair. He put off going to the hospital after a heart attack because he was worried about money.

"If I had the medical insurance, this wouldn't have happened," said Scott. "This would have been taken care of right then and there."

The researchers studied more than 3,700 patients who had heart attacks and came to emergency rooms for treatment. "We concluded that health care insurance plays a huge role in determining whether or not patients are able to come to the hospital promptly enough when they have symptoms of a heart attack," added Dr. Chan.

The researchers say this is the first study linking health insurance to the decision to seek treatment for a heart attack. The study reflects the ongoing problems in US health care. It was published in the Journal of the American Medical Association.

重难点评析

1. "The health care debate in the United States is far from over despite the passage of health care legislation". 译为"尽管已经通过了医疗改革立法,美国针对医疗保健的争论却远远没有结束。"此句中的"despite"表示让步关系。"far from"意思是"远非,不但不……",例如:Far from relieving my cough, the medicine aggravated it. 这药非但不镇咳,反而使我咳嗽得更厉害。His work is far from perfect. 他的工作远非十全十美。

2. "Others are pushing for a repeal of the health care legislation, and still others put off getting medical help even after a heart attack because they worry about paying for their care." 译为"其他人力图争取废除医疗改革法案,另外一些人则由于担心医疗保健的费用,甚至心脏病发的时候都推迟寻求医疗帮助。"翻译该句时,需要注意两个词组的翻译。"push for"指"急切、强烈地要求,为……奋力争取"。例如:People living near the airport are pushing for new rules about night flight. 住在机场附近的人们正强烈要求制订出夜航班机的新规。He pushed me for an answer. 他催我作出答复。"put off"意思是"延期,推

迟；拖延"。例如：They decided to put the meeting off until after Christmas. 他们决定把会议推迟到圣诞节以后。

3. "Women, adults under the age of 55 and less educated people in all the countries included in the study reported low satisfaction with health care access." 这句话的主干是：Women, adults and less educated people，而"in all the countries"是介词短语作后置定语。"included in the study"是过去分词作后置定语，修饰前面的这些人。

4. "If I had the medical insurance, this wouldn't have happened." 虚拟语气表示说话人主观上所说的话并不是事实，而是一种假设、愿望、建议、请求、命令、空想、猜测、必要性和可能性等。虚拟过去时（与过去事实相反），从句谓语形式用 had＋过去分词，主句谓语形式用 should(would，could，might)＋have＋过去分词。

5. "We concluded that health care insurance plays a huge role in determining whether or not patients are able to come to the hospital promptly enough when they have symptoms of a heart attack." 这句话的主语和谓语是：We concluded，后面是 that 引导的宾语从句。宾语从句的主干是：health care insurance plays a huge role，"in determining..."是说明在哪一方面发挥重大作用。"whether or not"引导"determine"的宾语从句。"when they have symptoms of a heart attack"是时间状语从句。

译文

研究表明，大约一半的美国人对他们的医疗保健体系缺乏信心。尽管已经通过了医疗改革立法，美国针对医疗保健的争论却远远没有结束。其他人力图争取废除医疗改革法案，另外一些人则由于担心医疗保健的费用，甚至心脏病发的时候都推迟寻求医疗帮助。

美国民众对医疗保健的分歧仍然像奥巴马总统医疗改革立法成为法律之前一样严重。

周四，华盛顿的抗议者手持标语，要求废止医改立法。他们说，这意味着支出不受控制。

美联社 GfK 进行的一项新的民意调查显示，50%的美国人反对新的医保法律，其中 64 岁以上的人群反对最为强烈。许多年长的美国人担心，由于联邦政府对医院和其他医疗提供机构的付款减少，他们的医疗保健将受到影响。

在路透社/Ipsos 进行的另外一项调查中，只有 51%的美国人认为他们可以获得足够的，能够支付得起的医疗保健。该调查覆盖了 22 个国家的民众。所有国家妇女，55 岁以下成年人和教育水平比较低的受调查者对医疗保健的可获得性满意度比较低。

然而，另外一项研究表明，没有医疗保险的人们通常会延迟去医院进行医治，即使心脏病发。Paul Chan 医生是研究人员之一。

"49%未参保的病人会等待 6 小时以上才去医院，而 45%的参保人群则因为担忧获得医疗保健的财务问题而等待 6 个小时以上才去医院。"

对于心脏病发的病人来说，每一分钟都非常重要。这名直升飞机乘务员非常了解这一点。医生表示，这些病人必须在两小时之内接受治疗才能获得最佳效果。到调查中的一些病人到医院寻求帮助的时候，他们的心脏已经受到了损害。

Larry Scott 现在必须以轮椅代步。在有一次心脏病发的时候，由于担心钱的问题，他推迟了去医院的时间。

"如果我有医疗保险,这样的情况就不会发生。我应该受到良好的照料。"

研究人员对 3 700 多名心脏病发后去医院急诊室进行治疗的病人进行调查。Dr. Chan 补充道:"我们得出结论,医疗保险起到非常重要的作用,可以决定病人表现出心脏病症状后是不是能够迅速前往医院。"

研究人员称,这是将医疗保险和寻求心脏病治疗的决定之间的关系的首份研究。该研究反映了美国医疗保健持续的问题。该研究发表在美国医学协会杂志上。

速 记

速记法被视为口译中的制胜绝招,其实,速记除了自身的技巧性,还是有很大的个人发挥空间的。每个人都能创建属于自己的一套速记符号系统,只要勤加练习,定能自成一派。

速记秘诀 1　速记本

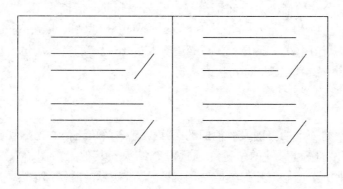

这张表模拟了一个手掌大小的迷你笔记本:

(1) 之所以手掌大小,因为它是人的眼睛最适宜的宽度,也是为了便于携带和翻页,以便用最快的手写速度和最方便的姿势进行记录。

(2) 之所以在中间画一条竖线,是为了使每行尽量不留空白,在一页纸上记下更多内容,充分利用空间。

(3) 之所以在每个段落结束的地方画一条斜线,也是为了强化意群组结束的位置,便于记录完毕后的语意分析。

速记秘诀 2　抓住实词

记录要迅速,就要抓住语篇中的"实词"。比如,"As a secretary he or she may have a lot of duties to fulfill."这句话中,Secretary, he or she, may have, duties, fulfill 这 5 个单词或词组是实词,而 As, a, a lot of, to 这 4 个单词或词组则是虚词。笔记的关键就是 5 个实词,而 5 个实词中最关键的还是名词和实义动词,即 secretary, duties 和 fulfill 这 3 个词。所以,在这个句子中,如果不借助手中的笔完全靠即时记忆掌握句义,方法就是马上判断并记住 secretary, duties 和 fulfill 这 3 个词。这样在随后的口译中,就能通过这三个关键词提炼出句子的大意。

速记诀窍 3　符号速记

速记时,记录笔记的时间非常有限,没有足够的时间记录完整的句子,而要紧抓要点,培养在语流中快速抓住关键词和逻辑关系的习惯和能力,很多时候需要运用缩略语或者只有自己才能识别的固定符号。不同的人对句子的理解速度和记忆时长各有不同，但无论快慢长短，只要能突出信息的关联性、抓住关键词并用生动的符号帮助记忆，都有助于听者对原文的理解。比如，当听到"Taiwan is an indispensable part of the People's Republic of China(台湾是中国不可分割的一部分)"这句话时，很多人尝试把每个词都记下来，结果还没记几个词，后面的内容就错过了。较理想的方法是用逻辑和图形的方式快速记录：

"台"字可能会写得慢，不如就用大写的 T 与 W 代替，表示 A 是 B 的一部分，可以用套圆圈的方式；而"中"字写起来比较快，当然也可以用 PRC 或 Ch 来表示，"不可分割"在两个圆圈的相互限制关系中便一目了然，不需要再做更多标记。

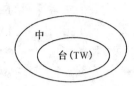

对于何时用中文记录、何时用英文记录的把握原则是：速度至上。而特殊符号则根据个人对符号的理解进行选择。比如：

"√"表示肯定、乐观、理解、赞同等；

"×"表示否定、悲观、误解、反对等；

"：" 表示观点、讲话内容、询问等；

"△"表示重要、重视；

"☆"表示非常重要、高度重视；

"‖"表示相对、并列关系；

"⊃⊂"表示演绎或归纳关系；

"＋－×/∑"表示四则运算和算术求和；

"←↑→↓↘↗⇒⇔⇐⇑⇓"各类箭头表示结论、支持、上升、下降；

"＜＞=≯≮≈≠≤≥"表示各种数量关系；

"∵∴"表示因果关系；

"⌒"、"&"表示联合、一起；

小节线"|"表示语意停顿；

重复符号"|: :|"表示不断重复。

速记诀窍 4　数字速记

原则一：自左至右，听到什么记什么

即按照书写习惯，自左向右只记录听到的数字，不考虑加几个零。比如，Thirty-thousand-and-twenty，记的时候就写"30,"和"20"，但在"20"之前留出一点距离，即：

$$30, \quad 20$$

原则二：自右至左，按位添零

即把所听到的数字自左至右记完之后，返回来从右向左为补足三位而添零：

$$30,020$$

原则三：自右至左，每四位画竖线

英文数字用阿拉伯数字记录下来，往往要用汉语说出来，这时再从右至左每四位数画一条竖线：

```
                    3|0,020
```

原则四:自左至右,按竖线读数

现在我们就可以按照竖线所在的位置读出中文的数字了,即"三万零二十"。

数字短时记忆小练习

我们常常遇到的是4位以下的数字,这时候就要通过重复来加强对短位数字的短时记忆。这里给大家介绍一个加强数字短时记忆的练习,这一练习也适用于速记专业词汇和其他类型的信息:

在同一行中写一串不超过4位的数字,大约2~5个,比如:

```
       9,393    1,000    203    323    11
```

用2~5秒的时间快速看,然后闭上眼睛,想想都有哪些数字。刚开始时,可能只能说出2~3个,多练几次,就可以记住一连串。

做到之后,可以在平行的两行中写两串数字,难度保持在4位以内。之后,还可以增加到三串,时间也可以适当加长。渐渐地,你会发现自己对数字越来越敏感,多位数的基数词掌握后,可以再熟悉一下分数、小数、百分数、电话号码、邮政编码、房间号、序数词、奇数、偶数以及数字升降变化的说法。

对大家来说,平时接触最多的可能是来自语言方面的信息,那就可以通过家人或者朋友口述的方式,培养短时记忆的习惯,不断提高这方面的能力。这其中最大的诀窍就是在心里默默地重复,即复诵。练习的时候,要慢慢让复诵的次数越来越多,间隔越来越短。

词类转移法

在翻译时,由于两种语言在语法和习惯表达上的差异,在保证原文意思不变的情况下,译文必须改变词类,这就叫词类转移法。这种方法促进词类的改变,而且还包括词类作用的改变和一定次序的变化。当然主要是指词类的变化,如原文中的名词可以转译成译文中的动词等词类。众所周知,语言是个无限生成的系统,在翻译实践中,词类转移的情形也是千变万化的。重要的是,要知道在翻译中为了保证译文忠实于原文并使译文合乎表达习惯,可以改变词类。下面所举的例子可以说明词类转移的一些常用情况。

1. 语言这个东西不是随便可以学好的,非下苦功不可。
The mastery of language is not easy and requires painstaking effort.

这句话的英译文应该说是忠实而地道的,但分析一下汉英文中的词类,却很少是对应的。原文中的词类到了译文中,差不多都发生了变化:"学好"是动词,意思上相应的英文词mastery是名词;"随便"是副词,意思上相应的英文词是作表语的easy,等等。假若译文中的英文词类、词序都与汉语完全相同,不作任何改变,那么这就不成一句英文句子。

2. In those years the Republicans were in.
那些年是共和党执政。(形容词→动词)

3. The music is a gas.
这音乐妙极了。(名词→形容词)

第十单元 医疗(Medical Care)

4. A week after his prelude to the President's visit, China was in.
在他为总统出访所作的序幕之行后一周,中国成了最时新的话题。(形→名)

5. Saud was a frustrated man at that time.
沙特那时已受挫折。(形→动)

6. The volume of trade has increased tremendously to the advantage of both countries.
贸易的巨增给两国带来了益处。(动+副→形+名)

7. Independent observers have commented favourably on the achievements you have made in this direction.
有独立见解的观察家们对你们在这方面取得的成就给予了很好的评价。(动+副→动+形+名)。

8. Traditionally, there had always been good relations between them.
它们之间一直有着传统的友好关系。(副→形)

9. Our age is witnessing a profound political change.
我们的时代是深刻的政治变化的见证。(动→名)

10. We have known a similar past of humiliation and exploitation.
在过去,我们都同样遭受到凌辱和剥削。(形→副)

11. We are enemies of all wars, but above all of dynastic wars.
我们反对一切战争,特别是反对王朝的战争。(系表结构+of→动)

12. Differences between the social systems of states shall not be an obstacle to their rapprochement and cooperation.
各国社会制度不同,但不应妨碍彼此和睦与相互合作。(to be+名+介→动)

13. His real mission in life was to contribute, in one way or another, to the overthrow of capitalist society.
他一生的真正使命是想办法为推翻资本主义社会而作出贡献。(名+of→动)

14. No wonder the sight of it should send the memories of quite a number of people of the old generation back 36 years ago.
难怪老一辈的许多人见了这个就会想到36年前的往事。(名+of 短语→动宾结构)

15. There is a big increase in demand for all kinds of consumer goods in every part of our country.
目前我国各地对各种消费品的需要量已大大增加。(形+名→副+动)

16. We also realize the growing need and necessity to industrialize certain sectors of the economy.
我们也认识到越来越需要使某些经济部门实行工业化。(形+名→副+动)

17. What kind of sailor are you?
你晕不晕船?(be a bad sailor 晕船;be a good sailor 不晕船)(形+名→动)

18. Parents' love of children is perfect and minute.
父母爱子女无微不至。(名+介→动)

19. Little by little they went along the entire coast of the Arctic Ocean, making careful observation on the way.

229

他们慢慢地沿着整个北冰洋岸航行,一路仔细观察。(形+名→副+动)

20. The cult of the individual is also a force of habit of millions and tens of millions.
个人崇拜也就是千百万人的一种习惯势力。(冠+名词 A+of+名词 B→形+名)

21. A man of talent is usually honest and modest.
有本领的人往往老老实实。(介词短语→形)

22. On these issues, Stalin was subjective and one-sided.
斯大林在这些问题上,陷入了主观性和片面性。(系表结构→动宾结构)

23. 凡不孤立而占有十分巩固阵地之地都不好打。
It is inadvisable to fight when an enemy force is not isolated but well trenched. (定语→状语)

24. It is impossible to live in society and be independent of society.
生于社会,不能脱离社会。(be+形+of→动词)

25. She was asked ten questions in the oral exam and answered every one correctly.
口试时,问了她10个问题,她一一答对了。(被动→主动)

26. 林则徐认为,要成功地禁止鸦片卖卖,就得首先把鸦片焚毁。
Lin Zexu believed that a successful ban of the trade in opium must be preceded by the destruction of the drug itself. (副+动→形+名;动→名)

27. 徐悲鸿画马画得很好。
Xu Beihong's drawings(paintings) of horses are exceptionally good. (动→名+of)

28. The delegates at the conference unanimously expressed their determination to oppose hegemonism on the part of that superpower.
会上,代表们一致表示坚决地反对那个超级大国的霸权主义。(名→副)

29. 这里就产生一个问题,你对发展重工业究竟是真想还是假想,想得厉害一点,还是差一点?
Here the question arises: Is your desire to develop heavy industry genuine or feigned, strong or weak?

30. 中国人民,百年以来,不屈不挠,再接再厉地英勇斗争,使得帝国主义至今不能灭亡中国,也永远不能灭亡中国。
Thanks to the Chinese people's unrelenting and heroic struggle during the last hundred years, imperialism has not been able to subjugate China, nor will it ever be able to do so. (此句中不但有词类转移现象,而且某些词语在句中的成分或作用也有改变。)

31. 一定要少说空话,多做工作。
There must be less empty talk and more hard work. (副+动+宾→形+名)

32. Thousands of Chinese overseas have asked to be permitted to return to China, but they have met with all sorts of unreasonable obstacles, which have prevented them from returning to their motherland.
成千上万的中国侨民要求回国,但受到种种无理阻挠,以致不能回到祖国。(定→状)

33. 在20世纪50年代初期,美帝企图征服朝鲜,从而进犯中国;但最后中朝军民打败了他们。

第十单元 医疗(Medical Care)

In the early 1950s, the US imperialists tried to conquer Korea and thereby to invade China, but were finally defeated by the army and people of Korea and China. (动宾结构→主谓结构)

34. 斯大林骄傲了,不谨慎了,他的思想里产生了主观主义,产生了片面性,对于某些重大问题作出了错误的决定,造成了严重的不良后果。

Stalin became conceited and imprudent. Subjectivism and one-sidedness developed in his thinking and he made erroneous decisions on certain important questions, which led to serious and harmful consequences. (状→定)

35. For 20 years we were passive witnesses to the deterioration of prices of our raw materials and an excessive increase of the prices of manufactured goods.

我们在20年内坐视原料价格下跌与工业品价格暴涨。(形+名→副+动)

36. The victory of justice over arbitrary acts, of reason over decadence and blindness, of democracy over imperialism, of good over evil, our victory of 25 October will represent one of the glorious pages of our history, and we shall be able to leave it to our heirs.

正义战胜了专断行为,理智战胜了堕落和盲目,民主战胜了帝国主义,善战胜了恶,我们在10月25日取得的胜利将作为光辉篇章之一载入史册,我们将把它传于子孙后代。(名+介→动)

37. It is incontestable that the advent of the People's Republic of China was a principal event in the evolution of international relations following World War Ⅱ.

中华人民共和国的成立无可置辩地是第二次世界大战以后国际关系演变中的大事件。(形→副)

38. Your Australian guests are immensely impressed by the splendor and warmth of our reception at the airport, along the boulevard and in the Great Hall of the People.

你们的澳大利亚客人对于你们在机场、在街道、在人民大会堂所给予我们盛大的、热情的接待,非常感谢。(名→形)

39. These qualities constitute a great attraction to any peace-loving country which believes in world peace and international friendship, cooperation and understanding.

仅就这些品质而言,它们就强烈地吸引着爱好和平并对世界和平与国际友谊、合作和了解抱有信念的任何国家。(从整个句子来看,有几种词类转移)

40. Out of all the glorious tales written about the U.S. revolution for independence from Britain the fact is hardly known that a black man was the first to die for American independence.

读遍了关于美国为摆脱英国统治争取独立而进行革命的堂皇纪事,也不容易知道第一个为美国独立而牺牲的原来是黑人。(介→动)

拓展阅读

选文A

国务院新闻办公室于2009年4月30日(星期四)下午15时举行新闻发布会,请卫生部、质检总局和农业部有关负责人介绍我国加强人感染猪流感防控工作情况,并答记者问。

在国新办新闻发布会上的谈话

国家质检总局副局长 刘平均

2009 年 4 月 30 日

最近,墨西哥、美国等国出现人感染猪流感疫情并在世界范围内广泛传播,党中央、国务院高度重视,就做好防控人感染猪流感疫情工作作出了一系列重要指示和部署。国家质检总局认真落实党中央、国务院领导的指示要求,立即启动了应急预案,成立防控猪流感疫情传入工作领导小组,在卫生部的统一协调下,切实履行职责,严格口岸检验检疫措施,积极防止疫情传入。

一、快速作出反应,加强出入境口岸检验检疫工作

4 月 25 日,接到世界卫生组织的通报后,国家质检总局高度重视,立即进行研究,并于当日发布了《关于防止人感染猪流感疫情传入我国的紧急公告》(2009 年第 30 号)。一是要求来自人感染猪流感流行地区的人员,如有流感样症状的,入境时应主动向出入境检验检疫机构口头申报。过去两周去过流行地区的人员,入境后出现流感样症状的,要及时与当地出入境检验检疫机构联系。二是前往人感染猪流感流行地区的人员,可以向出入境检验检疫机构及其国际旅行卫生保健中心了解该地区的疫情;旅行中或旅行后出现流感相关症状者,应立即就医,并在入境时向检验检疫机构申报。三是出入境检验检疫机构及其国际旅行卫生保健中心应向出入境人员进行猪流感防治知识宣传教育,增强出入境人员的防病意识。口岸检验检疫机构要加强对上述地区入境人员的体温检测、医学巡查等工作,对主动申报或现场查验发现有流感症状的人员要仔细排查,对受染人或受染嫌疑人采取公共卫生观察、隔离、送指定医院诊治等检疫措施,并发放《就诊方便卡》优先诊治,同时检疫人员做好自身防护工作。四是向社会发布应对疫情的预防措施。

4 月 26 日,质检总局联合农业部发布了《关于防止墨西哥和美国猪流感传入我国的公告》(2009 年第 31 号)。一是禁止直接或间接从墨西哥和美国疫区输入猪及其产品,停止签发从墨西哥和美国疫区进口猪及其产品的《进境动植物检疫许可证》,撤销已经签发的《进境动植物检疫许可证》。二是自公告发布之日起启运的来自墨西哥和美国疫区的猪及其产品,一律作退回或销毁处理。对公告发布之日前启运的来自墨西哥和美国疫区的猪及其产品,经猪流感(H1N1)检测合格后方可放行。三是禁止邮寄或旅客携带来自墨西哥、美国的猪及其产品进境,一经发现,一律作退回或销毁处理。四是在途经我国或在我国停留的国际航行船舶、飞机和火车等运输工具上,如发现有来自墨西哥、美国的猪及其产品,一律作封存处理;其交通员工自养自用的猪,必须装入完好的笼具中,其废弃物、泔水等,一律在出入境检验检疫机构的监督下作无害化处理,不得擅自抛弃。对来自疫区的交通工具作防疫消毒处理。五是对海关、边防等部门截获的非法入境的来自墨西哥、美国的非法入境的猪及其产品,一律在出入境检验检疫机构监督下作销毁处理。

在发出公告的同时,国家质检总局及时向全国出入境检验检疫机构发出通知,对防控工作作出具体部署。一是要求全国各口岸全面加强对出入境人员,尤其是来自猪流感流行地区人员的体温检测、医学巡查、交通工具运营人申报、出入境人员主动申报等工作,实施 24 小时值班制度,及时发现可疑病例。二是要求与墨西哥直接通航的口岸启动墨西哥入境人员(包括飞机乘务人员和船员)填写《出/入境健康申报卡》制度,对所有来自墨西哥的航班实行登机检疫,入境人员设立单独入境通道,发现可疑病例及时严格排查处置。三是加强出入境交通工具检疫工作。对墨西哥来华的飞机、船舶等交通运输工具实施消毒杀虫等防疫措施,对随机、随船携带的垃圾实施严格的无害化处理,对船舶压舱水实施消毒等卫生处理。

二、加大宣传力度,提高出入境人员的防病意识和能力

在采取上述措施的同时,质检总局还不断加大宣传力度。一是对疫情发生后采取的检验检疫措施广为告知,使全社会了解采取这些措施的目的是为了保护人类健康和生命安全。二是对疫病防范常识广泛普及。通过广大新闻媒体开展科学防控疫病宣传,质检总局网站开辟了专栏,介绍防病知识和注意事项。三是各口岸检验检疫机构及其国际旅行卫生保健中心也加强日常防疫宣传教育,针对性地印制人感染猪流感宣传材料,对出入境人员进行猪流感防治知识、口岸检疫要求等方面宣传教育,提高出入境人员的防病意识,争取出入境人员对检验检疫工作的支持。

三、加严检疫措施,进一步加大口岸疫病防控力度

根据疫情的发展变化情况,质检总局又采取了进一步加严口岸检验检疫的各项措施。一是派出由总局副局长带队的督查组,赴重点口岸进行督查,现场指导工作。二是继对来自墨西哥的国际航班实行登机检疫之后,对来自美国的航班也全部实行登机检疫。第一时间上机了解情况,进一步加大医学巡查力度。三是继设立墨西哥入境人员专用通道之后,要求从美国入境的人员也走机场专用通道,发现体温超过37.5℃的旅客,及时进行严格排查处置,定期对专用通道进行消毒处理。四是实行红外线体温检测前移,要求全国各口岸对从墨西哥、美国入境的人员,在专用通道即进行红外线体温检测,这些入境旅客与其他航班入境人员走共用通道时,再次接受红外体温检测,如发现体温超过37.5℃的旅客立即进行严格排查处置。五是加严出入境交通工具检疫工作。继墨西哥之后,对从美国来华的飞机、船舶等交通运输工具实施消毒杀虫等防疫措施,对随机、随船携带的垃圾实施严格的无害化处理,对船舶压舱水实施消毒等卫生处理。六是加强陆路边境口岸疫情防控工作,要求各陆路边境口岸检验检疫机构密切关注周边国家地区猪流感疫情动态,在当地政府的统一领导下加强联防联控,严防疫情通过陆路边境口岸传入我国。

国家质检总局及所属口岸检验检疫机构将密切关注国外疫情发展态势,在党中央、国务院的领导下,在卫生部的统一组织协调下,与有关部门紧密配合,沉着应对,科学防控,切实做好口岸检验检疫工作,严防猪流感疫病传入。

译文

AQSIQ's efforts on prevention and control of swine influenza

Liu Pingjun, Vice minister of General Administration of Quality Supervision, Inspection and Quarantine(AQSIQ)
April 30, 2009

Recently, the human cases of swine influenza were confirmed in countries including Mexico and the United States of America, and were now spreading widely in the world. The Party Central Committee and the State Council attached high importance to the issue and made a series of important instructions and arrangement. General Administration of Quality Supervision, Inspection and Quarantine (AQSIQ), carefully implementing the instructions of the Party Central Committee and the State Council, under the coordination of the Ministry of Health(MOH), performed our functions and responsibilities, launched contingency plan, set up the Leading Group of Preventing Swine Influenza and took a series of measures to actively combat the current pandemic situation and to prevent and control the epidemics, including intensifying the inspection and quarantine at the ports. Our major measures are the follows:

First, Rapid Response and Active Combat are performed.

Upon receiving notification by the World Health Organization(WHO) on April 25, AQSIQ attached great importance to the matter and immediately organized further study and promulgated on the same day *the Urgent Notice on Preventing the Swine Influenza from Entering into China* (Notice No. 30, 2009). The Notice requires: First, the people from the epidemic region, with any symptom of flu-like illnesses, shall voluntarily declare to the Entry-Exit Inspection and Quarantine Bureau(CIQ). For people who have been to the epidemic region in the previous two weeks, if he develops any flu-like symptom after entering into China, he shall contact the local CIQ in a timely manner. Second, people who are travelling to the epidemic region can consult the CIQ or its international travel health care center for information on the epidemic area. If he/she develops any influenza-like symptom during or after the travel, he/she shall immediately go to the doctor and declare to the CIQs upon entry. Third, the CIQs and their international travel health care centers shall educate the entry-exit personnel on the prevention and control of the swine influenza, and help them to increase the awareness of prevention. The inspection and quarantine agencies at ports shall intensify their work including the body temperature monitoring and medical inspection for travelers from the epidemic area, conduct careful examination for those who voluntarily declare problems and those who are found with symptoms of flu-like illness upon on-site inspection, took quarantine measures for the infected or the suspect including public health observation, isolation and sent them to the designated hospitals for medical treatment with the medical convenience cards. Meanwhile, the CIQs' staff is required to take necessary measures for self-protection. Fourth, we would notify to the public other precautionary measures in tackling the epidemics.

On April 26, AQSIQ, jointly with the Ministry of Agriculture(MOA) issued *the Notice on Preventing Swine Influenza from Spreading from Mexico and the United States of America into China* (Notice No. 31, 2009). The Notice requires: First, Suspend the direct and indirect importation of pigs and pig products from Mexico and the epidemic area of the United States. Stop the issuance of Import Quarantine Permit for pig and pig products from Mexico and epidemic area of the US, and those Import Quarantine Permit that have been issued for the above-mentioned regions shall be revoked. Second, the shipments of pig and pig products that depart Mexico and the epidemic area of the US since the day when the Notice is issued shall be returned or destroyed. Those shipments that depart before the notice issuance shall be released only when tested negative for the virus strain of H1N1 of swine influenza. Third, prohibit the mailing and carrying of pig and pig products from Mexico and the United States. Any pig and pig products from the above-mentioned region detected upon entry shall be returned or destroyed. Fourth, in case any detected pig and pig products from Mexico or the United States must be sealed on any vessel, aircraft, train, or other transportation means stop in China or across China; pigs raised by the crew for themselves use must be kept in intact cages, the pigs' disposal and swill must be hazard-free treated under the surveillance of CIQs, and the unauthorized disposal is prohibited. The transportation means coming from affected countries must be conducted with quarantine disinfection measures. Fifth, the illegal pig and pig products coming from Mexico and the US detected by customs or frontier defense inspection authorities must be destroyed under the surveillance of CIQs.

At the same time of issuing the joint notice, AQSIQ noticed all CIQs of the arrangement for swine influenza control and prevention. The measures are as follows: First, at all frontier ports, the inspection and quarantine measures undertaken to all entry-exit travelers, especially from swine flu epidemic areas including body temperature monitoring, medical inspection, conveyance operator declaration, traveler voluntary declaration should be intensified. And the 24-hour duty is required for timely detection of suspected cases. Second, the ports of direct flights to Mexico are requested to lunch the special system, which requires travelers from Mexico(including flight crew and sailors) to submit "entry-exit health declaration form". While, the boarding inspection and quarantine is required to all air flight from Mexico. Special passageway is set up for travelers from Mexico to get through inspection and quarantine, and any suspect case screened and detected must be timely treated. Third, strengthen the quarantine to entry transportation means, conduct disinfection and pest killing quarantine measures to the planes and vessels from Mexico, carry out the hazard-free treatment to the waste garbage with those air planes and vessels, and conduct disinfection hygiene treatment to the ballast water of the vessels.

Second, strengthen advocation to improve travelers' awareness and capacity of disease prevention.

In addition to the above measures, publicity is intensified by AQSIQ as follows: First, the inspection and quarantine measures undertaken after the epidemic outbreak will be publicized, so as to obtain the public understanding on that the purpose of those measures is protecting human health and life. Second, disease prevention and control knowledge will be extensively advocated. Through the media as well as setting special column on AQSIQ official website, the knowledge of how to prevent and control swine influenza is released. Third, the CIQs at ports and their international travel health care centers strengthen the routine quarantine advocation and education, print and distribute the public advocating materials on swine influenza, educate the entry-exit travelers with the knowledge of swine influenza control and prevention and port quarantine requirements, etc., so as to improve the entry-exit travelers' awareness of disease prevention and to obtain the travelers' support to inspection and quarantine work.

Third, further enhance entry-exit health inspection and quarantine measures based upon the epidemic situation development.

According to the development of epidemic situation abroad, AQSIQ further enhances the port inspection and quarantine measures as follows: First send a supervision group headed by vice ministers to take on-site review to key ports. Second, carry out boarding quarantine to all airplanes coming from the US after we have taken the same measures to the airplanes from Mexico, learning the situation in the first time by boarding the airplanes, further enhancing the medical inspection and conducting more strict inspection and quarantine measures to the personnel and commodities coming from the worst-hit epidemic areas; third, request the travelers coming from the US get through the airport special passageway after the special passageway has been set up for travelers from Mexico, while in case the passenger whose body temperature over 37.5 degrees Celsius are detected, they will be timely and strictly screened and treated, and the disinfection to the special passageway will be regularly conducted; fourth, the thermal imaging body temperature monitoring system will be moved forward to the gate. The travelers from the US and Mexico are requested to get through this system in the special passageway immediately after they get off the plane. Those targeted travelers will get through the body temperature monitoring system once again when sharing the passageway with other passengers, while in case the passenger whose body temperature over 37.5 degrees Celsius are detected, they will be timely and strictly screened and treated; fifth, strengthen the quarantine to entry-exit transportation means, conduct disinfection and pest killing quarantine measures to the planes and vessels from US and Mexico, carry out the hazard-free treatment to the waste garbage with those airplanes and vessels, and conduct disinfection hygiene treatment to the ballast water of the vessels; sixth, strengthen the control and prevention work in land boarder ports. Request the inspection and quarantine agencies in those land boarder ports to pay close attention to the swine epidemic situation development of the surrounding countries, to strengthen joint control and prevention under the leadership of local government and to strictly prevent swine influenza from spreading into China from those land boarder ports.

AQSIQ and its CIQs at ports will pay close attention to the development of epidemic situation abroad. Under the leadership of the Party Central Committee and the State Council, with coordination of MOH, we will closely work together with other relevant government departments, calmly and soberly tackle, scientifically control and prevent, faithfully undertake the port inspection and quarantine work, and prevent the swine influenza from spreading into China.

选文B

UN Secretary-General Ban Ki-moon's Message for World No Tobacco Day
31 May, 2010

This year's observance of World No Tobacco Day focuses on "Gender and tobacco, with an emphasis on marketing to women".

Although fewer than 1 out of 10 women are smokers, that still adds up to an estimated 200 million women around the world. Moreover, that number could grow, since the tobacco industry is spending heavily on advertisements that target women and associate tobacco use with beauty and liberation.

According to a recent study by the World Health Organization(WHO), the number of girls and boys who smoked was about equal in half the 151 countries surveyed. This finding is even more worrisome since young people who smoke are likely to continue in adulthood.

Evidence indicates that the prevalence rate of tobacco use among women is on the rise in some countries. Governments everywhere must take action to protect women from tobacco advertising, promotion and sponsorship, as stipulated in the *WHO Framework Convention on Tobacco Control*.

The Convention also calls on Governments to protect women from second-hand tobacco smoke — especially in countries where women feel powerless to protect themselves and their children. As WHO data show, of the 430,000 adults who die each year from second-hand smoke, nearly two thirds are women.

Around the world, more than 1.5 million women die each year from tobacco use. Most of these deaths occur in low- and middle-income countries. Without concerted action, that number could rise to 2.5 million women by the year 2030.

We must turn back the global tobacco epidemic. On World No Tobacco Day, I urge all Governments to address this public health threat. Tobacco use is not stylish or empowering. It is ugly and deadly.

译 文

联合国秘书长2010年世界无烟日致辞
2010年5月31日

今年世界无烟日活动的主题是"两性与烟草——关注针对女性的促销行为"。

虽然只有不到十分之一的女性吸烟,但这仍使全世界女烟民人数近达两亿。而且,由于烟草企业花巨资制作针对女性的广告,将烟草与美丽和妇女解放挂钩,这一数字还有可能增长。

世界卫生组织近期对151个国家的调查显示,有一半国家,男孩和女孩的吸烟人数不相上下。由于青少年在成年后很可能继续吸烟,这一结果越发令人担忧。

有证据表明,一些国家妇女烟草使用率在上升。各国政府必须采取行动,根据《世界卫生组织烟草控制框架公约》的规定,保护妇女远离烟草广告、促销和赞助活动。

这项公约还呼吁各国政府保护妇女远离二手烟雾,在妇女感觉无力保护自己和子女的国家尤应如此。世界卫生组织的数据显示,在每年因二手烟雾死亡的43万人当中,近三分之二为妇女。

在世界各地,每年有超过150万妇女死于烟草使用。其中大多数死亡发生在低收入和中等收入国家。如果不采取协调一致的行动,到2030年,这一数字将可能达到250万。

我们必须遏制全球烟草流行。值此世界无烟日之际,我敦促各国政府设法应对这一公共健康威胁。使用烟草既不时尚也不强身。使用烟草是一种致人于死命的陋习。

第十一单元　环境保护
(Environmental Protection)

单元要点

本单元共分五个层次,分别是:中国驻欧盟使团团长宋哲大使在东西方研究所气候变化专题研讨会上的演讲汉译英一篇;联合国秘书长潘基文2011年世界环境日致辞英译汉一篇;中国地名英译的注意事项;外国政要译名的策略;拓展阅读(汉译英、英译汉各一篇)。第一、二部分提供环境保护口译的例文及其翻译和重难点评析;第三、四部分主要是相关口译理论与技能的介绍;第五部分的拓展阅读中,提供汉、英原文和参考译文。

理论难点提示

1. 中国地名英译的注意事项。
2. 外国政要译名的策略。

选文A

积极应对气候变化,推动可持续发展
——中国驻欧盟使团团长宋哲大使在东西方研究所气候变化专题研讨会上的演讲
2010年2月16日

女士们、先生们:

很高兴参加此次会议,与大家进行交流。我想借此机会谈三个观点:第一,哥本哈根会议是应对气候变化的一个新起点;第二,国际社会应给予适应问题足够重视;第三,中欧应加强在应对气候变化方面的对话与合作。

大家对两个月前的哥本哈根会议一定还记忆犹新。会议虽然经历了不少曲折,但在各方共同努力下,最终取得了两方面重要成果,一是坚持了《联合国气候变化框架公约》、《京都议定书》和"巴厘路线图",明确了下一步继续谈判的方向;二是形成了《哥本哈根协议》,在发达国家强制减排和发展中国家采取自主行动上取得新进展,并就长期目标、资金、技术和透明度问题达成一定共识,为进一步加强应对气候变化国际合作奠定了基础,为未来阶段的谈判提供了政治动力。因此可以说,哥本哈根会议是成功的,也是现阶段所能取得的最好结果,应该得到珍惜。

应对气候变化的道路曲折漫长,哥本哈根会议不是终点,而是一个新起点。近一时期,陆续有近百个国家向《公约》秘书处通报了各自的减排或减缓目标。今年内还将举行波恩会议、墨西哥会议等一系列重要国际会议。作为国际社会负责任的一员,中方将继续发挥积极和建设性作用,同其他各方一道,以《哥本哈根协议》为基础,切实履行承诺,加强国际

合作,尽早完成"巴厘路线图"谈判,推动气候变化国际合作不断取得新进展。

日前,中国总理温家宝分别复函丹麦首相拉斯穆森和联合国秘书长潘基文,表示中方支持《哥本哈根协议》,同时重申中方将努力实现国内自主行动目标,即到2020年单位GDP二氧化碳排放比2005年下降40%至45%,非化石能源占一次能源消费比重达到15%左右,森林面积比2005年增加4 000万公顷,森林蓄积量比2005年增加13亿立方米。这是中国根据国情和发展阶段采取的自主行动,不附加任何条件,不与任何国家的减排目标挂钩,体现了中国政府所能做出的最大努力。

这里,我要特别说明的是,中国仍是一个发展中国家,处于工业化、城镇化快速发展的关键阶段,发展经济、改善民生的任务十分艰巨。中国人均GDP排在世界100位之后;按照联合国标准还有1.5亿人没有脱贫;每年要解决1 200万人的就业,比比利时全国人口还要多。此外,中国能源结构以煤为主,降低排放存在特殊困难。

即便如此,中国政府始终本着对民族、对人类负责任的态度,把应对气候变化作为重要战略任务。我们既要金山银山,更要绿水青山。中国决不会重复发达国家"先污染、后治理"的老路。中国将把自主采取的减缓目标作为约束性指标纳入国民经济和社会发展规划,坚定不移地走可持续发展道路,"言必信,行必果",为达到甚至超过承诺的减排目标而努力。

女士们,先生们:

减缓和适应是应对气候变化的两个有机组成部分。减缓是一项相对长期和艰巨的任务。适应则更加现实和紧迫,尤其对发展中国家而言。适应问题的核心是资金。《公约》明确规定,发达国家有义务向发展中国家提供资金和技术,帮助发展中国家适应气候变化。目前国际上已建立了包括最不发达国家基金在内的多个多边融资机制。但坦率地说,国际社会对适应问题的重视程度远未达到应有水平;现有机制所能落实到位的资金非常有限,与发展中国家的实际需要和期望值存在很大差距。

国际社会应改变"重减缓,轻适应"的错误做法,给予适应问题足够重视。特别是发达国家应承担责任,按照《公约》规定,切实兑现向发展中国家提供资金和技术的承诺。哥本哈根会议就资金问题达成初步共识,朝正确方向迈出了一步。但协议既未明确短期资金的来源以及如何落实,也没有明确各国在长期资金问题上承诺的具体金额,前景还存在很大不确定性。我们希望发达国家真正拿出政治诚意,采取切实行动,履行自己的义务,而不是企图推卸和转嫁责任。

女士们,先生们:

中欧气候变化合作由来已久。早在2005年双方就建立了气候变化伙伴关系。去年第十二次中欧领导人会晤决定提升气候变化伙伴关系,强化双方在气候变化领域的政策对话和务实合作。哥本哈根会议后,双方还拟定在近期要增加一次气候变化问题磋商。欧盟在节能和环保领域具有先进理念和技术,中国具有广阔的市场需求。双方可以进一步挖掘在能源和气候变化领域的合作潜力,特别是在以下几个领域:

一是节能和提高能效。中国在能源利用效率方面远远低于欧盟等发达国家,也有进一步降低单位GDP二氧化碳排放量的现实需要。

二是发展可再生能源。双方可通过清洁发展机制等促进中国可再生能源发展,改善能源结构,强化社会环保意识。

三是开发利用清洁能源。未来相当长时间内,中国能源生产和消费结构仍将以煤为主,这为双方提供了技术合作的重要平台。

女士们,先生们:

　　欧盟是世界上最大经济体,中国是世界上最大的发展中国家,加强中欧在应对气候变化和可持续发展等诸多领域的务实合作,不仅符合双方根本利益,也有利于世界的繁荣与发展。我们愿与欧盟各界通力合作,为应对气候变化和实现可持续发展而不懈努力。

　　谢谢大家!

重难点评析

　　1. "我想借此机会谈三个观点"是演讲常用词,译为:"I would like to take this opportunity to make three points."。

　　2. "《联合国气候变化框架公约》"译为"the United Nations Framework Convention on Climate Change","《京都议定书》"译为"the Kyoto Protocol","巴厘路线图"译为"the Bali road map","《哥本哈根协议》"译为"Copenhagen Accord"。

　　3. "……就长期目标、资金、技术和透明度问题达成一定共识,为进一步加强应对气候变化国际合作奠定了基础,为未来阶段的谈判提供了政治动力。"句中"就……达成共识"译为"reach consensus on","为……奠定基础"译为"lay the foundation for","为……提供动力"译为"give impetus to",此句译为:"It also reached certain consensus on issues such as long-term goals, funding, technology and transparency, which laid the foundation for further strengthening international cooperation on climate change and gave political impetus to future negotiations."。

　　4. "中方将继续发挥积极和建设性作用,同其他各方一道,以《哥本哈根协议》为基础,切实履行承诺,加强国际合作,尽早完成'巴厘路线图'谈判,推动气候变化国际合作不断取得新进展。"这是一个长句,全句首先使用了一系列谓语动词形成并列,最后用so as to引导目的状语。"发挥……的作用"译为"play an… role","履行承诺"译为"fulfill commitment","加强合作"译为"strengthen cooperation","推动……的不断进展"译为"promote continuous progress"。

　　5. "单位GDP二氧化碳排放"译为"carbon dioxide emissions per unit of GDP","非化石能源"译为"non-fossil energy","一次能源消费"译为"primary energy consumption"。

　　6. "中国人均GDP排在世界100位之后"译为:"China's per capita GDP ranks after the world's first 100."。

　　7. "没有脱贫"和"解决就业"采用了意译,分别译为:"remain in poverty"和"jobs need to be created",更加符合英语的习惯。

　　8. "中国能源结构以煤为主,降低排放存在特殊困难。"在翻译中采用了词序的调换译法将前半句译成:"以煤为主的能源结构。"——"China's coal-dominated energy mix poses special difficulties to emission reduction"。

　　9. "我们既要金山银山,更要绿水青山。"译员采用了增译法,表明说话人是在打比方"To use a metaphor, we want mountains of gold and silver, but first of all we want mountains of trees."。

　　10. "国际社会应改变'重减缓,轻适应'的错误做法。"翻译采用that引导主语从句译为:"It's been wrong that we put so much emphasis on mitigation but so little on adaptation."。

11. "我们希望发达国家真正拿出政治诚意,采取切实行动,履行自己的义务,而不是企图推卸和转嫁责任。"句中"拿出政治诚意"译为"demonstrate political sincerity","采取切实行动"译为"take concrete action","推卸和转嫁责任"译为"evade or shift to others their responsibilities"。

12. "双方可通过清洁发展机制等促进中国可再生能源发展,改善能源结构,强化社会环保意识。"句中"清洁发展机制"译为"the Clean Development Mechanism","可再生能源"译为"renewable energy"。

译文

Tackle Climate Change Actively and Promote Sustainable Development
—Speech at the East-West Institute Seminar by H. E. Ambassador Song Zhe,
Head of the Mission of the P. R. China to the EU
16 February 2010

Ladies and Gentlemen:

I am very pleased to be at this meeting and exchange views with you. I would like to take this opportunity to make three points: first, the Copenhagen Conference was a new starting point to tackle climate change; Secondly, the international community should give adequate attention to the issue of adaptation; Thirdly, China and the EU should strengthen dialogue and cooperation on climate change.

We still have fresh memories of the Copenhagen Conference which was held two months ago. The meeting experienced twists and turns, but thanks to the joint efforts of all parties, it ultimately obtained two important results. First, by adhering to the United Nations Framework Convention on Climate Change, the Kyoto Protocol and the Bali road map, the conference identified clearly the direction for the negotiations in the next step; Secondly, the conference issued the Copenhagen Accord, marking new progress in terms of binding reduction by developed countries and voluntary action by developing countries. It also reached certain consensus on issues such as long-term goals, funding, technology and transparency, which laid the foundation for further strengthening international cooperation on climate change and gave political impetus to future negotiations. It is fair to say that the Copenhagen conference was a success. It produced the best result that can be achieved at this stage, which should be cherished.

On tackling climate change, the road is long and tortuous. The Copenhagen Conference is not the end, but a new beginning. In recent weeks, there are nearly one hundred countries which notified the Secretariat of the Copenhagen Accord their respective emission reduction or mitigation targets. A series of important international conferences will be held in Bonn and Mexico this year. As a responsible member of the international community, China will continue to play an active and constructive role, earnestly fulfill its commitment, strengthen international cooperation, and with the Copenhagen Accord as the basis, work together with other parties for an early conclusion of the "Bali road map", so as to promote continuous progress of the international cooperation on climate change.

Recently, Chinese Premier Wen Jiabao sent letters to Danish Prime Minister Rasmussen and UN Secretary-General Ban Ki-moon and stated that China supports the Copenhagen Accord. Premier Wen reiterates that China will strive to achieve national voluntary reduction targets, that is, by 2020, carbon dioxide emissions per unit of GDP will drop by 40% to 45% than 2005, non-fossil energy will account for about 15% of primary energy consumption, forest area will increase by 40 million hectares and forest reserves by 1.3 billion cubic meters over 2005. This is a voluntary action China takes according to its own national conditions and stage of development. It is not attached to any conditions, or links to other country's emission reduction targets. It reflects the maximum efforts that the Chinese government can make.

Here, I would like to highlight that China is still a developing country. It is in the critical stage of rapid development of industrialization and urbanization. We are facing an arduous task of economic development and improving people's livelihood. China's per capita GDP ranks after the world's first 100. By the UN standard, 150 million Chinese remain in poverty. Every year jobs for 12 million people need to be created, even more than the entire population of Belgium. In addition, China's coal-dominated energy mix poses special difficulties to emission reduction.

Even so, the Chinese Government has always taken a responsible attitude towards the nation and mankind, and takes climate change as an important strategic task. To use a metaphor, we want mountains of gold and silver, but first of all we want mountains of trees. China will not repeat the model of "pollution first, treatment later" as it was in the history of the developed countries. China will set its own mitigation targets as compulsory targets of the national economic and social development plan and make efforts to meet our committed targets and do even more. We will unswervingly pursue sustainable development and honor our commitment by taking concrete actions.

Ladies and Gentlemen:

Mitigation and adaptation are two integral aspects in tackling climate change. Mitigation is a relatively longer-term and challenging task, whereas adaptation is more immediate and urgent, especially to developing countries. The core of adaptation is funding. The UNFCCC explicitly stipulates the obligation on the part of developed countries to provide funding and technology to developing countries. At present, the international community has established a number of multilateral financing mechanisms, including the Least Developed Countries Fund. But frankly speaking, the international community's emphasis on adaptation is far from enough. The funds that are available and can really be put in place by the existing mechanisms are very limited, and falling far short of the actual needs and expectations from the developing countries.

The international community should give more attention to adaptation. It's been wrong that we put so much emphasis on mitigation but so little on adaptation. The developed countries, in particular, should shoulder the responsibility, and in accordance with the Convention, deliver their promises to developing countries on financial and technology support. The Copenhagen Conference, having reached a preliminary consensus on the issue of funding, represented a step in the right direction. However, the Accord does not clearly specify the sources of funding in the short term or how they are going to be implemented. Neither does it stipulate the exact amount of long-term funding commitment of the countries concerned. There leaves much uncertainty. We hope that the developed countries will demonstrate political sincerity and take concrete action to fulfill its obligations, rather than evade or shift to others their responsibilities.

Ladies and gentlemen:

China-EU cooperation on climate change is already a long story. As early as in 2005, the two sides established partnership on climate change. At the 12th China-EU Summit last year, the two sides decided to upgrade such partnership and strengthen policy dialogue and practical cooperation in the field of climate change. Following the Copenhagen Conference, the two sides plan to add an extra round of consultations on climate change which will take place in the near future. The EU possess advanced concepts and technologies in the field of energy saving and environmental protection. China has a vast market demand. The two sides should further tap the potentials for cooperation on energy and climate change, especially in the following areas.

First, energy conservation and energy efficiency. China's energy utilization efficiency is far lower than the EU and other developed countries, and China needs to further reduce carbon dioxide emissions per unit of GDP.

The second area is renewable energy. By cooperation under the Clean Development Mechanism, the EU could help China to promote renewable energy development, improve energy structure, and strengthen social environmental awareness.

The third area is clean energy. For quite a long time in the future, China's energy production and consumption will continue to be dominated by coal, which presents us a vast platform for technical cooperation.

Ladies and Gentlemen:

The EU is the world's biggest economy, and China is the world's biggest developing country. To strengthen practical cooperation between China and the EU on climate change, and sustainable development not only serves the fundamental interests of both sides, but is also conducive to world prosperity and development. We are willing to cooperate with all communities in the EU and make unremitting efforts to cope with climate change and achieve sustainable development.

Thank you!

选文B

The Secretary-General's Message on World Environment Day
June 5, 2011

Nearly 20 years after the 1992 Earth Summit, the world is once again on the road to Rio — the site of the June 2012 UN Conference on Sustainable Development. Much has changed in the past two decades, geopolitically and environmentally. Hundreds of millions of people in Asia, Latin America — and, increasingly, in Africa — have risen from poverty. Yet, evidence is also accumulating of profound and potentially irreversible changes in the ability of the planet to sustain our progress.

Rapid economic growth has come with costs that traditionally rarely feature in national accounting. These range from atmospheric and water pollution to degraded fisheries and forests, all of which impact prosperity and human well-being. The theme of World Environment Day this year, "Forests: Nature at Your Service", emphasizes the multi-trillion dollar value of these and other ecosystems to society — especially the poor.

Despite growing global awareness of the dangers of environmental decline — including climate change, biodiversity loss and desertification — progress since the Earth Summit has been too slow. We will not build a just and equitable world unless we give equal weight to all three pillars of sustainable development — social, economic and environmental. To sustainably reduce poverty, guarantee food and nutrition security and provide decent employment for growing populations, we must make the most intelligent use of our natural capital.

India, the global host of World Environment Day in 2011, is among a growing number of countries working to address the pressures of ecological change. It is also helping to pioneer a better assessment of the economic value of nature-based services, with the assistance of the United Nations Environment Programme and the World Bank. India's Rural Employment Act and the country's encouragement of renewable energy are significant examples of how to scale up green growth and accelerate the transition to a green economy.

No single day can transform development onto a sustainable path. But on the road to Rio +20, this year's World Environment Day can send a message that those with influence in government and the private sector can — and must — take the necessary steps that will fulfill the promise of the Earth Summit. The global public is watching, and expects nothing less.

重难点评析

1. "Much has changed in the past two decades, geopolitically and environmentally." 句中两个副词"geopolitically and environmentally"在译文中为符合中文的表达习惯采用了

增译法"在地缘政治和环境方面。"

2. "These range from atmospheric and water pollution to degraded fisheries and forests."句中"range from... to..."译为"从……到……",此句采用了词类的换译,译文为:"这些代价从大气和水污染到渔业和森林的退化。"

3. "Despite growing global awareness of the dangers of environmental decline."这是一个让步句型,根据中文的表达习惯译为:"尽管全球越来越多的人意识到环境恶化的危险。""biodiversity loss"译为"生物多样性丧失","desertification"译为"荒漠化"。

4. "We will not build a just and equitable world unless we give equal weight to all three pillars of sustainable development — social, economic and environmental."句中"not... unless..."译为"除非……不……"。全句译为:"除非我们同样重视可持续发展的三个支柱——社会、经济和环境,否则我们无法建立一个公正和公平的世界。""give equal weight to"译为"同样重视"。

5. "guarantee food and nutrition security"译为"保证粮食和营养安全","provide decent employment"译为"提供体面就业","make the most intelligent use of"译为"以最明智的方式利用"。

6. "It is also helping to pioneer a better assessment of the economic value of nature-based services, with the assistance of the United Nations Environment Programme and the World Bank."本句采用了词序调换的译法更加符合中文的习惯,译为:"在联合国环境规划署和世界银行的援助下,它也在协助开创一种办法来更好地评估注重大自然的服务的经济价值。"

7. "scale up green growth"译为"扩大绿色增长","accelerate the transition to a green economy"译为"加快向绿色经济过渡"。

8. "The global public is watching, and expects nothing less."前文刚刚说过"fulfill the promise",所以这里"expects nothing less"根据上下文译成:"期望这些承诺能得到履行。"

译 文

联合国秘书长潘基文2011年世界环境日致辞
2011年6月5日

自1992年召开地球问题首脑会议之后,近20年已经过去。世界再一次踏上前往里约之路——2012年6月将在那里举行联合国可持续发展大会。在过去二十年里,世界在地缘政治和环境方面已发生巨大变化。有数亿亚洲和拉丁美洲人,以及越来越多的非洲人已从贫困中崛起。然而,越来越多的证据也表明,地球维持我们进步的能力已发生深刻的和可能无法逆转的变化。

经济快速增长产生了传统上很少包括在国民经济核算中的代价,这些代价从大气和水污染到渔业和森林的退化,所有这些均影响繁荣和人类福祉。今年世界环境日的主题是"森林:大自然为你服务",强调森林和其他生态系统对社会——特别是穷人所能带来的数万亿美元的价值。

尽管全球越来越多的人意识到环境恶化的危险,包括气候变化、生物多样性丧失和荒漠化,但自地球问题首脑会议以来的进展过于缓慢。除非我们同样重视可持续发展的三个支柱——社会、经济和环境,否则我们无法建立一个公正和公平的世界。为了可持续地减少贫困,保证粮食和营养安全,并为日益增长的人口提供体面就业,我们必须以最明智的方式利用自然资源。

印度是2011年世界环境日的全球主办国,它是世界上越来越多致力于应对生态变化压力的国家之一。在联合国环境规划署和世界银行的援助下,它也在协助开创一种办法来更好地评估注重大自然的服务的经济价值。印度的《农村就业法》和国家鼓励使用可再生能源的做法,是如何扩大绿色增长,加快向绿色经济过渡的显著例子。

促使发展走上可持续道路并非是一朝一夕之事,但在前往里约会议二十周年大会的道路上,今年的世界环境日可传达一个信息,即那些具有影响力的政府和私营部门能够——而且必须——采取必要步骤履行地球问题首脑会议的承诺。全世界各国人民都在关注,他们期望这些承诺能得到履行。

中国地名英译的注意事项

地名是历史的产物,是国家领土主权的象征,是日常生活的向导,是社会交往的媒介。在信息化社会中,地名在国际政治、经济、外交、外贸、科技、文化交流、新闻出版以及社会生活方面都起着非常重要的作用。

用汉语拼音字母拼写中国地名,不仅是中国的统一标准,而且是国际标准,全世界都要遵照使用。根据笔者英译中国地名的体会,本文拟谈谈中国地名英译的几点注意事项,供译者和读者参考。

一、专名是单音节的英译法

专名是单音节,通名也是单音节,这时通名应视作专名的组成部分,先音译并与专名连写,后重复意译,分写(汉字带点的字是通名,英语的画线部分是音译;括号内为该地所在省、市、地区或县,下同)例如:

1. 恒山　Hengshan Mountain(山西)
2. 淮河　the Huaihe River(河南、安徽、江苏)
3. 巢湖　the Chaohu Lake(安徽)
4. 渤海　the Bohai Sea(辽宁、山东)
5. 韩江　the Hanjiang River(广东)
6. 礼县　Lixian County(甘肃陇南地区)

二、通名专名化的英译法

通名专名化主要指单音节的通名,如山、河、江、湖、海、港、峡、关、岛等,按专名处理,与专名连写,构成专名整体(汉语带点的字和英语的画线部分即为通名专名化)。例如:

1. 都江堰市　Dujiangyan City(比较:the Dujiang Weir)(四川)
2. 绥芬河市　Suifenhe City(比较:the Suifen River)(黑龙江)
3. 白水江自然保护区　Baishuijiang Nature Reserve(比较:the Baishui River)(甘肃)

4. 青铜峡水利枢纽 Qingtongxia Water Control Project(比较:the Qingtong Gorge)(宁夏)

5. 武夷山自然保护区 Wuyishan Nature Reserve(比较:Wuyi Mountain)(福建)

6. 西湖区风景名胜区 Scenic Spots and Historic Sites of Xihu(比较:the West Lake)(浙江杭州)

三、通名是同一个汉字的多种英译法

通名是单音节的同一个汉字,根据意义有多种不同英译法,在大多数情况下,这些英译词不能互相代换。例如:

1. 山

(1) mount:峨眉山 Mount Emei(四川峨眉)

(2) mountain:五台山 Wutai Mountain(山西)

(3) hill:象鼻山 the Elephant Trunk Hill(广西桂林)

(4) island:大屿山 Lantau Island(香港)

(5) range:念青唐古拉山 the Nyainqentanglha Range(西藏)

(6) peak:拉旗山 Victoria Peak(香港)

(7) rock:狮子山 Lion Rock(香港)

2. 海

(1) sea:东海 the East China Sea

(2) lake:邛海 the Qionghai Lake(四川西昌)

(3) harbour:大滩海 Long Harbour(香港)

(4) port:牛尾海 Port Shelter(香港)

(5) forest:蜀南竹海 the Bamboo Forest in Southern Sichuan(四川长岭)

在某些情况下,根据通名意义,不同的汉字可英译为同一个单词。例如:"江、河、川、水、溪"英译为 river。

(1) 嘉陵江 the Jialing River(四川)

(2) 永定河 the Yongding River(河北、北京、天津)

(3) 螳螂川 the Tanglang River(云南)

(4) 汉水 the Hanshui River(陕西、湖北)

(5) 古田溪 the Gutian River(福建)

四、专名是同一个汉字的不同英译法

专名中同一个汉字有不同的读音和拼写,据笔者不完全统计,地名中这样的汉字有七八十个之多,每个字在地名中的读音和拼写是固定的,英译者不能一见汉字就按语言词典的读音和拼写翻译,而只能按中国地名词典的读音和拼写进行翻译(画线部分为该字的读音和拼写)。例如:

1. 陕

(1) 陕西省 Shaanxi Province

(2) 陕县 Shanxian County(河南)

2. 洞

(1) 洞庭湖 the Dong Lake(湖南)

(2) 洪洞县　Hongtong County(山西)

3. 六

(1) 六合县　Luhe County(江苏)

(2) 六盘水市　Liupanshui City(贵州)

4. 荥

(1) 荥阳市　Xingyang City(河南)

(2) 荥经县　Yingjing County(四川雅安地区)

5. 林

(1) 林甸县　Lindian County(黑龙江大庆市)

(2) 林芝地区　Nyingchi Prefecture(西藏)

(3) 林周县　Lhunzhub County(西藏拉萨市)

(4) 米林县　Mainling County(西藏林芝地区)

6. 扎

(1) 扎赉特旗　Jalaid Banner(内蒙古兴安盟)

(2) 扎兰屯市　Zalantun City(内蒙古呼伦贝尔盟)

(3) 扎囊县　Chanang County(西藏山南地区)

(4) 扎龙自然保护区　Zhalong Nature Reserve(黑龙江齐齐哈尔市)

(5) 扎达县　Zanda County(西藏阿里地区)

(6) 扎陵湖　the Gyaring Lake(青海)

五、专名是同样汉字的多种英译法

专名中的汉字是相同的,但表示不同的地点,每个地点的读音和拼写是固定的,应按"名从主人"的原则译写,不能按普通语言词典,而必须按中国地名词典英译。例如:

1. 浍河

(1) the Huihe River(河南、安徽)

(2) the Kuaihe River(山西)

2. 阿克乔克山

(1) Akqoka Mountain(新疆昭苏县)

(2) Akxoki Mountain(新疆塔城市)

3. 色拉寺

(1) the Sera Monastery(西藏拉萨市)

(2) the Sula Temple(四川色达)

4. 单城镇

(1) Dancheng Town(黑龙江双城县)

(2) Shancheng Town(山东单县)

5. 阿扎乡

(1) Arza Township(西藏嘉黎县)

(2) Ngagzha Township(西藏扎囊县)

(3) Ngarzhag Township(西藏浪卡子县)

6. 柏城镇
（1）Bocheng Town（山东高密市）
（2）Baicheng Town（河南西平县）

六、中国各民族名称的罗马字母拼写法

1991年8月30日,国家技术监督局批准了《中国各民族名称的罗马字母拼法和代码》(GB33041),该标准适用于文献工作、拼音电报、国际通讯、出版、新闻报导、信息处理和交换等方面,当然也适用于英译。特别值得一提的是,虽然汉字书写的民族名称有"族"字,但罗马字母拼写法无"zu"字的拼写,英译照抄,首字母大写(见附录:中国各民族名称法的罗马字母拼写法)。例如:

1. 双江拉祜族佤族布朗族傣族自治县
Lahu-Va-Blang-Dai Autonomous County of Shuangjiang（云南临沧地区）

2. 贡山独龙族怒族自治县
Derung-Nu Autonomous County of Gongshan（云南怒江）

3. 湘西土家族苗族自治州
Tujia-Miao Autonomous Prefecture of Xinangxi（湖南）

4. 金秀瑶族自治县
Yao Autonomous County of Jinxiu（广西柳州地区）

此外,朝鲜族和藏族的罗马字母拼写法,对外分别使用Korean和Tibetan。例如：
（1）延边朝鲜族自治州
Korean Autonomous Prefecture of Yanbian（吉林）
（2）甘孜藏族自治州
Tibetan Autonomous Prefecture of Garze（四川）

需要指出的是,如果专指"××族"通常就要译出"族"字。例如：
（1）回族　the Hui nationality（或 the Huis）
（2）彝族　the Yi nationality（或 the Yis）
（3）藏族　the Zang(Tibetan) nationality（或 the Zangs, the Tibetans）

但是,如果作形容词修饰名词,则又可省略"族"字。例如：维吾尔族医学 Uygur medicine,彝族人 the Yi people

七、以人名命名的地名英译法

以人名命名的地名英译,人名的姓和名连写,人名必须前置,通名后置,不加定冠词。这种译法多用于自然地理实全体地名,但有例外。例如：
（1）张广才岭　Zhangguangcai Mountain（吉林、黑龙江）
（2）欧阳海水库　Ouyanghai Reservoir（湖南桂阳）
（3）郑和群礁　Zhenghe Reefs（海南南沙群岛）
（4）李准滩 Lizhun Bank（海南南沙群岛）
（5）鲁班暗沙　Luban Ansha（海南中沙群岛）
（6）左权县　Zuoquan County（山西晋中地区）

如果以人名命名的非自然地理实体地名,姓和名分写,人名前置或后置按习惯用法,大

致有以下三种译法：

(1) 人名＋通名

黄继光纪念馆　Huang Jiguang Memorial(四川中江县)

(2) 人名's＋通名

中山陵墓　Sun Yat-sen's Mausoleum(江苏南京市)

(3) the＋通名＋of 人名

昭君墓　the Tomb of Wang Zhaojun(内蒙古呼和浩特市)

八、少数民族语地名的记音用加符字母

地名记音的几个符号可以加在特定的字母上面，代表特殊语音。蒙古语、维吉尔语和藏语音译转写的汉语拼音字母有无符和加符并列的，一般拼写用无符字母，地名记音用加符字母。例如：

乌鲁木齐市　Urumqi City(新疆)　巩乃斯河　Kunse River(新疆新源)　察隅县 Zayu County(西藏林芝地区)

改则县　Gerze County(西藏阿里地区)　德格县　Dege County(四川甘孜)　甘德县 Gade County(青海果洛)

九、地名中的符号不能省略

地名中的符号如果省略就会造成读音甚至语义错误。地名中有两种符号不能省略。

1. a,o,e 开头的音节连接在其他音节后面的时候，如果音节的界限发生混淆，用隔音符号，地名中的隔音符号不能省略。例如：

(1) (陕西)西安市　Xi'an City(如果省略隔音符号，就成为 Xian，可以读成仙、先、现、限、鲜、险、县等)

(2) (广西)兴安县　Xing'an County(如果省略隔音符号，就成为 Xingan County 新干县，在江西吉安地区)

(3) 建瓯市　Jian'ou City(福建)

(4) 第二松花江　the Di'er Songhua River(吉林)

(5) 东阿县　Dong'e County(山东聊城市)

(6) 天峨县　Tian'e County(广西河池地区)

2. 汉语拼音 ü 的韵母跟声母 n,l 拼的时候，ü 上面的两点不能省略。如果省略，就会造成误解。例如：

(1) (山西)闾河　the Lühe River(如果省略 u 上面的两点，就变成 the Luhe River 芦河，在江西)

(2) (台湾)绿岛　Lüdao Island(如果省略 u 上面的两点，就变成 Ludao Island 鹭岛，在黑龙江海林)

(3) 女山湖　the Nüshan Lake(安徽嘉山)

(4) 吕梁地区　Lüliang Prefecture(山西)

(5) 旅顺港　Lüshun Port(辽宁)

但是也有例外。例如：

(1) 绿春县　Luchun County(云南红河)

(2) 绿曲县　Luqu County(甘肃甘南)

外国政要译名的策略

中国人盼望着奥巴马，走下"空军一号"的却是"欧巴马"——这个笑话缘于11月12日美国驻华使馆发布的一张关于美国总统首次访华的纪念海报。海报上，红底金字的标题为"共同走过的日子"，底部则写着："美国总统巴拉克·欧巴马2009年11月首次访问中国的纪念海报"。随后，百科词条中多了"欧巴马"一项，许多人开始不明就里——到底是奥巴马还是欧巴马？奥巴马译名从何而来，其他政要的名字又是由谁第一个翻译？标准是什么？

中国外交部外语专家、前外交部翻译室主任过家鼎告诉《国际先驱导报》，"奥巴马"这个翻译没有问题，但美国人由发音来考虑倒也能理解。"提出讨论可以，但按照惯例，已经沿用一段时间的译名不会随便更改。"

奥巴马还是欧巴马？若要追溯到译名源头，一般来说，外国领导人的姓名翻译工作由中国唯一的综合性译名单位——新华社译名室来完成。

现任美国总统的全名在新华社的译名库里是"贝拉克·侯赛因·奥巴马"，这一姓名自2004年11月3日以来一直沿用至今。译名室负责人衷爽表示，奥巴马这个姓氏在非洲国家肯尼亚的一些部落很普遍，这么多年一直这么翻译。"如果他改了，那个家族的名字都会受影响。"而据2003年肯尼亚《联合报》的不完全统计，在Mahatali地区，姓Obama的人大概在7 000到8 000之间。所以，除非通过外交途径"强烈要求"，奥巴马这次想改名很难成功。

尽管人们猜不透"改名"的想法是不是奥巴马本人的意愿，但实际上，关心自己中文译名的外国政要还真不少。

2003年，被西方称为"强人"的时任柬埔寨首相洪森宣布将其中文名字更名为"云升"，尽管洪森首相不是中国人，但他希望自己有个更好的中文译名，而他同意改名"云升"正是听从身边华人朋友的建议。当地有报纸还说，金边的一位华人占卜师也为首相的中文译名发表了看法，认为"云升"比"洪森"的寓意好。为此，柬埔寨方面通过中国外交部致函新华社，新闻部国务秘书乔卡纳里表示"希望新华社今后对首相的改名予以理解"。

改名之后，麻烦却接踵而至。当时华文媒体亮出"云升"这个名字后，许多读者就不断打电话询问柬埔寨是不是换了新首相。一些华裔柬埔寨人则抱怨说，大家已经叫惯了"洪森"这个名字，忽然改称"云升"，觉得很别扭。更要命的是在政府部门颁布的一些具法律效力的文件中，两个名字竟然同时存在，一些法律上的麻烦就不可避免。不到一年，新华社便收到外交部来函，通知恢复洪森的原中文译名。

但偶尔也有例外的。比如法国总统萨科齐的名字就经过改动，原名"萨尔科奇"经法国政府要求改成"萨科齐"，他的夫人也由"布吕尼"改为"布鲁尼"。据新华社译名室译员李振洁解释，由于名字改动时，萨科齐刚刚当上总统，影响力远非今日，所以没有形成很大的冲击。

"名字毕竟是个符号，成为公众都认识的之后就不应该随便改动，要知道改动人名的一个字，有可能给我们带来很大的损失。"李振洁表示。毕竟，这可能涉及各类书本文摘乃至地图史册的改动。

许多人想不到的是，从上个世纪50年代初开始，新华社译名室便开始管理起中国大陆以及全世界的人名。几名译员天天对着枯燥的英文名字冥思苦想，绞尽脑汁；他们要和不同种类的语言打交道,要和不同的罗马字母、英文字母、希腊字母、韩文音节、片假名和平假名"搏斗"。凡是在中国大陆的报刊、书籍、广播电视中露面的外国人名,都与他们的工作息息相关。所以,该译名室也被人称为"国外人名信息进入中国所遇到的海关"。

在各类外文的中文汉字译名规则上,新华社译名室研究出一整套规范而细致的西文拼写与汉字对应系统。据陈有明介绍,为了在人名的汉字选择上提供一个借以依据的规范,目前新华社译名室以中国对外翻译出版公司出版的《世界人名翻译大词典》为标准。其本人也参与了词典的编撰工作。在词典的附录上,包含了 55 种语言的常用译音表,按照各种语言的发音规则和规律明确规定了对应的汉字发音用字和词语。

在翻译过程中,译名室强调的是"音译为主、名从主人、约定俗成"原则。例如许多驻华使节喜好起地道的中文名,比如历届的美国驻华大使们,从恒安石、芮效俭、尚慕杰到如今的洪博培,每个人都早早定好了自己的中文名字。而随着中国在国际上地位的不断提升,许多国际政要也赶起"时髦"。北约前秘书长夏侯雅伯(原名亚普·德霍普·斯海弗)便把外国人"名在前,姓在后"的习惯颠倒过来,加上中国化的音译而成。

由于早期的初始译著、译名个性化十足,延续至今形成了林林总总、五花八门的历史遗留译名,尽管从科学角度考证这些译名不符合标准,但由于已为中国人熟用并耳熟能详,改了反而不易被接受,容易产生歧义且引发争议,便仍保留旧译,比如凯瑟琳女皇为叶卡捷琳娜,萧伯纳不必改为伯纳·萧,仲马不必改为杜马,安徒生不必改为安德森,福尔摩斯就没有必要变成霍姆斯,拿破仑也不需要变成纳波里昂,哪怕其中被冠以一个刺眼的"破"字。

2008 年,译名室迎来一次前所未有的挑战。两个星期内,当时译名室的七人小组要为参加北京奥运会的 36 000 位外国人翻译正确的中文名字。他们中包括外国首脑、政府官员、行政人员、运动员、国外志愿者、记者,甚至连马匹的名字也需要翻译。

两百多个国家人员的名字、语言又是各不相同,译员们经常碰见土著语甚至光怪陆离的民族语言。比如柬埔寨的姓名是姓在前名在后,并且贵族有姓而平民无姓,老挝则相反;前也门国王正式用名有 11 段,真正的名字是第七段的"艾哈迈德"。

长期从事这项工作,李振洁也总结了一些经验。在她看来,外国名字除了根据音标、字形和字音多方面的配合,还需要译者自己的语感。

"翻译人名本身就不一定要死抠规则,遇到特殊情况未尝不能根据大众的喜好来选择译名。"她表示,比如 NBA 著名篮球运动员英文名为 Kobe Bryant(外界翻译为科比·布莱恩特),虽然根据规则应该翻译为科贝,但是这和公众已经认定的不一致,最后也没有修改。

与这些艰巨的翻译任务相比,让译员们更头疼的则是外界常常"望文生音"。译名室原负责人李纯曾举过最典型的"拉丹和拉登译名之争"和"国际金融大鳄索罗斯被错翻"两个典型例子,"拉登是媒体根据英语发音译的,但拉丹的名字来自阿拉伯语,阿拉伯语系里根本没有登这个音节,所以只能译成拉丹。从这点可以看出民间望英文而音译的做法是不负责任的。绍罗什错译成索罗斯也是同样的原因。因为他是匈牙利人,按照标准应该翻译成绍罗什。"

这些被译员们戏称为互联网时代带来的"弊端"。译名室的"权威性"在信息如此畅通的年代开始"打折扣",许多不严谨的翻译流传到网上很可能造成很大的影响。

政要译名　两岸三地大不同

第 44 任美国总统

英文:Barack Hussein Obama
大陆香港译名:奥巴马
台湾译名:欧巴马
第43任美国总统
英文:George Bush
大陆译名:布什
台湾译名:布希
香港译名:布殊
第42任美国总统
英文:Bill Clinton
大陆译名:克林顿
台湾译名:柯林顿
香港译名:两个译名都用
第40任美国总统
英文:Ronald Reagan
大陆译名:里根
台湾译名:雷根
香港译名:列根
第35任美国总统
英文:John Fitzgerald Kennedy
大陆译名:肯尼迪
台湾译名:甘乃迪
香港译名:甘乃地
美国国务卿
英文:Hillary Clinton
大陆译名:希拉里
台湾译名:希拉蕊
香港译名:希拉莉
美国前国务卿
英文:Henry Alfred Kissinger
大陆、香港译名:基辛格
台湾译名:季辛吉
英国第一位女首相
英文:Margaret Thatcher
大陆译名:撒切尔夫人
台湾译名:佘契尔夫人
香港译名:戴卓尔夫人
阿根廷的革命家
西文:Che Guevara

大陆、台湾译名：切·格瓦拉
香港译名：哲·古华拉

拓展阅读

选文A

香港海关关长袁铭辉2009年1月19日在"国际海关节"致辞

财政司司长、各位来宾、各位朋友：

我谨代表香港海关，热烈欢迎各位今晚驾临，与我们一起参与"国际海关节"。今年我们很荣幸，邀请到财政司司长曾俊华先生为我们的主礼嘉宾。大家都知道，曾先生是我的其中一位前任人。他于1999年3月至2007年7月出任关长期间，在提升香港海关的国际地位方面作出了很大的贡献。在曾先生的领导之下，香港于2000年首度获选为世界海关组织亚太地区副主席。曾先生随后在各副主席当中获选，主持于2001年6月举行的世界海关组织议会会议。作为该届议会会议的主席，香港海关对世界海关组织的整体政策方向作出重要的贡献。

我亦想多谢澳门海关关长徐礼恒先生、海关总署缉私局副局长王志先生，以及海关总署广东分署副主任刘广平先生，联同他们的高级官员远道从澳门、北京和广州前来，参与我们今晚的庆祝活动。我再次热烈欢迎你们和非常多谢你们！

世界海关组织每年都会为国际海关节订立特别的主题，以促进海关合作。今年的主题是"海关与环境：保护我们的自然遗产"。

我认为这个主题十分有意义，因为这个主题不单反映国际社会越来越关注保护环境和自然遗产的问题，亦突显现今海关人员的角色和责任越来越多元化。海关传统的主要角色，是征收入口税及消费税，以及防止走私和贩毒。自美国发生9·11袭击后，全球的海关当局在打击恐怖主义方面，已承担更重要的角色。同时，海关往往被正当的贸易商视为做生意的绊脚石，可见我们在透过利便商贸以促进经济增长方面，担当特别的角色。

在香港，海关人员具备多方面的知识和技能。我们不仅肩负海关的传统职责，例如征收税款和打击走私贩毒，而且还是执行保障知识产权法例、规管消费品安全和保障内地游客及本地消费者免受欺诈的唯一机关。

地球是全人类集体拥有的最宝贵资产。我们有责任为我们的后代好好保护我们的环境和自然遗产。随着贸易全球化和交通工具愈趋方便，海关人员必须担当重要的角色，遏止濒危动植物种的走私活动和"对环境敏感"的货物（例如耗蚀臭氧层物质、危险废物，以及化学武器）的非法贸易。

香港海关自2006年9月开始，已参与世界海关组织亚太区情报联络中心（或简称情报联络中心）筹办的"补天行动"计划。该计划旨在打击有关耗蚀臭氧层物质和危险废物的非法贸易。在2007年3月至2008年12月期间，香港海关共向其他海关当局提交222宗有关危险废物的货物报告，并四次就有关疑属耗蚀臭氧层物质的货物通知其他海关当局，以便采取执法行动。香港海关就"补天行动"作出的贡献得到赞赏，并有助情报联络中心获得由美国政府环境保护局颁发的2007年平流层臭氧保护奖。

255

在本港，我们与环境保护署携手推行危险废物的策略管制计划，以致自 2007 年开展该项计划以来已侦破并退回 271 个货柜的危险废物至出口国家。另外，我们亦与渔农自然护理署紧密合作，2006 年至 2008 年期间，成功阻截 391 宗涉及象牙、冷冻鱼翅、犀牛角、红檀香及其他濒危物种的走私案件，涉及物品总值 2 900 万元。

保护环境和我们的自然遗产是全球社会的共同责任。香港海关将会继续在这方面担当其角色。我们在这方面和履行其他职责所取得的成功，有赖本港和世界各国及各地的有关当局、其他政府部门、其他纪律部队及商界向我们提供的协助和合作，而这些机构中有很多已派代表出席今晚的活动。本人谨代表香港海关再次向各位致谢，希望在未来的日子，各位对我们的工作继续提供支持和协助。

谈及历史和传统，今年适逢香港海关成立一百周年。我们会举办一系列庆祝活动，以反映海关在过去一百年的各项重要发展。我们会在稍后时间公布活动详情，希望各位能从百忙中抽空参与我们的一些庆祝活动，分享这份喜悦。我深信只要得到各位支持，我们不单能完成工作和任务，并会在未来一百年继续取得成功。

多谢各位。

译文

Speech by the Commissioner of Customs and Excise, Mr Richard Yuen, on 2009 International Customs Day (January 19, 2009)

The Honourable Financial Secretary, distinguished guests, ladies and gentlemen,

On behalf of the Hong Kong Customs, I would like to extend a very warm welcome to you for being here with us this evening. This year we are most honoured to have the Financial Secretary, Mr John C Tsang, to be our guest of honour for the celebration of International Customs Day. As many of you know, Mr Tsang was one of my predecessors. During his term of office as the Commissioner between March 1999 and July 2001, he did a great job in extending Hong Kong Customs' international presence. Under Mr Tsang's leadership, in the year 2000, Hong Kong was for the first time elected Vice-Chair for the Asia Pacific Region of the World Customs Organisation (WCO). Mr Tsang was subsequently elected among all the vice-chairs to chair the WCO Council Session Meetings in June 2001. As the Chair of the Council Session, Hong Kong Customs made valuable contributions to the overall policy direction of the WCO.

I would also like to thank the Director-General of the Macao Customs Service, Mr Choi Lai Hang; the Deputy Director-General of the Anti-smuggling Bureau of the General Administration of Customs, Mr Wang Zhi, and the Deputy Director-General of the Guangdong Sub-Customs Administration, Mr Liu Guangping, who have come all the way from Macao, Beijing and Guangzhou with their senior colleagues to join our celebration this evening. A very warm welcome and big thank you to you all!

Each year, the World Customs Organisation dedicates International Customs Day to a special theme to promote international Customs co-operation to tackle an issue of common concern. This year, the theme is "Customs and the Environment: Protecting our Natural

Heritage".

I think this is a very meaningful theme, that not only reflects the growing concern of the international community about protecting our environment and our natural heritage, but that also helps to highlight the increasingly diverse roles and responsibilities of customs officers today. Traditionally, the main role of Customs is the collection of import and excise duties and the prevention of smuggling and trafficking in drugs. Since the 9.11 events, Customs administrations around the world have assumed an increasing role in the fight against terrorism. At the same time, the fact that Customs is often seen by bona fide traders as a stumbling block to doing business means that we have to play a key role in promoting economic growth through trade facilitation.

In Hong Kong, the versatility and resourcefulness of Customs officers are taken to such extremes that we are not only responsible for performing our traditional duties as tax collectors and smuggling and drug buster, but we are also responsible for enforcement of intellectual property rights, consumer products safety and acting as a tourist policeman to protect our Mainland tourists and local consumers alike from being ripped off by unscrupulous traders.

The earth is the most valuable common asset that we have as human beings. We owe our future generations a duty to protect the environment and our natural heritage. Globalisation of trade and convenience of travel means customs officers have to play a key role in stopping the smuggling of endangered fauna and flora and the illegal trade in "environmentally sensitive" commodities such as ozone depleting substances, hazardous and other wastes, and chemical weapons.

Since September 2006, Hong Kong Customs has participated in the "Sky-Hole-Patching" project organised by the WCO Regional Intelligence Liaison Office for Asia Pacific(or the RILO office in short). The project aimed at combating the illegal trade on ozone depleting substances and hazardous wastes. From March 2007 to December 2008, Hong Kong Customs had reported a total of 222 cases of hazardous waste shipments and four cases of suspicious shipments of ozone depleting substances to other Customs administrations for taking enforcement action. Our contribution to the "Sky-Hole-Patching" project is duly recognised through the award of the 2007 Stratospheric Ozone Protection Award to the RILO office by the Environmental Protection Agency of the US Government.

Locally, we have joined hands with the Environmental Protection Department in running a Strategic Control Scheme on Hazardous Waste which has led to the detection and return of 271 containers of hazardous wastes to the exporting countries since the scheme started in 2007. We also worked very closely with the Agricultural, Fisheries and Conservation Department and successfully intercepted 391 smuggling cases of ivory tusks, frozen shark's fin, rhino horns, red sandal wood and other endangered species, with a total seizure value of $29 million between 2006 and 2008.

It is the collective responsibility of the world community to protect the environment and our natural heritage. Hong Kong Customs will continue to play its part and our success in doing so would not have been possible without the help and co-operation given to us by our local and international counterparts, other government departments and the business community, many of which are represented here this evening. On behalf of Hong Kong Customs, I would like to thank you again and look forward to your continued support and assistance in future.

Talking about heritage, Hong Kong Customs will celebrate its centenary this year. We plan to organise a series of activities to mark the occasion and reflect on our milestones of development and achievements over the past 100 years. We will let you know the detailed programme when available and I hope you will find time from your busy schedule to join some if not all of our celebration activities and share our joy and the reminiscences of our "collective memories". With your support, I am sure we will not only be able to fulfil our tasks and missions but will also ensure our success in the next 100 years to come.

Thank you very much.

选文B

Proclamation by US President Obama on Earth Day, 2011
April 22, 2011

For over 40 years, our Nation has come together on Earth Day to appreciate and raise awareness about our environment, natural heritage, and the resources upon which generations of Americans have depended. Healthy land and clean water and air are essential to the health of our communities and wildlife. Earth Day is an opportunity to renew America's commitment to preserving and protecting the state of our environment through community service and responsible stewardship.

From the purity of the air we breathe and the water we drink to the condition of the land where we live, work, and play, the vitality of our natural resources has a profound influence on the well-being of our families and the strength of our economy. Our Nation has a proud conservation tradition, which includes countless individuals who have worked to safeguard our natural legacy and ensure our children can benefit from these resources. Looking to the future of our planet, American leadership will continue to be pivotal as we confront the environmental challenges that threaten the health of both our country and the globe.

Today, our world faces the major global environmental challenge of a changing climate. Our entire planet must address this problem because no nation, however large or small, wealthy or poor, can escape the impact of climate change. The United States can be a leader in reducing the dangerous pollution that causes global warming and can propel these advances by investing in the clean energy technologies, markets, and practices that will empower us to win the future.

While our changing climate requires international leadership, global action on clean energy and climate change must be joined with local action. Every American deserves the cleanest air, the safest water, and unpolluted land, and each person can take steps to protect those precious resources. When we reduce environmental hazards, especially in our most overburdened and polluted cities and neighborhoods, we prioritize the health of our families, and move towards building the clean energy economy of the 21st century.

To meet this responsibility, Federal and local programs will continue to ensure our Nation's clean air and water laws are effective, that our communities are protected from contaminated sites and other pollution, and that our children are safe from chemicals, toxins, and other environmental threats. Partnerships and community-driven strategies, like those highlighted by the America's Great Outdoors Initiative, are vital to building a future where children have access to outdoor places close to their homes; where our rural working lands and waters are conserved and restored; and our parks, forests, waters, and other natural areas are protected for future generations.

On Earth Day, we recognize the role that each of us can play in preserving our natural heritage. To protect our environment, keep our communities healthy, and help develop the economy of the future, I encourage all Americans to visit www. WhiteHouse. Gov/Earth Day to learn ways to protect and preserve our environment for centuries to come.

NOW, THEREFORE, I, BARACK OBAMA, President of the United States of America, by virtue of the authority vested in me by the Constitution and the laws of the United States, do hereby proclaim April 22, 2011, as Earth Day. I encourage all Americans to participate in service programs and activities that will protect our environment and contribute to a prosperous, healthy, and sustainable future.

IN WITNESS WHEREOF, I have hereunto set my hand this twenty-second day of April, in the year of our Lord two thousand eleven, and of the Independence of the United States of America the two hundred and thirty-fifth.

BARACK OBAMA

译文

美国总统奥巴马2011年地球日公告

2011年4月22日

40多年来,我们国家一直在"地球日"这天共同赞美我们的环境、我们的大自然遗产以及世代美国人所赖以为生的各种资源,同时提高对它们的认识。肥沃的土壤、清洁的水源和空气是我们的社区以及野生动植物的健康之本。我们在"地球日"之际重申,美国致力于通过社区服务和负责任的管理来维护和保护环境。

从我们呼吸的空气和饮水的清新纯净,到我们赖以生活、工作和娱乐的土地的状况,自然资源的活力对我们的家庭福祉与经济力量具有深刻影响。我国有着令人骄傲的保护自然资源的传统,其中包含着志在维护我国大自然遗产和确保子孙后代从中受益的无数个人努力。展望我们这个星球的未来,美国的领导力量将继续对战胜给我国和全球健康带来威胁的环境挑战具有关键作用。

今天,我们的世界面临着气候变化这一重大全球环境挑战。这个问题必须由我们整个星球来解决,因为没有一个国家,不论大小、贫富,能够摆脱气候变化的影响。美国可以在减少造成全球变暖的危险污染方面发挥带头作用,通过对清洁能源技术、市场和方式进行投资,推动进步。这将使我们赢得未来。

应对气候变化要求有国际化的领导力量,但是,针对清洁能源和气候变化的全球行动必须与地方行动相结合。每一个美国人都应享有最清新的空气、最安全的饮水和未受污染的土地,而且每个人都可以采取措施保护这些宝贵的资源。当我们减少环境危害,特别是在那些负荷过重、饱受污染的城市和街区这样做时,我们是在将家庭健康放在第一位,是在向建设21世纪的清洁能源经济前进。

为了履行这一责任,联邦和地方项目将继续保证我国清洁空气和水的法律行之有效,我们的社区不受污染区和其他污染源的危害,我们的孩子不受化学品、有毒物质和其他环境威胁的侵害。《美国大户外倡议》所体现的以合作伙伴关系和社区为动力的战略,对于建立这样一个未来至关重要——那就是:让孩子在自己住家附近有户外活动场所;让我们农耕地和水源得到保护和恢复;让我们的公园、森林、水域和其他自然环境为了子孙后代而受到保护。

在"地球日",我们认识到我们每一个人能够为保护大自然遗产所发挥的作用。为了保护我们的环境、维持我们社区的健康,并促进发展未来的经济,我敦促所有美国人登录www.WhiteHouse.Gov/EarthDay,了解如何将我们的环境千百年地保护与保存下去。

为此,我,美利坚合众国总统巴拉克·奥巴马,以美国宪法和法律赋予我的权力,特此宣布2011年4月22日为"地球日"。我敦促所有美国人参与环保服务与活动,并为建设一个繁荣、健康、可持续的未来贡献力量。

我谨于公元2011年,即美利坚合众国独立第二百三十五年之4月22日,亲笔在此签名为证。

巴拉克·奥巴马

第十二单元 法律事务
（Legal Affairs）

单元要点

本单元共分五个层次，分别是：加拿大驻华大使在中国杰赛普国际法模拟法庭辩论赛决赛开幕式上的讲话英译汉一篇；香港终审法院首席法官 2010 年法律年度开启典礼致辞（节选）英译汉一篇；口译中的跨文化因素；法庭口译的类别和特点；拓展阅读（汉译英、英译汉各一篇）。第一、二部分提供法律事务口译的例文及其翻译和重难点评析；第三、四部分主要是相关口译理论与技能的介绍；第五部分的拓展阅读中，提供汉、英原文和参考译文。

理论难点提示

1. 口译中的跨文化因素。
2. 法庭口译的类别和特点。

选文A

Remarks at the Opening Ceremony of China Finals of the Jessup International Law Moot Court Competition

by Canadian Ambassador David Mulroney

March 1, 2010

【用中文说】 今天，我很高兴来这里参加中国第八届杰赛普（Jessup）国际法模拟法庭辩论赛开幕式，这是迄今在中国举办的最大规模的杰赛普国际法模拟法庭辩论赛。

It is with honour — and humility — that I appear before you, surrounded by judges of the highest standing, as well as by China's best law students and professors, those who will shape the legal and judicial profession for decades to come.

During the week, you will be called to represent the interests of both sides of the moot case. You will use the legal analysis and advocacy skills you have developed at law school to convince judges with arguments based on established rules found in public international law. A body of normative, predictable, binding rules is inseparable from the rule of law. I therefore submit to you that the Jessup competition is, in itself, an exercise in the rule of law at work.

Now, domestically, the rule of law also constitutes a fundamental element of any thriving society. In Canada, our Supreme Court has described a number of core principles underpinning the rule of law. One of them is that "the relationship between the state and the individual be regulated by law". Another is that "the law is supreme over officials of the government as well as private individuals, and thereby preclusive of the influence of arbitrary power". Jurists have an important role to play in upholding these principles and giving them a concrete expression.

Let me now say a few words about lasting Canadian contributions to the development of international law over the years. I will draw on two examples.

John Humphrey, a Law Professor at McGill University in Montreal, was invited in 1946 to become the new United Nations' first Director of Human Rights and to take on the intimidating task of developing a basic document on this subject. His efforts led to the foundation of the Universal Declaration of Human Rights, famously called by Eleanor Roosevelt "the Magna Carta of all mankind". Now translated into 321 languages and dialects, the Declaration is the most cited legal document ever drafted by a Canadian.

More recently, Canada has played a leading role in the creation of the Rome Statute of the International Criminal Court, another turning point in the history and development of international justice. Its first President, from 2003 to 2009, was also a Canadian, Ambassador Philippe Kirsch.

In addition to legal cooperation, Canada and China work together in many fields. The recent visit to China of the Prime Minister of Canada, the Right Honourable Stephen Harper, and the ensuing Canada-China Joint Statement, have set the tone for a new era in Canada-China relations. 2010 will also be a hallmark year in terms of the Canada-China relationship, with a series of high-profile events.

—The Vancouver Winter Olympics saw Chinese athletes reach new summits in their medal tally — congratulations to Team China;

—We are excited about Canada's showcase Pavilion at the Shanghai 2010 World Expo and the appointment of Canadian cultural ambassador Da Shan as our Commissioner General;

—The G-20 Summit of leading world economies will be held in Toronto in June, and will see a return visit to Canada by China's leader;

—The 40th anniversary of diplomatic relations this year will be marked by a series of events.

The year ahead offers Canada and China opportunities to take our relationship to what Prime Minister Harper and Premier Wen Jiabao have described as a "significant new era."

Now, let me get to my brief. Canada is a prime destination for world-class, high-quality, affordable international education, in particular in law. Canada has the further advantage of being at the crossroads of the world's two main legal traditions, the civil law system and the common-law system. It is my respectful submission that students assembled here consider seriously Canada as their destination for top-quality graduate legal education.

In closing, I congratulate Renmin University for hosting this important event and wish you all a very good week at the Jessup Finals. This offers an exceptional opportunity to anticipate experiences you will have as jurists, when you argue real cases in China and internationally.

〔用中文说〕不管本周你们辩论的结果如何,请考虑去加拿大继续你们的法律教育。Thank you.

重难点评析

1. "shape the legal and judicial profession for decades to come"为符合中文的表达习惯译为"决定未来数十年法律和司法职业的走向"。

2. "the legal analysis and advocacy skills"译为"法律分析和控辩技巧","arguments based on established rules found in public international law"译为"国际公法中基于既定规则的论点"。

3. "A body of normative, predictable, binding rules is inseparable from the rule of law."句中"a body of/a lot of"译为"大量的","be inseparable from"译为"与……不可分离"。全句译为"大量的规范性、可预测性、约束性规则与法治是分不开的"。

4. "a number of core principles underpinning the rule of law"译为"支撑法治的一系列核心原则。"

5. "... and thereby preclusive of the influence of arbitrary power"句中"be preclusive of"译为"将……排除在外"。此句译为"从而排除肆意权力的影响"。

6. "..., another turning point in the history and development of international justice."此句采用了增译法,译为"这是国际司法历史和发展方面的另一个转折点"。

7. "set the tone for"译为"为……定下基调"。

8. "2010 will also be a hallmark year in terms of the Canada-China relationship, with a series of high-profile events."此句采用了增译法。"a hallmark year"译为"标志性的一年","a series of high-profile events"译为"一系列备受瞩目的活动"。

9. "The Vancouver Winter Olympics saw Chinese athletes reach new summits in their medal tally."此处不能将 saw 直译,应该意译为"在温哥华冬奥会上,中国运动员在奖牌榜上创造历史记录"。

10. "Now, let me get to my brief."译为"现在,让我总结一下。"

11. "... at the crossroads of the world's two main legal traditions, the civil law system and the common-law system."句中"at the crossroads of"意思是"位于……的交界口",此处根据上下文意译为"集……之大成"。"the civil law system and the common-law system"译为"民事法律制度和普通法制度"。

译 文

在中国杰赛普国际法模拟法庭辩论赛决赛开幕式上的讲话
加拿大驻华大使 马大维
2010年3月1日

[Said in Mandarin] I am delighted to be here today for the opening of the China Finals of the Jessup International Law Moot Court Competition, the largest Jessup finals ever held in China.

我站在你们面前,感到既荣幸又谦卑,我被最高法官们、中国最出色的法律专业学生、教授所围绕,你们将决定未来数十年法律和司法职业的走向。

在这一周里,你们将被要求代表假设案例双方的利益。你们将使用在法学院学到的法律分析和控辩技巧,寻找国际公法中基于既定规则的论点,以说服法官。大量的规范性、可预测性、约束性规则与法治是分不开的。因此我认为,杰赛普国际法模拟法庭辩论赛,本身就是一次法治的体现。

现在的国内,法治仍是构成任何繁荣社会的基本要素。在加拿大,我们最高法院已经描述了支撑法治的一系列核心原则。其中一条是,"国家与个人的关系由法律规定"。另一条是,"法律无论是对于政府官员还是平民百姓来说,都是至高无上的,从而排除肆意权力的影响"。法学家在坚持上述原则、具体体现这些原则方面,发挥重要作用。

现在让我谈一谈多年来加拿大对国际法发展所作出的持久贡献。我将引用两个例子。

约翰·汉弗莱是蒙特利尔麦吉尔大学的法学教授,他于1946年应邀成为新联合国的人权委员会第一任主任,并担负起一项挑战性十足的任务——就人权主题起草一个基本文件。他的努力产生了《世界人权宣言》,被埃莉诺·罗斯福称为"全人类大宪章"而著名。该宣言现已被翻译成321种语言和方言,是有史以来由加拿大人起草的最常被引用的法律文件。

最近,加拿大在制定国际刑事法院罗马规约方面起了主导作用,这是国际司法历史和发展方面的另一个转折点。2003年至2009年,国际刑事法院首任院长菲利普·基尔希大使,也是加拿大人。

除了法律合作以外,加拿大和中国还在许多领域合作。加拿大总理斯蒂芬·哈珀最近对中国的访问,以及随后发表的加拿大—中国联合声明,已为新时代的加中关系定下了基调。在加中关系方面,2010年还将是标志性的一年,我们将举办一系列备受瞩目的活动。

——在温哥华冬奥会上,中国运动员在奖牌榜上创造历史记录——我们向中国体育代表团表示祝贺。

——我们为2010年上海世博会加拿大展馆,以及任命加拿大文化大使大山为加拿大总代表而感到高兴。

——世界主要经济体二十国峰会将于6月在多伦多举行,并且中国领导人将回访加拿大。

——今年将举行一系列活动,庆祝加中建交40周年。

新的一年为加拿大和中国提供了机会,使我们两国关系进入到哈珀总理和温家宝总理所描述的"重要新时代"。

现在,让我总结一下。加拿大是世界级、高质量、可负担的国际教育主要目的地国,尤其在法律教育上。加拿大的进一步优势,是集世界两个主要法律传统——民事法律制度和普通法制度的大成。我的建议是,在座的学生可认真考虑加拿大作为他们高质量研究生法律教育的目的地。

最后,我祝贺人民大学主办这项重要活动,祝愿大家在杰塞普国际法模拟法庭辩论赛的一周里有出色表现。这提供了一个特殊的机会,当你们辩论在中国和国际上的真实案例时,你们将获得作为法学家的经验。

[Said in Mandarin] And no matter your results this week, think Canada for the continuation of your legal education.

谢谢大家。

选文B

CJ's Speech at Ceremonial Opening of the Legal Year 2010 (Excerpt)

Secretary for Justice, Mr Chairman, Mr President, Distinguished Guests, Ladies and Gentlemen,

On behalf of all my colleagues in the Judiciary, I would like to welcome all of you warmly to this Opening of the Legal Year. I thank you sincerely for your support by your presence. This is the 13th and the last address which I have the honour of giving at this event.

Role of the Judiciary

Each jurisdiction has its own constitutional arrangements distributing power between the executive, legislative and judicial branches and providing for the relationships between them. The arrangement for each jurisdiction reflects its own history and its own circumstances. The arrangement for one jurisdiction may not be appropriate for another.

It is important for the role of the independent Judiciary in Hong Kong to be reiterated and strongly emphasized and for its role to be clearly understood. The Hong Kong's system involves checks and balances between the Executive, the Legislature and the Judiciary. The independent Judiciary has a vital constitutional role to ensure that the acts of the Executive and the Legislature comply fully with the Basic Law and the law and that our fundamental rights and freedoms, which are at the heart of Hong Kong's system, are fully safeguarded.

Everyone, including all organs of government and all public officials, are subject to and equal before the law. The Judiciary is and must be seen to be impartial. Judges resolve all disputes, whether between citizens or between citizen and government in an impartial manner.

In dealing with cases involving the Executive or the Legislature, judges adopt neither a confrontational approach nor an approach designed to favour them. They simply administer justice without fear or favour. So where the Executive or the Legislature is successful in a case, this is not the result of the court seeking to favour them. Equally where a judgment goes against the Executive or the Legislature, the court is not seeking to confront them. In either case, the court is simply discharging its constitutional duty of adjudicating the dispute fairly and impartially.

Judicial review

A major development in the legal landscape since 1997 has undoubtedly been the growth of judicial review. Excluding the right of abode cases, 116 applications for judicial review were filed in 2001. In 2005, the number had grown to 149. In the last few years, the number ranged from 132 in 2006 to 147 in 2008. In 2009, 144 applications were filed.

This is a common phenomenon in many common law jurisdictions. I have previously explained publicly the factors which have led to it in the Hong Kong context: the growth in the volume of legislation to deal with an increasingly complex society, the enactment of the Bill of Rights and the Basic Law and the greater awareness on the part of citizens of their rights. I have also previously made clear that the court's role on judicial review is only to define the limits of legality. And that the solution to political, social and economic problems cannot be found through the legal process and can only be found through the political process.

The Court of Final Appeal

Over the last 12 years, the Court of Final Appeal has been functioning smoothly. The Court is now hearing about 40 appeals a year and dealing with about 150 applications for leave to appeal, of which about 50%~60% are disposed of on the papers without a hearing.

The participation of one non-permanent overseas judge in the collegiate court of five judges drawn from a panel of eminent judges from Australia, New Zealand and the United Kingdom has worked well. Of course, as is well appreciated by the overseas judges, when they sit on the Court, they function as and only as Hong Kong judges in Hong Kong's own circumstances under "one country, two systems". I am delighted to have on the platform today as part of our Judiciary, Sir Anthony Mason, the former Chief Justice of Australia, who has made such a signal contribution to our Court.

The Court is a relatively young court and we have much to learn. The Court's jurisprudence has been increasingly cited in other common law jurisdictions. I would venture to suggest that it has made good progress in establishing its stature.

Planning work is proceeding on the relocation of the Court to the present Legislative Council Building. Renovation works cannot start until the Council moves and the relocation may be made in around 2014. The Building will presumably be the Court's permanent home and in order to ensure that the people of Hong Kong can be justly proud of it, we should make haste slowly in getting it ready.

I for one shall be nostalgic for the French Mission Building where the Court spent its formative years and which holds so many memories of the challenges during my tenure. But it will be time to move on.

Exchanges with other Jurisdictions

Under "one country, two systems", it is of course important that judges in the Mainland and Hong Kong have a mutual understanding of each other's system and the differences between them. In the last 12 years, we have made great efforts to develop this through conferences, visits, courses and the like. As the only common law jurisdiction in

China under "one country, two systems", it is equally important that Hong Kong continues to maintain its links with leading common law jurisdictions through similar activities.

Civil Justice Reform and Mediation

Civil Justice Reform has been a major exercise. Under the leadership of the Chief Judge of the High Court and with the support of judges and supporting staff, its implementation in April 2009 went smoothly. But it will take some time for the Reform to fully settle in. A central feature is active case management by the court. In due time, this will bring about a change of culture in the conduct of litigation which would increase cost-effectiveness and ensure expedition. Another key feature is the facilitation by the court of the settlement of disputes by encouraging parties to engage in mediation. The relevant Practice Direction came into force on 1 January. It is expected that mediated settlements satisfactory to the parties will significantly increase. A Committee chaired by the Chief Judge is monitoring the working of the reformed system.

Conclusion

Since I shall only be stepping down at the end of August, I shall not be bidding farewell now. This will be done at a farewell sitting in the Court of Final Appeal in July.

On this occasion, I shall only say that it has been the greatest honour of my life to serve as your Chief Justice and to be given an opportunity to contribute at this dawn of the new constitutional order of Hong Kong as part of China under "one country, two systems".

It remains for me to wish you on behalf of all my colleagues in the Judiciary good health and every happiness in the new year. Thank you.

重难点评析

1. "This is the 13th and the last address which I have the honor of giving at this event."句中"have the honor of"译为"为……感到荣幸"。根据中文的表达习惯，此句使用分译法译成了两句话，"本人在法律年度开启典礼上致辞，实感荣幸；这是我上任以来第十三次，也是最后一次在这典礼上致辞"，并且在第一个分句中增译了"本人在法律年度开启典礼上致辞"。

2. "executive, legislative and judicial branches"译为"行政、立法与司法机关"。

3. "The Hong Kong's system involves checks and balances between the Executive, the Legislature and the Judiciary."句中"checks and balances"译为"权力制衡"，"the Executive, the Legislature and the Judiciary"译为"行政、立法和司法机关"。

4. "Everyone, including all organs of government and all public officials, are subject to and equal before the law."由于"be subject to"和"equal before the law"的两层含义，此句用分译法译成了两句话，"法律面前，人人平等。我们必须遵守法律，所有政府机关及全部公职人员均须如此"。

5. "In the last few years, the number ranged from 132 in 2006 to 147 in 2008."译为

"过去数年,司法覆核申请的数目介乎2006年的132宗至2008年的147宗。""range from...to..."译为"从……到……,介于……之间"。

6. "I have previously explained publicly the factors which have led to it in the Hong Kong context: the growth in the volume of legislation to deal with an increasingly complex society, the enactment of the Bill of Rights and the Basic Law and the greater awareness on the part of citizens of their rights."作为导致香港社会出现这个现象的三个因素,原话是三个名词短语,译者根据中文的习惯译成了三个并列的短句,"随着社会日趋复杂,法例的制定也日见繁多;还有是《人权法案》及《基本法》的制定;此外,社会各界对公民权利的意识亦日渐提高"。

7. "The participation of one non-permanent overseas judge in the collegiate court of five judges drawn from a panel of eminent judges from Australia, New Zealand and the United Kingdom has worked well."此处采用了分译法将这个长句分译成了几个小短句,层次分明,表述清楚,全句译为"终审法院合议庭由五位法官组成,包括一位海外的非常任法官,这做法一向运作良好,这些海外的非常任法官是澳洲、新西兰及英国的著名法官"。

8. "make haste slowly in getting it ready"译为"周详筹划,让大楼设施完备"。

9. "I for one shall be nostalgic for the French Mission Building where the Court spent its formative years and which holds so many memories of the challenges during my tenure."这是个长句子,对由where和which引导的定语从句成分在翻译时采用了分译法并且根据中文的表达习惯采用了意译,全句译为"日后,我定会怀念这座前法国外方传道会大楼,这个地方毕竟见证了法院的成长,还载有我在任期间经历挑战的回忆"。

10. "In due time, this will bring about a change of culture in the conduct of litigation which would increase cost-effectiveness and ensure expedition."主句和定语从句在翻译时根据上下文处理成了因果关系,全句译为"假以时日,这将改变我们的诉讼文化,从而提高成本效益,并确保案件得以迅速处理"。

译文

香港终审法院首席法官2010年法律年度开启典礼致辞(节选)

律政司司长、大律师公会主席、律师会会长、各位嘉宾:

我谨代表司法机构全体人员,热烈欢迎各位莅临本年度的法律年度开启典礼,并衷心感谢在座各位出席支持。本人在法律年度开启典礼上致辞,实感荣幸;这是我上任以来第十三次,也是最后一次在这典礼上致辞。

司法机关的角色

每一个司法管辖区都有各自的宪制安排,分配行政、立法与司法机关的权力,以及三者的相互关系。每一司法管辖区的安排,均反映本身的历史背景及本身的情况。一个司法管辖区的安排,对另一管辖区而言,未必适合。

对香港而言,一个独立司法机关所担当的角色,须予以重申及强调,并为各界清晰理解,这是很重要的。在香港的制度下,行政、立法和司法机关互相制衡。在宪制上,独立的司法机关肩负重要任务,确保行政、立法机关的运作完全符合《基本法》和法律的规定,以及确保市民的基本权利和自由得到充分保障。这些基本权利和自由正是香港制度的精义所在。

法律面前,人人平等。我们必须遵守法律,所有政府机关及全部公职人员均须如此。司法机关不单要不偏不倚,还要让人看得见我们行事是不偏不倚的。法官审理纠纷,不论是市民之间,或是市民与政府之间的纠纷,均以不偏不倚的态度作出裁决。

在处理涉及行政或立法机关的案件时,法官既不采取对抗态度,亦不刻意偏袒任何一方。法官的职责是执行司法工作,无惧无偏。若行政或立法机关胜诉,这不是因为法庭有意偏袒。同样,若判行政或立法机关败诉,也不是因为法庭有意对抗。无论判决如何,法庭都只是履行宪法职能,公平公正地审理案件。

司法覆核

自1997年以来,法律环境的其中一项重要发展,无疑是司法覆核案件的增加。撇除居港权案件,2001年共有116宗司法覆核申请,至2005年已升至149宗。过去数年,司法覆核申请的数目介乎2006年的132宗至2008年的147宗。2009年,入禀的司法覆核申请共有144宗。

这个现象在许多普通法适用地区亦属常见。我在此之前已公开阐明,引致香港社会出现这个现象的因素包括:随着社会日趋复杂,法例的制定也日见繁多;还有是《人权法案》及《基本法》的制定;此外,社会各界对公民权利的意识亦日渐提高。我亦早已表明,法庭在司法覆核程序的职能,仅是厘定合法性的界限。政治、社会或经济问题,只能经由政治过程,而非通过法律程序去谋求解决办法。

终审法院

终审法院在过去12年一直运作畅顺。法院现时每年聆讯约40宗上诉,以及处理约150宗上诉许可申请,其中约有50%~60%的申请是根据文件处理,而毋须进行聆讯的。

终审法院合议庭由五位法官组成,包括一位海外的非常任法官,这做法一向运作良好,这些海外的非常任法官是澳洲、新西兰及英国的著名法官。当然,来自海外的法官深明,参与终审法院的聆讯时,他们是在"一国两制"下的香港,履行香港法官的职责,亦仅限于香港法官的职责。今天,前澳洲首席法官梅师贤爵士,以我们司法体系一员的身份,一同在台上参与典礼,我实感高兴。梅师贤爵士对终审法院实在贡献良多。

相对来说,终审法院仍是一个比较新的终审法院,还需进一步累积经验,但终审法院在法理方面的论述,已日渐广为其他普通法适用地区援引。我敢说,终审法院在建立其地位的过程上,已取得良好进展。

终审法院迁往立法会现址的策划工作已经展开,至于修建工程,则须待立法会迁出方可进行。预计终审法院可于2014年左右搬迁,相信这会是法院的永久院址。正因如此,我们必须周详筹划,让大楼设施完备,使香港市民以此为荣。

日后,我定会怀念这座前法国外方传道会大楼,这个地方毕竟见证了法院的成长,还载有我在任期间经历挑战的回忆。然而,我们都总是要迈步向前。

与其他司法管辖区的交流

在"一国两制"下,内地与香港法官对两地制度,以及彼此的差异都应相互了解,这一点当然重要。过去12年,我们一直致力于举办会议、互访及研讨课程等活动,促进彼此交流。另一方面,香港是"一国两制"下中国境内唯一的普通法司法管辖区,我们透过同类交流活动,与其他主要的普通法适用地区继续维持联系,亦同样重要。

民事司法制度改革及调解

民事司法制度改革是大型的改革工作。在高等法院首席法官领导,及其他法官和支援人员协助下,民事司法制度改革已于2009年4月顺利实施。然而,要完全稳固改革后的制度,仍需要一段时间。积极的案件管理是改革的重点。假以时日,这将改变我们的诉讼文化,从而提高成本效益,并确保案件得以迅速处理。另一特点是由法庭鼓励争议各方采用调解来解决纠纷。有关的实务指示已于1月1日生效。通过调解而圆满解决纠纷的个案,预期会显著增加。至于改革后制度的运作,现正由高等法院首席法官担任主席的委员会监察有关情况。

结语

我于八月底才离任,所以不在此跟各位道别,还是留待七月我在终审法院的仪式时,才与各位话别。

今天,我只想说:香港在"一国两制"下回归中国,在新宪制下,我出任香港终审法院首席法官,有机会在这新时代出一份力,是我一生的最高荣誉。

最后,我谨代表司法机构全体人员,祝愿各位身体健康、新年快乐!多谢各位!

口译中的跨文化因素

一、理论学习

1. 跨文化交际的概念

语言既是思维工具,也是交际工具;不仅是语音文字的结合,更是文化的载体。语言是民族的重要特征之一。

因此,在架设两种语言世界的沟通桥梁中,口译具有两个基本功能:语言转换功能和跨文化交际功能。在实战中,口译员不仅要能够将两种语言熟练的转换,还要能够发挥文化协调的作用,清除文化差异引起的误解。

文化:与自然相对,英文中culture的本意便是"耕作"(与农业agriculture有关),它是人类认识自然、改造自然的成果。文化包括价值观念、语言、信仰、社会习俗、艺术等各个方面。

交际:信息的传播与共享。交际的三要素:发送者、信息、接收者。口译活动就是交际的一种。交际的特点是动态的、互动的、社会的。

跨文化交际:来自不同文化背景的人之间传递信息、交流思想的一种社会行为。

2. 如何培养跨文化交际意识

从认识的角度:

增强母语文化底蕴,这是学习口译的立足点和根本。

了解文化的多元性,加强对中西方文化的对比学习。

树立文化间的平等意识,端正态度,一视同仁,不贬低或崇拜某一文化。

从行为的角度:

广泛学习,扩大视野,扩大知识面。

具体问题具体对待,掌握跨文化交际技巧。

从实践中积累经验、总结教训。

二、口译中的文化因素

1. 思维因素

英语文化：直线思维，直接明了，强调理性、分析、逻辑关联，看重结果。例：英语信函地址是由小到大的顺序。

中国文化：曲线思维，含蓄婉转，强调整体、铺陈、隐含、象征，看重过程。例：外国人有时候抱怨中国人谈判时兜圈子。

2. 时间观念

西方人：侧重于客观认知，发明了钟表，准确到分秒，重视守时。

中国人：侧重于主观感受，时间的准确性比较模糊，古代2个小时为一个时辰，提到时间可能是"一炷香的功夫"，不是特别守时。

西方人：看重未来，多关注之后的展望，更具创新精神。

中国人：看重过去，"前事不忘后事之师"、"5000年历史的文明古国"。

例如，对于"老"的概念，中国文化中体现的是"资历"、"经验"，带有尊敬的意味。而在英语文化中"old"的概念往往体现的是"past"、"out of date"，带有歧视的意味。因此中文中提到"老教授、老专家、老先生……"时，口译为英语时通常不要提到"old"的概念，而是直接译为"professor, expert, sir..."

3. 认知差异

（1）颜色喜好

以红白颜色为例，中国人提到红色联想到的是太阳、火焰的颜色，感到温暖和喜庆。例如：而白色在中国文化中常常与丧事相关，因此中国人的传统结婚礼服会选择红色。

西方人提到红色联想到的是鲜血的颜色，感到暴力和血腥。例如："red alert（红色警报）、red battle（血腥的战斗）"。而白色在西方文化中是"干净"、"纯洁"的象征，因此西方的结婚礼服不会选择红色，而是白色的婚纱。

以下表达中同样反映出中西方文化对颜色的感官和认知差异：

红糖 brown sugar；红茶 black tea；黄色电影 blue film

（2）动物喜好

以猫狗为例，中国文化中很多时候将狗视为贬义：狗腿子、狗崽子……而在西方文化中狗被视为人类最好的朋友，带有宠爱之意：lucky dog，clever dog... 对于猫，中国人喜好一般，偏褒义，由猫捉老鼠联想到猫的勇敢："不管白猫黑猫，能捉到老鼠就是好猫。"而在西方文化中cat往往是恶毒、邪恶的象征：old cat（臭老太婆）。

除了颜色、动物喜好外，类似的认知差异还有很多，在此不一一举例。

4. 数量概念

（1）数量的表达

汉语四位数一断，英语三位数一断；

汉语看重过程，说八折；英语看重结果，说20%off。

（2）数量的认知

中国人对于数字注重综合，而西方人注重分析。

以购物付钱为例，中国人付钱先想到的是总数，付款时由大到小。而西方人先想到的是零头,付款时先付小数目的钱,再付大面额的钱。

(3) 数字的象征意义

中西方文化对于数字都情有独钟,中国人往往因数字的发音对数字产生好恶,而西方人多因数字的宗教内涵对数字产生好恶。

① 中西方都喜爱的数字

中国人用"三"代表全部和总括。"三个代表"、"三大纪律"、"三番五次"

西方人同样把"three"看做完美,主要是受到基督文化的影响。"圣父圣子圣灵三位一体"。

All good things go by three. (Shakespeare)

近代中国人因"八"与"发"谐音而偏爱这一数字,认为它是财富的象征。

西方人提到"eight"也多联想到"好运、幸福"的含义。

② 中国人偏爱的数字

中国人认为"九"是个位数中最大的数字,表示"最高、最大、最久":"九五至尊"、"一言九鼎"、"九天揽月"……数字9在西方文化中没有如此尊贵,但也可以表示"多、深"的含义:cloud nine(非常高兴)。

中国人普遍认为"六"代表和谐和顺利之意。"六六大顺"、"一路(陆)顺风"。而在西方文化中 six 却带有不吉利的内涵。

③ 中国人讨厌的数字

因为"四"与中文的"死"谐音,数字"四"往往不被中国人喜欢,而在西方文化中,数字4常有公平正义之意。

④ 西方人偏爱的数字

西方人视 seven 为神圣,上帝造万物用了七天,很多好的事情都与七有关。而中国人有时会认为"七"与"气"谐音,表示"生气";而且"七"在中国传统文化中经常与"头七"产生联系,是不吉利的象征。

⑤ 西方人讨厌的数字

5是西方文化中公认的 unlucky number,主要原因是在《圣经》中背叛耶稣的犹大被认为是耶稣的第 13 个门徒,耶稣受难的日子是在星期五,如果某一天既是 13 号,又赶上星期五,那这一天便被称为 Black Friday(黑色星期五),历史上很多不好的事情都巧合的发生在黑色星期五,更增加了西方人的迷信。

5. **价值观念**

中国人谦虚客气,经常会让西方人感到谦虚过度,莫名其妙。例如,中国主人经常会说"招待不周"、"饭菜不好"这样的谦虚客套话,而西方人听来就会信以为真,感到诧异。

例:一路上您辛苦啦!

误译:You must be very tired! 这会让听者认为自己是否面容憔悴才让对方说出此话。

正译:How was the flight?

东方文化注重整体,看重集体;而西方文化强调个体,看重个人。因此对于中国人来说可以接受的询问个人隐私的话题在西方文化中是一大禁忌。这些禁忌包括不要询问个人的年龄、婚姻状况、宗教信仰、政治主张等。

如果在外事活动中一旦由于中方发言人不了解或不经意提到了这些禁忌,而又为了

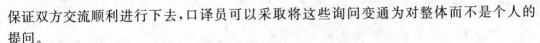

保证双方交流顺利进行下去,口译员可以采取将这些询问变通为对整体而不是个人的提问。

例如:当中方发言人不经意间对外方客人问道:"我想您这个高级经理年薪怎么也得有5万美元吧?"译员便可以译为:"I guess a senior manager working for big companies would get paid around 50 thousand dollars per year, am I right?"

6. 风俗礼仪

中西方文化中都有大量不同的风俗礼仪,在口译活动中译员还要注意避免由于风俗礼仪不同造成的尴尬和误解。例如西方人口中经常会有"dear(亲爱的)"这样的称呼,译员要注意说话对象之间的关系,以免引起误会。

三、跨文化交际口译的三大难点

1. 成语、习语、俗语的口译

对等口译:英汉两种语言中有一部分 idioms 彼此存在对应的表达(不是词的对等,而是意义的对等),或者由于文化交流的影响一方对另一方的表达已经熟知,这时可以直接采取对等口译。译员平时要注意积累这样的对等表达,口译时便可驾轻就熟。

例:七上八下 at sixes and sevens;

Trojan Horse 特洛伊木马。

舍形取义:更多的时候是 idioms 仅在单一文化中出现,无法找到另一种语言的counterpart,这时可以采取意译的方法。

例:一条龙服务中心 one package service center;

Achilles' heel 致命要害。

借用:如果在一种语言中的表达所反映的内涵刚好能在另一种语言中找到类似的表达,这时可以不妨采取借用加补充的方法。当然,这种方法还是需要译员平时有敏锐的观察和大量的积累。

例:游泳馆池里人多得像下饺子一样。The swimming pool is packed like sardines.

清明节:如果一时忘记了 Tomb-sweeping Day 的译法,可以说:It's a Chinese traditional Memorial Day(美国对阵亡战士的纪念日),but it is usually in memory of our ancestors.

2. 诗词、名言、警句的口译

阐释补充:在中西方交流中,发言人还经常有引用诗词、名言等情况。口译时通常采取"意译诗词原句+补充背景知识"的方法。

To be or not to be, that is the question.

莎士比亚在《哈姆雷特》中说过一句名言:生存还是死亡,这是个问题。

温总理答记者问的经典口译片段:

"在我当选以后,我心里总默念着林则徐的两句诗:苟利国家生死以,岂因祸福避趋之。这就是我今后工作的态度。"

Since I became premier, I have been whispering two lines written by Lin Zexu(a patriotic Qing Dynasty official in the 19th century) to myself. And they are: I will do whatever it takes to serve my country even at the cost of my own life, regardless of fortune or misfortune to myself. This will be the attitude in which I will start my work.

我总记得一句古训:生于忧患,死于安乐。

I always pay a lot of attention to an ancient motto, that is, one prospers in worries and hardship, and perishes in ease and comfort.

3. 幽默、玩笑、讽刺的口译

幽默或开玩笑是口译最难的一种情况,然而在很多场合发言人为了调动听众的情绪,增加讲话的感染力,往往乐于使用幽默的表达,译员这时要具体情况具体对待,如果幽默比较容易理解,直接口译即可,如果幽默翻译到另一种语言中会失去效果(如双关语),译员可以采取向听众交代说明并适当翻译的方法。

例:现在是年轻人的天下了,不是有句流行语嘛:长江后浪推前浪,把老爸拍在沙滩上。

Just now the speaker quoted a popular Chinese saying in joke. And the meaning is:as in the Changjiang River the waves behind drive on those before, so each new generation excels the last one.

讽刺、不恰当的玩笑如果出现在双方交流中,译员要引起高度警觉,有时为了避免双方的矛盾出现,口译中可以采取减轻语气、略译等办法。

法庭口译的类别和特点

法庭翻译(court interpreting)一般是指在民事或刑事诉讼过程中,当事人或证人由于不通晓当地(国)的通用/官方语言造成理解和表达上的困难时所得到的翻译服务。从事这一翻译工作的人被称为法庭译员。法庭口译主要分为同声传译(simultaneous interpreting)、交替传译(consecutive interpreting)和视译(sight interpreting)三种。同声传译是指讲话人讲话的同时,拖后几个词开始口译,这种方法对口译人员的要求较高。"同声传译通常只为在庭审过程中只听不说和/或暂时不发言的有关人员而实行(如陪审员、陪审团成员、被告等),多数时候需要同传设备以便口译员在工作时不受干扰。"同声传译在美国、香港地区等是法庭口译的主要形式,但在大陆这种方式几乎没有被采用过。一是同传需要专用设备,而法院基本没有;二是同传对译员要求太高,而我国能做同传的法庭口译员非常缺乏。"视译可以说是一种口译和笔译的混合体,因此既可以叫做视觉翻译(sight translation),也可以叫做视觉口译(sight interpreting)"。视觉口译的材料往往不会在庭审前给译员,所以需要译员当场口译,材料难度大(如判决书、证词等),时间紧迫,对译员的语言能力、法律知识和心理素质都是一种考验。

法庭口译的特点主要体现在几种口译方式交替进行,对译员的语言素质要求特别高。如上所述,法庭口译不是单一的某种口译方式。在庭审的时候根据需要,译员一会儿被要求使用同声传译,瞬间又转到交替口译,抑或又转到视觉口译;同时,法庭口译实际也包含了开庭前后的笔译部分。首先,在法庭这样庄重、紧张的气氛中,译员还要在多种口译方式之间来回转换,难度颇大。其次,法庭口译对译员的语言水平要求超过一般的口译。这是因为法庭上的任何一字一词都有可能是法官断案的关键,译员的任何错误都有可能引起误解,造成误判。所以要求法庭口译员必须完整准确、一字不差地翻译源语信息,不得修饰和省略源语信息,不得更改原话语的语体和语域。译员对两种语言都要有较强敏感性,不仅要对语言特征和副语言特征有识别能力,还要有相应的转换能力。说话人的迟疑、重复、口误等都要求被忠实的传译,同时还要注意其说话时的表情、语音、语调。说话人往往还要面对两种语言的地域方言和社会方言。例如,汉语可能是粤语、山东话、客家话、四川话,等等,而外语,比如英语有可能是苏格兰英语、威尔士英语、黑人英语、澳大利亚英语、印度英语,等等。从社会方言的角度来讲,"语言会因不同职业、阶层、年龄、性别等因素而形成诸多语言变体。俚语、黑话、行业语等会使口译环境非常复杂,难度亦很大"。

1. 法庭口译员的基本素质

法庭口译员是一种复合型人才,其人才的培养和资格认证应基于多种素质要求,包括双语能力、双文化知识、法律知识、心理素质。

双语能力,具体地讲,包括听、说、读、写、译五种基本素质。口译人员要能熟练地使用两种语言,其外语水平达到或接近母语者的水平(native-like proficiency)。

双文化知识是指对两种语言的文化背景要有一定了解。任何犯罪活动、诉讼纠纷都是在特定的时间、地域、社会背景下发生的;而且,对法庭话语的解读,必须依据特定的文化背景,译者要有能力识别文化背景对法庭话语解读造成的差异,在口译时注意双方的文化沟通障碍,在必要的时候可以"向法庭反映,由法庭出面解释和解决"。

法律知识是指译员要掌握相关法律基本条文,熟知法律的运作过程和庭审的运作模式,在接到法庭口译的任务后,译员还应当查阅与本次诉讼相关的法律条文,比如与知识产权相关的诉讼,译员要查阅《中华人民共和国著作权法实施条例》和《中华人民共和国专利法》等。

法庭口译人员心理素质要好,这是因为口译行为本身就充满压力,而法庭庭审自身也是火药味甚浓,场面紧张而庄严,这两个特点相互叠加,对口译员的要求不言而喻。而且法庭上控诉双方经常哭哭啼啼,情绪激动,有时又会遇见凶杀案等骇人听闻的案件,看见或听见惨不忍睹的证据证言,这时候,译员要沉着冷静,口译时要尽量客观,避免个人感情和情绪。

2. 法庭口译的标准和职业道德

忠实和准确是法庭口译的最基本要求。要达到忠实和准确,译员要完整地、一字不差地传译说话人的话语,不得随意增加、删减、解释、改述,也不能有遗漏、曲解、误传等现象发生。"口译时,在保持语言的自然以及语域、语体、语气不变的基础上,应使语言结构与语义和原语言一致,对模棱两可的话语、错误的开头语以及重复等都应如实翻译。如果没听清或没听懂,口译人员应征得法官的同意后进行澄清;如果在同声传译时没听清或没听懂,通常的做法是由口译人员自己判断插话澄清或继续口译"。

中立、保密是法庭口译员的职业道德。回避原则是使法庭口译员保持中立的有效方法。法庭口译人员和控辩双方不应有任何私人关系或其他能够影响译员中立立场的特殊关系,如亲戚、朋友、同学、邻居等。同时,在开庭和休庭前后或期间,法庭口译员都不应和控辩双方人员和其家属等进行交谈和接触;在整个庭审期间,译员也不应观看和收听对本案进行的相关报道,也不应和他人对本案进行讨论,以免受到其他观点的影响,从而最终影响到译员的中立性。由于特殊的身份,译员在庭审前后有可能接触到一些材料,如卷宗、专家证词和法庭判决书等等,这时,译员应严守保密要求,不应向任何人透露任何相关信息。

法庭口译是一项复杂程度和劳动强度都非常高的职业,要成为一个合格的法庭口译员,必须经过专业培训,掌握各种复合技能。鉴于当前和今后一段时间,对法庭口译的需求将有大幅增加,鉴于法庭口译在维护法律公平、公正和当事人权利方面的重要作用,应该在高校开设法庭口译专业,并有相关的法庭口译资格认证体系和专门立法,规范法庭口译,提高法庭口译质量,明确法庭口译员的社会地位并提高其工资水平。

拓展阅读

选文A

中国人民银行副行长胡晓炼在《物权法》担保物权司法解释座谈会上的讲话
2010年5月27日

今天我们在这里召开由最高人民法院和中国人民银行主办、世界银行集团国际金融公司协办的《物权法》担保物权司法解释专题座谈会。欢迎大家一起来交流担保法律制度改革经验以及国内动产、权利担保创新实践,积极推动《物权法》第四编担保物权司法解释的制定起草工作。

我国担保信贷在信贷总量中占比80%以上,担保物权法律制度改革与创新,是一项重要的金融基础设施建设。动产担保是物权法体系中最活跃的领域,与经济发展水平、经济结构调整有着极为密切的关系。基于理想动产担保框架四大支柱——宽泛的担保物范围、统一的登记公示系统、清晰的优先权规则和快速的执行程序,人民银行提出了将应收账款、存货等纳入担保物范围、初步创建浮动抵押、保护善意取得第三人所有权、拓宽当事人自治空间、明晰优先顺位原则、明确应收账款担保登记机构、明确动产抵押登记原则以及担保物权登记收费规则等八项建议,已被2007年3月16日通过的《物权法》吸收为具体条文。

《物权法》的出台,对促进信贷市场健康发展、防范化解金融风险、缓解中小企业融资难问题均具有重要意义。

应该说,中小企业融资问题是一个世界性难题,在发展中国家比较突出。虽然也有企业经营风险大、财务制度透明度差、银行贷款难于管理等诸多方面的原因,但是,中小企业融资瓶颈在于欠缺合法担保物。我国商业银行接受的信贷担保物中70%左右是土地和建筑等不动产,而广大中小企业资产70%以上表现为应收账款和存货,普遍欠缺不动产担保资源。据估算,我国中小企业大约有16万亿的资产由于受到法律等方面的限制,不能用于担保借入信贷资金。允许存货和应收账款担保融资,对解决中小企业融资难问题意义重大。

《物权法》还明确了应收账款质押登记机构,人民银行"应收账款质押登记公示系统"、"融资租赁登记公示系统"分别于2007年10月1日、2009年7月20日上线运行。担保登记产生公示、对抗效力,登记实行形式审查原则,对于保护金融机构作为担保权人的合法权益发挥了重要作用。"应收账款质押登记公示系统"对保理业务也进行登记,一定程度解决了商业银行附回购型保理业务存在的法律风险。

《物权法》的出台,基本解决了我国动产担保立法相对滞后的问题。但是,我们也看到,《物权法》出台后,国内商业银行依托客户资源和经营关系积极进行担保创新,围绕应收账款、存货等出现了多种物权组合担保形式。在农村地区,针对土地使用权、宅基地等,一些商业银行也尝试进行产品创新。但同时,"应收账款质押登记公示系统"、"融资租赁登记公示系统"运行中也存在登记依据、范围、效力等方面的问题。以上问题迫切需要法律予以明确规范。

今明两天,我们在这里召开专题座谈会,目的就是广泛了解担保创新实践和《物权法》实施中亟待规范的问题,推动担保物权司法解释尽快出台,以全面反映国内担保创新实践,更好地适应和服务国内经济金融发展的需要。

最后,预祝本次座谈会圆满成功!谢谢大家!

译文

Deputy Governor Hu's Speech at the Symposium on Judicial Interpretation of *Law on Real Rights*

I am delighted to attend the symposium on judicial interpretation of the Law on Real Rights of the People's Republic of China organized by the Supreme People's Court and the People's Bank of China with the support of International Finance Corporation. We have gathered here today to discuss the experiences of reforming the legal system on security interest, security interests in personal property and innovative practices on warranty of titles, so as to promote the drafting of judicial interpretation of the *Law on Real Rights* Part Four on Security Interest.

Secured credit accounted for more than 80 percent of China's aggregate credit. Therefore, reform and innovation of legal framework concerning security interest is an important part of financial infrastructure. Security interest in personal property is one of the most frequently discussed area in property law system and it is closely related to economic development and restructuring. Based on the four pillars of an ideal framework of security interest in personal property, namely wide range of eligible collateral, a centralized registration and public display system, well-defined rule of priority and streamlined process for implementation, the PBC put forward 8 proposals, i. e. making account receivables and inventory eligible collaterals, establishing a floating charge system, protecting bona fide purchase, expanding party autonomy, defining the rule of priority in a clear-cut manner, designating the institution for the registration of account receivables, defining the principles for the registration of floating charge and rules for the registration and charging of security interest, which have already been written into the Law on Real Rights enacted on March 16, 2007.

The launch of the *Law on Real Rights* is of great significance to the development of the credit market, prevention and mitigation of financial risks and easing the financing difficulties of small and medium-sized enterprises (SMEs).

SME financing is a worldwide challenge, and it is more difficult in developing countries. Out of multiple problems such as large SMEs' exposure to operational risks and lack of financial transparency and banks' difficulties in managing lending to SMEs, the lack of legitimate collateral is the real bottleneck. Approximately 70 percent of the credit collateral received by commercial banks in China is real estate, while more than 70 percent of the assets of SMEs are account receivables and inventory. It was estimated that 16 trillion yuan worth of assets of SMEs could not be accepted as loan collaterals. Making account receivables and inventory eligible collaterals is an important solution to the financing difficulties of SMEs.

The *Law on Real Rights* also identifies a dedicated agency for account receivables finance registration. The PBC's account receivables finance registration and public display system and the financial leasing registration and public display system started to operate on October 1st, 2007 and July 20th, 2009 respectively. The registration of collateral puts collateral information on public display and holds third parties involved legally accountable, playing an important role in protecting legitimate rights and interests of financial institutions as the secured party. The system also registers factoring business, mitigating legal risks of commercial banks' factoring business with repurchase agreement attached.

The enaction of the *Law on Real Rights* has largely filled in the gap in China's legislation on taking floating charge as collaterals. However, after the *Law on Real Rights* was promulgated, commercial banks have explored taking a mixture of real right as collateral, and they are promoting innovation to include land use right and rural housing site as eligible collaterals. What's more, the two registration systems still need improvements in terms of basis of registration, scope and effectiveness of the registration, underpinning the urgency of legal definition. These need to be clarified by legislations.

This symposium aims to understand innovative practices concerning collaterals, discuss issues to be solved in the implementation of the *Law on Real Rights*, so as to promote judicial interpretations of security interest to be released as soon as possible based on latest developments in collaterals and serve economic and financial development in a more effective manner.

I wish the symposium a complete success. Thank you.

 选文B

Remarks at the Intellectual Property Summit in Hong Kong
US Attorney General Eric Holder
October 18, 2010

Thank you, Superintendent O'Grady. I appreciate your warm welcome, and I am grateful for the support — and the inspiring example — that you and your colleagues in the An Garda Siochana are providing to the international law enforcement community.

I would also like to thank INTERPOL, Hong Kong Customs, and Underwriters Laboratories for hosting this important conference — and for bringing together so many leaders, experts, and partners from law enforcement agencies across the world.

During my service as the Attorney General of the United States, I have had the privilege of working with many of you on a broad range of issues. I have seen, firsthand, the power of our joint efforts. And I am convinced that the work of our nations' law enforcement agencies — to combat terrorism, to dismantle drug cartels and human trafficking rings, to stop childpornographers and others who would prey on our most vulnerable citizens — is more effective because of our collaboration. To address new and emerging threats — and to protect the security, and defend the liberties, of the people we serve — this cooperation must continue.

It is fitting that we are gathered here in Hong Kong — a center of global innovation — to chart our course forward. Not only is Hong Kong one of the world's most vibrant and modern cities, it is headquarters for so many leading international organizations and corporations. It is a hub for international politics, law, education, and commerce. And, this week, I hope it is the meeting ground for unprecedented international cooperation.

This conference is an important opportunity — a chance to focus the attention, and to harness the talents and resources, of the international law enforcement community in protecting intellectual property rights, safeguarding innovation, ensuring the health and safety of our citizens, and combating the international networks of organized criminals now seeking to profit from IP (Intellectual Property) crimes.

As global criminal networks increasingly fund their illicit activities through intellectual property crimes, our challenge is not simply to keep up. Our strategies must become more sophisticated than those employed by the criminals we pursue. Our collaboration across borders must become more seamless. And our determination must not waver.

Like many of your own governments, the Obama Administration recognizes that our nation's economic prosperity is increasingly tied to industries — like software or life sciences — that rely on strong IP enforcement. That is why we have created a new framework, and called for an increased level of activity, to better protect intellectual property rights.

As many of you know, last year, President Obama created a new leadership role in the White House — Intellectual Property Enforcement Coordinator and appointed Victoria Espinel to fill this position. I am pleased that Victoria is here with us today. As IP Enforcement Coordinator, her first order of business was to develop a comprehensive strategic plan to guide our government's efforts to protect intellectual property, including copyrights, trademarks, and trade secrets. The strategic plan was released by the White House this summer. Already, it is strengthening and streamlining our efforts to detect and prosecute IP crimes. This work is just one example of the administration's renewed focus on IP protection.

Last December, Vice President Biden convened the administration's first intellectual property summit, which brought together cabinet officials and industry leaders to discuss intellectual property rights and policies — and to identify ways to improve our enforcement efforts. During that summit, I had the chance to discuss the Justice Department's intellectual property enforcement strategy and the critical work being done by some of our most talented lawyers and investigators.

A key part of this strategy is led by Justice Department prosecutors — many of whom are focused exclusively on computer and intellectual property crimes. I am committed to making sure that these prosecutors have the resources and the specialized training necessary to prevent, identify, and stop IP violations — and to spot emerging crime trends more quickly.

Of course, the outstanding work of our prosecutors isn't done, and couldn't be accomplished, in isolation. It is supported by the skills and dedication of the investigative agents who develop the cases we bring in court. At every level of the Justice Department, we are committed to improving partnerships with our federal law enforcement colleagues — and with leaders across the international law enforcement community. In particular, I would like to note the great work being done through the National Intellectual Property Rights Coordination Center, which is led by our colleagues in U.S. Immigration and Customs Enforcement. The IPR Center brings together investigators and analysts from a number of federal agencies to coordinate our efforts to investigate counterfeiting, online piracy, and other IP violations.

To build on the contributions and achievements of our prosecutors and investigators, in February of this year, I reestablished the Justice Department's Task Force on Intellectual Property. Chaired by the Deputy Attorney General, the Task Force includes senior leaders from across the Department. And, as many of you know, it's focused on facilitating coordination among international law enforcement partners. A cornerstone of this effort is the Intellectual Property Law Enforcement Coordinator program.

With the help of our colleagues in the Department of State, the Justice Department has deployed two federal prosecutors — based in Bangkok, Thailand, and in Sofia, Bulgaria — to manage our IP protection efforts in Southeast Asia and in Eastern Europe. They work closely with our international counterparts to share information and evidence regarding joint investigations and to enhance IP enforcement training programs. Here in Asia, one of our law enforcement coordinators is actively engaged in efforts to strengthen the work of the IP Criminal Enforcement Network.

But this work is not just for our coordinators alone. Following this conference, I will travel to Beijing, where I look forward to meeting with my counterparts and other officials to discuss how we can build on our nations' bilateral enforcement efforts through the Intellectual Property Working Group of the U.S.-China Joint Liaison Group for Law Enforcement Cooperation. Together, I hope we can work to identify the most pressing, and perilous, gaps in our enforcement mechanisms — and begin taking the steps required to close these gaps, strengthen IP protections, and fulfill the most critical obligations of public service: ensuring opportunity, fostering prosperity, and protecting the safety and health of our people.

In this work, I pledge my own best efforts. And, today, I ask for yours. I will continue to seek out and seize opportunities to foster stronger relationships, and greater cooperation, among international law enforcement agencies. But I also know that, without your help — and until every nation makes a commitment, and takes action, to ensure aggressive IP enforcement — we will not solve the challenges that now bring us together.

Each of us — and every member of the international law enforcement community — has pledged to protect the rights and security of the citizens we serve. But none of us can fulfill that promise alone. In this age of instantaneous global communication, when criminal activity knows no bounds, our enforcement work must extend beyond our own before our own borders. Working together is no longer just the best way forward. Now, it is the only way forward.

On behalf of the United States, I am grateful for your partnership, your leadership, and your cooperation in protecting the safety of our citizens, the strength of our markets, and the intellectual property rights of our nations' innovators and entrepreneurs.

Our task is great — but our success is possible. Only if we work in common cause, only if we put the full measure of national commitment in our efforts, and only if we honor the values we share, can we — and will we — create a world in which intellectual property crime is not the domain of the future, but a marker of the past.

Thank you.

译文

在香港国际知识产权峰会上的演讲

美国司法部长　埃里克·霍尔德

2010年10月18日

谢谢你,奥格雷迪侦警司,感谢你的热情欢迎和支持,并感谢你和爱尔兰国家警察局的同事们为国际执法界树立鼓舞人心的榜样。

我同时也感谢国际刑警组织、香港海关和保险商试验所联合举办此次重要会议,使全世界执法机构的众多领导、专家和合作伙伴有机会聚集在一起。

作为美国司法部长,我有幸在广泛的领域与你们当中的很多人一起合作。我亲眼见证了我们合作努力的成果。我坚信,我们的合作将使各国执法部门能更有效地打击恐怖主义、贩毒集团和人口贩卖,制止儿童色情和其他伤害弱势群体的行为。为了应对出现的新威胁,保护我们公民的安全和自由,必须继续有这种合作。

香港作为一个全球创新中心,是我们相聚和规划未来的一个恰如其分的地点。香港不仅是世界上最充满活力的现代化城市之一,也是众多国际主要机构和公司总部所在地,它是一个集政治、法律、教育和商业为一体的国际中心。我希望,它也将在本周成为一个空前的国际合作的场所。

本次会议是一个重要的机会,使国际执法界更加关注并投入更多的人力和资源来保护知识产权和创新,保障我们公民的健康和人身安全,并与正在试图通过知识产权牟利的国际有组织犯罪网络进行斗争。

随着全球犯罪网络越来越多地利用知识产权犯罪手段资助其非法活动,我们面临的挑战是不能仅限于跟上应付。我们的战略必须变得比我们所追踪的犯罪分子所使用的更高超。我们与其他国家的合作必须更加天衣无缝。我们的决心绝不能动摇。

就像许多你们各自的政府一样,奥巴马政府认识到,我们国家的经济繁荣越来越与一些行业联系在一起——如软件或生命科学——这些都依靠强有力的知识产权执法。这就是为什么我们创建了一个新的框架,并要求有更多行动,更好地保护知识产权。

你们很多人都知道,去年,奥巴马总统在白宫设立了一个新的领导角色,即知识产权执法事务协调员,并任命维多利亚·埃斯皮内尔担任这个职务。我很高兴,维多利亚今天也在这里。作为知识产权事务协调员,她的第一项任务就是制定一项全面的战略计划来指导我国政府保护知识产权的努力,包括版权、商标权和贸易机密。这项战略计划已于今年夏天由白宫公布,并已增强了我国侦破和起诉侵犯知识产权犯罪行为的努力,提高了这方面的工作效率。这项工作仅仅是本届政府更加重视保护知识产权的一个例子。

去年12月,副总统拜登召集了本届政府的首次知识产权峰会,与会的内阁官员和产业界领袖讨论了知识产权及政策问题,确定了改善我们执法工作的途径。在峰会期间,我有机会阐述了司法部的知识产权执法战略以及我国一些最有才智的律师和调查人员正在开展的极其重要的工作。

这项战略的一个重要部分由司法部检察官领导实施,他们当中的很多人专注于与电脑和知识产权相关的罪行。我将尽最大努力确保这些检察官获得必需的资源和专门训练,以防止、识别和制止侵犯知识产权行为,并能更快地发觉新的犯罪趋势。

当然,我们的检察官的出色工作不是,也无法是孤立完成的;它得到调查人员的技能和敬业精神的支持,我们的法庭工作是基于调查人员的立案。在司法部的每一个层次,我们都致力于改善与联邦执法同行们的伙伴关系,改善与整个国际执法部门领导者的伙伴关系。我要特别指出由美国移民与海关执法局领导牵头的国家知识产权协调中心所作的出色工作。这个中心集中了多个联邦机构的调查员和分析员,为我们调查伪造产品、互联网盗版和其他侵犯知识产权的行为提供协调努力。

为了进一步发展我们的检察官和调查人员所作的贡献和取得的成果,我于今年2月重新设立了司法部知识产权特别工作组。这个工作组由司法部副部长领导,成员包括司法部各部门的高级领导官员。你们很多人都知道,这个工作组的重点是促进国际执法伙伴之间的协调。它的一个核心努力是知识产权执法协调员项目。

在我们的国务部同事的帮助下,司法部在泰国的曼谷和保加利亚的索菲亚派驻了两名联邦检察官,分别管理我们在东南亚和东欧的知识产权保护工作。他们同我们的国际同行密切合作,分享信息和联合调查的证据,并加强知识产权执法培训项目。在亚洲,我们的一位执法协调员在积极从事加强知识产权刑事执法网的工作。

但该项努力并不仅仅是我们的协调员们的工作。在本次大会结束后,我将前往北京,在那里我期待会晤我的同行和其他官员,讨论我们如何通过美中执法合作联合联络组的知识产权工作组扩大两国的双边执法努力。我希望我们能够共同找出我们执法机制中最紧迫、最危险的缺口,并开始采取必要措施予以弥补,加强知识产权保护,并履行公共服务中最为关键的责任:保障机会、促进繁荣、保护我们人民的安全和健康。

在这项工作中,我保证将尽自己的最大努力,今天,我请各位也尽你们的最大努力。我将继续寻求和抓住机遇,在国际执法机构之间促进更牢固的关系和更紧密的合作。但是,我也非常清楚,没有你们的帮助——而且除非每一个国家都作出承诺并采取积极的执法行动保护知识产权——我们就不可能解决让我们汇聚到一起的这些挑战。

我们每个人——国际执法界的每个成员——都作出承诺,要保护我们所服务的公民的权利与安全。但我们没有人能单独履行这项承诺。在这个全球即时通讯的时代,犯罪活动无国界,我们的执法工作必须超越我们自己的国界。共同合作不再仅仅是我们前进的最佳道路,而是我们前进的唯一道路。

我谨代表美国向你们致谢,感谢你们展现的伙伴合作精神、你们的领导作用、你们在保护我们的公民安全、市场实力及保护我们各国创新者与企业家的知识产权方面提供的合作。

我们的任务巨大,但我们有可能成功。只有当我们为共同的事业而努力,只有当我们在这一努力中投入国家承诺的全部力量,只有当我们尊重维护我们共同具有的价值观,我们才能——我们就能——创造出这样一个世界,在那里知识产权犯罪已不属于未来的前景,而只不过是昔日的一个烙印而已。

谢谢各位。

第十三单元　外贸政策
(Foreign Trade Policy)

单元要点

本单元共分五个层次,分别是:国家主席胡锦涛在美中企业界领导人圆桌会议上的讲话汉译英一篇;英国财政大臣奥斯本在第三次"中英经济财金对话"新闻发布会上的致辞英译汉一篇;数字口译;口译中的中文称谓翻译;拓展阅读(汉译英、英译汉各一篇)。第一、二部分提供外贸政策口译的例文及其翻译和重难点评析;第三、四部分主要是相关口译理论与技能的介绍;第五部分的拓展阅读中,提供汉、英原文和参考译文。

理论难点提示

1. 数字口译。
2. 口译中的中文称谓翻译。

选文A

在美中企业界领导人圆桌会议上的讲话
中华人民共和国主席　胡锦涛
艾森豪威尔行政大楼
2011年1月19日

各位企业家代表,今天很高兴同奥巴马总统一起同各位企业界代表见面。在座的各位都是两国杰出的代表,不仅为各自国家的经济,也为中美关系发展作出了贡献。我向你们表达我诚挚的谢意。

在座的两国企业家把握经济全球化深入发展的机遇,积极开拓对方国家市场,促进两国互利合作。我愿在这里列举一些数据,展示我们取得的成就。

1979年,当我们两国正式建立外交关系的时候,我们的双边贸易额不足25亿美元,而去年已经上升到了3 800亿美元,增长了150多倍。双向投资从无到有,累计超过了700亿美元。

中美两国经贸和投资合作给两国人民带来了实实在在的利益,给两国企业带来了重要商机。数据表明,我们两国的总贸易已经为美国消费者带来了近600亿美元的财富。

展望未来,我们的贸易合作前景广阔。在这里我想告诉大家的是,中国正在加快转变经济发展方式和调整经济结构,着力扩大内需特别是消费需求。

近年来,中国的国内消费每年以两位数的速度增长。2010年,中国国内市场规模超过2万亿美元,美国也在全力振兴经济。

奥巴马总统已开始实施出口倍增计划。在昨晚的晚宴和刚刚举行的会谈中,我同奥巴马总统讨论了推进中美全面经济合作问题。我们一致同意加强两国金融、经贸、能源、环境、科技、农业、基础设施建设等领域务实合作。中美经贸和投资合作前景十分广阔。希望两国企业把握机遇、积极作为。

我还要告诉美国的企业家们,中方欢迎美国企业到中国发展。中国将坚持改革开放,一如既往为包括美国企业在内的外国企业提供透明、公平、高效的投资环境。所有在中国注册的企业都享有国民待遇,中国政府在自主创新产品认定、政府采购、知识产权保护上对它们都会一视同仁、平等对待。

在这里,我也要告诉中国的企业家们,中国政府一贯并将继续支持中国企业到美国投资兴业。希望你们能继续积极进取、开拓创新,并同时不忘回馈当地社会。相信奥巴马总统和美国政府会为来美投资的中国企业提供公平竞争的环境。

最后,我祝在座各位的企业在新的一年里实现更大的增长,希望你们为促进两国的贸易投资合作作出更大的贡献。

现在,我愿回答各位提出的问题。谢谢。

重难点评析

1. "我愿在这里列举一些数据,展示我们取得的成就。"句中"列举数据"译为"cite a set of statistics","展示我们取得的成就"省译了"成就",译为"show how far we have come"。

2. "1979年,当我们两国正式建立外交关系的时候,我们的双边贸易额不足25亿美元,而去年已经上升到了3 800亿美元,增长了150多倍。"外贸口译会经常涉及数字口译,要对"增长了""上升到","翻了……倍","是……的……倍"等不同的表达特别注意。此句是两个时期的双边贸易额的对比,采用了分译法译为两个句子,全句译为"In 1979, when we firmly established diplomatic ties, our two-way trade was less than $2.5 billion U.S. But the figure for last year was $380 billion U.S., which is more than 150-fold increase."

3. "中国正在加快转变经济发展方式和调整经济结构,着力扩大内需特别是消费需求。"该句采用了合译法和词类换译将两个动词"转变"和"调整"合译成一个名词"transformation"。全句译为"China is speeding up this transformation of economic growth pattern and economic restructuring."

4. "扩大内需"译为"boost domestic demand","以两位数的速度增长"译为"grow at a double-digit rate"。

5. "美国也在全力振兴经济。"译为"And here in the United States, you are also working all-out to stimulate your economy."译者非常灵活地进行了人称的转译,译文使用了第二人称符合实际的情况非常自然。

6. "希望两国企业把握机遇、积极作为。"句中将"积极作为"进行了意译"take active options and achieve great things."。

7. "透明、公平、高效的投资环境"译为"a transparent, just, fair, highly efficient investment climate"。

8. "中国政府在自主创新产品认定、政府采购、知识产权保护上对它们都会一视同仁、平等对待。"句中"自主创新产品认定、政府采购、知识产权保护"译为"in terms of innovation products, accreditation, government procurement, IPR protection","一视同仁、平等对待"意思近似,故译为一个短语"give them equal treatment"。

9. "一贯并将继续支持"译为"... will, as it has always done, support you...。"

10. "继续积极进取、开拓创新"译为"continue to be enterprising and creative。"

译文

Remarks in Roundtable Discussion with American and Chinese Business Leaders

by H. E. Hu Jintao, President of the People's Republic of China

Eisenhower Executive Office Building

January 19, 2011

Business leaders, today it gives me a great pleasure to be here with President Obama and meet with you, business leaders. All of you around this table and your companies are leading performers of the two countries. You have not only made positive contribution to the economic growth of your respective countries, but also to China-U. S. relations. So I wish to offer you my sincere appreciation.

All business leaders around this table have seized the opportunities presented by the deepening economic globalization. You have been working vigorously to expand market in each other's countries. You have grown your business, but also promoted mutual beneficial cooperation between the two countries. I will cite a set of statistics to show how far we have come.

In 1979, when we firmly established diplomatic ties, our two-way trade was less than \$2.5 billion U. S. But the figure for last year was \$380 billion U. S., which is more than 150-fold increase. Our mutual investment also started from virtually nothing to an accumulation of \$70 billion U. S.

The trade and investment cooperation between our two countries have indeed brought real benefits to the people of our countries and important business communities — opportunities for our business communities. According to figures, our total trade has brought about \$60 billion U. S. of benefits to U. S. consumers.

If we look ahead to the future, our trade cooperation enjoys a promising future. Here I have a message to all of you — that is, China is speeding up this transformation of economic growth pattern and economic restructuring. We are focusing our efforts to boosting domestic demand, especially consumer spending.

In recent years, China's domestic spending has been growing at a double-digit rate every year. In 2010, our domestic market has surpassed a scale of \$2 trillion U. S. And here in the United States, you are also working all-out to stimulate your economy.

President Obama has launched a program to double your exports. Both in the dinner last night and in my meeting with President Obama just now, we discussed how to advance economic cooperation between our two countries across the board. We agreed to strengthen our cooperation in the financial, economic, trade, energy and the environment, science and technology, agriculture, infrastructure and many other fields. So, indeed, there is a promising future for trade and investment cooperation between our two countries. I do hope that companies from both countries can seize the opportunities, take active options and achieve great things.

I also have a message to American entrepreneurs. That is, we welcome you as companies to China. China follows reform and opening up. We will, as always, try to provide a transparent, just, fair, highly efficient investment climate to U.S. companies and other foreign companies. I also wish to tell you that all companies registered in China are given national treatment. In terms of innovation products, accreditation, government procurement, IPR protection, the Chinese government will give them equal treatment.

Here, I also have a message to Chinese entrepreneurs. That is, the Chinese government will, as it has always done, support you in making investments and doing business here in the United States. I hope that you can continue to be enterprising and creative, and at the same time, don't forget to give back to the local communities. I do believe that President Obama and the U.S. administration will provide a level playing field for Chinese companies to make investments here in the United States.

To conclude, I wish the companies you represent even greater growth in the new year. And I also expect that you can make even greater contribution to promoting trade and investment cooperation between our two countries.

And now I'm ready to listen to your views. Thank you.

选文B

Closing Comments at Economic and Financial Dialogue Press Conference
by UK Chancellor George Osborne
9 November 2010

Thank you very much Vice Premier Wang Qishan. And let me thank you again for welcoming us to Beijing today to this Economic and Financial Dialogue.

I agree with you that we have had very friendly and successful talks, covering a whole range of issues of relevance to both our countries.

China is now the world's second largest economy. Its contribution to prosperity in the UK is becoming increasingly important. That is why we have come to China as the strongest ministerial delegation ever to visit from the UK. We look forward to this afternoon, when the Prime Minister David Cameron and Premier Wen will take part in the UK-China summit.

Today the Vice Premier and I talked about the economic relationship between our two countries. We both agreed to further strengthen bilateral cooperation. We both agreed to continue implementing economic policies conducive to sustainable economic growth. The UK has committed to a clear, credible, ambitious and growth-friendly medium-term fiscal consolid ation plan which will ensure fiscal sustainability. And as the Vice Premier has said China is committed to accelerate the restructuring to further strengthen the role of domestic demand. This action by both sides will support confidence and mitigate risks to recovery.

We also agreed to work together through the G20. We both strongly support the G20 as the premier forum for our international economic cooperation, where the world's largest economies work together to support their mutual aspirations and ambitions. We both welcomed the ambitious agreement reached by G20 Finance Ministers & Central Bank Governor at Gyeongju, Korea, to reform the IMF's quota and governance that will help deliver a more effective, credible and legitimate IMF. At Gyeongju we also agreed to strengthen multilateral cooperation to promote external sustainability and the full range of policies conducive to reducing excessive imbalances and maintaining current account imbalances at sustainable levels. We need to move further forward in Seoul this week. I hope that China will seize the opportunity to play a leading role on this.

We also discussed the trade links between our countries. It is worth remembering that China is the world's largest exporter of goods and the UK is the world's second largest exporter of services. This complementary in our relationship will provide a strong foundation to strengthen our trade and investment links. Both sides will uphold the principles of free trade and resist all forms of protectionism. We will work together to achieve Doha — the UK sees 2011 as a key window of opportunity for achieving this, and I hope China will take a leading role in driving this agenda forward at the G20 Summit in Seoul.

We also discussed how to encourage Chinese investment in the UK and how to enable Chinese companies to do business in the UK. The UK is already one of the most open economies in the world to trade and inward investment and welcomes more Chinese investment, including from sovereign wealth funds. We noted that UK firms are doing well in China's growing market. For example, UK firms play a key role in China's financial markets. UK banks account for 23 per cent of the foreign banking market. Our insurers are among the leading foreign players.

And we agreed that it is not just bilateral trade that matters. The UK and China can work in partnership elsewhere, and we discussed how we can support greater partnerships between UK and Chinese companies in third countries. We discussed the business environment in both our countries. There are lots of opportunities in China's growing market and I highlighted some areas where British companies believe China's business environment could be improved. We also noted the challenges in the business environment and will work to address this. I encouraged China to respond constructively to the views of the business community. We noted the importance of effective protection of intellectual property rights to promote innovation and encourage bilateral trade, especially in high-technology goods and services. We agreed ambitious plans for deepened technical collaboration on intellectual property administration and enforcement. We also agreed to establish a working-level dialogue on tax issues for businesses engaged in bilateral trade and investment.

We discussed the economic outlook for our countries. I outlined the decisive steps we have had to take to deal with Britain's deficit. And I assured the Vice Premier that Britain's economic and financial strengths will be further enhanced. Our business sector remains top-class with world-beating research, innovation and enterprise. London is the world's largest and leading international financial centre and I was pleased that we have agreed to strengthen our financial sector collaboration. We both agreed that further deepening of financial services ties between the UK and China will benefit both sides. We reiterated our commitment to work together to drive forward the reform of international financial regulation and supervisory standards, and strengthen transparency and accountability in the financial sector.

We are announcing an expansion of our unrivalled programme of bilateral technical collaboration and joint research on financial sector reform and development. This includes development of the offshore renminbi market, SME financing, corporate and government bond market development. We welcome the fact that China will soon allow foreign-invested banks to conduct bond underwriting business. We agree to explore the possibility of cross-cutting Exchange Trade Funds on our respective stock markets. We both reiterated our support for mutual listings arrangements that will allow Chinese companies to list in London and foreign firms to list in China.

So, Vice Premier, let me conclude. Successful talks, between ever closer economic partners. Once again, thank you for hosting us. And I look forward to the 2011 dialogue in the United Kingdom.

重难点评析

1. "covering a whole range of issues"译为"(会谈)涉及了一系列的事务"。

2. "We both agreed to continue implementing economic policies conducive to sustainable economic growth."译文将后置的定语部分"conducive to sustainable economic growth"提前，进行了词序调译，根据中文的表达习惯译为"双方一致同意继续实施有利于经济可持续发展的经济政策"。

3. "The UK has committed to a clear, credible, ambitious and growth-friendly medium-term fiscal consolidation plan which will ensure fiscal sustainability."在定语从句处进行了断译，分成了两个部分，更符合中文的表达习惯，译为"英国已承诺要实施明确的、可靠的、雄心勃勃的、有益于发展的中期财政整顿计划，以确保财政的可持续性"。

4. "support confidence and mitigate risks"译为"提升信心，缓和风险"。

5. "We both welcomed the ambitious agreement reached by G20 Finance Ministers & Central Bank Governor at Gyeongju, Korea, to reform the IMF's quota and governance

that will help deliver a more effective, credible and legitimate IMF."句中"G20 Finance Ministers & Central Bank Governor at Gyeongju, Korea"译为"韩国庆州G20财长和央行行长会议","to reform the IMF's quota and governance"译为"就国际货币基金组织份额和治理改革"。

6. "reducing excessive imbalances and maintaining current account imbalances at sustainable levels"译为"减少过度失衡和在可持续的水平上保持经常账户失衡"。

7. "It is worth remembering that…"句中that引导主语从句译为"值得一提的是……"。

8. "driving this agenda forward at the G20 Summit in Seoul"译为"在首尔的G20峰会上推进这个议程"。

9. "… welcomes more Chinese investment, including from sovereign wealth funds."译为"欢迎更多来自中国的投资,包括主权财富基金的投资"。

10. "We also noted the challenges in the business environment and will work to address this."此处"address"为动词,意为"设法解决,处理,对付"。

11. "We agreed ambitious plans for deepened technical collaboration on intellectual property administration and enforcement."这里根据中文的习惯增译了动词"启动",全句译为"双方同意启动雄心勃勃的计划,在知识产权管理和实施方面深化技术合作"。

12. "the decisive steps we have had to take to deal with Britain's deficit"译为"采取的解决英国赤字问题的决定性措施"。

13. "We reiterated our commitment to work together to drive forward the reform of international financial regulation and supervisory standards, and strengthen transparency and accountability in the financial sector."句中"international financial regulation and supervisory standards"译为"国际金融监管标准","transparency and accountability"译为"透明度和问责制"。

14. "the offshore renminbi market, SME financing, corporate and government bond market"译为"离岸人民币市场、中小企业融资、公司和政府债券市场";"conduct bond underwriting business"译为"开展债券承销业务"。

15. "We agree to explore the possibility of cross-cutting Exchange Trade Funds on our respective stock markets."译为"我们同意探索研究交易型开放式指数基金(ETF)在对方国家相互上市的可能性"。

16. "We both reiterated our support for mutual listings arrangements that will allow Chinese companies to list in London and foreign firms to list in China."句中that引导的定语从句给出了"mutual listings"的具体解释,即"允许中国企业在伦敦上市以及外国企业在中国上市"。

译文

在第三次"中英经济财金对话"新闻发布会上的致辞
英国财政大臣 奥斯本
2010年11月9日

非常感谢王岐山副总理。对于您今天欢迎我们到北京来参加本次经济财金对话,我再

第十三单元 外贸政策(Foreign Trade Policy)

一次表示感谢。

我和您都认为:我们的会谈是非常友好而有成效的,涉及了一系列有关我们两国的事务。

中国现在是世界上第二大经济体。它对于英国经济繁荣的贡献日益重要。这也是我们此次作为英国有史以来最强大的部长级代表团到中国访问的原因。我们期待着今天下午首相戴维·卡梅伦和温家宝总理参加的英—中峰会。

今天副总理和我探讨了我们两国间的经济关系。双方一致同意进一步加强双边合作。双方一致同意继续实施有利于经济可持续发展的经济政策。英国已承诺要实施明确的、可靠的、雄心勃勃的、有益于发展的中期财政整顿计划,以确保财政的可持续性。副总理也谈到,中国要致力于加快经济结构调整,进一步加强内需对经济增长的作用。双方的这一举措将有助于提振市场信心、减少经济复苏风险。

双方赞同在G20峰会上共同努力。双方坚定支持G20,这是各国实现国际经济合作的重要论坛,其间,全球最大的经济体为实现他们共同的愿望和前景而协同努力。双方欢迎在韩国庆州G20财长和央行行长会议上就国际货币基金组织份额和治理改革达成的重要共识,这将有助于提高国际货币基金组织的有效性、可信度和合法性。在庆州,我们也赞同加强多边合作,推动外部发展的可持续性以及实施一系列有益于减少过度失衡和在可持续的水平上保持经常账户失衡的政策。我们希望在本周的首尔峰会上能够取得更多进展。我希望中国抓住机会,发挥领导作用。

双方探讨了两国间的贸易关系。值得一提的是,中国是世界上最大的商品出口国,而英国是世界上第二大服务出口国。两国在这方面的互补将为加强我们的贸易和投资关系提供强有力的基础。双方都赞成自由贸易的原则,抵制各种形式的贸易保护主义。双方将协同努力推动多哈回合成果。英国认为2011年是实现这一目标的关键机会,我希望中国在首尔召开的G20峰会上可以发挥领先作用,推动此项议程的开展。

双方探讨了如何鼓励中国在英国投资、如何促使中国企业在英国开展业务。英国作为世界上贸易和投资最开放的经济体之一,欢迎更多来自中国的投资,包括主权财富基金的投资。我们注意到,英国企业在中国日益发展的市场上表现出色。例如,英国企业在中国金融市场上发挥着关键作用。英国银行占外国银行市场的23%。英国的保险公司也处于领先的外国企业行列。

双方同意,发挥重要作用的不仅仅是双边贸易。英、中两国可以在其他领域合作,双方探讨了如何在第三国进一步发展英、中两国企业间的合作。双方探讨了两国的商业发展环境。在中国日益发展的市场上有大量的机会,我曾强调了在一些领域英国企业相信中国的商业环境会进一步完善。双方也注意到商业环境中面临的挑战,将共同努力解决这些问题。我希望中国对于这些来自商界的意见可以有建设性地应对。双方认识到有效保护知识产权对促进创新和鼓励双边贸易的重要性,特别是在高科技产品和服务领域。双方同意启动雄心勃勃的计划,在知识产权管理和实施方面深化技术合作。双方同意,建立企业双边贸易和投资的税收问题的工作层面的对话机制。

双方探讨了两国的经济发展前景。我概述了我们所采取的解决英国赤字问题的决定性措施,并且我可以和副总理确定的是英国的经济和金融实力将进一步增强。我们的商业依然是一流的,拥有世界上最强大的研究、创新能力以及企业。伦敦是世界上最大的国际金融中心,发挥着引领的作用。我很高兴我们能够一致同意加强金融领域的协作。双方一致认为,进一步加深英国和中国之间的金融服务关系对双方都是有利的。我们重申致力于合作推动国际金融监管标准的改革,加强金融领域的透明度和问责制。

我们宣布,进一步拓展现有成果,继续致力于双边技术合作以及金融领域改革与发展方面的共同研究。包括离岸人民币市场、中小企业融资、公司和政府债券市场的发展。我们期待着中国将尽快允许外资银行开展债券承销业务。我们同意探索研究交易型开放式指数基金(ETF)在对方国家相互上市的可能性。双方重申了对两国企业相互上市的支持,即允许中国企业在伦敦上市以及外国企业在中国上市。

副总理,我确信,这是日益密切的经济合作伙伴之间的成功的会谈。再一次对您给予的款待表示感谢。

我期待着2011年在英国的对话。

数字口译

作为口译实战中的重点和难点,数字口译历来是口译教学中的重要组成部分。在训练中口译学员有轻视简单基础练习和排斥枯燥机械训练的情绪,而一旦进入实战,往往被数字难住,以致口译失败。因此,要想学好数字口译并真正获得提高,学员必须静下心来认真按照老师的要求完成每一个部分的训练任务。

数字口译的过程分为听记和转换两个阶段:

在听记阶段,口译员必须有非常敏锐的数字反应识别能力,无论是听到中文还是英文,无论听到的是什么样的数字,译员必须能够在第一时间立即辨别出来,尤其是对于类似含有-ty和-teen这样发音容易产生混淆的数字,必须进行一个阶段的辨音识数的训练。

同时,由于受到人的记忆能力所限,为了保证口译中的数字准确无误,口译过程中还要借助笔记的辅助,因此口译员必须坚持听数字记笔记的习惯。

关于数字的记录:

中文数字可以采用"数字+单位"的记录方法,如:12万3456 13亿

英文数字可以采用"数字+符号"的记录方法,如:123,456 1.3b 1B 234M 567T 890

下图为汉英两种语言中的数位对照表:

Figure Interpreting

兆	千亿	百亿	十亿	亿	千万	百万	十万	万	千	百	十	个
T			B			M			T			
4	3	2	1	2	3	4	5	6	7	8	9	0

数字口译的第二个阶段便是数字转换，通过上图我们可以看出，汉英两种语言中的数字单位不是一一对应的，除了个、十、百（hundred）、千（thousand）和万亿/兆（trillion）外，其余的数字单位使用的表达是不同的。这主要是由于中西方在认知和历史上留下的表达差异，英语中以3个位数作为一个停顿单位，而汉语中是以4个位数作为一个停顿单位。

因此，要想成功地进行数字转换，译员必须能够非常熟练地将英汉两种语言中没有对等词的位数进行自动化转换。这是数字口译训练的起点，也是数字口译的关键点。

例如：在做汉英口译时，当我们听到"万"这个位数，脑子里要立即反应出"十个千"（ten thousand）这个英文概念，然后将"万"前面的数字乘以十，落款改为"thousand"。

1万＝10 thousand；5万＝fifty thousand。

这样，"几万"这个数用英语思维时就变成了"几十个千"。同理，"几十万"要变成"几百个千"。

20万＝200 thousand；80万＝800 thousand。

除了汉语的"万"和英语的"thousand"之间要进行思维转换，汉语中的"千万""亿""百亿"和"千亿"也要与英语中的"million"和"billion"达到自动化转换的程度。如：

1百万＝1 million；1 200万＝12 million；2亿＝200 million；

13亿＝1.3 billion（1 billion 300 million）

100亿＝10 billion；5000亿＝500 billion

在完成第一步"数位转换"强化训练后，学员还要进行复杂数字的快速朗读训练，通常在学习初期，可以采用从后往前英语三位一个逗号，中文四位一个竖线的"断位读数法"。如：

1234567890　英文：1,234,567,890　中文：12|3456|7890
25269056　英文：25,269,056　中文：2526|9056

以上的训练是数字口译的准备阶段，学员要排除掉轻视和抵触的情绪，坚持做下去，很快便会发现自己的双语思维和数字转换能力会有显著的提高。

除此之外，在真正的口译实战中，译员往往要遇到含有度量衡单位、表示增加减少的变化趋势以及许多特殊的数字表达形式，因此在训练的后期必须要进行专项的数字转换训练，逐个解决掉数字转换和表达上的具体问题，坚持将遇到或收集到的各种单位整理到学习笔记中。

数字概念转换：必须了解中英两种语言中诸多常见的数字概念的表达。

例：五又三分之一＝five and one third；7.5折＝25 percent off；three squared＝三的二次方

数字单位转换：必须熟练掌握中英两种语言中大部分常见的单位表达。

960万平方公里＝9.6 million square kilometers；100加仑＝100 gallons；180,000 light-years＝18万光年

数字增减表达：必须牢牢记住两种语言中表示增加、减少、倍数等形式的正确表达。

例：

同比增长17.1%＝with a year-on-year increase of 17.1%；up by 17.1% year on year
环比下跌2.5%＝decreased by 2.5% over that of the previous month
年均增长15.9%＝grew at an average annual rate of 15.9%

增加了 5 771 万＝increased by 57.71 million

达到 39.8 万亿元＝to reach 39.8 trillion yuan

从 3.16 万亿元增加到 8.31 万亿元＝increased from 3.16 trillion yuan to 8.31 trillion yuan

比上年增加 1 304.8 亿元＝an increase of 130.48 billion yuan over last year

占总额的 80.6％＝accounting for 80.6％ of the total value

2008 年,我国的国民生产总值将是 1980 年的四倍。By 2008, our GNP will have been four times/fourfold as much as it was in 1980.

2008 年,我国的国民生产总值将在 1980 年的基础上翻两番。By 2008, our GNP in 1980 will have been quadrupled.

2008 年,我国的国民生产总值将比 1980 年增加三倍。By 2008, our GNP will have increased by 300％ over 1980.

以上的学习和训练只要经过不长的时间就可以完成,而且会让初学者很快就有较大的能力提高。

但是,这里必须指出,在口译实战中真正困扰译员的决不限于这些数字的转换和表达,而是与数字相关联的各种经贸、金融等社会各个领域的概念和术语。因此,要想胜任实际的口译工作,学员必须要整理和识记大量的背景知识和术语表达。

例:

消费价格指数:Consumer Price Index,英文缩写为 CPI

货币供应量:money supply

tertiary industry:第三产业

carry-over effect:翘尾因素;延期生效;结账效应

口译中的中文称谓翻译

在外事接待活动中,译员首先面临的一道难题是称谓的口译。称谓代表了一个人的职位、职衔或学衔,体现了一个人的资历和地位。称谓的误译不仅是对有关人员的不尊重,而且也会产生种种不良的后果。称谓的准确翻译其关键在于译员对有关人员的身份及其称谓的表达是否有一个正确的理解,尤其是对称谓语的认识。一种称谓语很可能表示多种身份,例如,英语的头衔语 president,译成汉语时可视具体情况分别译作共和国的总统、国家主席、大学的校长、学院的院长、学会或协会的会长或主席、公司的总裁或董事长,等等。

一般说来,各类机构或组织的首长其汉语称谓译成英语时虽可套用通用词 head,但从比较严格的意义上看,应使用特定的、规范的称谓语。例如:

校长(大学)　President of Beijing University

校长(中小学)　Principal/Headmaster of Donghai Middle School

院长(大学下属)　Dean of the Graduate School

系主任(大学学院下属)　Chair/Chairman of the English Department

会长/主席(学/协会)　President of the Student Union, Shanghai University

厂长(企业)　Director of the Machine Tools Manufacturing Plant

院长(医院)　President of Huadong Hospital

主任(中心)　Director of the Business Center

主任(行政)　Director of Foreign Affairs Office
董事长(企业)　President/Chairman of the Board of Directors
董事长(学校)　President/Chairman of the Board of Trustees

首席长官的汉语称谓常以"总……"表示,而表示首席长官的英语称谓语则常带有 chief general, head, managing 这类词,因此当翻译冠以"总"字的头衔时,需遵循英语头衔的表达习惯:

总书记　general secretary
总工程师　chief engineer
总会计师　chief accountant
总建筑师　chief architect
总编辑　chief editor; editor-in-chief; managing editor
总出纳　chief cashier; general cashier
总裁判　chief referee
总经理　general manager; managing director; executive head
总代理　general agent
总教练　head coach
总导演　head director
总干事　secretary-general; commissioner
总指挥　commander-in-chief; generalissimo
总领事　consul-general
总监　chief inspector; inspector-general; chief impresario
总厨　head cook; chef

有些部门或机构的首长或主管的英译,可以用一些通用的头衔词表示,例如下列机构的负责人可以用 director, head 或 chief 来表示:

司(部属)　department
厅(省属)　department
署(省属)　office(行署为 administrative office)
局　bureau
所　institute
处　division
科　section
股　section
室　office
教研室　program/section

例:
局长　director of the bureau; head of the bureau; bureau chief。
国务院　the State Council,下属的部为 ministry,所以部长叫作 minister。
另外,公署专员叫作 commissioner,其办事机构叫作"专员公署",英语为 prefectural commissioner's office。

汉语中表示副职的头衔一般都冠以"副"字,英译时需视词语的固定搭配或表达习惯等情况,可选择 vice, associate, assistant, deputy 等词。相对而言,vice 使用面较广。例如:

副总统(或大学副校长等)　vice president

副主席(或系副主任等)　vice chairman

副总理　vice premier

副部长　vice minister

副省长　vice governor

副市长　vice mayor

副领事　vice consul

副校长(中小学)　vice principal

行政职务的副职头衔与学术头衔的"副"职称往往用不同的词表达,最为常用的英语词是 associate。例如:

副教授　associate professor

副研究员　associate research fellow

副主编　associate managing editor

副编审　associate senior editor

副审判长　associate judge

副研究馆员　associate research fellow of... (e.g. library science)

副译审　associate senior translator

副主任医师　associate senior doctor

当然,有些英语职位头衔,如 manager 和 headmaster,其副职头衔可冠以 assistant。例如:

副总经理　assistant/deputy general manager; assistant/deputy managing director

大堂副理(宾馆)　assistant manager

副校长(中小学)　assistant headmaster

以 director 表示的职位的副职常以 deputy director 表示。此外,secretary, mayor, dean 等头衔的副职也可冠以 deputy,例如:

副秘书长　deputy secretary-general

副书记　deputy secretary

副市长　deputy mayor

副院长　deputy dean

学术头衔系列除了含"正""副"级别的高级职称和中级职称外,还有初级职称,如"助理","助理"常用 assistant 来表示。例如:

助理教授　assistant professor

助理研究员　assistant research fellow

助理工程师　assistant engineer

助理编辑　assistant editor

助理馆员　assistant research fellow of... (e.g. library science)

助理教练　assistant coach

助理农艺师　assistant agronomist

还有一些行业的职称头衔,其高级职称不用"正"或"副"表示,而直接用"高级"或"资深"来表示,我们可以用 senior 来称呼。例如:

高级编辑　senior editor

高级工程师　senior engineer

高级记者　senior reporter

高级讲师　senior lecturer

高级教师　senior teacher

高级农艺师　senior agronomist

有一些行业的职称或职务系列中,最高级别的职位冠以"首席"一词,英语常用 chief 来表示。例如:

首席执行官　chief executive officer(CEO)

首席法官　chief judge

首席顾问　chief advisor

首席检察官　chief inspector/prosecutor

首席仲裁员　chief arbitrator

首席监事　chief supervisor

首席播音员　chief announcer/broadcaster

首席代表　chief representative

首席记者　chief correspondent

除了用"总"、"高级"、"首席"等词语来表示一些机构或行业的最高级职务之外,还有一些高级职务则使用带"长"字的头衔。例如:

检察长　procurator-general

审判长　presiding judge;chief judge;chief of judges

护士长　head nurse

秘书长　secretary-general

参谋长　chief of staff

厨师长　head cook,chef

有些头衔会含诸如"代理"、"常务"、"执行"、"名誉"这类称谓语。例如:

代理市长、代理总理、代理主任

常务理事、常务副校长

执行主席、执行主任、执行秘书

名誉校长、名誉会长

一般说来,"代理"可译作 acting。例如:

代理市长　acting mayor

代理总理　acting premier

代理主任　acting director

"常务"可以用 managing 表示。例如:

常务理事　managing director

常务副校长　managing vice president

"执行"可译作 executive。例如：

执行主任　executive director

执行秘书　executive secretary

执行主席　executive chairman（也可译作 presiding chairman）

"名誉"译为 honorary。例如：

名誉校长　honorary president/principal

名誉主席、会长　honorary chairman/president（也可用 emeritus 表示，如 emeritus chairman/president）

有些职称或职务带有"主任"、"主治"、"特级""特派"、"特约"等头衔，英译不尽相同。例如：

主任编辑　associate senior editor

主任秘书　chief secretary

主任医师　senior doctor

主任护士　senior nurse

主治医师　attending/chief doctor; physician; consultant

特级教师　special-grade senior teacher

特派记者　accredited correspondent

特派员/专员　commissioner

特约编辑　contributing editor

特约记者　special correspondent

许多职称、职务的头衔称谓其英语表达法难以归类，需要日积月累，逐步记录在自己的称谓语料库中。以下所列举是其中的一部分：

办公室主任　office manager（如"校长办公室主任"manager of president's office）

财务主任　treasurer

车间主任　workshop manager/director

编审　senior editor

博导（博士生导师）　doctoral student supervisor

研究生导师　graduate student tutor

客座教授　visiting professor

院士　academician

译审　senior translator

村长　village head

领班　captain; foreman; gaffer

经纪人　broker

税务员　tax collector

研究管员　research fellow of...（如"图书馆研究管员"research fellow of library science）

股票交易员　stock dealer

红马夹　(stock exchange) floor broker

业务经理　service/business/operation manager
住院医生　resident(doctor); registrar
国际大师　international master
注册会计师　chartered/certified public accountant; registered/incorporated accountant

我国有一些常见的荣誉称号(honorary title)在许多英语国家没有对应的表达语,现列举部分英译供参考:

标兵　pacemaker
学习标兵　student pacemaker; model student
劳动模范　model worker
模范教师　model teacher
优秀教师　excellent teacher
优秀员工　outstanding employee; employee of the month/year
青年标兵　model youth/youth pacemaker
青年突击手　youth shock worker
三好学生　"triple-A" outstanding student; outstanding student
三八妇女红旗手　"March 8th Red Banner" outstanding woman pacemaker

拓展阅读

选文A

商务部副部长钟山在"中意工商晚宴"上的致辞
2011年6月3日　意大利米兰

尊敬的习近平副主席:
尊敬的罗马尼部长,特莱蒙蒂部长,各位来宾:
大家晚上好!

为推动中意两国工商界的交流与合作,中国商务部与意大利经济发展部在习近平副主席访问之际,共同主办"中意工商晚宴"。首先,我代表中国商务部向承办此次活动的中国机电产品进出口商会、意大利对外贸易委员会和意中基金会表示诚挚的感谢,同时对意大利官方代表和企业家朋友们放弃假期出席晚宴表示衷心的感谢和热烈的欢迎。

中意建交41年来,在两国政府的积极推动和企业界的共同努力下,双边贸易高速增长。今年1~4月的双边贸易同比增长36.6%。双向投资快速发展,今年前4个月意对华投资同比增长42%,中国对意投资则比去年全年的总额增长一倍。两国经济技术合作不断加强,发展态势令人高兴。

中意两国经贸合作互补性强、基础牢固、潜力巨大。去年10月,两国总理提出到2015年双边贸易额达到800亿美元的新目标。中国愿继续扩大从意大利进口有竞争力的产品,促进两国贸易平衡。中国还将进一步鼓励企业到意大利投资;同时我们也欢迎意大利企业家来华投资;中国希望与意大利开展节能环保等高新技术领域的合作。

我相信,只要两国政府和企业界共同努力,不断拓展合作领域、创新合作方式,实现优势互补、互利共赢,为两国的经济社会发展做出新的贡献,造福两国人民。

谢谢大家。

译文

Opening Speech by Vice Minister Zhong Shan at China-Italy Business Dinner

Milan, Italy

June 3, 2011

Respected Vice President Xi Jinping,

Respected Minister Romani and Minister Tremonti,

Dear Guests,

Good evening!

In order to promote exchanges and cooperation between the business communities of China and Italy, the Chinese Ministry of Commerce and the Italian Ministry of Economic Development co-sponsored the China-Italy Business Dinner for Vice President Xi Jinping's visit to Italy. First, may I express, on behalf of the Chinese Ministry of Commerce, sincere gratitude to the organizers, namely, China Chamber of Commerce for Import and Export of Machinery and Electronic Products, Italian Foreign Trade Commission and Italy-China Foundation, as well as my heart felt thanks and a warm welcome to Italian officials and entrepreneurs who gave up holidays to attend the dinner.

Since China and Italy established diplomatic ties 41 years ago, bilateral trade has been growing rapidly thanks to the joint efforts of the governments and business circles of the two countries. In the first four months of 2011, bilateral trade was up 36.6% year-on-year. Bilateral investment has been developing rapidly, with investment from Italy to China soaring by 42% year-on-year, while investment from China to Italy doubled the total volume of 2010. Economic and technological cooperation between the two countries has strengthened, and kept a strong momentum.

China and Italy are highly complementary in trade and economic cooperation, with solid foundation and great potential. In October 2010, the Premiers of the two countries set a new target of bringing bilateral trade volume to US$ 80 billion in 2015. China will continue to expand imports of competitive products from Italy, and promote balanced trade between the two countries. China will also encourage enterprises to invest in Italy, and welcome Italian entrepreneurs to invest in China. China hopes to carry out cooperation with Italy in such high-tech sectors as energy conservation and environmental protection.

I believe that with the joint efforts of governments and business communities of both countries, we will expand and innovate cooperation, draw upon each other's advantages, realize mutual benefit and win-win, make new contribution to the economic and social development and bring benefit to the peoples of both countries.

Thank you.

选文B

Speech of H. E. Mr. Zhang Yan, Chinese Ambassador on the Inauguration Ceremony of Sany Heavy Industry India

April 12, 2010

H. E. Mr. Zhang Chunxian, Secretary of Hunan Provincial Committee of Communist Party of China

Mr. Sachin Ahir, Minister for Industries, Government of Maharashtra

Mr. Li Jiang, Secretary of Political and Legislative Affairs Committee of Hunan Province

Mr. Liang Wengen, Chairman of Sany Group

Distinguished guests, Ladies and Gentlemen,

It is my great pleasure to visit Pune, a beautiful and the second largest city of the state of Maharashtra, and attend the Inauguration Ceremony of the production plant of Sany Heavy Industry India. On behalf of the Embassy of the People's Republic of China in India and Chinese Consul-General in Mumbai, I would like to extend my warmest congratulations to Sany Heavy Industry India.

China and India border on each other by mountains and rivers and share long-standing history of friendship. With the joint efforts of China and India, our bilateral economic and trade cooperation has entered into a period of unprecedented development in recent years. According to the statistics of China Customs, China-India trade volume reached USD 51.8 billion in the year of 2008, achieving an average annual growth rate of 43% over the past 8 years. This year we are aiming at a total volume of 60 billion USD.

Cooperation in infrastructure construction has also witnessed a rapid development. Since 2006, Chinese companies have completed engineering projects in India with a cumulative value of USD 11.1 billion. These projects have improved the local infrastructure, and the social economic development in India. Meanwhile, investments between the two countries are also growing fast. The total volume of investment from both sides has exceeded USD 600 million. In addition, the two countries have been working closely to safeguard the rights and interests of developing countries in the multilateral trading system and the climate change negotiations.

Sany Group is a leading company in the field of heavy industry. As the biggest concrete machinery manufacturer in the world, Sany has been awarded a series of honors, such as one of the Global Top 50 Construction Machinery Manufacturers, China's Most Competitive Brand, and the Benchmarking Brand of the Chinese Construction Machinery Industries etc. In recent years, Sany Group has payed much attention to Indian Market. We are happy to see that the Sany Heavy Industry India today is launching its new production plant in Pune which is one of the four biggest construction machinery manufacturing bases of Sany overseas and the first entering into production. It is a concrete step in implementing the instruction made by Chinese President Hu Jintao during his visit to India in 2006, and another living testimony of growing economic cooperation between China and India. I believe, the Sany Heavy Industry India will not only provide high quality products and services to Indian customers, but also create more job opportunities through its efforts in the future. I also wish that Sany Heavy Industry India could create a win-win situation in cooperation with their Indian partners.

This year marks the 60th anniversary of the establishment of diplomatic relations between China and India. I believe in the 21st century China and India, two newly emerging economic powers, will live in greater harmony, work closely in a spirit of mutual benefit to further advance our strategic and cooperative partnership, and create a brighter future for both countries.

Today's Inauguration Ceremony marks a significant development of bilateral economic relations of China and India. I want to express my sincere congratulations to Sany India again and hope Sany India to achieve a great success in the future. I wish China-India friendly cooperative relationship growing stronger and stronger and last forever!

Thank you!

译文

中国驻印度大使张炎在三一重工印度产业园开业仪式的致辞
2010年4月12日

(中国共产党湖南省委书记)张春贤先生,
(马哈拉施特拉邦工业部长)萨钦先生,
(湖南政法委书记)李江先生,
(三一重工董事长)梁稳根先生,
各位嘉宾、女士们、先生们:

我很高兴能来到美丽的马哈拉施特拉邦第二大城市普那,出席三一重工印度产业园开业仪式,我谨代表中国驻印度大使馆和驻孟买总领事馆,向三一重工印度产业园致以热烈的祝贺。

中印两国山水相连,友谊源远流长,近年来在两国的共同努力下,双方经贸合作已进入前所未有的发展时期,据中国关税数据显示,2008年中印贸易总额达到了518亿美元,过去8年来平均每年增长43%,今年预计贸易总量将达到600亿美元。

中印基础设施建设合作迅速发展,自2006年来,中国企业已经在印度工程项目累计投资111亿,这些工程改善了印度本地的基础设施,促进了社会经济发展。同时,两国之间的投资也迅猛发展,双方投资总额已经超过了6亿。此外,我们两国还在确保发展中国家在多边贸易体系和气候变化谈判的权益方面紧密合作。

三一重工是重工业领域的佼佼者,作为世界混泥土机械制造商,三一拥有全球工程机械制造商50强、中国最具竞争力品牌、中国工程机械行业标志性品牌等荣誉称号。近些年来，三一重工高度重视印度市场，我们很高兴地看到今天三一重工在普那建立新的产业园，这是中国三一集团在海外四大基地中第一个投产的基地，是落实中国国家主席胡锦涛2006年访印期间有关加强中印经济贸易合作意见的具体成果之一，也是两国日益增长的经贸合作的明证。我相信，三一印度公司不仅会为印度市场生产高质量的基建工程机械产品，而且将为当地带来更多的就业机会。我祝愿三一印度公司与印度合作伙伴一道共同开创合作双赢的局面。

今年是中印建交60周年，我相信21世纪的中印两大新经济强国定能和谐共存，以互惠互利的精神紧密合作，进一步发展我们的战略合作伙伴关系，为两国创造更加美好的未来。

今天的开业仪式标志着中印双方经济关系的重大发展，我要再次表达对三一印度公司的诚挚祝贺，祝愿三一印度公司未来获得更大的成功，祝愿中印两国的友好合作关系不断加强，万世永存！

谢谢！

第十四单元　科　技
（Science & Technology）

单元要点

本单元共分五个层次，分别是：驻联合国大使刘振民在第64届联大四委关于"和平利用外空的国际合作"议题的发言汉译英一篇；2002年国务院副总理李岚清在国际数学家大会开幕式上的贺词英译汉一篇；科技口译的特点；口译前准备工作概述；拓展阅读（汉译英、英译汉各一篇）。第一、二部分提供科技口译的例文及其翻译和重难点评析；第三、四部分主要是相关口译理论与技能的介绍；第五部分的拓展阅读中，提供汉、英原文和参考译文。

理论难点提示

1. 科技口译的特点。
2. 口译前准备工作概述。

选文A

驻联合国大使刘振民在第64届联大四委关于"和平利用外空的国际合作"议题的发言
2009年10月21日

主席先生：

请允许我代表中国代表团向和平利用外空委员会主席团和联合国外空司表示感谢，对外空委第52届会议的工作成果表示祝贺。今年是联合国第三次外空大会召开10周年，我们高度评价第三次外空大会的积极意义，很高兴看到这次会议的各项建议得到不同程度地落实，取得很多惠及全人类的重要成果。

主席先生，

中国积极支持和始终坚持和平利用外空。我们呼吁国际社会共同努力，建设有利于和平、发展、合作和法治的"和谐外空秩序"。中国认为，任何违背和平利用外空原则的行为，包括外空武器化和外空军备竞赛，都是违背人类共同利益的。

去年，中国与俄罗斯共同向日内瓦裁谈会提交了"关于防止在外空部署武器以及对外空物体使用武力或威胁使用武力条约草案"，受到许多国家欢迎，我们期待各方早日就该条约草案启动正式谈判。

主席先生，

过去一年间，中国在和平探索和利用外空领域取得可喜成绩，在进入空间、卫星研制与应用、航天基础与保障、载人航天以及空间探索等五大方面的能力均得到提高。2009年3月，"嫦娥一号"飞船成功撞月，为中国绕月探测工程画上圆满句号。前不久，中国首个低纬度发射场——海南航天发射场破土动工。该发射场建成后,将大大提高中国航天发射的综合能力。

另外,空间技术在中国被广泛应用于农业、林业、国土、教育、水利、城乡建设、环境、测绘、交通、气象、海洋、地质科学研究等领域,给人民生活带来深刻变化。

中国在自身发展的同时,积极开展外空领域的国际交流与合作,促进各国共同发展。中国一直支持和帮助建立"联合国灾害管理和应急信息平台"北京办公室,目前已与联合国外空司就东道国协议基本达成一致。中国作为亚太空间合作组织的东道国,积极支持该组织各项工作,并于今年7月与该组织签署了东道国协议。中国支持该组织成为外空委观察员,希望该组织进一步加强与外空委的合作。

中国支持扩大外空领域合作,今年5月,中国与巴西签署协议,通过在南非、埃及和西班牙的接收站向非洲地区提供中巴地球资源卫星02B数据,以实际行动支持非洲各国探索和和平利用外空的努力。

主席先生,

外空是人类共同财富,发展外空事业应促进人类文明和社会进步,其所带来的利益应让全世界人民分享,特别应考虑发展中国家的需求。中国愿以开放和负责任的态度与更多国家,包括广大发展中国家开展空间技术合作,为使外空造福全人类贡献力量。

谢谢主席先生。

重难点评析

1. "我们高度评价第三次外空大会的积极意义",句中"高度评价"是致辞和发言的常用语,译为"We highly value the positive outcomes of UNISPACE Ⅲ."。

2. "得到不同程度地落实"译为"be implemented to varying degrees"。

3. "我们呼吁国际社会共同努力,建设有利于和平、发展、合作和法治的'和谐外空秩序'"。这句话中"和谐外空秩序"之前的定语比较长,故在英译中采用了词序的调译将其处理成定语从句后置,译为"We call for joint efforts by the international community to build a 'harmonious outer space order' which is conducive to peace, development, cooperation and the rule of law."。

4. "外空武器化和外空军备竞赛"译为"weaponization and arms race in outer space"。

5. "我们期待各方早日就该条约草案启动正式谈判。"外交常用辞令"期待启动正式谈判"译为"look forward to the initiation of formal negotiations",这里的"启动"进行了词类的换译。

6. "进入空间、卫星研制与应用、航天基础与保障、载人航天以及空间探索等五大方面的能力"译为"its capacities in five major areas, namely, entry into space, satellite development and applications, space infrastructure and ground support, manned space flights and deep space exploration"。

7. "为……画上圆满句号"译为"put a perfect period to"。

8. "……将大大提高中国航天发射的综合能力"。根据英语表达习惯采用了语态的换译,译文用了被动语态,"China's overall space-launching capabilities will be greatly enhanced."

9. "空间技术在中国被广泛应用于农业、林业、国土、教育、水利、城乡建设、环境、测绘、交通、气象、海洋、地质科学研究等领域",这些领域是口译中经常会被说到的,要熟悉它们各自的笔记符号和正确的英文表达,全句译为"Space technology has been widely used in agriculture, forestry, national land use and survey, education, irrigation and water conservancy, rural and urban development, environment protection and monitoring, mapping, traffic, meteorology, oceans, and geo-scientific research."。

10. "目前已与联合国外空司就东道国协议基本达成一致",外交常用辞令"与……就……达成一致",译为"has basically reached agreement with UNOOSA on a host country agreement."。

11. "亚太空间合作组织的东道国"译为"host to the Asia-Pacific Space Cooperation Organization(APSCO)";"东道国协议"译为"the host country agreement"。

12. "其所带来的利益应让全世界人民分享,特别应考虑发展中国家的需求"。译文中将句子中的两个部分都处理成了被动语态,工整简洁,全句译为"the benefits thereby generated should be shared among all the people of the world, and in particular, the need of the developing nations should be taken into account."。

译文

Statement by H. E. Ambassador Liu Zhenmin at the Fourth Committee of the 64th Session of the UN General Assembly on Agenda Item 30: "International cooperation in the peaceful uses of outer space"

New York, 21 October 2009

Mr. Chairman,

Please allow me, on behalf of the Chinese delegation, to extend our thanks and congratulations to the Bureau of the Committee on the Peaceful Uses of Outer Space (COPUOS) and the United Nations Office for Outer Space Affairs (UNOOSA) for the positive outcome of the 52nd Session of COPUOS. This year marks the 10th anniversary of UNISPACE III. We highly value the positive outcomes of UNISPACE III, and are pleased to note that its recommendations have been implemented to varying degrees with significant achievements that benefit mankind as a whole.

Mr. Chairman,

China has all along adhered to peaceful uses of Outer Space. We call for joint efforts by the international community to build a "harmonious outer space order" which is conducive to peace, development, cooperation and the rule of law. China is of the view that any act that contravenes the principle of peaceful uses of outer space, such as weaponization of and arms race in outer space, runs counter to the common interest of mankind.

Last year, China and the Russian Federation jointly tabled at the Conference on Disarmament in Geneva a draft Treaty on the Prevention of the Deployment of Weapons in

Outer Space, the Threat or Use of Force against Outer Space Objects, which was welcomed by many States. We look forward to the initiation of formal negotiations on the draft at an early date.

Mr. Chairman,

Over the past year, China has scored encouraging achievements in the exploration and peaceful uses of Outer Space, and strengthened its capacities in five major areas, namely, entry into space, satellite development and applications, space infrastructure and ground support, manned space flights and deep space exploration. In March this year, the successful impact on the Moon by the lunar probe "Chang-E1" put a perfect period to our lunar exploration program. Not long ago, the construction of China's first low-latitude space launch site — Hainan Spaceport — was started. Once completed, China's overall space-launching capabilities will be greatly enhanced.

Moreover, space technology has been widely used in agriculture, forestry, national land use and survey, education, irrigation and water conservancy, rural and urban development, environment protection and monitoring, mapping, traffic, meteorology, oceans, and geo-scientific research, bringing about profound changes in people's life in China.

While developing its own space capabilities, China is actively engaged in international exchange and cooperation in peaceful uses of outer space in an effort to promote common development. China has all along supported and helped the establishment of a UN-SPIDER (United Nations Platform for space-based information for Disaster Management and Emergercy Responses) office in Beijing, and has basically reached agreement with UNOOSA on a host country agreement. As host to the Asia-Pacific Space Cooperation Organization(APSCO), China actively supports its work in all aspects and signed the host country agreement with APSCO in July this year. China supports its application for observer status with COPUOS in the hope that it will further strengthen cooperation with COPUOS.

We support broadening international cooperation in outer space area. Last May, China signed an agreement with Brazil to provide Africa region with CBERS-02B(China-Brazil Earth Resources Satellite) data through ground stations in South Africa, Egypt and Spain, thereby supporting the African countries in their efforts to explore and use outer space peacefully.

Mr. Chairman,

As common wealth of mankind, outer space should be developed in the interest of promoting progress of human civilization and human society; the benefits thereby generated should be shared among all the people of the world, and in particular, the need of the developing nations should be taken into account. With an open mind and a sense of responsibility, China is ready to conduct cooperation in space technology with more countries, including developing countries, to contribute to the efforts of making outer space benefit mankind as a whole.

Thank you, Mr. Chairman.

选文B

Speech at the Opening Ceremony of International Congress of Mathematics
by Li Lanqing Vice-Premier of the People's Republic of China

Respected President Jiang Zemin, Respected IMU President Mr. Palis, Distinguished guests, ladies and gentlemen

Today, mathematicians from all over the world are gathering here for the first International Congress of Mathematicians in the new millennium. On behalf of President Jiang Zemin and the Chinese government, I have the pleasure to extend to you our warmest welcome.

No one could have imagined the extraordinary evolution of science and technology over the past century. Space exploration, nuclear energy, computers and information technology, not to mention biological engineering, are all milestones that mark a new era of knowledge for humankind. Our social progress depends on scientific innovation, and mathematics is fundamental to science. Mathematics expressed the theory of relativity and the quantum mechanics in the early 20th century; since then mathematicians have played a vital role in inventing computers, designing space and energy programs, and investigating the structure of DNA molecules. Mathematics is the language of the universe.

Mathematical methods are used extensively in economics, medicine, agriculture, architecture, arts and all other fields of modern knowledge. As Roger Bacon pointed out, mathematics is the key to all branches of science. Today mathematics is the keystone of high technology, and, in a sense, the symbol of modern civilization.

In this light, the Chinese government is especially delighted to see this congress being held in Beijing. As President Jiang Zemin clearly expressed when he met with Professor Chern Shing-shen, IMU President Palis and other mathematicians in October 2000, "the Chinese government fully supports hosting the 2002 International Congress of Mathematicians in Beijing. China wishes to take this opportunity to promote math research and education in the country, in an effort to bring them up to the world advanced level in the early 21st century and lay a solid foundation for the future progress of science and technology in China."

As a developing country, China is marching on the road toward modernization. It has been a century-long pursuit for the Chinese people to revitalize their country through development of science and education. This historical process has been even further accelerated in the last two decades by reform and opening up policies, as both young talents and accomplished experts emerge in great numbers on the international scientific scene. The Chinese government has fully supported all endeavors to pursue this development, including a series of programs launched nationwide to promote basic scientific research, especially in mathematics. For example, in the past four years, the National Science Foundation of China has doubled its funding for mathematics, and the government has allocated thousands of millions of yuan to support the Pilot Knowledge Innovation Program in the Chinese Academy of Sciences.

We are aware that China still has a long way to go before reaching the advanced world levels in science and technology. Science knows no boundaries. The advancement of science requires peace, stability and cooperation. In this regard, I believe that the International Congresses of Mathematicians, with over a hundred years of tradition, sets the example. Hosting the 24th Congress in Beijing is a good opportunity for Chinese scientists to learn from and to cooperate with their colleagues abroad. I hope that this congress will mark a new starting point for the development of mathematics and science in China. As the first congress ever held in a developing country, I also hope that this congress will inspire a new era of international cooperation for global scientific community.

In about 10 minutes' time, the new Fields medallists and the winner of the Nevanlinna Prize will be announced and awarded. I would like to take this opportunity to offer them my sincere congratulations. Their achievements not only represent their distinguished contributions to mathematics, but to world cooperation and the well-being of all humankind.

In conclusion, I wish this congress a great success, and all our guests a memorable stay in China.

Thank you!

重难点评析

1. "Space exploration, nuclear energy, computers and information technology, not to mention biological engineering, are all milestones that mark a new era of knowledge for humankind."本句采用了词的省译,将"milestones"略去未译,更加符合英文习惯,全句译为"太空探索、核能、计算机信息技术,当然还有生物工程,这一切都标志着人类进入了一个崭新的知识时代"。

2. "the theory of relativity and the quantum mechanics"译为"相对论与量子力学"。

3. "Mathematicians have played a vital role in inventing computers, designing space and energy programs, and investigating the structure of DNA molecules."译为"数学家们在计算机的研制、空间与核能计划的发展乃至DNA结构的探索中都发挥着重要的作用"。

4. "… and, in a sense, the symbol of modern civilization."译为"……在一定意义上可以说是现代文明的标志"。

5. "… in an effort to bring them up to the world advanced level in the early 21st century and lay a solid foundation for the future progress of science and technology in

China." 译为"力争在下世纪初将中国的数学研究与人才培养推向世界前列,为中国今后的科技发展奠定坚实雄厚的基础"。

  6. "It has been a century-long pursuit for the Chinese people to revitalize their country through development of science and education." 句中的 it 是形式主语,真正的主语是不定式 to 引导的,应译为"科教兴国是中国人民一个多世纪以来始终奋力追求的目标"。

  7. "the National Science Foundation of China has doubled its funding for mathematics"译为"中国国家自然科学基金委员会对数学的资助就翻了一番/是原来的两倍之多"。

  8. "the Pilot Knowledge Innovation Program in the Chinese Academy of Sciences"译为"中国科学院知识创新试点工程"。

  9. "Science knows no boundaries"译为"科学无国界"。

  10. "mark a new starting point for sth."译为"成为……的新起点","inspire a new era of sth."译为"开辟……的新时代"。

  11. "In about 10 minutes' time, the new Fields medallists and the winner of the Nevanlinna Prize will be announced and awarded."原句是被动语态,翻译时为符合中文的表达习惯使用了主动语态并省译了主语,全句译为"再过10分钟时间,将要宣布新的菲尔兹奖与奈瓦林纳奖获得者"。

译文

2002年国务院副总理李岚清在国际数学家大会开幕式上的贺词

尊敬的江泽民主席,尊敬的帕利斯教授,
贵宾们,女士们,先生们:
  今天,来自世界各地的数学家聚集一堂,举行新世纪的第一次国际数学家大会。我谨代表江泽民主席和中国政府向各位表示热烈的欢迎。
  在过去一个世纪里,科学技术发生了前人无法想象的巨大发展。太空探索、核能、计算机信息技术,当然还有生物工程,这一切都标志着人类进入了一个崭新的知识时代。社会的进步依赖于科学的创新,而数学对于科学的发展则具有根本的意义。数学在20世纪初相对论与量子力学的创立中建有奇功;自那时以来,数学家们在计算机的研制、空间与核能计划的发展乃至DNA结构的探索中都发挥着重要的作用。数学是宇宙的语言。
  数学方法在经济、医学、农业、建筑和艺术等现代知识的所有领域中都得到了广泛的应用。正如罗杰·培根所说,数学是所有学科的钥匙;而今天,数学则是高技术的基础,并且在一定意义上可以说是现代文明的标志。
  基于以上认识,中国政府非常高兴地看到2002国际数学家大会能在北京举行。正如中华人民共和国主席江泽民在2000年10月接见陈省身教授和国际数学联盟主席帕利斯等中外著名数学家时所表示的那样:"中国政府支持2002年在北京召开国际数学家大会,并希望藉此契机力争在下世纪初将中国的数学研究与人才培养推向世界前列,为中国今后的科技发展奠定坚实雄厚的基础。"
  作为发展中国家,中国正在现代化建设的道路上迈进。科教兴国是中国人民一个多世纪以来始终奋力追求的目标。在过去的20多年里,这一历史过程在改革开放方针的指引下获得了加速发展。年轻人才和有造诣的专家大量涌现并活跃在国际科技舞台。中国政府全力支持一切有利于这一发展的努力,制定了一系列促进包括数学在内的基础科学研究的国家计划和规划。例如,在过去4年里,中国国家自然科学基金委员会对数学的资助就翻了一番;在国家支持中国科学院知识创新试点工程的拨款中有一亿元左右用于数学研究。

我们清楚地认识到,中国的科学技术要达到世界先进水平还要经过长期的努力。科学是没有国界的,科学的发展需要和平、稳定与合作。在这方面,我认为已有百年传统的国际数学家大会为我们提供了范例。在北京举办第24届国际数学家大会,为中国科学家带来了向国际同行学习并在更广泛的规模上展开合作的难得机遇。我希望本次大会将成为中国数学与科学发展的一个新的起点。同时,作为首次在发展中国家举办的国际数学家大会,我希望本次大会也将为全世界的科学界开辟一个国际合作的崭新时代。

再过10分钟时间,将要宣布新的菲尔兹奖与奈瓦林纳奖获得者。我愿借此机会向他们表示衷心的祝贺。他们的研究成果不仅是对数学发展的卓越贡献,也是对全世界的合作和人类的幸福作出的卓越贡献。

最后,预祝大会圆满成功,预祝各位代表和各位来宾在中国度过难忘的时光!
谢谢大家。

科技口译的特点

与其他类型的口译相比,科技口译有其自身的特点。它要求译员不仅要具备坚实的语言基础,还要懂得相关专业知识,具备敏捷的思维能力和灵活的应变能力。科技口译的特点可以归纳如下:

1. 口译的服务对象多是中外专业技术人员,故对口译人员口译质量的要求很高。谈话双方谈论的都是一些与专业有关的问题。因此,翻译时要准确、精炼,切忌不懂装懂、含糊其辞或凭直觉作出不确切的翻译,引起双方的误解。

2. 科技口译涉及的专业种类较多。这一特点要求译员必须熟悉某一或数种专业基本知识,掌握这些专业的中英文含义及词汇,并能在较短的时间内掌握所承担翻译任务的专业知识。

3. 虽然科技口译对准确性要求很高,但也不乏灵活性。译员除了要精通两种语言、有非凡的记忆力以及广博的知识面之外,还要有灵活的应变能力、敏捷的思维能力和快速的反应能力。这是一项复杂的综合能力,绝非一朝一夕就能获得,需要长期不懈的积累和训练。

4. 在我们所能遇到的口译现场中,所使用的词汇大部分为非技术词汇(non-technical words)或半技术词汇(semi-technical words),而所谓纯专业词汇(specialized words)所占比例较小。因此我们在担任现场翻译时,要特别注意多用词汇(multi-purpose words)的用法,因为有些词汇既可用于日常生活口语,又可用于技术领域。

5. 科技口译中会遇到不少缩略词。有些在词典上查得到,有些查不到。译员不仅平时要多记缩略词,还要不断掌握新出现的缩略词,做到脱口而出。对于查不到的词,如有可能,提前向专家请教,排除障碍。

由于科技口译有上述特点,译员必须做好翻译前的准备工作,掌握专业术语和专业词汇。平时要注意阅读,搜集并整理新词汇、新术语,扩大知识面。勤于实践,不断提高自己的业务水平和能力。

口译前准备工作概述

大发明家贝尔(Alexander Graham Bell)有句名言:Before anything else, preparation is the key to success. 这句话在任何工作中都适用。充分的译前准备是成功完成口译任务的关键。

按照从接受任务到进入现场的时间顺序,译前准备包括以下几个步骤:

1. 任务准备

译员接受一项口译任务后,首先要向组织者了解和获取此次任务的相关详情:

A. 口译类型:是交替传译还是同声传译;是正式口译还是非正式口译;是联络口译、商务谈判还是会议翻译等。

B. 行业类型:是教育、金融、医药还是外事等行业。

C. 活动安排:时间地点、日程安排、活动名称、人员规模、组织联络、工作环境、现场设施、特殊要求等。

D. 服务对象:发言人和听众的情况,包括国籍、语言、身份、背景等。

E. 相关资料:是否有发言稿、发言提纲、PPT 幻灯片、参考资料、相关网站等。

2. 专题准备

在第一课中我们已经介绍,好的口译员要具备扎实的双语知识、广博的百科知识和快速学习新知识的能力。在一个具体的口译任务中,译员除了要调动平时长期的知识储备和经验积累外,还要能够在短时间内进行专题知识和任务的更新与准备。这一过程由于任务日程和难易程度的不同通常要经历几天到几周的时间:

(1) 专业知识

通过组织方、工具书、参考文献、互联网等各种途径搜集整理与口译任务相关的各类资料,进行全面、深入、细致的专业知识学习和准备。

组织者提供的资料:高度重视、熟烂于心。

自己搜集和整理的资料必须至少包含以下三个方面的内容:

① 专题词汇术语(双语对照);

② 概念理论及常识;

③ 相关参考文章或发言资料(双语对照)。

(2) 任务模拟

由于译员接受口译任务时获得的任务信息和官方材料的不同,口译任务可以分为明确型、模糊型和未知型任务,译员可以在准备好专业知识后针对不同情况进行任务模拟:

明确型任务:译员已知任务的主题、详细安排、具体内容、发言稿或相关材料时,要重点研究发言稿或材料的内容,对材料进行笔译、视译,模拟口译任务的全过程。

模糊型任务:译员仅知道大概任务主题、行业类型、口译类型、服务对象、少量发言内容和材料时,要根据任务介绍和仅有的官方材料进行联想和预测,熟悉发言人可能涉及的各方面内容,分析发言可能出现的话语类型、主要内容和逻辑思路,建立大概的发言框架进行口译模拟。

未知型任务:译员仅知道大概任务主题、行业类型、口译类型时,需要准备的内容会更加广泛,同样按照上面的方法进行框架推理和内容预测,并在接下来的准备时间、乃至临场之前继续保持与组织方的密切沟通,以获得更多任务信息和资料。

3. 身心准备

身体准备:调整作息时间,注意饮食,保证身体健康、精力充沛。

心理准备:调整情绪,准备好可能遇到的临场状况,放松心态,增强自信心。

4. 行前准备

在临行前要做好个人和工作的各类准备:

着装、交通、文件、材料、文具、电子词典、电脑

手机、联络簿、饮用水、含片、点心

……

5. 现场准备

与联络人密切沟通,核实工作流程,获取最新信息和资料。

尽快确定好工作位置,熟悉工作环境,检查工作设备。

在可能的情况下与发言人进行简单沟通,熟悉发音特点,了解发言内容。

如果是同传任务,与工作伙伴进行交流沟通,协调配合,增强互信。

整理好工具、着装,提前去好洗手间。

调节情绪,做好深呼吸,舒缓紧张心情,全身心投入到接下来的工作中。

拓展阅读

选文A

在国务院新闻办新闻发布会上的讲话

全国政协副主席、科学技术部部长　万　钢

(2008年5月8日)

各位记者朋友,女士们,先生们:

上午好!

感谢大家来出席这次新闻发布会。下面,我向各位简要介绍一下"科技奥运"的情况。

现代奥运会离不开科技的有力支撑。为了把北京奥运会办成一届"有特色、高水平"的奥运会,实现"绿色奥运、科技奥运、人文奥运"的承诺,全国科技界结合北京奥运会建设的重大科技需求,发挥团结协作和联合攻关的优势,开发和应用了大批先进、适用的创新技术成果,一方面为北京奥运建设提供了全方位的技术支持和服务,另一方面也大大地促进了科技及其产业化的发展。我们有理由相信,即将开幕的2008年北京奥运会,一定会成为奥运史上科技含量最高的一届奥运会,也会成为奥运史上节能环保程度最高的一届奥运会。

七年来,科技奥运建设取得了以下主要成效:

一是为北京奥运会建设提供了全面的科技支撑,把"科技奥运"理念变成了实际行动。

申奥成功后,科技部会同北京市等有关部门,制定了"奥运科技(2008)行动计划",以实

践"科技奥运"理念、支撑"绿色奥运"建设为重点,围绕与举办奥运会直接相关的场馆建设、大型活动、赛事组织等方面的科技需求,组织开展技术攻关和技术应用,攻克了一系列技术难题。一大批先进技术应用于北京奥运会建设中,显著提高了北京奥运会的科技含量。

二是集成应用了一批绿色环保和节能减排技术,以科技创新支撑"绿色奥运"理念。

围绕"绿色奥运"建设和节能减排目标,重点开展了绿色建筑、清洁能源、生态环境等方面的技术开发和应用示范。一批先进的新能源汽车、绿色能源、高效节能和环保新技术、新工艺和新产品得到了广泛的应用,并将在北京奥运会期间发挥重要作用。尤其是,500多辆新能源汽车投入应用,将在奥运史上首次实现在奥林匹克中心区域的交通"零排放"。这些新能源和节能环保新技术在北京奥运会的成功应用,将对全世界起到积极的示范作用,并对世界人类进步产生重要影响。

三是大量运用了信息通讯和智能交通等先进技术成果,丰富了"人文奥运"内涵。

围绕实现"4个ANY"的奥运承诺,通过应用信息通信、智能交通和安全保障等当代最先进的高新技术成果,使北京奥运会的信息通信、城市交通、食品安全和气象预报等服务更加快捷和方便,更加人性化和个性化,体现并丰富了"人文奥运"的理念。

四是"科技奥运"建设明显提升我国自主创新能力,带动和促进了信息、环保等新兴产业的发展。

奥运建设已经明显推动了我国交通、建筑、气象等传统产业的整体提升,同时也促进了新能源汽车、能源环保和信息等新兴产业的跨越式发展。这些科技创新成果的推广应用和产业化发展,有力地提高了我国的科技水平和自主创新能力。

另外,为了让世界各国和国内公众了解科技奥运取得的重大成效,体验和感受"科技奥运"理念的内涵,科技部、北京市政府、北京奥组委会同其他有关部门将在今年5月20—25日召开的"第11届中国北京国际科技产业博览会"期间,举办以"让北京更美好、让奥运更精彩"为主题的科技奥运展览,主要内容将以科技支撑绿色奥运、丰富人文奥运为主线,围绕科技奥运"六大目标"展开。参展项目将达到150多项。欢迎各位届时参观!

下面,我和北京市科委马林主任、北京奥组委技术部杨义春部长、科技部计划司秦勇副司长愿意回答大家的提问。

译 文

Speech at the Press Conference held by the State Council Information Office

Vice chairman of the National Committee of CPPCC,

minister of Ministry of Science and Technology 8 May, 2008

Ladies and gentlemen,
Good morning!

Thank you for attending this press conference. I wish to brief you on our work regarding High-tech Olympics.

A modern Olympics needs to be supported by science and technology. In order to make the Beijing Olympics a characteristic and high-level one and realize the commitments of "Green Olympics, High-Tech Olympics and People's Olympics", by our concerted efforts, the science and technology community has developed and applied a great number of advanced and practical innovative achievements according to the major scientific and technological demands of the construction for Beijing Olympics. By doing so, we shall provide an all-round technological support and service to the construction for the Beijing Olympics on the one hand, and greatly facilitate the development of science and technology as well as its commercialization on the other. We are convinced that the 2008 Beijing Olympics will turn out to be one that not only takes the lead in its application of science and technology but also does the best in energy conservation and environmental protection. During the past seven years, our endeavor in "High-tech Olympics" has achieved the following results:

Firstly, we have provided the construction for Beijing Olympics with an all-round scientific and technological support and turned the concept of "High-tech Olympics" into action.

After the success in Olympic Bid, together with Beijing Municipality and related government departments, MOST (Ministty of Science and Technology) promulgated *The Action Plan for High-tech Olympics 2008*. Focusing on realizing "High-tech Olympics" concept and supporting "Green Olympics" construction, our efforts aim to meet the scientific and technological demands from venue building, large-scale events and competition organization, which are directly related to the Olympic Games. We have made technological breakthroughs and applications, and solved a series of technological difficulties. A batch of advanced technologies will be adopted in the construction of the Olympics, which serves to significantly improve the scientific and technological level of the Beijing Olympics.

Secondly, we have integrated and applied many environmentaly friendly, energy saving and emission reducing technologies, underpinning the concept of "Green Olympics" with science, technology and innovation.

In order to achieve the goals of "Green Olympics" construction, energy conservation and emission reduction, we have attached great importance to technological development and applicable demonstration in the areas of green buildings, clean energies and eco-environment. A group of advanced new energy vehicles, green energies, highly efficient and environmentaly friendly new technologies, new techniques and new products are extensively utilized and will play a significant role during the Beijing Olympics. In particular, over 500 new energy vehicles will be used, which is the first time for Olympic central zones to realize zero emission in the history of Olympic Games. The successful application of new energies and energy saving, emission reducing technologies in the Beijing Olympics will set a good example for the whole world and contribute to the progress of the humanity.

Thirdly, we have employed advanced technologies including ICT (Information and Communication Technology) and ITS (Intelligent Transportation System), which enriches the connotation of "People's Olympics".

We have made the commitment that by 2008, information services will be inexpensive, rich in content, free of language barrier, customized and available at any terminal for anyone, at anytime and anywhere. Honoring this commitment, we have applied the most advanced new and high technologies such as ICT, ITS and Security Guarantee. By doing so, we aim to make information and communication, urban transportation, food safety, weather forecast as well as other services more convenient, considerate and individualized during the Olympic Games. Thus, it will embody the concept of "People's Olympics".

Fourthly, our endeavor in "High-tech Olympics" has markedly upgraded China's innovation capacity and facilitated the development of emerging industries such as information and environmental protection.

The Olympic constructions have noticeably promoted the upgrade of China's traditional industries such as transportation, construction, and meteorology. In the meantime, they have also accelerated the leapfrog development of emerging industries including new energy vehicles, energy and environmental protection, and information. The promotion, application and commercialization of those scientific and technological innovation results serve to improve China's science and technology level as well as innovation capacity.

Further more, in order that people both at home and abroad can be informed of major achievements and experience the concept of "High-tech Olympics", the Ministry of Science and Technology, Beijing Municipal Government, the Beijing Organizing Committee of the Olympic Games (BOCOG) and other related agencies will co-host High-tech Olympic Achievements Exhibition with the theme of "Making Beijing more beautiful and making the Olympics more wonderful". This exhibition is to be held during the 11th China Beijing International High-tech Expo from May 20—25, 2008. Aiming at six objectives of High-tech Olympics, the main contents for the exhibition will focus on science and technology as a support to Green Olympics and enrichment to People's Olympics. There will be over 150 projects on show. Welcome to the exhibition.

Next, Mr. Yang Yichun, Director of Technology Department of BOCOG, Mr. Ma Lin, Director General of Beijing Municipal Science and Technology Commission, Mr. Qin Yong, Deputy Director General of the Department of Development Planning of MOST, and I are delighted to take a few questions.

选文B

Better Life in Rural Communities with ICTs
Message from Dr. Hamadoun Touré, ITU Secretary-General
World Telecommunication and Information Society Day, 17 May 2011

ICTs are constantly reshaping the way the world communicates while creating opportunities for a better life through long-term, sustainable development, not least among the most disadvantaged sections of our society.

This year, as we celebrate ITU's 146th anniversary, we focus our attention on the world's rural communities in our quest to connect the remotest corners to the benefits of ICTs.

Today, ICTs are the powerhouses of the global economy and offer real solutions towards generating sustainable economic growth and prosperity. ICTs also act as catalysts in accelerating progress towards meeting the Millennium Development Goals.

In the rural context, ICTs provide enhanced opportunities to generate income and combat poverty, hunger, ill health and illiteracy. ICTs and related e-applications are key instruments in improving governance and rural services, such as providing community health care, safe drinking water and sanitation, education, food and shelter; improving maternal health and reducing child mortality; empowering women and the more vulnerable members of society; and ensuring environmental sustainability.

Half the world's population — nearly 3.5 billion people — resides in rural districts and far flung communities, representing the poorer, less educated, and more deprived cousins of the world's urban citizens. Among them are as many as 1.4 billion of the world's extremely poor people, who are also among the least connected to the benefits of ICTs. We cannot allow this situation to continue. It is time for global action to connect rural communities to the opportunities offered by ICTs.

ITU is committed to connecting the world and to ensuring that the benefits of ICTs reach the remotest corners as well as the most vulnerable communities. I am proud to say that our work at ITU in developing the standards for ICTs, managing vital spectrum and orbital resources, mobilizing the necessary technical, human and financial resources, and strengthening emergency response in the aftermath of devastating natural disasters has met with unprecedented success as we enter the second decade of this millennium.

Although mobile penetration has spread rapidly with over 5.3 billion subscribers worldwide, the thrust now is to drive content through enhanced broadband access aimed at establishing the information and communication highways — networks that will feed both rural communities and urban centres with the means to meet their development goals and aspirations. ITU's leadership role in the Broadband Commission for Digital Development is aimed at increasing the roll out of this state-of-the-art technology to firmly establish a universally accessible knowledge-based information society.

I urge you to celebrate World Telecommunication and Information Society Day this year by focusing on connecting people around the world and harnessing the full potential of ICTs so that we can all enjoy a more productive, peaceful and — in every way — a better life, particularly in rural areas.

译 文

信息通信技术让农村生活更美好
国际电信联盟秘书长　哈玛德·图埃博士的致辞
世界电信和信息社会日,2011年5月17日

信息通信技术(ICT)不断改变着世界上人们交流的方式。与此同时,长期、可持续的ICT发展亦为人民,尤其是我们社会中的最弱势群体,创造着过上更好生活的机遇。

今年国际电联146周年的庆典活动将关注全球的农村社区,以体现我们为使世界最偏远角落的人们享受到ICT的福祉所做出的努力。

如今,ICT大力推动着全球经济发展,为实现可持续的经济增长和繁荣提供了现实的解决方案。ICT还是加速实现千年发展目标的催化剂。

在农村,ICT为增加收入和战胜贫困、饥饿、疾病和文盲提供了机遇。ICT及相关电子应用是完善管理和提供农村服务的重要工具,这些服务包括提供社区医保、安全饮水与卫生服务、教育、食品和居所;提高产妇健康水平并降低儿童死亡率;赋予妇女和社会较弱势群体各种能力;确保环境的可持续性。

全球半数人口(近35亿人)居住在农村地区和偏远社区,他们是全球城市居民的同胞,但往往比城市居民贫穷,教育水平低、生活条件差。他们当中有多达14亿人是世界上最贫困且极少受益于ICT的人口。我们不能允许这种状况持续下去。现在是开展全球行动,让农村社区迎来ICT提供的机遇的时候了。

国际电联致力于连通世界,致力于确保最边远地区和最弱势群体亦能受益于ICT。在我们跨入本世纪第二个十年之际,我可以自豪地说,国际电联在所开展的ICT标准制定、关键的频谱和轨道资源管理、必要的技术、人力和财力资源筹措以及加强毁灭性自然灾害发生后的应急反应机制等方面,均取得了前所未有的成果。

移动业务发展迅猛,全球用户已突破53亿,目前的工作重点是通过强化宽带接入推进内容的发展,从而建成信息通信高速公路——即,建成能够利用各种手段,使农村社区和城市均能实现其发展目标与抱负的网络。国际电联在宽带数字发展委员会中发挥的领导作用就是,大力推广此类最先进的技术,为一个面向大众的知识型信息社会奠定坚实基础。

在庆祝今年的世界电信和信息社会日之时,我谨敦促各位特别关注连通世界各国人民和充分利用ICT潜力的问题,只有这样才能让人人(尤其是农村地区的人们)都过上更富成效、更为祥和以及在方方面面均更为美好的生活。

第十五单元　网络时代
（Network Times）

单元要点

本单元共分五个层次，分别是：中国互联网协会理事长胡启恒在第四届中美互联网论坛上的讲话汉译英；康柏公司主席及首席执行官埃克哈德·费佛关于中国青少年信息网络工程的讲话英译汉一篇；口译员的临场应变策略；中文网络流行词汇英文译解；拓展阅读（汉译英、英译汉各一篇）。第一、二部分提供网络时代口译的例文及其翻译和重难点评析；第三、四部分主要是相关口译理论与技能的介绍；第五部分的拓展阅读中，提供汉、英原文和参考译文。

理论难点提示

1. 口译员的临场应变策略。
2. 中文网络流行词汇英文译解。

选文A

在第四届中美互联网论坛上的讲话

中国互联网协会理事长　胡启恒

2010年11月8日

尊敬的钱小芊副主任，

尊敬的罗伯特·赫马茨先生，

克瑞格·蒙迪先生，

女士们，先生们，

大家下午好，由中国互联网协会和美国微软公司联合发起的第四届中美互联网论坛于今天正式拉开帷幕。首先，我谨代表中方主办者中国互联网协会对来自中美两国互联网行业的各位嘉宾，表示热烈的欢迎，向参与本次论坛报道的新闻媒体朋友们表示欢迎和感谢，向积极支持和组织筹办本次论坛的中美双方的业界同仁表示衷心的感谢。

本届中美互联网论坛的主题是为了更加有用，更加可信赖的互联网。在为期两天的会议期间，双方代表将围绕云计算、网络犯罪和隐私保护的国际合作、在线知识产权保护和标准、互联网法制和新媒体等议题进行交流和对话，共同分享有意义的实践，增进彼此之间的认识和理解，对于促进中美两国互联网行业的健康发展和交流协作，造福两国网民，将起到积极的作用。

近两年来中国网民规模急剧扩大，网络基础设施日益完善，互联网普及率不断提高，截至 2010 年 6 月,中国网民规模达到 4.4 亿,互联网普及率攀升到 33%,宽带网民规模是 3.6 亿,使用电脑上网的群体中宽带普及率达到 98%,国际出口带宽近 1 000 G,农村网民达到 1.15 亿,占整体网民的 27.4%,网民每周上网的时间继续增加,人均每周上网时长达到 19.8 小时。特别值得一提的是中国手机网民的规模达到 2.77 亿,其中只使用手机上网的网民占整体网民的比例提升到了 11.7%,使用手机作为上网设备的占比攀升到了 65.9%,移动互联网用户在全部移动用户的渗透率达到 33%,手机网民在信息获取和交流沟通类的应用上,使用率比较高,手机的即时通信使用率位居首位,达到 61.5%,手机搜索以 48.4% 的使用率排名第二。

手机网民快速增长的一个重要驱动力是移动互联网的快速发展,3G 的普及,基于 3G 的使用丰富多彩,阅读、音乐、互动社区、支付、应用程序商店等各种应用争奇斗艳,日新月异,吸引着越来越多的手机上网用户。随着三网融合试点工作的不断深入和推进,移动互联网在我国尤其农村地区的发展和普及,还将要进一步加快。当前我国拥有自主知识产权的移动互联网相关产品不断涌现,产业链的参与者越来越多,为用户提供更加便捷和舒适的个性化服务,成为移动互联网产业各方的共识。例如优视科技公司开发的 UC 浏览器,它拥有完整的自主产权,不但使用方便还可以为用户节省流量,良好的用户体验,使之拥有超过了全球四亿次的下载量。当前北京、上海、南京、杭州、广州等多个城市都开展了无线城市建设,在广州召开的亚运会和亚洲残运会期间北京实行全程的无线网络 WIFI 上网。运营商提供了随时随地达到了 3 MB 的网速,用户可以通过手机、笔记本等方式享受移动互联网高速冲浪随时随地关注亚运的赛况。可以肯定地说,随着移动通讯技术的不断升级发展,移动互联网在中国有着非常广阔的发展空间。

微博的流行也使无线网迅速流行,国内以新浪微博为代表的一批微博发展壮大,开展了中国微博时代。相关机构预测,到 2010 年底,国内微博服务商的累计注册活跃账户数将突破 6 500 万个。在今年的 8 月,中国互联网协会主办的 2010 中国互联网大会期间,会场上首次启用微博互动,腾讯微博在会场安装两块大型显示屏显示会议期间发表的所有的有价值有趣味的内容。大会也首次提供大会嘉宾回答微博提问的环节,大众的参与度提高了,由此诞生了一个网络热词——上墙。这个例子充分展现了微博强大的互动效果,及潜在的巨大营销潜力和舆论影响,引起了各方的关注。如何利用好微博等新媒体手段,进一步服务经济发展和促进公共事务透明化,是我们将要深入探讨和研究的问题之一。

中国的电子商务不断向传统产业渗透、融合,带动相关产业快速发展,并成为基于互联网的新兴服务业。大型企业电子商务应用水平显著提高,并逐渐向网上设计、制造、计划、管理等纵深发展,中小企业在以销售、采购为代表的生产经营各环节的电子商务应用中保持高速增长,并呈现出"多渠道,主动性"的特征。电子商务服务业的作用也将随着电子商务应用的日益广泛和深入而显得更加突出,在与电子商务相关的信用、支付、物流、IT、金融等领域涌现出越来越多的服务商和服务模式,为电子商务活动提供多样化的服务。据统计 2009 年中国电子商务交易额达 3.8 万亿元,其中大中型工业企业电子商务交易额达到 1.57 万亿元人民币,中小企业电子商务交易额达到 1.99 万亿元人民币,网络购物交易额达到 2 586 亿人民币,占社会零售总额的 2.06%。

政府对互联网技术的发展与创新也非常重视,近年来一直积极推进和加快下一步互联网、物联网以及云计算等关键技术的研发和产业化,引领产业快速发展。以云计算为例,当前已有阿里巴巴、腾讯、百度、中国石化等一些大型企业建立自己的云计算平台。在云计算应用过程中,如何保护用户数据和隐私安全一直是各方关注的焦点,九月于立陶宛召开的联合国互联网治理论坛第五次会议上业界针对这个问题也进行了专门的探讨,微软提出建议进一步加强云计算提供商在隐私和安全保护的透明度以及联合打击犯罪方面加强合作,肯尼亚会议建议建立一套全球云计算安全与隐私保护的标准等。

尽管近年来中国互联网的发展取得了一定成绩,但仍然有些地方需要继续努力和积极推动,例如缩小数字鸿沟,抵制网络色情,深化网络版权保护和网络安全工作等;此外中国互联网行业的整体创新能力不够,对互联网的理解利用程度和深度上,仍与国际同行存在一定差距。由于国家所处的发展阶段技术水平和文化方面的差异,中美两国互联网产业在发展过程中出现不同的特点和情况,同时也存在着许多共同的话题和关注点,因此双方需要进一步加强相互之间的理解、交流和合作。中国互联网协会非常愿意继续积极推动双方交流。

本届论坛,为双方提供了一个良好的交流互动平台,在接下来的会议过程中希望来自中美两国互联网的企业和专家代表们畅所欲言,各抒己见,特别希望中国互联网界的代表们,珍惜本次宝贵的机会认真借鉴和学习美国同仁在互联网创新当中的成功经验和有效做法。

女士们、先生们,

让我们脚踏实地,真诚合作,携手并进,为营造一个和谐、绿色、更加有用、更加可信赖的互联网不懈努力,共同创造互联网的美好明天,最后衷心祝愿本届中美互联网论坛圆满成功!

谢谢大家。

重难点评析

1. "正式拉开帷幕"译为"formally raise its curtain"。

2. "双方代表将围绕云计算、网络犯罪和隐私保护的国际合作、在线知识产权保护和标准、互联网法制和新媒体等议题进行交流和对话"句中由于"围绕"后的议题部分内容很长,故采用倒译的方法,将"交流和对话"提前译出,全句译为"delegates from both sides will carry out direct communication and conversation on the topics like 'cloud computing', 'International cooperation on Internet crime prevention and privacy protection', 'online intellectual property rights protection and criteria' and 'Internet law and the development of new media'."。

3. "手机网民快速增长的一个重要驱动力是移动互联网的快速发展"译文中将名词"驱动力"换译成了动词"has driven";将"手机网民快速增长"和"互联网的快速发展"进行了倒译,全句译为"The fast development of the mobile Internet network has driven the growth of mobile Internet users."。

4. "三网融合试点工作",译者将"三网"进行了解释性的增译,译为"telecom, radio and TV"。

5. "为用户提供更加便捷和舒适的个性化服务,成为移动互联网产业各方的共识"本句根据英文的表达习惯倒译为"It has become a consensus to provide more convenient and

personalized services for users. ".

6. "这个例子充分展现了微博强大的互动效果,及潜在的巨大营销潜力和舆论影响,引起了各方的关注",为符合英文的表达习惯,译者使用了定语从句将并列的部分"强大的互动效果,及潜在的巨大营销潜力和舆论影响"进行分译,全句译为"The example displays the strong interactive function of micro-blogs, whose great marketing potential and public influence have drawn huge attention. ".

7. "在与电子商务相关的信用、支付、物流、IT、金融等领域涌现出越来越多的服务商和服务模式,为电子商务活动提供多样化的服务",这句话采用倒译的方法,将"在与电子商务相关的信用、支付、物流、IT、金融等领域"的翻译后置,全句译为"There are more service providers and modes in relevant trust, billing, logistical, IT and financial sectors. ".

8. "政府对互联网技术的发展与创新也非常重视"句中"对某事非常重视"译为"attach great importance to"。

9. "以云计算为例,当前已有阿里巴巴、腾讯、百度、中国石化等一些大型企业建立自己的云计算平台",为避免译文的重复,译员省译了"以云计算为例",全句译为"At present, some big enterprises, such as Alibaba, Tencent, Baidu and Sinopec, have established their own cloud-computing platforms. ".

10. "缩小数字鸿沟,抵制网络色情,深化网络版权保护和网络安全工作"译为"narrowing the digital divide, cracking down on online pornography and strengthening Internet copyright protection and online security"。

11. "畅所欲言,各抒己见"译为"speak their minds without reservation"。

译 文

Speech at the Plenum of 4th China-U. S. Internet Forum

By Hu Qiheng, Chairperson of the Internet Society of China

8 November, 2010

Your Excellency Vice Minister Qian Xiaoqian,
Your Excellency Mr. Robert Hormats and
Mr. Craig Mundie,
Ladies and Gentlemen:

Good afternoon! The 4th China-U. S. Internet Forum, co-hosted by the Internet Society of China(ISC) and Microsoft Corp. , formally raises its curtain today. At first, on behalf of the Chinese host — the Internet Society of China, I would like to extend a warm welcome to the guests from Chinese and US Internet industry. I'd also express my welcome and gratitude to all media friends covering this forum, and thank all my colleagues from China and the United States who have paid great efforts to organize and prepare for this forum.

This year, the theme of the forum is "for the more useful and reliable Internet". During the two-day event, delegates from both sides will carry out direct communication and conversation on the topics like "cloud computing", "International cooperation on Internet crime prevention and privacy protection", "online intellectual property rights protection and criteria" and "Internet law and the development of new media". They will also discuss how to innovate and manage Internet industry, share useful experiences and practices as well as enhance mutual recognition and understanding. Through these discussions, the forum will further promote the healthy development of and deepen the cooperation and communication between the Internet industries in China and the USA, and therefore benefit the people in the two countries.

In the last two years, the population of Internet users in China has grown rapidly. As the basic network facilities gradually improve, China increasingly expands the coverage of the Internet. By June 2010, China had registered a total of 440 million Internet users and the penetration of the Internet had risen to 33 percent. The broadband users in China have reached 360 million and 98 percent of the Internet users who surf the Internet on computers have access to broadband networks. The export of Internet bandwidth had reached nearly 1,000 gigabytes. About 115 million people in rural areas have access to Internet, accounting for 27.4 percent of the total Internet users. The time people spent online continues to increase — each person spending 19.8 hours per week. What deserves to be mentioned is that 277 million people surf the Internet on mobile phones, which accounts for 65.9 percent of the total Internet users and 33 percent of the total mobile phone users, and 11.7 percent of them only get access to mobile Internet. People usually use mobile Internet to acquire information and communicate with others. Instant messaging service tops the usage of the mobile Internet, accounting for 61.5 percent, followed by mobile search, which accounts for 48.4 percent.

The fast development of the mobile Internet network has driven the growth of mobile Internet users. As the 3G networks expand, mobile Internet services based on the networks, such as reading, music, interactive communities, online payment and application stores, have attracted more and more people to surf the Internet on mobile phones. The coverage of the mobile Internet will further expand in China, especially in rural areas, as the integration of telecom, radio and TV, and Internet networks deepens. At present, there are increasingly more mobile Internet products that have independent intellectual property rights, and more parties joining the industrial links. It has become a consensus to provide more convenient and personalized services for users. UC explorer, developed by UC Mobile Limited, is a successful example. The product enjoys core technology and full IPR (Intellectual Property Right) of its own. It's convenient to use and saves online traffic. The good user experience has resulted in more than 400 million downloads globally. In addition, China also attaches importance to building wireless cities. At present, the cities of Beijing, Shanghai, Nanjing, Hangzhou and Guangzhou have started building wireless networks. During this year's Guangzhou Asian Games and Asian Para Games, a free wireless service will be available via mobile phones and laptops to acquire competition information in Beijing. The operators will provide an Internet access with the speed of 3Mbps and the speed will reach as fast as 10 Mbps in some popular areas. Certainly, as the mobile communication technique develops, mobile Internet has vast development space in China.

The emergence of microblogging is another highlight of China's Internet industry in recent years. The popularity of Twitter has made the concept of "microblogging" accepted by the public. In China, microblogging services, represented by Sina Microblogging, have rapidly developed, opening the era of microblogging in China. According to a relevant institution's prediction, by the end of 2010, the active accounts on domestic service providers will accumulatively reach 65 million. In August, at the China Internet Conference hosted by ISC, microblogging was used as an interactive platform for the first time. Tencent installed two screens in the conference hall, rolling the valuable and interesting contents posted by micro-bloggers about the conference. Speakers were also invited to answer the questions on the micro-blogs. Participation was expanded and a buzzword "on screen" was therefore produced. The word refers to micro-bloggers commenting on the conference and expressing their opinions on their blogs that would be screened at the conference. The example displays the strong interactive function of micro-blogs, whose great marketing potential and public influence have drawn huge attention. How to use new media, especially microblogging, to better serve economic development and promote transparency of public affairs is one of the issues that we are going to thoroughly discuss and research.

China's e-commerce continues to integrate with traditional industries and promote the development of relevant industries, forming the new service sectors based on the Internet. Big enterprises have developed their e-commerce levels, expanding to online design, manufacture, planning and management. The applications of e-commerce of medium and small enterprises for producing and operating, especially sales and purchasing, have kept fast growth, with the characteristics of "multi-channels and activeness". As the expansion of e-commerce, its service sectors become more and more important. There are more service providers and modes in relevant trust, billing, logistical, IT and financial sectors. Statistics show that the transaction volumes of China e-commerce reached 3.8 trillion yuan in 2009, of which 1.57 trillion yuan were between large and medium-sized industrial enterprises, 1.99 trillion yuan between medium and small ones. The transaction volumes of online shopping reached 258.6 billion yuan, accounting for 2.06 percent of the total retail sales.

The Chinese government attaches great importance to Internet technique development and innovation. In recent years, China has been promoting and accelerating the research and industrialization of key technique, such as the next generation Internet, the Internet of things and cloud computing, to speed up industrial development. At present, some big enterprises, such as Alibaba, Tencent, Baidu and Sinopec, have established their own cloud-computing platforms. A method to protect users' data and privacy during the application of cloud computing remains a focus for relevant parties. At the fifth annual Internet Governance Forum (IGF) meeting in September in Lithuania, the issue was specifically discussed. Microsoft suggested further enhancing the transparency of the privacy protection and security services provided by cloud-computing providers and the collaboration on combating digital crimes. The Computer Society of Kenya suggested stipulating a global standard for cloud-computing security and privacy protection.

China's Internet industry has scored a lot during the past few years, but there is still room for improvement, such as narrowing the digital divide, cracking down on online pornography and strengthening Internet copyright protection and online security. In addition, the general lack of innovation lags behind international counterparts in understanding and utility of the Internet. Due to differences on development phases, technique levels and cultural backgrounds, the Internet industries of China and the USA have different characteristics, but also share many common concerns. Therefore, the two sides need to further strengthen mutual understanding, communication and cooperation. ISC is willing to continue promoting bilateral communication.

The forum provides a good communication and interactive platform for both sides. In the following sessions, I hope the delegates and experts from Chinese and the US Internet enterprises will speak their minds without reservation. And in particular, I hope Chinese delegates will cherish this opportunity to learn from successful US experiences and effective measures on Internet innovation and governance.

Ladies and gentlemen,

Let's cooperate earnestly and join hands to create a harmonious, green, more useful and reliable Internet environment. Let's work together for a better future! I sincerely wish this forum a complete success!

Thank you!

选文B

Compaq's Commitment to the China Youth Information Online Project
—Speech on China Youth Information Online Project

Echhard Pfeiffer, President and Chief Executive Officer of Compaq Co.

Beijing, 11 March, 1999

Distinguished guests, Ladies and Gentlemen,

It is a great honor for me to be here today to announce Compaq's commitment to the China Youth Information Online Project. I have participated in several events during my four days here in Beijing, but this one is particularly special to me because it involves the young people who represent our future.

Based on what I have seen during my brief stay here, that future is very bright. I could see it in the faces of the several hundred students I had the honor of addressing at Beijing University. I see it in the Chinese government's commitment to build an information technology infrastructure that will enable China to compete on an equal footing with other major economies of the world. And I see it in the promise of programs like this one.

From Western Europe to the Far East, Compaq is working with governments and educators to help improve access to information technology and to incorporate the Internet into the educational process. We often talk about how the Internet is revolutionizing the world of commerce. But the Internet has just as much potential to revolutionize education.

First, it is a tool for communications. With the Internet, students can interact with other online students and schools in China and around the world. More and more schools are setting up their own web pages to share information, exchange ideas and learn more about other cultures. In fact, at least one school in Beijing — the Number One Middle School of Beijing — is already on line as part of the School World Internet Education program based in Australia. And I'm sure there are others.

Second, the Internet is in many ways the world's largest research library. With the right direction from their teachers, students can find information that contributes to their studies in a wide variety of fields. They can visit an online museum, read the latest research papers from leading scientific institutions, and learn even more about current events.

Third, the Internet makes possible new approaches in long-distance learning. This will be particularly valuable in a country as large as China. As you build your Internet infrastructure and begin to provide Internet access to schools, you will be able to provide enhanced educational resources to schools in rural and remote areas of the country.

The China Youth Information Online Project is consistent with Compaq's vision of a world where virtually all information is on line and people can securely access the information they need from anywhere at any time. We are pleased to be working in partnership with the China Youth Association and the China Commodities Exchange Commission to bring education to the classroom via the Internet.

Compaq is donating 370 personal computers and 13 servers to youth palaces and schools in twelve cities to set up an Internet classroom. I had the honor of attending the opening ceremony of the Beijing Youth Palace earlier this week and was proud to see that Compaq was making such a large contribution to China's youth.

Through these efforts, youngsters will not only improve their education by using the Internet, they will also learn skills that are critically needed to help China achieve its information technology and e-commerce goals. It is also important for young people to understand the Internet because it is driving significant changes in our world; changes in how we communicate, how we buy and sell, how we compete, and how we live and work.

Today's students are tomorrow's information technology leaders. By building an

Internet infrastructure, you will give these students the tools they need to help establish China as one of the leaders in the Internet Age. The China Youth Information Online Project is a good start, and Compaq is honored to be part of this effort.

We are committed to working with you and with other organizations and institutions in China to help make the Internet an integrated part of your educational system and your economy.

Thank you.

重难点评析

1. "I could see it in the faces of the several hundred students. I had the honor of addressing at Beijing University. I see it in the Chinese government's commitment to build an information technology infrastructure that will enable China to compete on an equal footing with other major economies of the world."译者分开翻译了两个并列的"I see it in..."，在后一句作了补译"……，我从中看到了光明的前景"，译文为"我有幸在北京大学发表了演讲。我能够从几百名学生的面孔上看到这一点。中国政府致力于建设信息技术基础设施，它将使中国能够在平等的基础上，与世界其他主要国家开展竞争。我从中看到了光明的前景"。

2. "improve access to information technology and to incorporate the Internet into the educational process"译为"改进对信息技术的利用，并将互联网技术应用于教育发展"。

3. "In fact, at least one school in Beijing — the Number One Middle School of Beijing — is already on line as part of the School World Internet Education program based in Australia."两个破折号中间的插入语部分被分译成一个独立的句子，更符合中文的表达习惯，全句译为"实际上，北京至少有一所学校已经联网，成为澳大利亚校际互联网教育计划的一个组成部分。它就是北京第一中学。"

4. "find information that contributes to their studies in a wide variety of fields"译为"从许多领域发现有利于他们学习的信息"。

5. "makes possible new approaches in long-distance learning"译为"使远程教学中的新方法成为可能"。译文是典型的倒译法，因为"make"的宾语很长，在英语的表达中是置于"possible"之后的。

6. "The China Youth Information Online Project is consistent with Compaq's vision of a world where virtually all information is on line and people can securely access the information they need from anywhere at any time."译者将where引导的定语从句分译成了独立的句子，全句译为"中国青少年信息网络工程，与康柏公司对未来世界的看法是一致的。我们预见，未来世界的所有信息都是联网的，人们可以在任何时间和任何地点，以安全可靠的方式，访问他们需求的信息"。

7. "Compaq is donating 370 personal computers and 13 servers to youth palaces and schools in twelve cities to set up an Internet classroom."译者使用了分译和增译的方法，将其译成了两个句子，全句译为"康柏将为12个城市的少年宫和学校，捐赠370台个人计算机和13部服务器。这些设备将允许每个少年宫和学校，各设置一个互联网教室"。

8. "changes in how we communicate, how we buy and sell, how we compete, and how we live and work."为使得上下文更为紧凑和符合中文的表达习惯,译者采用了词性的转换,将名词"changes"译成了动词"改变",全句译为"改变我们的通信方式,改变我们购买和销售商品的方式,改变我们的竞争方式,而且改变我们的工作和生活方式"。

译 文

康柏致力于中国的青少年信息网络工程——关于中国青少年信息网络工程的讲话
康柏公司主席及首席执行官　埃克哈德·费佛
1999年3月11日北京

尊敬的嘉宾,女士们,先生们:

今天,我十分荣幸地在这里宣布康柏公司决定致力于发展中国青少年信息网络工程。最近四天,我在北京参加了许多活动。但今天的这项活动对我具有特殊意义,因为它是为了代表着未来的青年而开展的。

根据我在这里短暂逗留期间的所见所闻,我认为我们的未来是十分光明的。我有幸在北京大学发表了演讲。我能够从几百名学生的面孔上看到这一点。中国政府致力于建设信息技术基础设施,它将使中国能够在平等的基础上,与世界其他主要国家开展竞争。我从中看到了光明的前景。我从今天这样的工程项目中也看到了前途的光明。

从西欧到远东,康柏公司跟各国政府和教育机构展开了合作,目的就是改进对信息技术的利用,并将互联网技术应用于教育发展。我们经常谈论互联网如何使商务领域发生了革命性变化。不过,互联网同样具有实现教育革命的潜力。

首先,它是一种通信工具。通过互联网,学生可以跟中国和世界各地联网的学生以及学校进行交互式通信。越来越多的学校在竞相设置他们自己的网页,以便共享信息,交流思想,更多地学习其他文化知识。实际上,北京至少有一所学校已经联网,成为澳大利亚校际互联网教育计划的一个组成部分。它就是北京第一中学。而且,我相信,还有其他的学校也联网了。

第二,从许多方面来看,互联网是世界上最大的科研图书馆。在教师的正确指导下,学生可以从许多领域发现有利于他们学习的信息。他们可以访问联机博物馆,阅读领先科研机构的最新研究报告,了解有关当前科研活动的更多信息。

第三,互联网使远程教学中的新方法成为可能。这对于像中国这样面积广大的国家来说,具有特别重要的意义。你们通过建设互联网基础设施和在学校提供互联网访问,就可以为农村和偏远地区的学习提供更多更好的教育资源。

中国青少年信息网络工程,与康柏公司对未来世界的看法是一致的。我们预见,未来世界的所有信息都是联网的,人们可以在任何时间和任何地点,以安全可靠的方式,访问他们所需求的信息。我们乐意跟中国青少年协会和中国商品交易中心开展合作,以实现通过互联网把教育送到课堂。

康柏将为12个城市的少年宫和学校,捐赠370台个人计算机和13部服务器。这些设备将允许每个少年宫和学校,各设置一个互联网教室。本周早些时候,我荣幸地出席了北京市青少年宫的开幕仪式,并对康柏公司为中国青少年作出如此巨大的贡献感到自豪。

通过这些努力,青少年不仅可以利用互联网提高他们的学习成绩,而且可以学到帮助中国实现信息技术和电子商务所迫切需要的技术。让年青人了解网络,也具有重要意义。因为它正推动我们的世界发生显著变化,改变我们的通信方式,改变我们购买和销售商品的方式,改变我们的竞争方式,而且改变我们的工作和生活方式。

今天的学生就是明天的信息技术领导者。通过建设互联网基础设施,你们将为这些学生提供帮助中国成为互联网时代领先者的所需要的工具。中国青少年信息网络工程是一个良好的开端。康柏公司能够成为该工程的一部分,感到非常荣幸。

我们将跟你们以及中国其他组织与机构开展密切合作,为使互联网成为你们教育系统和经济的一个有机组成部分提供帮助。

谢谢诸位。

口译员的临场应变策略

口译实战中,经常会出现各种各样的现场状况,译员除了要对自身的知识水平、口译技能有充分的准备外,还要具备应对特殊情况和突发状况的素质和能力。从某种意义上说,口译过程也是危机处理的过程,以下是口译过程中可能会出现的临场问题及应变策略:

1. 译员问题

(1) 听记问题

没听清:由于讲话人的口音、语速、现场环境噪音,或译员受到外界干扰、本人疲惫分神等问题,译员可能出现没听清某部分段落内容的情况。

没听懂:受到译员自身的语言能力、知识水平和准备程度的限制,译员在现场会遇到某些术语、表达、引语没有立即理解明白的情况。

没记全:由于类似以上各种因素的影响,译员也会出现大脑没有记住或笔记没有记全的情况。

在听记阶段如果出现上述问题,译员要分清缺失的这部分内容是否重要,是否影响自己和听众对其他部分的理解。如果是次要内容,并不影响大局,可以省略不译或采取模糊处理的办法。如果是关键内容,可采取礼貌地询问发言人、请教现场人员的办法,避免误译或信息丢失。

(2) 表达问题

不会译:如果听懂了讲话人的发言内容,但一时找不到正确的表达,可以采取直译、解释或重复原文原词的办法。

译漏或译错了:如果译员意识到自己译漏或译错了部分内容,可以立即或在适当的时机采取补全的办法,或以解释的语气引出正确的译文。如果在口译时被他人现场指错,译员应该不卑不亢、平静虚心地向讲话人或指错人询问确认,并有风度地更正自己的错误。

听众不明白:如果是译员的表达、音量、语速等自身问题导致听众听不懂、有意见,译员要进行解释、补充甚至重译,并在接下来的口译中注意听众的反应,加强与听众的沟通。

2. 发言人问题

讲话人语速快、说不停:讲话人如果没有意识到译员的存在,或者没有与译员配合的经验,常常会有此种情况,这时译员应首先稳住情绪,不要乱了阵脚,接下来专注地听记,语速快的以听为主,说不停的以记大意和逻辑为主,并在恰当的时机有礼貌地打断或者提醒讲话人,以便更好地完成口译任务。

讲话人说错话:如果译员能够意识到讲话人的发言明显是有违常识的错误或口误,译员可以在译文中予以纠正;如果无法肯定,可以视现场情况向讲话人确认;如果是在极为正式的场合或发言人有特别的主张倾向,应按原话口译。

讲话人表达不流利、逻辑混乱:如果讲话人自身的思维和语言水平存在问题,出现表达不流利、逻辑关系混乱的情况,译员可以对原文进行梳理,删繁就简,不要再重复讲话人的表达问题。

讲话人语言不得体:由于英汉两种语言的文化差异,如果讲话人的某句发言在翻译后会产生冒犯失礼或引起误解的情况,译员可以采取淡化、变通或略译的方法。

3. 配合问题

在工作中由于发言人听不懂外语,或译员没有把握好节奏,偶尔会出现发言人与译员彼此抢话等配合上的问题,这时译员要尽快适应发言人的讲话节奏,并在口译完毕后给发言人以眼神等信号,力争互相保持一种无形中的默契。

4. 工作环境问题

设备问题:在译前准备时译员应该对设备进行检查和确认,但在口译过程中偶尔也会出现麦克风没声音、耳机有问题、设备不工作等情况,这时译员要随机应变,例如交传时如果麦克风没声音,译员要迅速检查是否是麦克风按钮忘记打开,而如果是麦克风确实坏了,在现场环境比较安静或不是很开阔的情况下,译员不妨放下麦克风大声口译,并等待工作人员前来帮忙。如果出现重要设备无法工作而导致口译无法进行时,译员应立即示意工作人员前来处理。

现场环境:在活动中出现外界干扰,或者听众不配合,人员走动、说话等情况,译员要观察确认产生上述问题的原因是译员、设备还是其他原因造成的,如果非译员或设备的问题,只要讲话人没有停下,译员就要继续进行下面的口译工作。如果需要临时暂停发言和口译以便处理现场状况,译员要与发言人和组织者进行配合协调。

中文网络流行词汇英文译解

语言是社会的镜像。透过不断发展和变化的词汇尤其是网络"流行词汇",人们不仅可以捕捉到当今社会的热点事件和现象,把脉时下变迁的社会心理和文化心态,还能准确预测未来的流行趋势。下文挑选了一些中文网络流行词汇,以期帮助广大英语学习者及时把握英汉语言的动态变化,领悟语言所折射的文化信息。

闪婚族　wedding rusher

点评:"闪婚族"是对急于要找结婚对象且匆忙结婚的人的简称,这些人或迫于长辈压力而匆匆成家,或迫于就业压力而欲通过婚嫁"曲线就业"。此类人士的共性在于"急"(rushing),故闪婚族可译为"wedding rusher"。

背景:近年来,社会上开始涌现越来越多的"闪婚族"。相关统计表明,2012春年出现的"闪婚族"增幅近三成。专家分析,这一现象反映了社会转型期人们对婚姻关系理解的变化,在某种程度上,是由社会压力、生活节奏等原因造成的。

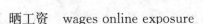

晒工资　wages online exposure

点评："晒工资"并非将工资拿到太阳底下去晒,而是将工资条拿到网上去曝光。基于这一意蕴,该词可译为"wages online exposure"。

背景:《中国青年报》近日所做的民意调查显示,47.5%的人上网看过工资条,37.7%的人愿意本着"匿名填写,保证真实"的原则,将自己的工资条在网上公开。相关人士分析,"晒工资"表达了人们呼唤收入分配透明的社会心态;但是,此类事件也可能会给社会带来负效应,如导致部分人心理失衡或无意间泄露商业秘密等。

钟点养老　special old-age care by hour

点评:"钟点养老"是某社区为解决部分空巢老人在节日期间无人照料而推出的"节日钟点养老"服务项目,不同于月付费或年付费的规范性养老服务,故不能直译为"hour care/service for the old",只可意译为"special old-age care by hour"。

背景:北京海淀区建材西里社区创建全市首家"即购票即入门"的新型敬老院,这种敬老院集娱乐、运动、住宿、医疗为一体,老人只需花上几元钱,就可在此吃、喝、玩、住一整天。春节期间,多位空巢老人通过购买此类"门票"欢度了佳节。

拼客　mass bargainer

点评:"拼客"是集体团购者的别称,此类人士在节假日通过结群团购达到优惠购物的目的。因此,该词可译为"mass bargainer",用来表示为讨价还价占便宜而拼凑搭伙的意思。

背景:每逢佳节,一些家电商场都会迎来一群由5至10人组成的特殊的消费者——"拼客团"。据调查显示,"拼客"族主要集中在北京、上海、深圳、广州等全国主要的大中型城市,以青年白领、学生人群为主,他们时尚却不奢侈,期待用最小的经济成本追求高品味的生活。

最牛钉子户　the most willful anti-mover

点评:"钉子户"是对不愿搬迁的住户的称呼。如果按其字面意思应将该词直译为"nail family"。在英语语境中则有不明所以之嫌,故根据其实际的意义,将该词译为"anti-mover",意为"抗拒搬迁的人"。"牛"字来源于中国俗语,在英语词典中并无现成的词汇与该词对应,根据其"死硬到底"的意义,以"willful"(恣意而为、一意孤行)译之。故整个词组可译为"the most willful anti-mover"。

背景:2007年3月19日,重庆市九龙坡区人民法院给"中国最牛钉子户"的户主杨某下达了限期履行通知书。逾期不履行,法院将强制执行。4月2日晚,杨某与开发商达成和解,重庆"最牛钉子户"房屋正式被拆除。据此,喧嚣一时的重庆"史上最牛钉子户"事件终于尘埃落定。

流氓软件　hooligan software

点评:"流氓软件"是指某些影响电脑正常运行、一旦装上就难以卸载的电脑软件的称谓,可直译为"hooligan software"。

背景:从中国互联网协会正式公布的"流氓软件"定义来看,流氓软件主要指那些在未明确提示用户或未经用户许可的情况下,在网友计算机上安装运行、侵害网民合法权益的软件,但不包含我国法律法规规定的计算机病毒。近日在新西兰召开的国际反病毒大会上,微软公司公布的报告显示,中国的流氓软件数量居世界第八,美国居第一。

解约门　agreement-canceling fever

点评:"解约门"是指当前娱乐圈盛行的解约跳槽的做法,根据该词的本意,将其中的

"门"字译作"door""gate"或"entrance"都不合适,故根据该词的内涵意义将该词语译为"agreement-canceling fever"。

背景:近年,娱乐圈出了个最新热门词汇"解约门"。继国内一线女星范冰冰和陈好跳槽后,亚洲人气第一天王周杰伦也难耐"七年之痒",在与老东家阿尔发公司的7年合约到期后,也铁了心要与老东家"劳燕分飞",欲自立门户。

版本位　official-rank-oriented publishing standard

点评:"版本位"是与"官本位"如影随形的词汇,是指依领导官位高低来确定新闻头条的潜规则。如果直接将"版本位"译为"publishing standard",则看不出其"版本位"的潜在内涵,因此该词语可译为"official-rank-oriented publishing standard"。

背景:据2007年4月3日的《中国青年报》报道,在市委书记汪洋的提议下,重庆市专门出台文件,规定"要腾出大量头条的版面和时段用于面向基层、服务群众的报道"。市领导除涉及全局性重要活动以外的常规性调研活动,一律刊发在二版,且有严格的字数限制,此举在全国为革除版本位积弊开了先河。

医德档案　medical morality record

点评:"医德"是医务人员的职业道德,可译为"medical morality";而"医德档案"是对医务人员职业道德状况的记录,因此可译作"medical morality record"。

背景:据《东方早报》2007年4月4日报道,上海市卫生局向全市医疗机构下发了《关于在全市卫生系统建立医德档案制度的通知》。《通知》明确规定,上海今年将为14万医务人员全部建立医德档案。一旦发现有收受"红包"、商业贿赂等行为,医务人员将被取消当年评优、评职称或给予缓聘、解职待聘等处理。

拓展阅读

选文A

中国的云计算发展面临三大挑战——在第四届中美互联网论坛的发言
腾讯首席执行官　马化腾
2010年11月8日

腾讯作为中国最大的互联网企业之一,12年来的成长经历可以说鉴证了中国互联网产业从无到有、从弱到强的发展奇迹,今天关注中美两国互联网发展的朋友们聚集一堂共同分享腾讯如何看待云计算在中国的发展状况和前景,以及我们所关注的关键的技术,以及它对于未来互联网行业乃至整个IT行业的影响。

首先我简单介绍一下腾讯,腾讯是为全国4亿网民提供高质量服务的企业,它提供从及时通讯、网络媒体、网络游戏、SNS、搜索引擎到电子商务完整的电子服务,如此广泛的服务范畴在中国和世界其他地区都是少有的。今天随着云计算的兴起,为所有的互联网用户提供更方便的应用提供可能性,也为我们互联网今后的发展提供广阔的空间。

云计算从概念到实现只有短短几年时间,腾讯也赶上了这一次的浪潮,不同的公司对云计算有不同的解读,对我们来说云计算就是应用公共网络设施对逻辑的组建,像水和电一样融入大家的生活,为用户提供海量一站式的服务,通过云计算可以让用户在任何时间地点访问任何信息,让他们获得在 PC 时代和网络初期无法得到的方便。

近年来,我们在云计算投入了大量的人力、资金和物力。我们正在建立亚洲最大的数据中心以及对云计算提供硬件资源的支撑,同时开发用于支持分布式存储,变形计算支持云计算的平台,中国一些其他的互联网企业在云计算的基础上做了一些布局,中国政府和我们企业界也在共同制订云计算的国家标准。

我们想结合我们的特点谈谈云计算,除了超级数据中心,等等的云计算平台以外,我想着重讲三方面的技术和挑战。

首先是信息安全。如果我们把以往个人和企业的计算机比做自己家里的保险柜,把信息比作现金,过去把信息存储在自己计算机的做法相当于把现金放在自己的保险柜里,这样当然是既不利于使用也不利于流通。云计算就是相当于现在的银行,把现金存在银行里面,实际上比自己的保险柜更安全、方便,首先是这个银行是安全、有信用的。云计算能够得到普及和得到所有互联网用户的认可,关键在于互联网安全能否做好。一方面使用户可以方便使用云端的服务,一方面是这些服务和隐私是得到保护的。我们知道便利性和安全性是矛盾的。在技术上如何解决这个问题,关系到云计算得到广大用户的认可。在过去几年,云计算在 24 小时不间断地保护用户的信息,基本上满足了用户随时随地使用在线产品的便利性,保证他们的安全性,这样的前提下用户可以放心地把原本在本地存储的终端信息放到云端的数据银行当中。另外一方面我们要在法律和政策上制止任何危害用户信息安全问题的发生,保证云计算产业有良好的发展。

第二大点就是通用和标准开放的平台。云计算的一个好处就是不受终端系统限制,给用户带来连贯性的体验,比如我们的个人电脑从传统的 PC 向手机和平板电脑、互联网电视、车载资讯的娱乐终端等智能终端发展,操作系统也出现新兴系统百花齐放的局面,云计算要支持这些系统就要做好标准化通用性。在标准化方面,微软和中国工业界正在制定统一的标准,云计算的目的之一是要将计算资源以最经济的方式提供给社会。由于它的规模巨大,不可能每一个企业和机构都发展自己的云计算平台,而是由主要的互联网公司提供给全社会,为了强调这个目的我们强调云计算平台是在通用的标准上提供的,能否做到开放和合作,关乎到云计算技术能否普及,以及能否带动整个 IT 产业上下游的发展。云计算要像提供水和电一样为中小机构提供计算能力、海量输出和带宽资源。如果云计算的提供商将它作为垄断资源,将云计算作为控制中小企业及互联网上下游的工具,用一些条条框框把这些属于产业链中下游的业务变成约束在自己的业务中,从长远来说会伤害到整个 IT 产业链。腾讯本着互通互利的原则,希望共同发展完善云计算的产业链,不仅让广大用户通过云计算平台共享信息和服务,也要让中小企业机构分享云计算的成果,基于云计算发展增值服务。

第三大点就是我想谈一下基于云计算的应用和服务。云计算是个载体,它上面的各种服务才是实质,没有这些应用和服务,云计算就成了一个摆设,一个泡沫。我们要在云计算的基础上整合各种已经有的 IT 服务,从通信、媒体、办公自动化、网络游戏、SNS、搜索引擎到电子商务,等等完整的各种各样的互联网应用,这样才能真正给用户带来好处。下面我有一个腾讯的例子是我们 QQ 的云应用,分享我们在云应用方面的策略。从这个例子里面我们可以看到云计算为互联网用户带来的价值,以及对互联网和 IT 产业的影响。我们的目标是创建一个用户携带自己的服务组合、在线习惯,以及隐私数据的任何平台。首先我们要提供一个跨终端跨系统的体系,现在终端的大量涌现,我们QQ的云是搭建一个云体系,确保用户可以得到完善的云服务体验,QQ云提供了一个免下载、免安装、即插即用的平台,为用户解决了各种烦恼。同时云也可以携带各种组合到任何一个场景,也可以为用户提供量身定做的个性化服务,以及用户的关系网络,完成社区化的服务。基于云计算平台,可以做到客户不仅可以按照时间场景选择不同的组合,也可以同步到自己每个终端甚至共用的设备上,以及处理方式的选择信息接受,等等方面。我们在云计算倡导市场性的开放心态,为了营造一个健康的生态环境和产业连,QQ云平台对第三方开发者和商业伙伴来讲是完全开放和透明的。我们希望不仅是腾讯还是合作伙伴,第三方开发者还是个人都可以创造自己的云应用,并分享和提供到应用市场上去。QQ将云应用提供商作为基础服务,比如终端兼容、个性化设置、关系链传播、支付体系,等等,通过丰富的应用、便捷的管理、安全的使用,让客户的个性化使用得到体现,同时让应用提供商能够接触到巨大的用户群和关系链,共同开拓新的市场机会。

刚才谈了三个挑战性问题,我们希望基于云计算平台为客户提供更多价值,通过开放和合作,为IT行业提供新的商机。

中美互联网论坛已经举行了四届,成为两国互联网业界最重要的交流和合作的机制,腾讯也在积极布局海外,包括美国在内的其他市场的网络用户提供产品和服务,我们也希望通过中美互联网论坛这一平台,与两国的互联网企业加强交流,共同探讨互联网行业新的趋势、新的技术和新的理念,为推动中美乃至全球互联网的繁荣与发展做出贡献!

谢谢大家。

译文

Cloud computing in China: prospects, key technologies, major challenges

By Ma Huateng

Chairman of the Board and CEO of Tencent

November 8, 2010

Tencent is China's largest privately owned enterprise oriented toward comprehensive Internet business. Founded 12 years ago, it is a testament to the miraculous development of China's Internet industry. Today, all friends connected with the industry gather together here, giving me a precious opportunity to share with you some of our thoughts on the development and prospects of cloud computing in China, our technological focuses, and the influence of cloud computing on the Internet industry and the entire IT industry.

As China's largest Internet company, Tencent offers high-quality network services to 400 million users across the country. We boast all kinds of Internet businesses, including instant-communication tools, online media, online games, SNS societies, search engines and e-business. Such a wide service range is rare both in China and in the other parts of the world. The advanced cloud computing technology has made it possible for Internet users to enjoy good services more conveniently and opened a spacious room for the development of the Internet industry in the following years.

It only took cloud computing a few years to change from a vague idea to real technology. Chinese Internet companies, including Tencent, caught the trend fortunately. Different companies may have a different understanding on this technology. For Tencent, the key value of cloud computing is that it can utilize the public network structure to make our computing ability, processing ability and logic components as assessable as household tap water and electricity. With the aid of cloud computing, we can help users to acquire any information anytime, anywhere. This is an unprecedented convenience as compared with the PC era and the initial periods of the Internet era. This is our understanding of cloud computing platform.

In recent years, We have invested large quantities of funds, devices and personnel to develop cloud computing technologies. For instance, Tencent is building Asia's largest data center to support a cloud computing platform and developing a cloud computing platform to support distributed storage, parallel computing and intelligent resource management. Other Chinese enterprises are also working on cloud computing hardware and related support. At the same time, the government is working with the industry to set up relative national standards.

Now, I would like to talk about the major technologies and challenges Tencent is focusing on. Since you are all familiar with super data centers, high-speed broadband network and the cloud computing platform that can manage these hardware devices and systems, I will show you three other key technologies and challenges.

First, information security. Let's make a comparison. If personal computers and company computers are like one's safe, and if information is money, the practice of storing information in a computer is like putting money in his safe, which is, of course, inconvenient and not good for liquidity. Instead, depositing money in a bank is more convenient and safer, on the condition that the bank is secure and credible. In this sense, the key to popularizing cloud computing technology and gaining users' recognition is how safe the Internet is. In terms of technology, efforts should be made to ensure that users can conveniently use services in the cloud and that the services are safe and that users' privacy is protected. We all know that in the online world, it's difficult to realize convenience and safety at the same time. How to address the issue becomes the key to popularizing cloud computing. In the past years, Tencent has made continuous efforts to develop technologies on information security. A professional team is working 24 hours a day to protect user information with the best devices and solutions. Generally speaking, we are now able to offer users easy access to our online products and services anytime, anywhere and ensure their information is safe. In this situation, users are willing to use our cloud services and move data from their own terminals to our cloud-based "data bank". With regard to laws and policies, efforts should be made to prohibit acts that may harm the safety of user information, thus to foster an environment conducive to the development of cloud computing and the entire industry.

The second thing I want to talk about is the platform, which should be universal, standardized and open to all. An advantage of cloud computing is the consistent experience it offers users on all terminals and systems. Currently, the scope of "personal computer" has expanded from traditional PC and Mac computers to smart terminals like cell phones, flat-panel computers, Internet TV and car infotainment systems. And computer operating systems have seen a rigorous development, with Android, iOS, Meego and other new systems emerging in addition to Windows. To support all these terminals and systems, cloud computing must be standardized and universal. Now, the government is working with Internet enterprises, including Tencent, to set up unified standards. An objective of cloud computing is to make computing resources accessible to the whole society in the most economic way. Given the large scale of the work, it's impossible and unnecessary for every enterprise and institution to develop its own cloud computing platform. This work can be done by major Internet companies. To achieve the objective, Tencent insists that the cloud computing platform be universal, standardized and open to all. The openness and cooperativeness of the platform is key to its popularity and its influence on IT Industry and national economy. Platform suppliers should ensure their computing abilities, mass data storage and bandwidth resources can be as available as water and electricity for small- and medium-sized enterprises and research institutions. If suppliers take cloud computing as a monopolized resource, use it to control enterprises in the midstream and downstream industry and make special rules to force the enterprises to use these services, the entire IT industry will be ruined in the long run. In the principle of openness, cooperation and mutual benefit, Tencent hopes to work with other Internet companies to promote technological development and industry development based on cloud computing. We hope to help Internet users share information and services on the cloud platform, help small-and medium-sized enterprises and research institutions share cloud computing results and make our contributions to the development of value-added, cloud-based products and services.

The third thing I want to talk about is the key role of cloud applications and services. Cloud computing is only a bearer. Services and applications based on it are the most important. Without the services and applications, cloud computing is useless. Therefore, Tencent will integrate all IT services, including instant communication tools, online media, office automation, online games, SNS societies, search engines and e-business, on the basis of cloud computing. Only in this way can we bring real benefits to users. Next, I will take the QQ cloud as an example to show you our strategy on cloud application. After my explanation, you will see the values cloud computing can bring to users, and you will see the influence cloud computing can leave on the Internet and IT industries. The objective of the QQ cloud is to build an application platform where users can safely bring their service portfolio, online habits and private data to any other scenes. To achieve this, we will first offer users consistent trans-terminal, trans-system services. Currently, there are a variety of terminals and systems, such as the PC, smart phons and flat-panel computers, but they all use the Web as the application platform. Based on the Web, the QQ cloud tries to build a complete cloud-application system to ensure that users can enjoy consistent cloud services. The QQ cloud offers a browser-server, plug-and-play cloud platform, saving users from troubles caused by various terminals. Meanwhile, it allows users to safely bring their cloud service portfolio, user habits and private data to any other application scene. Based on the cloud platform, the QQ cloud can provide users with customized services and social services based on users' contact chain. Users' demands and habits differ. In the past, such information was stored on their own terminals, unable to be taken to other places. Now, based on the cloud platform, we can help users choose different service portfolios according to the time and the scene and safely synchronize the portfolios between various terminals or public devices. Users can use the portfolios, including UI, application settings and message receiving and processing mode, in a familiar environment in their accustomed way. Meanwhile, users can share their cloud applications, experiences and creations with friends in their societies. We always stress that cloud computing development needs the efforts of the entire IT industry and the whole society. We advocate an open, market-oriented business environment. The QQ cloud is an open platform. It's impossible to have any single company develop all applications and services. To build a healthy, win-win industrial environment, the QQ cloud platform is open and transparent to all third-party developers and commercial partners. We hope that in addition to Tencent, our partners, competitors, independent developers and even individual users can create their cloud applications and share or sell them in application market. The QQ cloud will provide application suppliers with basic services, such as terminal compatibility, customized settings, cloud storage, contact chain spreading, application management and payment system. With abundant applications, convenient management and safe usage, the QQ cloud is able to meet users' customized demands and better achieve user values. At the same time, it will give application suppliers access to users and contact chains, to better integrate upstream industry with downstream industry and make a joint exploration of new market potentials.

By developing the aforementioned technologies, by solving the three challenges I just talked about, Tencent hopes to bring more benefits to users with the support of cloud platform. In the principle of openness and cooperation, we hope to find more business opportunities for the IT industry.

Four sessions of the China-U. S. Internet Forum has been successfully held. This forum has become a major communication and cooperation mechanism for the Internet industry of the two countries. Tencent is working hard to explore overseas markets to offer products and services to network users in the U. S. and other countries. We sincerely hope to take the advantage of this forum to enhance our communications with Internet companies in the two countries, discuss new trends, new technologies and new ideas of the industry and make our contribution to the development of the Internet in both China and the U. S. , as well as other countries of the world!

Thank you!

选文B

Secretary-General Message on World Telecommunication and Information Society Day

New York, 17 May 2010

In today's world, telecommunications are more than just a basic service — they are a means to promote development, improve society and save lives. This will be all the more true in the world of tomorrow.

The importance of telecommunications was on display in the wake of the earthquake which devastated Haiti earlier this year. Communications technologies were used to coordinate aid, optimize resources and provide desperately sought information about the victims. The International Telecommunications Union(ITU) and its commercial partners contributed scores of satellite terminals and helped to provide wireless communications to help disaster relief and clean-up efforts.

I welcome those efforts and, more broadly, the work of ITU and others to promote broadband access in rural and remote areas around the world.

Greater access can mean faster progress toward the Millennium Development Goals (MDGs). The Internet drives trade, commerce and even education. Telemedicine is improving health care. Earth monitoring satellites are being used to address climate change. And green technologies are promoting cleaner cities.

As these innovations grow in importance, so, too, does the need to bridge the digital divide.

The theme of this year's observance, "Better Cities, Better Life with ICTs", is a reminder that communications technologies must be employed — and disposed of — in a manner that raises living standards while protecting the environment.

The United Nations is committed to ensuring that people everywhere have equitable access to information and communication technologies. On this International Day, let us resolve to fully harness the great potential of the digital revolution in the service of life-saving relief operations, sustainable development and lasting peace.

译文

联合国秘书长2010世界电信和信息社会日致辞

纽约 2010年5月17日

在当今世界,电信不仅仅是一项基本服务,而是一种促进发展、改进社会和拯救生命的手段。未来的世界将更是如此。

在今年初发生了摧毁海地的地震之后,电信的重要性体现出来。通信技术被用来协调援助、优化资源和提供迫切需要的伤亡人员的信息。国际电信联盟及其商业伙伴捐赠了数十部卫星终端,并帮助提供无线通信服务,以协助救灾和清理工作。

　　对于这些努力,更广泛地讲,对于电联和其他各方促进世界各地农村和偏远地区宽带接入的工作,我表示欢迎。

　　更广泛的宽带接入可能意味着在实现千年发展目标方面取得更快的进展。因特网推动了贸易、商业、甚至教育的发展。远程医疗正在改善保健服务。地球监测卫星正被用于应对气候变化。绿色技术正在使城市更加清洁。

　　随着这些创新的重要性日益加强,也越来越有必要弥补数字鸿沟。

　　今年的纪念活动以"利用信通技术优化城市和生活"为主题,它提醒我们,必须以提高生活水平并同时保护环境的方式采用和处理通信技术。

　　联合国致力于确保任何地方的人们均可公平地利用信息和通信技术。值此国际日之际,让我们下定决心,在拯救生命的救济活动、可持续发展和持久和平中充分发挥数字革命的巨大潜力。